S0-BAM-512

Economics, Ethics, and Public Policy

Economics, Ethics, and Public Policy

EDITED BY
CHARLES K. WILBER

ROWMAN & LITTLEFIELD PUBLISHERS, INC.
Lanham • Boulder • New York • Oxford

ROWMAN & LITTLEFIELD PUBLISHERS, INC.

Published in the United States of America
by Rowman & Littlefield Publishers, Inc.
4720 Boston Way, Lanham, Maryland 20706

12 Hid's Copse Road
Cumnor Hill, Oxford OX2 9JJ, England

British Library Cataloguing in Publication Information Available

Library of Congress Cataloging-in-Publication Data

Economics, ethics, and public policy / edited by Charles K. Wilber.
p. cm.
Includes bibliographical references and index.
ISBN 0-8476-8789-9 (cloth : alk. paper).—ISBN 0-8476-8790-2 (pbk. : alk. paper)
1. Economics—Moral and ethical aspects. 2. Economic policy—Moral and ethical aspects. 3. Economic development—Moral and ethical aspects. 4. Social justice. I. Wilber, Charles K.
HB72.E273 1998
338.9—dc21 97-30482
CIP

Printed in the United States of America

∞ ™ The paper used in this publication meets the minimum requirements of American National Standard for Information Sciences—Permanence of Paper for Printed Library Materials, ANSI Z39.48–1984.

For Meme
a woman of virtue

CONTENTS

INTRODUCTION

This book focuses on the interaction between ethics and economics, in both economic theory and economic policy. There are three ways in which ethics are important in economics: (1) Economists have ethical values that help shape the way they do economics; (2) Economic actors have ethical values that help shape their behavior; and (3) Economic institutions and policies impact people differently and thus ethical evaluations must supplement economic evaluations. In this book, philosophical moral theories will be introduced and used as the framework for later discussion of public policy issues.

Part I: Economists, Value Judgments, and Economic Theory deals with the following issues. Economists, as persons, bring a viewpoint with them that structures the questions they ask, the methods they use, the evidence and answers they deem acceptable. Is this merely Joseph Schumpeter's "preanalytic vision" or does it lead to the value permeation of theory? If there is no objective access to the "real" world an economist is forced to see that world through the lenses of theory. Does that mean "facts" are theory-laden? And value-laden? What would this mean for economic theory?

Part II: Rationality, Ethics, and the Behavior of Economic Agents focuses on the following issues. All evidence indicates that economic actors (consumers, workers, firms) act out of more than calculated self-interest. Thus the assumption of rationality may be insufficient or inappropriate depending on the situation. People's behavior is influenced by many things including ethical norms. What impact does this have upon the ability of economic theory to predict outcomes of economic policies? For example, given imperfect information actors might be tempted into strategic behavior that will result in suboptimal outcomes. Morally constrained behavior might reduce that opportunism.

Part III: Ethical Theories and Theories of Justice surveys the major ethical theories that dominate discussion in philosophy and then attempts to show how they might help a decision maker in an organization—whether a business firm, a government agency, or some other group. These ethical theories focus on guiding individual decision making. They are analogous to microeconomic theories. Theories of justice are analogous to macroeconomics. They are concerned with the way the economic system as a whole is organized and operated.

Part IV: Economic Institutions and Ethics addresses the fact that institutions—such as markets and property rights—have an impact on people's welfare that needs to be evaluated in ethical terms. Specific examples—future generations, surrogate motherhood, discrimination, development—are analyzed to discover the ways they embody ethical issues.

Part V: Economic Policies and Ethics considers economists' use of the concept of Pareto optimality as their measuring rod when evaluating economic policies, a convention based on the notion that individual preferences are the ultimate measure of welfare. This assumption has caused considerable controversy, raising the question of where individual preferences come from and whether some preferences are unworthy. Cost-benefit analysis, a primary tool of policy evaluation based on the assumption that individual preferences are what count, is treated at length.

This is a book that emphasizes questions, not answers. The various articles claim that ethics are important to economics—both its study and its practice. Economic ethics is a more wide-ranging field than business ethics or medical ethics and far less studied. From the economist's side, this might be because of the value-free claims made for so long by economists. As the value-free position becomes more difficult to sustain, there is hope that discussion of ethics by economists will become less self-conscious and better informed. If this book helps promote that discussion the work will have been worthwhile.

I want to thank my friend and noted moral philosopher, James Sterba, for his help and willingness to listen patiently to an amateur ethicist rambling on. His guidance was invaluable. My research assistants, John Blanford and Greg Hannsgen, contributed bibliographic searches, draft summaries of readings, and insightful conversation that contributed significantly to the completion of this work. I also want to thank the undergraduate students in my Economics, Ethics, and Public Policy class over the past three years for their enthusiasm and criticism of successive versions of the readings. Finally, I must thank all those people who responded to my bibliographic requests on the ACE, IDEAL, and SOC-ETHIC listservs. They gave me many great suggestions for readings.

PART I

ECONOMISTS, VALUE JUDGMENTS, AND ECONOMIC THEORY

This section deals with the role of values in economics. Many economists argue that while values might have a place in what is termed normative economics, they should be kept out of the everyday scientific business of the profession—the development and testing of falsifiable propositions—which is often referred to as positive economics. This separation, as the writers in this section show, is problematic. Economists, as persons, necessarily work from a viewpoint that structures the questions asked, the methods, the evidence, the answers deemed acceptable. Is this merely Joseph Schumpeter's "pre-analytic vision" or does it lead to the value permeation of theory? If there is no objective access to the "real" world an economist is forced to see that world through the lenses of theory. Does that mean "facts" are theory laden? And value laden? What would this mean for economic theory? The question becomes: How does one do economics in a world where facts and values cannot be conveniently disentangled?

In looking for an answer to this question, economists might find, to their surprise, that they have much to learn from Adam Smith. Jerry Evensky, in the first chapter of this section, shows that Smith's economic theory was closely related to his moral thought. For example, while Smith often used the metaphor of the watch in describing how the self-interested actions of individuals worked for the good of the whole, he saw the "machine" itself as the product of a beneficent God, which moreover depended on the virtues of individual actors to operate smoothly. As Evensky points out, Smith's *Theory of Moral Sentiments,* written before the *Wealth of Nations,* offers a rich moral vision of society that contrasts with the thin gruel of "rational economic man." Smith argued that over the course of history, society advanced through successive stages, each requiring more advanced values than the previous. Smith became less sanguine about moral progress over the course of his life, but moral standards continued to play a crucial role in his work.

Since the work of Thomas Kuhn and other historians of science, it has been increasingly recognized that scientists cannot be neutral in matters of value. The next two chapters in this collection agree that values are inevitably part of economics, though they disagree on the exact nature of their role. Charles Wilber and Roland Hoksbergen survey what others have had to say about value neutrality in economics, showing that there has been a lively debate on the subject in the years since 1970. One group of economists argue that economists can successfully separate values from facts, which are "out there" in the world, by adhering to a positivist methodology. According to this group, a failure to maintain this distinction will lead to a disastrous slide into relativism.

Critics of value neutrality, on the other hand, marshal a wide variety of arguments to make their case. It is argued, for example, that since there is no access to objective reality except through the lenses of a theory, the values shared by the community of economists color their judgment in determining just what the relevant "facts" are.

Wilber and Hoksbergen themselves come down on this side of the issue in the final part of their paper, in which they argue that economists share a "world view"—a notion of the good, which shapes their analysis of the economy. This world view includes three main elements:

1. People are rational and self-interested.
2. The purpose of life is to pursue happiness as people define it.
3. The ideal world is one in which people are free to compete to meet their ends and in which market forces lead to optimal equilibrium outcomes.

This is certainly a set of value judgments, in need of justification like any other; if these judgments indeed correctly characterize economics, they should be openly debated, rather than tacitly assumed.

Samuel Weston, in the following chapter, concedes that value judgments are inevitably part of economics, but argues that nevertheless it is possible and desirable to maintain the positive/normative distinction. Economists must recognize the inevitable value-permeation of their doctrine, even as they attempt to sort out positive from normative aspects of the field. Because of value permeation, economists cannot avoid taking sides on normative issues.

There are several benefits of nevertheless continuing to make the distinction between the two types of issues. First, it is necessary to distinguish different types of questions and avoid fallacious reasoning from positive to normative statements. Second, economists should label certain subjects as "normative" to acknowledge economists' lack of competency to deal with them in an authoritative way. Third, the distinction should be made in order to avoid casting factual issues inappropriately in terms of "good" versus "evil." Finally, facts and values should be kept separate in order to maintain objectivity, which Weston characterizes as an openness to critical scrutiny. To sum up Weston's prescription, "if freedom from ethical values ceases to be viewed as an attainable goal for economics, the next step might be the 'legalization' of normative economics" (p. 15). If Weston's prescriptions were accepted, the kind of value judgments pointed out by Wilber and Hoksbergen would be brought out into the open for discussion and debate.

The authors mentioned so far have emphasized how economists bring certain values to their interpretation of the facts, for example, by imposing a neoclassical template on the world they observe. Robert Frank, Thomas Gilovich, and Dennis Regan go a step further. They experimentally demonstrate that economists' values can affect the "real world" itself—and not just economists' interpretations of it. This happens when economists "export" values in the classroom by teaching the economic theory of rationality. The authors report several experiments, in one of which they put students in a prisoners' dilemma situation, with actual cash at stake. In a regression model of the resulting data, with the decision to defect as the dependent variable, an economics-major variable was significantly positive; those who had studied economics the most were more likely to take the most self-interested action. If this kind of effect is common, then even clearly self-interested behavior may not constitute an independent verification of the theory of rational self-interest, but instead may be a *product* of that theory.

The authors in this section thus provide us with several different approaches to the relationship between facts and values in economics. They demonstrate that the role in economics of ideals such as objectivity are unsettled. The debate is a longstanding one, and it continues.

1.

ETHICS AND THE INVISIBLE HAND

Jerry Evensky

Introduction

As modern economists, we use Adam Smith's "invisible hand" metaphor confident that we all know what it means in our discourse: it reflects our admiration for the elegant and smooth functioning of the market system as a coordinator of autonomous individual choices in an interdependent world. But in Adam Smith's moral philosophy, the invisible hand has a much broader responsibility: if individuals are to enjoy the fruits of a classical liberal society, the invisible hand must not only coordinate individuals' choices, it must shape the individuals into constructive social beings—ethical beings. Revisiting Smith's metaphor provides a valuable lesson: the foundation of success in creating a constructive classical liberal society lies in individuals' adherence to a common social ethics.[1]

I begin by presenting the philosophical basis for Smith's invisible hand, describing the sense in which the hand is invisible, and whose hand it is.[2] I then describe the story Smith tells of the invisible hand creating and maintaining a constructive classical liberal society, and show how Smith's story evolved as his faith in the ability of the invisible hand to shape an appropriate ethical foundation waned. I conclude with some thoughts on the legacy of Adam Smith and of our predecessors in economic inquiry more generally.

Journal of Economic Perspectives 7, no. 2 (Spring 1993): 197-205.

The Philosophical Basis of the Invisible Hand

Smith did not believe that philosophers are engaged in discovering Truth. In his view, philosophers can only *imagine* what connecting principles give rise to the order we observe. To illustrate this point, Smith (1980, pp. 42–43) contrasts a philosopher's perspective on nature with that of a spectator who is awed by the wonder of the special effects at an opera.

> Upon the clear discovery of a connecting chain of intermediate events, it [our wonder] vanishes altogether. Who wonders at the machinery of the opera-house who has once been admitted behind the scenes? In the Wonders of nature, however, it rarely happens that we can discover so clearly this connecting chain. With regard to a few even of them, indeed, we seem to have been really admitted behind the scenes.

Nature's Truth lies in the machinery behind the scenes. "Philosophy . . . *pretends* [emphasis added] to lay open the concealed connections that unite the various appearances of nature," wrote Smith (1980, p. 51). The great philosophers are the ones who have the creativity to imagine what those "concealed connections" might be. And the greatest of all philosophers, according to Smith, was Sir Isaac Newton.

Smith's essay on the "History of Astronomy" concludes with a review of Newton's work. There Smith (1980, pp. 104–105) asserts that Newton's representation of the connecting principles that order the physical universe "prevails over all opposition . . . with principles [that], it must be acknowledged, have a degree of firmness and solidity that we should look in vain for any other system." Smith sees Newton's work as a triumph of the imagination and is awed by its brilliance. In fact, Newton's representation is so powerful that it is easy to be seduced into using the language of Truth when one describes it. Nevertheless, Smith concludes his review of Newton's work with a reminder to his reader, and it seems to himself, that even this great philosophical triumph is simply a flight of imagination, a great story. Smith (p. 105) writes:

> And even we, while we have been endeavouring to represent all philosophical systems as mere inventions of the imagination . . . have insensibly been drawn in, to make use of language expressing the connecting principles of this one, *as if* [emphasis added] they were the real chains which Nature makes use of to bind together her several operations.

Smith seeks to do for moral philosophy what Newton had done for natural philosophy. He wants to tell a story of the connecting principles of the human order with commanding and compelling persuasive power. But, as with Newton, Smith's story does not begin with these principles. Both men take the story back to the origin of these principles, and it is here that we meet the "invisible hand." Newton and Smith believed that the connecting principles which give rise to the order we observe reflect the planning and handiwork of a designer. But who is the artificer that designed and constructed this great work? Smith and Newton both believed in the Deity as designer.

In the classic enlightenment analogy, the Deity is to the universe as the watchmaker is to a watch. In each case it is the hand of the designer that arranges the springs and pins and wheels, and sets the system in motion. But in both cases that hand is invisible to the spectator who observes only the product of the effort: the orderly progress of the hands of the watch, or of the sun, the moon, and the planets; we see nothing of the designer, we see only the effects of the design.[3]

The Invisible Hand and Ethics

Smith's "invisible hand" metaphor reflects his view that he is representing the invisible connecting principles of the "immense machine of the universe" (Smith, 1976b, p. 236) that are the handiwork of the Deity. To fully appreciate the impact of this perspective on Smith's moral philosophy, however, one must bear in mind that Smith (1976b, p. 166) saw the Deity as not only handy, but also benevolent.

> The happiness of mankind, as well as of all other rational creatures, seems to have been the original purpose intended by the Author of nature, when he brought them into existence. No other end seems worthy of that supreme wisdom and divine benignity which we necessarily ascribe to him . . .

This is the Deity who endowed all humans with self-love, and in so doing set the spring that gives motion to human industry. This is the Deity who arranged the connecting principles such that the actions of all those seeking their own advantage could produce the most efficient allocation of resources, and thus the greatest possible wealth for the nation. This is indeed a benevolent designer.

Smith's *Wealth of Nations* is the story of those socially desirable unintended consequences of individual action that result when events are allowed to follow their "natural course," the course consistent with the Deity's design. But while that course is natural, it is not inevitable (Smith, 1976b, p. 316):

> Human society, when we contemplate it in a certain abstract and philosophical light, appears like a great, an immense machine, whose regular and harmonious movements produce a thousand agreeable effects. As in any other beautiful and noble machine that was the production of human art, whatever tended to render its movements more smooth and easy would derive a beauty from this effect, and, on the contrary, whatever tended to obstruct them would displease upon that account: so virtue,

> which is, as it were, the fine polish to the wheels of society, necessarily pleases; while vice, like the vile rust, which makes them jar and grate upon one another, is as necessarily offensive.

For the wheels to turn easily, for the machine to run smoothly, there must be virtue. Human virtue is the *sine qua non* of the fruitful classical liberal society Smith envisioned.

In *The Theory of Moral Sentiments,* Smith explores the ethics consistent with the Deity's design, the ideal of ethics, presenting his view of how an individual would in theory personally define and enforce that ethical position. With this limiting point of the ethical ideal as a reference, he then turns to the real.

Smith takes human frailty as a given and thus recognizes the impossibility of achieving the ideal in any individual, much less in society as a whole. For example, remembering his dear, recently deceased friend David Hume, Smith wrote: "Upon the whole, I have always considered him, both in his lifetime and since his death, as approaching as nearly to the idea of a perfectly wise and virtuous man, as perhaps the nature of human frailty will permit" (Smith, 1977, pp. 217, 221).

Smith saw Hume as a model of the kind of being society should seek to nurture. For, in Smith's moral philosophy, it is the degree to which individuals in society approach the ethical limit that determines the degree to which society as a whole will enjoy the fruits of living in the classical liberal construct of the Deity's design.

Much of *The Theory of Moral Sentiments* is dedicated to an examination of ethics at a social level. According to Smith, hope for improving human virtue and thus for improving society lies in social evolution and socialization. Social evolution brings the improvement of the human condition through stages: from the rude state of hunting and gathering, through the progressively more productive and refined stages of pasturage and agriculture, to the most advanced stage, a commercial society. Since each stage requires a progressively more refined system of human values, the movement of a society from stage to stage is simultaneous with the development of that society's value system. For human progress to occur, each generation must refine the values it inherited from the last, and then must pass those enhanced values on to the next generation through the socialization of its children.

Smith sees each individual as being shaped by and in turn, given that person's experience, shaping society. The dynamic and continuity of human social evolution derive from this coevolution: communities contribute the continuity as individuals come and go, and individuals contribute the dynamic to the degree that they draw on their extra-community experience to act on the community during their stay. This coevolution of individual and society makes human improvement possible, for through this process individuals and factions can meld into a community, sharing common values that provide common ground for constructive competition among all parties.

Smith recognized that any given society might move forward, and then stagnate or even regress. But at the level of humankind, we again encounter the power and beneficence of the invisible hand. It not only guides the elegant, frictionless ideal human society; the invisible hand guides the evolution of the human condition through the stages toward that ideal. Or so Smith saw it as a young man. Experience brought Smith more of an appreciation for the dynamic power of factions, and with that experience his faith in the dexterity and strength of the invisible hand seemed to fade.

In particular, prior to the 1770s, Smith did not fully appreciate the dynamic nature of mercantilism. It was upon his arrival in London (1773) to publish *The Wealth of Nations* that he encountered firsthand the stark reality of the growing influence of commercial interests in Parliament.[4] This influence, reflected in the immense expense incurred in the wars to protect and preserve the colonies[5] (a classic mercantilist policy), seems to have disabused Smith of much of his optimism.

The "Additions and Corrections" to *The Wealth of Nations,* published in 1784, represents the only major revision of that text. The focus of those changes is how mercantilism was distorting commercial society, the last stage in the sanguine dynamic Smith had envisioned as guided by the invisible hand. This concern represented more than a change of perspective from sanguine to skeptical; it struck at the heart of Smith's analysis. If the invisible hand would not guide society toward the ideal, how could we hope to get there? Smith addressed this question in revisions to *The Theory of Moral Sentiments* made in the last year of his life.

In the 30 years since *The Theory of Moral Sentiments* was first published, Smith had made no significant revisions to that work. But in 1789, in advanced age and weakened frame, he set to that task. Smith made revisions throughout the text, but by far the most significant change was the addition of (Smith, 1977, pp. 319–20) "a compleat new sixth part containing a practical system of Morality, under the title of the Character of Virtue." In these revisions, Smith appeals to all citizens to put the well-being of the society before that of any particular faction to which they might belong, and he makes a special plea to those who might be statesmen to step forward and construct a moral society by deed and example.

Smith's conception of how to develop a moral society is driven by his notion that society is made up of a layered web of communities with divergent interests,[6] and that these differences can be the seeds of destructive factions. He argues that to avoid this destructive tendency there must be a balance: the values of the society must respect the diversity of values among the communities it encompasses, and these communities' values must not undermine the commitment of individuals to the core set of values that give order to society.[7]

In Smith's view, this balance of respect and commitment is crucial for the society to be a constructive environment within which the individuals and groups that make up society can not only survive but flourish (Smith, 1976b, pp. 219–20, 235–37). And as they flourish, so too will society.

By the end of his life, Adam Smith was no longer looking to the invisible hand to guide society to the conditions necessary for a constructive classical liberal state. Instead, he called upon the visible hand of moral leadership from all individuals, and especially statesmen, to create those conditions and thereby that society. This appeal and the sacrifice he makes to present it (the work on the revisions weakened him so that he died within six months of completing them) reflect the centrality of ethics to his vision of a classical liberal society.

Smith's Legacy and the Mentoring Past

The image of individual actions guided as if by an invisible hand to an unintended optimal outcome has been passed down to modern economic discourse. For example, listen to Arrow and Hahn in their introduction to *General Competitive Analysis* (1971, pp. vi–vii):

> There is by now a long and fairly imposing line of economists from Adam Smith to the present who have sought to show that a decentralized economy motivated by self-interest . . . would be compatible with a coherent disposition of economic resources that could be regarded, in a well-defined sense, as superior to a large class of possible alternative dispositions. . . . It is important to understand how surprising this claim must be to anyone not exposed to this tradition. The immediate "common sense" answer to the question "What will an economy motivated by individual greed and controlled by a very large number of different agents look like?" is probably: There will be chaos.

But the Smithian story told by Arrow and Hahn—and they are representative of modern economists—is an abridged edition. The spring that motivates action in Smith's story has been carried forward, but much of the rest of his tale has been forgotten. Unfortunately, this has become the standard treatment of the works of the great economists of the past. They are not read for the fullness of their vision; they are cited for the pieces we have inherited.

This approach to our past reflects a modern sense that the development of economic thought has been an inexorable progress toward greater understanding. In this view, the greats among our predecessors have in their own time pushed understanding of the world into new frontiers. Like other trailblazers of the past, their once freshly cleared path is now well-trod and the cutting edge lies far beyond. We appreciate them, not for where they reached, but for where their efforts have allowed us to reach. The actual works of those greats are treated as "classics," cited by many, and read by few.

The cost of this approach to our past is the loss of much of our rich legacy. The modern adaptation of Smith's invisible hand story is, I believe, a case in point. To tell that story without ethical dimension is to lose much of its richness and relevance. Smith's story weaves self-love and the invisible hand into a tale about the human condition that is much more telling than can be developed with those concepts alone. He begins with an exploration of the ethical ideal, moves on to the evolution of social ethics and socialization as a dynamic that ameliorates the corrosive effects of human frailty, and then develops this evolutionary foundation into a tale about the emergence and functioning of an elegant and efficient classical liberal society. In Smith's story ethics is the hero—not self-interest or greed—for it is ethics that defend the social intercourse from the Hobbesian chaos. Once the veil of "classic" is lifted from Smith's work, it can be read again as a thoughtful commentary on the state of modern classical liberal societies, and as an underutilized resource for the development of the models that economists use to analyze and construct those societies.

Notes

I would like to express a special thanks to Joe Persky for encouraging me to do this piece, and to Celia Kamps and Timothy Taylor for excellent editorial assistance. Needless to say all opinions and errors are my own.

1. There is a growing interest in this subject. In recent years we have seen, for example, works by James Buchanan (1991), Amitai Etzioni (1988), Robert Frank (1988), Jane Mansbridge (1990), as well as Pope John Paul II's Encyclical Letter "Centesimus Annus" address this issue. The presentation here builds on my earlier work (Evensky, 1987, 1989, 1992a, 1992b, forthcoming).

2. Smith actually uses the "invisible hand" metaphor only once in *The Wealth of Nations* (Smith, 1976a, p. 456), once in *The Theory of Moral Sentiments* (Smith, 1976b, p. 184), and once in the *Essays* (Smith, 1980, p. 49); but the image is central to his moral philosophy.

3. See Smith (1976b, p. 87) for an example of his use of this watchmaker image. This "design argument" (Hurlbutt, 1965) is expressed in eloquent and absolute terms by Cleanthes in David Hume's *Dialogues Concerning Natural Religion* (Hume, 1947, p. 143):

> Look round the world: contemplate the whole and every part of it: you will find it to be nothing but one great machine, subdivided into an infinite number of lesser machines, which admit of subdivisions, to a degree beyond what senses and faculties can trace and explain. All of these var-

> ious machines, and even their most minute parts, are adjusted to each other with an accuracy which ravishes into admiration all men, who have ever contemplated them. The curious adapting of means to ends, throughout all nature, resembles exactly, though it much exceeds, the productions of human contrivance; of human design, thought, wisdom, and intelligence. Since therefore the effects resemble each other, we are led to infer, by all rules of analogy, that the causes also resemble; and that the Author of Nature is somewhat similar to the mind of men; though possessed of much larger faculties; proportioned to the grandeur of the work, which has been executed. By this argument a posteriori, and by this argument alone, do we prove at once the existence of a Deity, and his similarity to human mind and intelligence.

Ironically, by the end of the *Dialogues,* Cleanthes' case is destroyed by the skeptic Philo. Smith's adherence to the philosophy of design seems more akin to that position taken by Hume's character Demea: it's a matter of faith, not proof.

4. See Kammen (1970, p. 10) for more on this "modern conception of interest."

5. About the policy of retaining the colonies, Smith wrote in the "Additions and Corrections" (Smith, 1976a, p. 661): "For the sake of that little enhancement of price which this monopoly [(the American colonial trade)] might afford our producers, the home-consumers have been burdened with the whole expense of maintaining and defending that empire. For this purpose, and for this purpose only, in the two last wars, more than two hundred millions have been spent. . . . The interest of this debt alone is not only greater than the whole extraordinary profit, which, it ever could be pretended, was made by the monopoly of the colony trade, but than the whole value of that trade or than the whole value of the goods, which at an average have been annually exported to the colonies."

6. Society can be thought of as the Community-at-large. The scope of the Community-at-large depends on the level of analysis one has in mind. Smith sometimes writes in terms of nation-states; but the ultimate scope Smith had in mind was the whole of human society, for his moral philosophy is a global analysis.

7. "Concern for our own happiness recommends to us the virtue of prudence; concern for that of other people, the virtues of justice and beneficence . . ." Beneficence "is the ornament which embellishes, not the foundation which supports the building. . . . Justice, on the contrary, is the main pillar that upholds the whole edifice. If it is removed, the great immense fabric of human society must in a moment crumble into atoms" (Smith, 1976b, pp. 262, 86). In Smith's moral philosophy the definitions of prudence, justice, and beneficence, and the standard for the proper balance of these sentiments were determined by the sympathy of an impartial spectator. The roots of this construct are in the same ground as John Rawls' (1971) "veil of ignorance," for the virtue of an impartial spectator derives from the same lack of an invested location that the veil creates.

References

Arrow, Kenneth, and Frank Hahn, *General Competitive Analysis*. San Francisco: Holden-Day, 1971.

Becker, G., *The Economic Approach to Human Behavior*. Chicago: The University of Chicago Press, 1976.

Buchanan, James, *The Economics and the Ethics of Constitutional Order*. Ann Arbor: The University of Michigan Press, 1991.

Etzioni, Amitai, *The Moral Dimension: Toward a New Economics*. New York: The Free Press, 1988.

Evensky, Jerry, "The Two Voices of Adam Smith: Moral Philosopher and Social Critic," *History of Political Economy,* Fall 1987, *19*:3, 447–68.

Evensky, Jerry, "The Evolution of Adam Smith's Views on Political Economy," *History of Political Economy,* Spring 1989, *21*:1, 123–45.

Evensky, Jerry, *Economic Ideas and Issues: A Systematic Approach to Critical Thinking*. Englewood Cliffs: Prentice-Hall, 1990.

Evensky, Jerry, "Ethics and the Classical Liberal Tradition in Economics," *History of Political Economy,* Spring 1992a, *24*:1, 62–77.

Evensky, Jerry, "The Role of Community Values in Modern Classical Liberal Economic Thought," *Scottish Journal of Political Economy,* February 1992b, *39*:1, 21–38.

Evensky, Jerry, "Adam Smith on the Human Foundation of a Successful Liberal Society." *History of Political Economy,* forthcoming.

Frank, Robert, *Passions within Reason: The Strategic Role of the Emotions*. New York: W. W. Norton and Co., 1988.

Hume, David, *Dialogues Concerning Natural Religion*. Introduction by Norman Kemp Smith, 1947. Indianapolis: Bobbs-Merrill Educational Publishing, [1985].

Hurlbutt, Robert H., III, *Hume, Newton, and the Design Argument,* 1965. Lincoln: University of Nebraska Press, [1985].

Kammen, Michael, *Empire and Interest, the American Colonies and the Politics of Mercantilism*. Philadelphia: Lippincott, 1970.

Mansbridge, Janet, *Beyond Self-Interest*. Chicago: University of Chicago Press, 1990.

Pope, John Paul II, "'Centesimus Annus': Encyclical Letter," *Catholic International,* 1990, *2*:12, 552–89.

Rawls, John, *A Theory of Justice*. Cambridge: Harvard University Press, 1971.

Smith, Adam, *An Inquiry into the Nature and Causes of the Wealth of Nations,* (1776), Edited in two vol. by W. B. Todd. In Vol. 2 of *The Glasgow Edition of the Works and Correspondence of Adam Smith,* General editing by D. D. Raphael and Andrew Skinner, Oxford: Clarendon Press, [1976a].

Smith, Adam, *The Theory of Moral Sentiments,* (1759), Raphael, D. D., and A. L. Macfie, eds. In Vol. 1 of *The Glasgow Edition of the Works and Correspondence of Adam Smith,* General editing by D. D. Raphael and Andrew Skinner, Oxford: Clarendon Press, [1976b].

Smith, Adam, *The Correspondence of Adam Smith,* (1740–90), Mossner, E.

C., and T. S. Ross, eds. In Vol. 6 of *The Glasgow Edition of the Works and Correspondence of Adam Smith,* General editing by D. D. Raphael and Andrew Skinner, Oxford: Clarendon Press, [1977].

Smith, Adam, *Lectures on Jurisprudence,* (1762–63, 1766), Meek, R. L., D. D. Raphael, and P. G. Stein, eds. In Vol. 5 of *The Glasgow Edition of the Works and Correspondence of Adam Smith,* General editing by D. D. Raphael and Andrew Skinner, Oxford: Clarendon Press, [1978].

Smith, Adam, *Essays on Philosophical Subjects,* (1795), Wightman, W. P. D., and J. C. Bryce, eds. In Vol. 3 of *The Glasgow Edition of the Works and Correspondence of Adam Smith,* General editing by D. D. Raphael and Andrew Skinner, Oxford: Clarendon Press, [1980].

Smith, Adam, *Lectures on Rhetoric and Belles Lettres,* manuscript notes of lectures on Jurisprudence, Bryce, J. C., ed. In Vol. 4 of *The Glasgow Edition of the Works and Correspondence of Adam Smith,* General editing by D. D. Raphael and Andrew Skinner, Oxford: Clarendon Press, [1983].

2.

ETHICAL VALUES AND ECONOMIC THEORY: A SURVEY

Charles K. Wilber and Roland Hoksbergen

The issue of ethical value judgments in economic science stubbornly refuses to go away. The problem is at least as old as the John N. Keynes argument which would divide economics into three areas: positive (economic theory), normative (welfare economics), and practical (economic policy). The first deals with "what is," the second with "what ought to be," and the third with how to get from one to the other. Although the majority of mainstream (neoclassical, monetarist, Keynesian) economists admit that ethical values permeate welfare economics and economic policy, they proceed confidently on the belief that their work in economic theory is ethically neutral. Methodologists studying the question are much more cautious.[1]

There are numerous issues involving ethical value judgments in welfare economics and in economic policy. However, it is more challenging to deal with values in the scientific core of economic theory. Thus, in this article we survey the current state of debate over the role of ethical values in economic theory. We refer to the historical development of the debate, but our attention is focused primarily on work since 1970. The debate has always revolved around larger issues in the philosophy of science. This is also true in the current debate and thus the value question must be situated in the context of developments in the philosophy of science.

Religious Studies Review 12, no. 3/4 (July/October 1986): 208–14.

Recent Arguments in Defense of Value-Neutrality

In recent years there has been a flurry of literature on methodological issues in economics, much of it dealing explicitly with the impact of ethical value judgments on economics as a science. Of this literature, a greater amount argues the value-permeation thesis than defends the idea of value-neutrality. However, value-neutrality of economics as a science is the dominant position in the day-to-day work of contemporary economists. It seems expedient to begin by laying out its arguments.

There are two pervasive tenets to the value-neutrality argument. The first is a reliance on the Humean guillotine which categorically separates fact ("what is") from value ("what ought to be"). This is also known as the positive/normative dichotomy (Robbins, 1935, 148). The second basic tenet strongly supports the first by claiming that since we have objective access to the empirical world through our sense experience, scientists need not concern themselves with "what ought to be." This second tenet is the really crucial point (Friedman, 1979, 19), and the one which post-positivist philosophy of science has sought to undermine (Thomas, 1979).

Although the defense of value-neutrality has become more philosophically sophisticated over the years, recent arguments draw heavily on their predecessors. In his well thought out and carefully argued defense of Lakatosian falsificationism, Mark Blaug (1980) follows in the tradition of Coats (1964) and Hutchinson (1964)[2] by arguing that scientific economics is comprised of three separate components: pre-scientific decisions, scientific analysis, and post-scientific application. According to Coats and Hutchinson, value judgments inevitably are wrapped up in the first and third components, but the realm of science escapes untainted.

Blaug, however, recognizes that any scientific analysis so grounded in admitted value judgments will likely be seen as value-permeated. He thus points out a difference between the value judgments of pre-science and of post-science. Drawing on Nagel (1961, 492–95) Blaug seeks to protect Hume's guillotine against precisely this sort of objection by drawing a distinction in social science between two types of value judgments—characterizing value judgments and appraising value judgments. In Nagel a *characterizing value judgment* "expresses *an estimate* of the degree to which some commonly recognized (and more or less clearly defined) type of action, object, or institution is embodied in a given instance." An *appraising value judgment* "expresses *approval or disapproval* either of some moral (or social) ideal, or of some action (or institution) because of commitment to such an ideal" (Nagel, 1961, 493). Some value judgments are thus not really value judgments of any ethical significance, but judgments that merely allow one to carry on the scientific enterprise.

Fritz Machlup is another writer on methodology who frequently has tackled the issue of value-neutrality. *Methodology of Economics and Other Social Sciences* (1978) compiles some twenty-six of his articles, many of which discuss precisely this issue. Machlup always has spoken as a logical empiricist, one of whose tenets is that value judgments are not to be allowed into true scientific analysis. Machlup lists twelve ways in which value judgments may enter into economic analysis,[3] finding only that welfare economics is inevitably value-laden. This is not serious for value-free economics, since welfare economics is explicitly policy related and hence normative.[4]

Machlup also addresses the crucial issue of the value-ladenness of the very concepts and terms used in scientific statements. Machlup bails out on this one, suggesting that we may develop neutral language over time, and that even though "transgressions into normative territory are possible on these counts . . . the implied threats to scientific objectivity are not serious enough to make even the purist fret and squirm" (1978, 444). But while Machlup dismisses rather casually the problem of value-laden language, it continually crops up in criticisms of the value-neutrality position.

Ian M. T. Stewart (1979), in a book intended for beginning students of economic methodology, also banks heavily on the clear-cut division between positive and normative economics. Like Machlup, Stewart is a logical empiricist. He relies on the emotive theory of value, which renders value judgments totally out of the realm of science because any normative statement is untestable against empirical facts.

In yet another recent attempt to reconcile value judgments and objective science, Timothy J. Brennan (1979) denies that economics necessarily is value-permeated. It is only when a scientist goes beyond observed relationships and attributes cause that he has stepped over the boundary between the positive and normative. As Brennan says,

> It is the teleological nature of explanation which adds evaluative judgments to empirical study as a facet of economics. (1979, 920)

In stating his case Brennan reintroduced the notion of "brute fact." This is the notion that facts are in some sense "out there" for all to see, independent of scientific theory. Unfortunately for Brennan, the idea of brute fact has fallen on hard times in the philosophy of science literature (Thomas, 1979). Today it is generally recognized even by sophisticated logical empiricists that facts are theory-laden and that theories are tested by the facts designated as of interest by the theory.[5] The more important question then becomes whether theory itself is, in part, value determined, for if it is, then theory-laden facts would also appear to be value-laden.

The defense of value-neutrality still stands, but the pillars seem to be weakening. Recent defenders are often forced to resort to warnings about possible consequences should value-permeation be accepted. Blaug contends that:

> If there are not at least some descriptive factual assertions about social uniformities that are value-free (apart from the characterizing value judgments implied in methodological judgments), it seems difficult to escape the conclusion that we have the license to assert whatever we please (1980, 136).

This is why the second tenet—we have objective access to the empirical world-is crucial for the classical defense of value-neutrality. Brennan says, "linking facts to values can make facts a matter of opinion or value objective," and that, moreover, "we may dismiss sound factual research simply because we disagree with the researcher's values, using permeation as an excuse . . ." (1979, 920). Hutchinson goes so far as to characterize the antipositivist rejection of the distinction between positive and normative statements in the social sciences as an attempt "to legitimize and validate the propagation of ideology" (1981, 279).[6]

It almost seems as if these authors are persuaded by the value-permeation arguments, but find the consequences so unsettling that it must be wrong. Blaug and Machlup appear to defend value-neutrality more out of their own fears of (their own interpretation of) the logical consequences of value-permeation than out of a concern for the cogency of the arguments themselves. Blaug concedes that both "factual" and "moral" arguments rest "at bottom" "on certain definite techniques of persuasion, which in turn depend for their effectiveness, on shared values of one kind or another" (1980, 132).[7]

In an article first published in 1952, Machlup admits that, perhaps complete freedom from value judgments in economics can be achieved if a great many things remain unsaid which ought to be said and which only an economist is qualified to say (1978, 121). Machlup questions the economist's use of terms like efficiency, optimality, misallocation, etc., and suggests that pronouncements, and even analysis, on these issues necessitate some basic value judgments about the goodness of efficiency. But despite wavering, he and Blaug hold fast to the position that economics as a science must remain free from evaluative (as opposed to methodological) value judgments.

For the most part, then, present-day arguments in support of value-neutrality tend to toe the traditional line. Hutchinson, Friedman and Robbins have each recently reaffirmed earlier positions. Machlup has recirculated his previously written articles with little, if any, changes in argumentation. Stewart and Blaug, while updating the arguments, retain the crucial positive/normative dichotomy. Let us now consider recent criticisms of the value-neutrality thesis.

Recent Criticisms of Value-Neutrality

It is of paramount interest that criticism of the value-neutrality thesis is generally made by those who do not view logical empiricism or Popperian falsificationism as adequate philosophies of science. In general, when one finds an attack on the thesis of value-neutrality, one also finds an attack on the philosophy of science that is perceived to generate the thesis. In recent years most assaults on value-neutrality have been based on the arguments of Thomas S. Kuhn, sometimes misinterpreted, about the nature of normal science and scientific progress. These more substantive Kuhnian arguments will be taken up after a brief review of some of the general criticisms of the idea of value-neutrality.

A common complaint against value-neutrality is that there is a fundamental difference between the natural and the social sciences, not just in degree (as Friedman, Robbins, Hutchinson, Machlup, et al. would admit), but in kind. Robert L. Heilbroner argues that

> the economic investigator is in a fundamentally different relationship *vis-à-vis* his subject from that of the natural scientist, so that advocacy or value-laden interpretation becomes an inescapable part of social inquiry—indeed a desirable part (1973, 130).

This fundamental difference is due to the fact that "the objects observed by the social scientist all possess the attribute of consciousness—of cognition, of 'calculation,' of volition . . . social events are not merely interactions of forces, but contests of wills" (133–34). Royall Brandis adds to this the fact that humans cannot change the laws according to which the physical universe operates, but humans do have the power to change the structure of the social universe (1963, 49–50).

In his presidential address to the Canadian Economics Association in 1977, Scott Gordon argued that Nagel's differentiation of characterizing and appraising value judgments may be appropriate for the natural sciences, but not for the social sciences. Gordon points out that, in part, what Nagel means by characterizing value judgments are judgments of classification. If so, then defining the classification "imperialism" with its attributes or activities involves no ethical value judgments. Gordon confesses to be uncomfortable with such a consequence, for social scientists "have to operate with many terms that can be made neither descriptively precise nor free of value loadings" (1977, 535). Terms like "'unemployment,' 'economic development,' 'monopoly,' 'competition,' 'income,' 'savings,' 'labor,' and 'capital'" are value-laden just as the term "imperialism" is.

Jon D. Wisman argues further that in emulating the methodology of the natural sciences, economics "has misunderstood its knowledge and research-guiding interests" (1978, 277). Wisman adds that knowledge does not stand outside human society, but is grounded in it and "is steered by human interests" (278). The unfortunate result of striving for value-neutrality is that these interests are concealed and economics serves as "apologetics and ideology" of the ruling capitalist order (280).[8]

Larry Dwyer makes a point similar to Wisman's by arguing that while science is driven by a search for truth, it is not interested in just any truth. The relevant truth must be both "interesting" and "valuable," and thus all science is goal-directed activity (1982, 79). He continues by arguing that ". . . putative criteria for a 'good' or 'acceptable' scientific theory cannot be ranked in terms of their importance per se, but only in relation to the extent to which each serves specific ends of scientific inquiry" (79).

Theory choice is not, therefore, based objectively on noncontroversial criteria (e.g., degree of verification or corroboration), but on criteria that are inevitably value-laden (i.e., the extent to which each theory serves specific ends). According to Dwyer, the scientists' search for "valuable truth" is directed by what they think society (and science) *ought to do*. Dwyer summarizes by arguing that: no amount of evidence ever completely confirms or disconfirms any empirical hypothesis but only renders it more or less probable. The decision regarding the sufficiency of evidence is a function of the importance in the typically ethical sense of making a mistake in accepting or rejecting the hypothesis (86). While the arguments presented to this point may be valid, the defenders of value-neutrality still do not grant general validity to the value-permeation arguments.

Another line of reasoning, Kuhnian in character, seems more convincing to many. Kuhn, referring to the natural sciences, speaks of paradigms, characterized by the shared values of a given scientific community. While Kuhn does not deal with the social sciences, it is in them that his arguments have been applied most extensively. Among those who have made reference to the Kuhnian logic are Boulding (1969), Heilbroner (1973), Gordon (1977), Fusfeld (1980), Duhs (1982), Caldwell (1982) and Johnson (1983).

It is Kuhn's rejection of the second tenet—that we have objective access to the empirical world through our sense experience—that is important for those opposed to the value-neutrality position. Kuhn argues that the empirical world can be known only through the filter of a theory; thus, facts are theory-laden. The natural sciences achieve objectivity through empirical testing. Decisive anomalies become "acid tests" within the paradigm. Since in the social sciences there are no decisive anomalies, testability does not perform the same function.

Many in economics have misinterpreted Kuhn by arguing that he believes science proceeds through periodic revolutions that are analogous to religious conversions (Fusfeld, 1980). Such an (mis)interpretation clearly would oppose Kuhn to the idea of value-neutrality. Imre Lakatos is seen as reintroducing objectivity into Kuhn's scientific revolutions (Blaug, 1975, 1980). Actually much of Kuhn's work and Lakatos's sophisticated Popperianism[9] are similar: they agree that historical and sociological analyses are important in determining the actual methods of evaluations used by scientists; that the unit of ultimate scientific choice is holistic (paradigm/research program); and that the elements of a scientific paradigm/research program are internally unfalsifiable and are rejected only by moving to a new paradigm/research program that answers the accumulated anomalies. The characteristics of Kuhn's "paradigm in crisis" are those of Lakatos's "degenerating research program," and Lakatos is committed to the rationality or irrationality of science to the same degree as Kuhn (Kuhn, 1971; Thomas, 1979).

Kuhn differs from Popper and Lakatos in his rejection of the need for methodological rules to safeguard the objectivity of science. Kuhn argues that the cognitive authority of science does not reside ultimately in any body of neutral data or atemporal methodological rules, but in the judgment of the scientific community. Both the interpretation of data and the formulation of methodological rules are the products of a historically formed consensus of scientists. This consensus or shared judgment is the ultimate basis of the cognitive authority of science (Gutting, 1981). Kuhn argues that this account of science depicts science as a rational enterprise. Lakatos, influenced by Popper, calls it "mob rule" and claims there must be methodological norms to safeguard rationality and objectivity. This is where the battlelines are today in post-empiricist philosophy of science.

It comes as a surprise, then, that Mark Blaug finds "Lakatos' picture of scientific activity . . . much richer than Kuhn's" (1975, 408), for agreement with Lakatos versus Kuhn is not a defense of objectivity in the social sciences. It is also of interest that Blaug holds a unity of science view, for he finds Lakatos perfectly applicable to the social sciences, even when Lakatos himself speaks exclusively of the natural sciences. What appears to have occurred in the literature is that opponents of value-neutrality have built their arguments upon the Kuhnian characterization of science and scientific progress. Frequently they have misinterpreted Kuhn's work as depicting science as lacking in rationality and objectivity. The defenders of value-neutrality have counter-attacked by building their arguments upon Lakatos's work, sometimes misrepresenting his work as defending the old positivist positions. But, in addition to all of the other areas of agreement mentioned above, Lakatos agrees with Kuhn that data are not theory-independent.

The Role of World Views

One major argument of those who build on the Kuhnian[10] approach might run as follows: A world view greatly influences the scientific paradigm out of which one works; value judgments are closely associated with the world view; theories must remain coherent with the world view; facts themselves are theory-laden; therefore, the whole scientific venture is permeated by value judgments from the start.

Dwyer contends that "science is done from what might be called a *Weltan-*

schauung or *Lebenswelt*" (76). This world view shapes the interests of the scientist and determines the questions asked, the problems considered important, the answers deemed acceptable, the axioms of the theory, the choice of "relevant facts," the hypotheses proposed to account for such facts, the criteria used to assess the fruitfulness of competing theories, the language in which results are to be formulated, and so on.[11] Such a view entails that neoclassical economics, which generally has embraced the philosophy of logical empiricism, also is subject to a broader world view (McKenzie, 1981, 706; Katouzian, 1980, 146–47).

The Neo-Classical World View: A Case in Point

At this point let us illustrate the world view argument with neo-classical economics. It is our position that the world view of mainstream neo-classical economics is closely associated with the notion of the good embedded in its particular scientific paradigm.

Neo-classical economics is founded on a world view made up of the following propositions:

1. Human nature is such that humans are:
   a. Self-interested.
   b. Rational. That is, they know their own interest and choose from among a variety of means in order to maximize that interest.
2. The purpose of human life is for individuals to pursue happiness as they themselves define it. Therefore, it is essential that they be left free to do so.
3. The ideal social world is a gathering of free individuals who compete with each other under conditions of scarcity to achieve self-interested ends. As in the natural world with physical entities, in the social world too there are forces at work which move economic agents toward equilibrium positions.

Neo-classical economists either accept the preceding empirically unverifiable and unfalsifiable statements or, barring overt acceptance, conduct scientific inquiry with methods based thereon.[12] To state it simply, neoclassical economists believe that humans are rational maximizers of their own self-interest and that humans act in a rational world characterized by forces which move things toward equilibrium.[13] The first two propositions contain the motivating force in economic life (satisfaction of self-interest), and the third proposition spells out the context in which that force works itself out.

It seems fairly clear that judgments of value, of a particular notion of the good, are directly implied by propositions one and two of this world view. If the purpose of life is that individuals pursue happiness, and if they do so self-interestedly, then it certainly would be good for individuals to receive what they want. Here is the basic notion of the good permeating all neo-classical economics: individuals should be free to get as much as possible of what they want. Other value judgments of the neo-classical paradigm either qualify what types of individual wants will be considered or are derivative from this basic value judgment. That this basic position is, in fact, a judgment of value, or of the good, is a point willingly granted by Pearce and Nash (1981). They argue that there are two basic judgments in any use of economic theory, such as cost-benefit analysis. The first of these is that individual preferences should count. Pearce and Nash also agree that use of economic theory requires a value judgment on distributional equity. But this value judgment is rather superficial, for it is external to the neo-classical paradigm. Because it is external it often obstructs our view of the more fundamental value judgments, those deeply embedded in the paradigm itself.

These other value judgments, along with the basic value judgment, can be summarized in this way:

1. Individuals should be free to get what they want.
2. Competitive market equilibrium is the ideal economic situation.
   a. Competitive market institutions should be established whenever and wherever possible.
   b. Market prices should be used to determine value.
3. Means and ends should be bifurcated into two mutually exclusive categories.
4. Means and ends should be measured quantitatively.

The second value judgment derives from elements one and three of the neo-classical world view and from the basic value judgment that individual preferences should count. If one takes the core ideas of individualism, rationality and the social context of harmony among diverse and conflicting interests, along with a goodly number of limiting assumptions, it can be shown that competitive equilibrium maximizes the value of consumption and is therefore the best of all possible economic situations. The second value judgment is thus a different sort than the first, because it is conditional on the first. It does not stand alone. Competitive market equilibrium is good, in part, *because* it allows the greatest number of individual wants to be satisfied. Moreover, this value judgment is also determined by the world view. Without the third proposition such a judgment could not be made, for then some other economic condition could be found to satisfy individual wants. Competitive market equilibrium is good because the world view insists that only this condition can be ideal.

The notion of competitive equilibrium carries out two basic functions: it serves as an ideal and as a standard by which to measure the real value of current economic conditions. Because it serves as an ideal for which we strive, it leads directly to the value judgment that wherever competitive markets do not exist or are weak, they should be instituted or promoted. Wherever markets do not exist, the natural competitiveness of human beings will be channeled into other nonproductive directions. It would be better to establish markets where this competitiveness and self-interest seeking behavior could be channeled into mutually satisfying activities. Wherever markets are weak and distorted due to monopoly power or government interference there is sure to be a reduction in actual consumption. Therefore, perfectly competitive markets should be promoted so that the ideal competitive equilibrium can be achieved.

The third and fourth value judgments do not spring directly from the world view. Instead, they make the paradigm based thereon operational. The separation of means and ends is not strictly required by the world view itself, but is an operational requirement, without which the paradigm could generate no meaningful research or study. If means and ends were not mutually exclusive, then neo-classical economics would be nothing more than a simple statement that humans do what they do because they wish to do it. There could be, for example, no inquiry into how satisfaction is maximized by choosing among various alternatives. If some activity (e.g., production or consumption) could be both means and end, then one could not determine which part is which. As Jerome Rothenberg concedes, the intermixing of means and ends "does violence to our paradigm"[14] (1975, 57). This results in the value judgment that consumption is the end or "good" to be achieved. In so doing, any good inherent in the process or means for obtaining higher consumption is ignored. The splitting of economic activities into means and ends by its very nature promotes a particular notion of the good. It may be an operational necessity, but it is also a judgment of value. With means and ends separated, it becomes convenient to measure the satisfaction given by particular ends and the dissatisfaction (costs) resulting from employing various means. It becomes possible to measure how much better one situation is than another, by comparing numbers instead of concepts or ideas. Things that are apparently incommensurable thus become commensurable. This is evident in many branches of neo-classical analysis; when money values are unavailable or inappropriate, quantified units are used in their place.

Exactly why neo-classical economics has become so enamored of quantification is hard to say. It is not required by the world view, nor is it absolutely necessary for conducting research within the paradigm, as is the case with the previous value judgment. A likely reason is that neo-classical economics has, in general, adopted the methodological practices prescribed by logical positivism. For the logical positivist, precision and objectivity are held in highest regard. There is no more precise or objective unit than a number.

The emphasis on quantification in neo-classical economics adds another element to its particular notion of the good. While the third value judgment separates means and ends, the fourth value judgment tells us to focus on means and ends that can be quantified. One practical outcome of this is a heavy emphasis on "things" over interpersonal relationships, education, cultural affairs, family, workplace organization, etc. Things are countable while the quality of these other spheres of human life is not. In the area of economic policy especially, such concerns are treated often as obstacles to be removed or overcome. To the extent that this occurs, the notion of the good which focuses on quantifiable inputs and outputs is embedded in the paradigm. Within neo-classical economics there are thus judgments of value which are rooted in a fundamental world view. There are also judgments of value which operate in concert with the world view and which allow the neo-classical approach to be operational. Together these judgments make up the neo-classical position on the character of the good, and when an economic policy is planned, implemented and evaluated, it is done on the basis of these clearly defined standards.

To conclude this discussion, the paradigm or research program of any scientific community is circumscribed by boundaries laid out in a world view which, while not perhaps individually subjective, is nevertheless empirically untestable, or metaphysical as Boland (1981) would say. How then do value judgments about the good, the just and the right enter into scientific analysis? Such value judgments are themselves entailed by the same world view which gives rise to theoretical and factual analysis. "What is" and "what ought to be" are thus inextricably comingled in the data, the facts, the theories, the descriptions, the explanations, the prescriptions, and so on. All are permeated by the a priori world view.

Concluding Remarks

Whether one gives any credence to the arguments of value-permeation will depend largely on whether Kuhn's rejection of the second tenet of value neutrality—objective access to the empirical world through sense experience—applies to economic science. Even if the argument were accepted, it would not necessarily mean the death knell of orthodox economics. It would mean merely that the "presuppositions" (i.e., the world view) on which it is founded would have to be opened up to greater scrutiny.

Amartya K. Sen has already come a long way in his critique of Samuelson's revealed preference theory toward this position. He argues that faith in the axioms underlying the theory derives not from empirical support but rather from the fact that they are "sensibly" chosen psychological assumptions (Wong, 1978, 59). From whence do the psychological assumptions derive? Followers of the Kuhnian logic would point to the foundational world view. Should one find oneself in accord with the world view underlying neo-classical economics, then the admission of value-permeation will not have a very dramatic impact on the way one goes about scientific work.

One last remark concerns the impact of the Kuhnian approach on the positive/normative dichotomy. Obviously the dichotomy cannot hold strictly. Bruce J. Caldwell, a tentative adherent of the Kuhnian position, notes that Kuhn's approach "pinpoints where values enter science, and why they are important." Thus, his contribution is more instructive than "endless arguments about whether science is, or can be, or should be either value-free or value-laden" (1982, 226).[15] Under a Kuhnian approach the positive/normative dichotomy disappears into the broader concept of the scientific paradigm. The normative and the positive are inextricably intertwined in each area of analysis.

In most present-day criticisms of value-neutrality, acceptance or rejection of it stands or falls on the decision to accept or reject the second tenet. Despite misunderstanding by economists, both Kuhn and Lakatos do reject it. As stated above, the issue may be shifting to the impact on economic science of theory-laden facts and value-laden theory. This appears to be the new battleground which economic methodologists will occupy in the future.

Notes

1. There are even those who might agree with neo-classical theory, but would nevertheless regard it as being value-permeated to the core. See, e.g., McKenzie (1981).

2. Blaug, being a falsificationist, would not likely be in agreement with Hutchinson in most other areas. Machlup, for example, has referred to Hutchinson as an ultra-empiricist (see Caldwell, 1982, 139–72). Nevertheless, on the role of value judgments in economics, Blaug and Hutchinson are in close agreement.

3. Chapter 17, "Positive and Normative Economics," 425–50. Reprinted from Robert L. Heilbroner, ed. *Economic Means and Social Ends: Essays in Political Economics,* Englewood Cliffs, NJ: Prentice-Hall, 1969, pp. 99–129.

4. Although there are a few (e.g., Archibald, 1959) who argue that welfare economics is also value-free, there is general agreement as to the importance and inevitability of value judgments in welfare economics. But this in no way precludes the possibility of value-free positive economics (see, e.g., Little, 1957 and Mishan, 1981).

5. See, for example, Blaug (1980, 14–15), Coddington (1972, 10), Machlup (1978, 101–30), Boland (1982, 19) and Caldwell (1982, 48).

6. This is very similar to Schumpeter's point that ideology (which is of necessity value-laden) fills in where true knowledge is not available (1954, 42–43). See also Hutchinson (1964) for a more extensive discussion of this point.

7. Or consider the following statement made by Blaug in 1975: "no doubt

Hume's Guillotine tells us that we cannot logically deduce ought from is or is from ought. We can, however, influence ought by is and vice versa: moral judgments may be altered by presentation of the facts, and facts are theory-laden so that a change of values may alter our perception of the facts" (1975, 406).

8. Wisman actually leans toward arguing, as opposed to Heilbroner, Brandis and Gordon, that natural science is heavily influenced by value judgments as well. This point is made more carefully by Homa Katouzian (1980) who argues explicitly that there is no fundamental difference: all science is value-permeated (see esp. 138).

9. See Lakatos (1970) for a full development of the concept of scientific research programs. See also the response by Kuhn in the same volume.

10. This argument could be built upon Lakatos as well and it is probably the historical fact that Kuhn's work appeared first that accounts for its being utilized. Kuhn and Lakatos laid the groundwork for the reintroduction of world views into the discussion on methodology, even though they themselves did not consider the idea. By introducing the ideas of "paradigm" and "scientific research programs," they left the door open to the reinstatement of world views as the foundation of scientific work. For example, Lakatos's "hard core" is hardly distinguishable from a world view.

11. See also Duhs (1982, 230–31), O'Brien (1981, 31), Gordon (1977, 534), Finn (1979) and Fusfeld (1980, 34–43) for similar references to the fundamental nature of the world view.

12. Many contend that they do not ultimately "believe" these propositions, only that they accept them and some logically consistent and consequent propositions as "useful assumptions" in the conduct of their work. From a philosophy of science perspective, however, such a position is wholly untenable, the product of shoddy methodology. In the philosophy of science it is known as intrumentalism and receives a severe denunciation from Imre Lakatos: "instrumentalism is a degenerate version of [conventionalism], based on a mere philosophical muddle caused by a lack of elementary logical competence" (Caldwell, 1982, 52).

13. Reading recently an article on Friedman and monetarism, we came unexpectedly upon the following statement: "Friedman takes consistent optimization as an article of faith." In other words, it is part of his world view. See Hoover (1984, 69).

14. For example, if the production activity of human labor were more than just a means; say, if work was good in and of itself regardless of the final product; then it would be impossible for the neo-classical economist to discover how much individual wants are satisfied by the activity. The ends and the means would be all mixed together and it would be impossible to speak of the value of the product and the cost of the resources independently.

15. Boland (1982, 17) argues that the positive/normative distinction is a relic from earlier attempts to save inductivism. And Wisman (1978, 277–79) and Mini (1974, 127 ff.) contend that the positive/normative dichotomy arises from the incorrect Cartesian dichotomy between the mental and the physical worlds.

References

Alexander, Sidney S. 1967 "Human Values and Economists' Values." In Sidney Hook (ed.) *Human Values and Economic Policy*. New York University Press.

Archibald, G. C. 1959 "Welfare Economics, Ethics and Essentialism." *Economica* (November).

Blaug, Mark 1975 "Kuhn vs. Lakatos, or Paradigms vs. Research Programs in the History of Economics." *History of Political Economy* (Winter).

Blaug, Mark 1980 *The Methodology of Economics: Or How Economists Explain*. Cambridge University Press.

Boland, Lawrence 1981 "On the Futility of Criticizing the Neo-classical Maximization Hypothesis." *American Economic Review* (December).

Boland, Lawrence 1982 *The Foundations of Economic Method*. London: Allen & Unwin.

Boulding, Kenneth E. 1969 "Economics as a Moral Science." *American Economic Review* (March).

Brandis, Royall 1963 "Value Judgments and Economic Science." *Quarterly Journal of Economics and Business* (2).

Brennan, Timothy J. 1979 "Explanation and Value in Economics." *Journal of Economic Issues* (December).

Caldwell, Bruce J. 1982 *Beyond Positivism: Economic Methodology in the Twentieth Century*. London: Allen & Unwin.

Coats, A. W. 1964 "Value Judgments in Economics." *Yorkshire Bulletin of Economics and Social Research* (November).

Coddington, Alan 1972 "Positive Economics." *Canadian Journal of Economics* (February).

Duhs, L. A. 1982 "Why Economists Disagree: The Philosophy of Irreconcilability." *Journal of Economic Issues* (March).

Dwyer, Larry 1982 "The Alleged Value-Neutrality of Economics: An Alternative View." *Journal of Economic Issues* (March).

Finn, Daniel Rush 1979 "Objectivity in Economics: On the Choice of Scientific Method." *Review of Social Economics* (April).

Friedman, Milton 1979 "The Methodology of Positive Economics." In Frank Hahn and Martin Hollis (eds.), *Philosophy and Economic Theory*. London: Oxford University. Reprinted from Friedman, *Essays in Positive Economics*. University of Chicago, 1953, Part I, sections 1, 2, 3, & 6.

Friedman, Milton 1967 "Value Judgments in Economics." In Sidney Hook (ed.), *Human Values and Economic Policy*. New York University.

Fusfeld, Daniel 1980 "The Conceptual Framework of Modern Economics." *Journal of Economic Issues* (March).

Gordon, Scott 1977 "Social Science and Value Judgments." *Canadian Journal of Economics* (November).

Gutting, Gary 1984 "Paradigms and Hermeneutics: A Dialogue." unpublished ms.

Heilbroner, Robert L. 1973 "Economics as a 'Value-Free' Science." *Social Research* (Spring).

Hoover, Kevin D. 1984 "Two Types of Monetarism." *Journal of Economic Literature* (March).
Hutchinson, T. W. 1964 *Positive Economics and Policy Objectives*. London: Allen & Unwin.
Hutchinson, T. W. 1977 *Knowledge and Ignorance in Economics*. University of Chicago.
Hutchinson, T. W. 1981 *The Politics and Philosophy of Economics: Marxians, Keynesians and Austrians*. New York University.
Johnson, L. E. 1983 "Economic Paradigms: A Missing Dimension." *Journal of Economic Issues* (December).
Katouzian, Homa 1980 *Ideology and Method in Economics*. New York University.
Kuhn, Thomas S. 1970 "Reflections on My Critics." In Imre Lakatos and Alan Musgrave (eds.), *Criticism and the Growth of Knowledge*. Cambridge University Press.
Kuhn, Thomas S. 1970 *The Structure of Scientific Revolutions*. Chicago University.
Kuhn, Thomas S. 1971 "Notes on Lakatos." In R. C. Buck and R. S. Cohen (eds.), *Boston Studies in the Philosophy of Science*. Dordrecht.
Lakatos, Imre 1970 "Falsification and the Methodology of Scientific Research Programmes." In Lakatos and Musgrave (eds.), *Criticism and the Growth of Knowledge*. Cambridge University Press.
Little, I. M. D. 1957 *A Critique of Welfare Economics*. Clarendon Press.
Machlup, Fritz 1978 *Methodology of Economics and Other Social Sciences*. New York: Academic.
McCloskey, Donald N. 1983 "The Rhetoric of Economics." *Journal of Economic Literature* (June).
McKenzie, Richard B. 1981 "The Necessary Normative Context of Positive Economics." *Journal of Economic Issues* (September).
Meek, Ronald L. 1964 "Value Judgments in Economics." *British Journal for Philosophy of Science* (August).
Mini, Piero 1974 *Philosophy and Economics: The Origins and Development of Economic Theory*. University Presses of Florida.
Mishan, E. J. 1981 *Introduction to Normative Economics*. Oxford University.
Myrdal, Gunnar 1958 *Value in Social Theory*. London: Routledge and Kegan Paul.
Myrdal, Gunnar 1969 *Objectivity in Social Research*. Pantheon.
Nagel, Ernest 1961 *The Structure of Science: Problems in the Logic of Scientific Explanation*. Harcourt, Brace and World.
O'Brien, John Conway 1981 "The Economists' Quandary: Ethical Values." *International Journal of Social Economics* (3).
Pearce, D. W. and C. A. Nash 1981 *The Social Appraisal of Projects*. John Wiley & Sons.
Robbins, Lionel 1948 *An Essay on the Nature and Significance of Economic Science, 2nd Ed*. London: MacMillan.

Robbins, Lionel 1979 "On Latsis' Method and Appraisal in Economics: A Review Essay." *Journal of Economic Literature* (September).

Rothenberg, Jerome 1975 "Cost-Benefit Analysis: A Methodological Exposition." In M. Guttentag and S. Strueninge (eds.), *Handbook of Evaluation Research,* Vol. II. Sage.

Schumpeter, Joseph A. 1954 *History of Economic Analysis*. Oxford University.

Stewart, Ian M. T. 1979 *Reasoning and Method in Economics*. London: McGraw-Hill.

Streeten, Paul 1950 "Economics and Value Judgments." *Quarterly Journal of Economics* (November).

Thomas, David 1979 *Naturalism and Social Science: A Post-Empiricist Philosophy of Social Science*. Cambridge University Press.

Ward, Ben 1972 *What's Wrong with Economics?* Basic Books.

Weber, Max 1949 *Methodology of the Social Sciences*. Translated and Edited by Henry A. Shils and Henry A. Finch. Free Press.

Wisman, Jon D. 1978 "The Naturalistic Turn of Orthodox Economics: A Study of Methodological Misunderstanding." *Review of Social Economics* (December).

Wong, Stanley 1978 *The Foundations of Paul Samuelson's Revealed Preference Theory*. Routledge and Kegan Paul.

3.

TOWARD A BETTER UNDERSTANDING OF THE POSITIVE/NORMATIVE DISTINCTION IN ECONOMICS

Samuel C. Weston

Introduction

This essay argues in favor of retaining the positive/normative distinction in economics, in spite of developments in methodology and epistemology that have cast doubt on the possibility of a "value-free" economics. The central claim is that it is worthwhile to distinguish between positive economic analysis and normative judgments, even if economics is viewed as being permeated with ethical values. This argument is presented without trying either to demonstrate that there is (or is not) a profound epistemological difference between science and ethics or to show that positive science can (or cannot) afford us access to objective reality.

The author of a widely used introductory economics textbook has called for "a universal agreement to abandon the positive-normative distinction" (Paul Heyne, 1978, pp. 184–85). At the core of Heyne's argument is the not uncommon contention, inspired by Thomas Kuhn, that "economics is inescapably grounded upon nonscientific commitments." For this reason he argues that it is "untenable" for economists to "continue to affirm the possibility of a positive science of economics, continue to assure their students and one another that economists possess or can create a purely scientific, purely descriptive,

Economics and Philosophy 10 (1994): 1–17.

value-free, logical-empirical system of thought and knowledge, and continue to condemn as unscientific any attempt to derive economic generalizations with the explicit aid of value judgments."

It is possible to agree with Heyne's latter assertion and still have misgivings about dropping the positive/normative distinction from economics, as will be shown below. Section 1 examines the meaning and function of the positive/normative distinction. The conceptual distinction is distinguished from the putative behavioral standard often thought to be implied by such a distinction. Section 2 then presents four reasons why a value-free economics is probably not attainable. Section 3 considers the usefulness of the positive/normative distinction. The paper concludes with a summary and some further thoughts that follow from the recognition that economics cannot be a value-free science.

1. What Does It Mean?

A. Conceptual Distinction vs. Behavioral Standard

It seems unlikely that very many economists, if asked to think about it, would argue that the existence of a conceptual device, the positive/normative distinction, would, by itself, imply the existence of a behavioral standard, that economists should strive to be ethically neutral or value-free. It would be surprising if they did, since this would be a fairly clear-cut case of deriving an "ought" from an "is." Probably the putative value-free behavioral standard is the result of a conjunction of making the positive/normative distinction, accepting the scientific norm of objectivity, and embracing a moral skepticism such as that embodied in what Subroto Roy calls "Hume's Second Law."[1]

Discussions concerning the role of value judgments in economics, while generally mentioning the positive/normative distinction, more often than not fail to make clear the precise nature of the connection between this distinction and the notion that economists should attempt to be ethically neutral toward their subject matter. As a consequence, there is a danger that those who argue against the possibility of a value-free economics will cast out the positive/normative baby along with the value-free bathwater. This would be a mistake, as will be shown.

The first thing to make clear in the present essay is that the positive/normative distinction is merely a conceptual distinction. It cannot by itself direct economists to avoid advocating ethical positions in the classroom and in their writing.[2] What it might help to do will be discussed in section 3.

B. Definitions

A problem with the positive/normative distinction in economics is the lack of unanimous agreement as to what exactly it is supposed to communicate. The meaning of "positive" economics has not been too much of a problem, except where it has become enmeshed with the issue of philosophical positivism. What constitutes "normative" economics is more problematic. The widely used connection between "normative" and "ought" or "should" in introductory economics texts leaves it unclear whether normative economics includes all policy advice or only that advice which asserts standards of ethical desirability.

J. N. Keynes ([1917] 1973, pp. 34–35) distinguished between "positive," "normative," and "the art" of economics. In Keynes's scheme positive science is the "body of systematized knowledge of what is," normative science is "a body of systemized knowledge relating to criteria of what ought to be," and art is "a system of rules for the attainment of a given end." The subsequent reduction of Keynes's tripartite distinction to a dichotomy has resulted in a lack of accord as to which of the remaining categories should encompass Keynes's "art."[3]

Keynes's three-way distinction brought together two related, but different, concerns expressed by earlier writers. Richard Whately and his protégé Nassau Senior, while not using those terms, were two of the earliest economists to voice the special motivations for distinguishing between positive and normative economics.[4] Whately wanted it understood that an economist's advice is always about the efficacy of means to some end, not the morality of the end itself. The category in need of special delineation according to Whately would be advice containing assertions of ethical desirability. Senior considered any policy advocacy to be outside of the proper business of economics. His stress is on economists not flinching from the truth in the face of many factors, including moral and political concerns likely to be encountered in actual policy deliberations, which might tempt one to do so. The special category according to Senior would be policy advice. Whatever the history of the distinction, for the purpose of this paper it will be made as follows:

1. Positive economics. Positive economics consists of nonethical true-or-false claims about economies or aspects of economies. It can include empirical statements, such as, "Defense accounts for approximately 25 percent of government spending in the United States." It can include conclusions of hypothetical arguments, such as, "Minimum wage laws will tend to cause higher unemployment." In some cases the asserted truth claim is of a mathematical sort. To a student who says, "We know by Young's Theorem that the cross-partials are equal," we might reply, "That's true." We are saying that it is true that the student's statement is consistent with definitions and axioms that define the system. We are not necessarily saying anything about what is true outside of that system.

Positive economics can also include a proposition such as, "Minimum wage laws are a significant cause of high unemployment among black teenagers in the United States." By changing the predicate of the more formal statement we have introduced empirical content. The truth claim of this statement now depends more for its content on the hiring practices of employers than on its logical consistency. Perhaps because of racism or perceived risk, many employers are reluctant to hire black teenagers at any wage. It is a positive statement because it is believed to be either true or false. Minimum wage laws either have a significant bearing on black teenage unemployment or they do not.

2. Normative economics. Normative economics consists of, or refers to, propositions concerning economics that contain at least one assertion as to what is ethically preferable.[5] This definition deviates from the broader dictionary sense of the term "norm," which could be understood to include standards that are merely prudential; however, it follows Machlup (1969), and has some precedence, if not unanimity, in economic jargon. It has the advantage of giving prominence to the role of ethical values in economics, which is a more difficult philosophical problem than the role of the economist as policy advisor.

Providing examples of normative economic statements can be trickier than it might first seem. There are statements such as, "Unequal income distribution is evil," which would almost always be taken as unambiguously normative. More problematic is a statement such as, "All other things being equal, a market economy will outperform a centrally planned economy." Even if the speaker is careful to note that this declaration does not automatically entail advocacy of a market economy, the verb "outperforms" implies an appraisal with respect to some standard, in this case the production of goods and services. This points toward Myrdal's criticism of positive economics (see below, section 2.C.), which intimates that it is impossible to do economics without evaluations, and that, due to the nature of inherited language, we may not even be fully aware of all the evaluations that we make.

However, the point of the positive/normative distinction, as it is being presented here, is not to ban advocacy by economists, nor is it to claim that there exist clearly and easily identifiable bodies of thought called "positive economics," and "normative economics." As a conceptual device, the primary function of the positive/normative distinction is to help us to sort things out, where there is a need for this.

2. The Impossibility of a Value-Free Economics

Conceptually distinguishing between positive and normative economics does not automatically entail the practical possibility of a purely positive, that is, value-free or ethically neutral economics. There are at least four reasons for this.

A. Inherent Professional Norms[6]

Kenneth Boulding (1970, p. 118) sees sets of commonly held values as being the defining characteristic of cultures and subcultures. In this context, he views science as a subculture, characterized by such a set of values. The scientific subculture holds veracity, curiosity, measurement, quantification, careful observation, experimentation, and objectivity in high regard (Boulding, 1970, p. 119). Insofar as the scientific subculture values these traits and activities, that is, considers them good, science has an "essential ethical basis" (*Ibid.*, p. 120).

The important thing to realize here is that those traits that characterize the scientific subculture are not automatically considered to be good. To do so is to take an ethical stance. Even if the economist were determined to avoid any expression of "what should be" concerning social, political, and economic goals, he or she is still unavoidably inculcating a normative message that to pursue science, to seek the truth, is good.

This would seem trivial, except that it is an issue in contemporary academia. If it is the case, as is now being alleged, that reports of "political correctness" on college campuses have been exaggerated, the response to these reports has not been. What is being responded to is, in many cases, the perception that some academic leaders are declaring the norm of truth-seeking to be secondary to other normative goals.[7]

B. The Normative Context of Economics

Hume ([1777] 1960, pp. 15–16) pointed out that scarcity was the basic cause of the need for justice more than a century before Carl Menger (1871) was to identify this as the basic cause of the economic problem. This suggests a primal entanglement of the two questions. Conceptually distinguishing ethical questions from positive economic questions is an act of intellectual analysis. That such a dissection is possible implies that there is a pre-existing raw material to be operated on in which the two things are interwoven or in some way bound together. This raw material is what Schumpeter (1954, pp. 34–43) calls "vision." It is also the basis on which he distinguishes "economic analysis" from "economic thought."

Richard McKenzie (1981, p. 715) calls for us to admit that economics exists in a "necessary normative context." Part of his argument echoes Schumpeter's point. This is that ethical and other concerns are almost inevitably involved in the choice of questions to take up. The choice of questions that define economics suggests prior concerns with prosperity, individual freedom, distribution, justice, and so on.

That it is possible to conceptually distinguish positive economic questions from ethical questions does not mean that it is possible to separate the practical effects of answers to these. The context in which economics is discussed is more than a source of questions. The attempt to develop a picture of how the world works is often subsidiary to the question of what we are going to do (Samuels, 1988, pp. 349–52). The public at large expects advice from economists, and this advice is liable to be translated into actions. Economics has consequences.

Fortunately, or unfortunately, depending on one's point of view, the law does not allow malpractice suits against economists. If the world works a certain way, if we are mistaken in our understanding of this, and if this misunderstanding gets translated into misinformed policies, it is not mainly economists who bear the brunt of the ensuing pain and misery. Even if we are not mistaken, implementation of any particular policy will have costs to someone.

Different economists may have different ways of dealing with the consequences of economics. Some may claim to exist outside of the ethical life (Williams, 1985, chap. 2). Others may claim that they are deontologically committed to the search for truth, and they are content to let the consequentialist chips fall where they may. Some may work on ethical justification of the results of their favored policies. There may even be those who tamper with evidence, because an apparent truth is too distasteful to confront. Whatever the approach taken, the consequences of economics require an ethical stance, or at least a stance toward ethics, by the economist. The raw material that motivates economics and the practical consequences of economics place economics in a normative context.

C. Values Embedded in Our Terminology

Gunnar Myrdal ([1954] 1984, 1958) made a well-known attack on the "implicit values" held by economists. One angle of his attack was aimed at the value-laden terminology used in economics. Examples of such terms include: "economic integration," "productivity," "equilibrium," "balance," "adjustment" (Myrdal, [1954] 1984, p. 256; 1958, p. 1). Myrdal believed that terminology represented "involved structures of metaphysical ideas, which are firmly anchored in our tradition of thought" ([1954] 1984, p. 257). Specifically with regard to economics, the terms are "permeated with the maxims of natural law philosophy, and, later, of utilitarianism" (*Ibid.,* p. 255).

Part of the problem, according to Myrdal (*Ibid.,* p. 255), is that almost all the terms in economics have at least two meanings. A century ago it was a matter of some contention whether economics needed a precisely defined set of terms such as those of physics. One might recall Bohm Bawerk's heroic and futile efforts to define the term "capital" once and for all, and Pareto's coining of *ophelimite* in an effort to purge economics of all utilitarian content. But it was Marshall who appears to have carried the day, with his refusal to get involved in disputes over the meanings of words, and his insistence that the reasonings of economics must be "expressed in a language that is intelligible to the general public" (Marshall, [1920] 1982, p. 43). One of Marshall's defenses of this practice is that by keeping our usage "in harmony with the traditions of the past," "we might be quick to perceive the indirect hints and the subtle and subdued warnings, which the experiences of our ancestors offer for our instruction" (*Ibid.,* pp. 42–43). This could be interpreted as saying that it is desirable to preserve a terminology replete with double meanings that invoke the involved structures of metaphysical ideas referred to by Myrdal.

Williams (1985, pp. 128–31) points out that if there does exist a fundamental difference between facts and values, knowledge of this is a discovery. It is not something which we can take as apparent from the language we have inherited. It is not a distinction that is, or has been, universally recognized. If this is the case, it would suggest that even were the world to reach some sort of consensus that a meaningful distinction can be drawn between science and ethics, given the dynamics of linguistic evolution, it would take a very long time for languages to change to the point where they automatically reflect this awareness.

This does not necessarily imply that economics cannot be a source of useful information about how the world works. It does suggest that economists will continue to run into Myrdal's problem for the foreseeable future. It probably means that economics will continue to be vulnerable to the charge that it is "part of the manipulation of the social and political psychology of masses of people" (Samuels, 1988, p. 352). This will require that economists must at least be alert to their own and other economist's usage. Insofar as this alertness is aimed at detecting intended and unintended ethical messages, it is an ethical awareness that is required. This is another case of an unavoidable ethical involvement by economists.

D. Implications of Giving Policy Advice

Machlup (1969, pp. 114–29) argues that it is impossible for economists to avoid making value judgments when they act as policy advisors.[8] The reason for this is that situations will inevitably arise in which the economist must substitute his own value judgments (which he will generally assume are those in the best interest of society) for the value judgments of his real or hypothetical clients. Such situations occur because it is generally impossible to fully and unambiguously specify the client's objectives, except in the most restricted and artificial cases.

Even when the choice is between only two conflicting goals, it would most often require rather heroic assumptions to believe that it is possible to specify the acceptable rate of trade-off between them. The interdependence of the economy implies that actual policies involve partial conflicts among a large number of quantifiable entities, such as unemployment, inflation, growth of GNP, tax revenue, government expenditure, private investment, interest rates, income inequality, and so on. Effects on all of these are likely to be matters of concern.

Moreover, the real or imagined client will probably be interested not only in the aggregate magnitudes, but also in the policy effect on the composition of these magnitudes. The situation is made worse by the fact that nonquantifiable magnitudes are apt to be important also. What effect will a policy have on various political, religious, economic, and intellectual freedoms? What is the esthetic impact? How will the policy affect the way this nation is seen by other nations?

The policy advisor hence is confronted with a staggering task even to imagine completely the array of trade-offs involved in almost any economic policy. Yet conclusions about the desirability of a policy aimed at some objective require, at least implicitly, that answers have been arrived at regarding the entire spectrum of acceptable rates of trade-off. Machlup (1969, pp. 119–22) contends that the only way that it is possible to arrive at a unique solution is for the value system of the economist to serve, consciously or unconsciously, as a proxy for the value system of the client so as to fill in the gaps in the specifications of the client's preferences.

Machlup (1965, pp. 3–5) makes another point relevant to the discussion of the ethical entanglement involved in giving policy advice. It is perhaps not inevitable, but surely empirically significant, that economists' (and other social scientists') ethical values become involved when they are called upon to make factual assumptions. This might not be the case were the appropriate evidence available. But, of course, all too often it is not. Hence we witness arguments concerning facts, which are conflated with ethical disputes. Does pornography cause sex crimes? Would restrictive handgun legislation make us safer? Can the unemployment rate be lowered by a fiscal stimulus? Will a high tax on luxury goods harm the poor more than the rich?

One could argue that the norm of objectivity and other professional norms are different enough from assertions of what is best for society as to constitute a special case. With regard to the ethical content of the language, one could acknowledge the situation, claim purity of scientific intent, and promise to be cautious. To the assertion that economics takes place within an ethical context, one could agree with this and still maintain that the impersonal methodological procedure eliminate any bias caused by this context, and that by concentrating on the administration of this, one could be a purely scientific economist. It is not so easy to argue past the point that giving policy advice almost inevitably means asserting one's own values. If Machlup's argument is correct, then the requirement of a "value-free" economics is a demand for something close to impossible.

3. Why Bother?

If one is willing to accept one or more of the arguments against the possibility of economics being value-free, the point of the positive/normative distinction cannot be to direct economists toward ethical neutrality. One is then left with the question of whether this distinction serves any useful purpose. The main reason it might is that economics bears on matters of urgent interest to people, which makes it often controversial. The reasons for conceptually distinguishing between positive and normative economics in such a setting are (1) to be clear as to what question is being discussed; (2) to issue a caveat regarding credentials; (3) to maintain an environment in which any premise or line of reasoning can be questioned without raising doubts as to the moral character of the questioner; and (4) to promote the scientific norm of objectivity.

A. Keeping the Questions Distinct

There is a certain peculiarity about economics, which it shares with other attempts at developing human sciences. This shows up in enduring controversies surrounding the works of Machiavelli, Hobbes, Darwin, and Freud, for example. The assumed premises or the conclusions involved in attempts to describe how the world is can offend ethical sensibilities. At the same time the assumptions or the conclusions might be mistaken. There are two separate issues. That a person might find a human science assumption or conclusion unpalatable could provide a strong motive for that person working to show it mistaken. But only under strong and peculiar assumptions could ethical offensiveness itself entail mistakenness. However, when the grounds for judging a proposition to be true or false are fairly tenuous, as often is the case in economics and other human sciences, and when there is a strong ethical aspect to issues to which the proposition pertains, this simple claim can get lost in the heat of battle. The principle of comparative advantage and the claim that citizens have a moral obligation to purchase the products of their countrymen both pertain to arguments concerning international trade policies. Intellectual clarity requires that we know which we are discussing.

It is important to stress at this point that the claim being made is the modest one that the ethical appraisal of an assumption or proposition and a judgment of its truth content are two distinct issues, and that distinguishing between positive and normative economic statements helps to illuminate this. Acceptance of this point does not require accepting ethical skepticism. It may well be the case, as Roy (1992, chaps. 1 and 2) argues, that "Hume's Second Law" has been the predominant position regarding ethics among economists, and that this has been historically closely associated with acceptance of the positive/normative distinction. While ethical skepticism might require the positive/normative distinction, the latter does not imply the former.

While employing the positive/normative distinction does not require one to hold any particular position with regard to moral epistemology, it does have the effect, at least in certain settings, of attaching an asterisk to ethical issues. This seems prudent and responsible in view of serious philosophical questions concerning the difference between science and ethics, and the ultimate basis of ethical judgments, which warrant deeper inquiries than time is likely to allow, say, in most undergraduate economics classes. The asterisk, on the one hand, suggests that we read more philosophy to find out why these are difficult issues. On the other hand it might serve the desirable role of undercutting the authority of anyone trying to push a certain point of view by means of unsupported assertion.

B. Issuing a Caution about Credentials

One of Max Weber's (1949, pp. 3–5) concerns was the abuse of scientific credentials. How is it that a PhD earned by running regressions on wage patterns in some industry or by creating a highly abstract mathematical model qualifies one to know what is ethically best for society? The asterisk suggested by the positive/normative distinction also serves to remind us that an economist who would tell us, explicitly or implicitly, what is ethically desirable for society may have no more formal preparation for that role than the guy who pontificates at the corner saloon. This might be most important in lower-level undergraduate classes or public arenas where the audience has not yet even begun to think about matters such as the scope of economics, and where the halo effect of one's certification might be most pronounced.

In normal practice, laypersons expect credentialed experts to have a large array of information at their disposal, and they are prepared to accept this information as true, based on little more than the authority of the expert. The positive/normative distinction is a safeguard against the economist slipping in an assertion such as, "equality of income distribution is not a legitimate concern of government," along with facts about the size and composition of GNP or the history of the Federal Reserve System.

This is similar to, but not quite the same as, being reminded that a veterinarian's license does not qualify one to practice law. If asked a legal question, the veterinarian might refer her client to a lawyer. The difference is that it is not clear that there are credentialed ethical authorities to whom economists can refer people. The economist therefore cannot get off the hook so easily. If economics is permeated with ethical values, then there is every reason to expect that economists must deal with ethical arguments. The question is how best to do this. Perhaps economists need more training in ethical philosophy than they now receive. The point of issuing a caution concerning economists' professional credentials is not to prevent them from engaging in reasoned ethical arguments, but to undercut the authority of those who would abuse those credentials.

C. Maintaining a Scholarly Environment

There are a number of things about economics that can make it a touchy subject. One is the basic conception of the human agent. It is very easy for "self-interested" to be taken as meaning "selfish," causing economics to be viewed as a celebration of greed. Another is that the basic cost/benefit analysis essential to economically rational behavior is liable to be presented or interpreted as focusing on pecuniary costs and benefits, ignoring "higher" values. Yet another is the concern with distributional issues. Directly or indirectly almost everything in economics bears upon distribution.

These and other aspects of economics can be sensitive subjects as the result of various factors. The rational self-interested model of human behavior or the Marxian analysis of class may threaten or vindicate someone's self-concept or their interpretation of other people. Economists may argue that some social program, which a person may support or reject for a variety of reasons—ethical, psychological, sociological, and so on—can be counterproductive with respect to the goal it is supposed to achieve. A piece of legislation seen by some people as being vital to maintaining a traditional way of life experienced by friends and relatives may be viewed by an economist as an example of economic rent-seeking. Responses to such ideas presented in economics are liable to be affected by an amalgam of beliefs, attitudes, and concerns, without which interest in economics could not be initiated or sustained.[9]

It often happens that concern for the future of self, family, friends, the nation, and/or the world becomes tightly bound with one or more moral claims. For example, "The North American Free Trade Agreement will allow greedy capitalists to get richer by exploiting Mexican labor," or, "The environmental movement is just another excuse for socialists to further abridge the right to private property." When this happens an "us versus them" dimension is introduced into the debate. Because it is entangled with the moral claim, "us versus them" can easily take on overtones of "good versus evil."

One effect of this is that a person presenting a proposition bearing on immediate human concerns, such as the principle of comparative advantage or Marx's theory of the extraction of surplus value, could possibly be seen as an agent of "them" (or "us"). If this occurs, economic propositions can come to be classified "ad hominem." They either originate from the "good guys" or the "bad guys."[10] Such classification can serve as a substitute for evaluating the argument on its own merits, particularly when the argument is difficult to evaluate. Even worse, the perception that scholarly discourse is essentially a battle of good versus evil might have a dampening effect on free inquiry itself.

Consequently, a third desirable effect of retaining the conceptual positive/normative distinction would be to help create and sustain an environment in which disagreement about truth content is not seen as a battle of good versus evil. One could certainly argue that it appears to have thus far failed to achieve this. It may have even exacerbated the situation, because the positive/normative distinction itself has at times been the bone of contention in us-versus-them disputes. It remains to be seen whether this will still be the case when, as advocated here, the conceptual distinction is removed from its association with value-freedom.

D. Promoting the Norm of Objectivity

There is a norm of objectivity in economics similar to that expressed by Senior (see note 4). Put most simply, this is merely an ethical commitment to truthfulness. The positive/normative distinction is one step toward inculcating this attitude. If we allow that the truthfulness of a proposition is a separate issue from the ethical appraisal of the proposition, then the norm of objectivity could be seen as a requirement that economists and students of economics acknowledge the results of tests of truthfulness, even if these results are ethically disturbing. The commitment is to a process of public and self-administered critical examination.

For economists to claim they are "objective," meaning that they are trying to maintain an attitude of openness to critical scrutiny, can be confused with an assertion of having achieved a nonperspectival point of view. An ethical commitment to truthfulness is not the same thing as a claim of possessing a means of attaining access to objective reality. It does involve a conception of truth, and, if put into operation, it does involve a working commitment to the hypothesis that certain tests, that is, logical and empirical, may be the best determinants available for deciding the truthfulness of propositions. One implication of a commitment to critical scrutiny is that the presumed tests of truthfulness are themselves subject to critical examination.

Ultimately, the judgment of the usefulness of distinguishing between positive and normative economics depends on what one considers to be the goal of scholarly economics. The underlying premise in the preceding argument is that the primary goal is to understand the world. There may be those who argue that the "point is not to understand the world, but to change it." Even here, if the intent is to change the world in a purposeful manner, the ability to effect such alterations would seem to be contingent on an understanding of how the world is.

4. Conclusion and Further Thoughts

To summarize the argument: (1) There are at least four reasons to doubt that it is possible for economics to be ethically neutral or value-free. (2) The raw material of economics is highly likely to involve a mixture of factual and ethical propositions. It is useful to distinguish these in order to (1) be clear as to what question we are addressing, and to remind ourselves that the ethical offensiveness of a proposition cannot determine its truthfulness; (2) remind ourselves and others of the limitations of our professional credentials; (3) lessen the influence of "good guys versus bad guys" as a determinant of truthfulness, thereby helping to maintain a scholarly environment; and (4) help inculcate the norm of objectivity.

It should be clear that this essay is not being offered as a defense of "business as usual" in economics, where the positive/normative distinction might be seen as a wall behind which economists can pretend to avoid ethical issues. Rather it is addressed to a future in which the extent to which economics is permeated with ethical values, and the implications of this, are becoming better understood and appreciated. If freedom from ethical values ceases to be viewed as an attainable goal for economics, the next step might be the "legalization" of normative economics.

One concern about admitting the impossibility of a value-free economics is that this will give economists "the license to assert whatever we please" (Blaug, 1980, pp. 183–84). Unless critical scrutiny is abandoned, it seems more likely that the effect of legalized normative economics will be to have economists presenting reasoned arguments about different sorts of propositions than has hitherto been the case. This could be an improvement. One effect of interpreting the positive/normative distinction as implying a sanction against getting involved in ethical issues has been to drive these issues underground.

The Cambridge Controversies offer an example of the worst sort of covert battle over ethical values (Blaug, 1983, pp. 211–17). Rather than a detailed working out of the economic and ethical implications of holding different ethical stances with regard to the right to private property, distributive justice, and the role of government—something which would have been very valuable and which was explicitly endorsed by Weber (1949, pp. 20–21)—what we inherit from this debate is an immense body of technical literature that obfuscates more than illuminates the ethical issues at the root of the controversy.

Another example of distortion engendered by the presumed norm of ethical neutrality is in the apparent use of Pareto optimality as a way to have something to say about welfare. In intermediate micro texts the Pareto criterion is typically unobtrusively justified in an early chapter on the grounds that "no one would object to making someone better off if this could be done without making anyone else worse off." Later this becomes the standard for judging policies toward, for example, monopoly. This is extremely misleading if it has the effect of teaching the fledgling economist that she has acquired a scientific tool that renders arguments about property rights, act versus rule utilitarianism, and so on superfluous.

The first thing, then, is to bring ethical issues in economics out into the open air. This is no more than Machlup's (1969, p. 129) advice. Bring the value assumptions out into the open and justify them. Better yet, present alternate scenarios embodying different value assumptions. Machlup's prescription is consistent with the Popperian "critical attitude" in that, by openly displaying the ethical positions they are exposed to criticism. Once in the open the naturally expected development would be that economists would start to become ethical philosophers of a specialized sort, as Smith was and a few modern authors such as Sen are already.

Most of the glory in economics, and in any scholarly discipline, goes to those whose activities cause advances in knowledge. Yet it seems that most economists, most of the time, are engaged in more mundane pursuits. One of these is remedial math teaching. Economists are peculiarly positioned in this regard. On the one hand, it is necessary to bring the students up to mathematical par in order to proceed with the economics lesson. On the other hand, economics provides semi-concrete, sustained examples that permit the student the repetitious practice needed to develop confidence in the math. One can lament that this is needed, but given the circumstances, this is a valuable service that economists perform.

Economics has a similar, though undeveloped, relationship to ethics. Professional ethical philosophers tend to deal with the subject in the most general way. Economics is concerned with some particular questions, such as private property and distributive justice, along with a practically infinite number of variations on those themes. One thing that economists could do is to divert more resources to the study of ethics, in an effort to become as proficient at philosophical ethics as they now are at mathematics.

Notes

I would like to thank Samuel Bostaph, Mark Perlman, the referees, and especially Daniel Hausman for their helpful comments and suggestions.

1. Roy (1992, p. 20) states this as: "After every empirical question and every logical and mathematical question has been answered in an economic problem, there is no further scope for common reasoning to work. If an evaluative statement is made at such a point, then it can express no more than a subjective attitude or feeling of the individual economist towards the subject."

2. One might wonder who, in fact, does believe it can do this. The contention here is that the two often tend to be regarded as being part of the same package, without the link being made explicit. The Heyne quote in the introduction does make the connection, in the way that this paper is arguing against. Also doing this is O'Brien (1981, p. 29), who says (referring to Lionel Robbins), "He still insists on the necessity of preserving the idea of a neutral science of economics and regards the distinction between positive and normative economics as one of the achievements in the history of economic thought. . . ." Likewise, Balabkins (1987, p. 53), after giving J. N. Keynes credit for the distinction, writes that afterward, "English speaking economists remain *value free*" (emphasis in original). Wilber and Hoksbergen (1984, p. 191) argue that under a Kuhnian approach "the positive/normative dichotomy disappears completely into the broader concept of the scientific paradigm."

3. For evidence of this see Warren Samuels's (1980) survey of his Michigan State colleagues' views on how advocacy of free trade affects the status of economics as a science.

4. Whately ([1832] 1966, pp. 19–20) says, "When a physician tells his patient, "You ought to go to the sea," or, "You ought to abstain from secondary employments," he is always understood to be speaking in reference to *health*

alone. He is not supposed to imply by the use of the word "ought," that his patient is *morally* bound to follow the prescription at all events; which would perhaps imply the incurring of ruinous expense, or the neglect of important duties" (emphasis in original). Senior (1836, p. 3) says, "The business of a Political Economist is neither to recommend nor to dissuade, but to state general principles, which it is fatal to neglect, but neither advisable, nor perhaps practicable, to use as the sole, or even the principle, guides in the actual conduct of affairs. In the meantime the duty of each individual writer is clear. Employed as he is upon a Science in which error or even ignorance, may be productive of such intense and such extensive mischief, he is bound, like a juryman, to give deliverance true according to the evidence, and allow neither sympathy with indigence, nor disgust at profusion or at avarice—neither reverence for existing institutions, nor detestation of existing abuses—neither love of popularity, nor of paradox, nor of system, to deter him from stating what he believes to be the facts, or of drawing from those facts what appear to him to be the legitimate conclusions."

5. It may be noted that this definition of normative economics excludes the rationality principle, which also might not fit into the category of positive economics offered here. The rationality principle could be a key ingredient in a normative claim. If an economist claims, for example, that it is "irrational" for a seller to regard sunk costs as relevant to a current decision to sell, this could be interpreted as a strictly descriptive rule that helps to specify the hypothetical behavior of *homo economicus*. It could also be viewed as practical advice as to how one ought to behave, since "irrational" is commonly used as a term of condemnation. Much depends on the intent and context. Whether the rationality principle belongs to positive economics or to metaphysics is an unsettled question, complicated by various possible interpretations of the principle itself, and its role in economic explanations (Caldwell, 1991, pp. 18–20).

6. Modern scientific norms arose historically as defenses of science and the individual inquirer against the dogmatism and tyranny of medieval authoritarianism. They thus had a blatantly ethical purpose in their initiation (Roy, 1992, pp. 35–47).

7. A referee points out that "political correctness" is not an assault on truth, but an expression of the view that values are embedded in terminology. This may be correct; however, the claim here is merely that the backlash to P.C. is a response to the *perception*, correct or incorrect, of an assault on truth.

8. Machlup (1965, p. 4n) defines a "policy advisor" as "anybody offering advice, paid or unpaid, upon request or unsolicited, in the government or in the opposition, as an interested party or as a disinterested expert."

9. I am thinking here of something like Schumpeter's (1954, p. 41) "vision," which he defines as, "the pre-analytic cognitive act that supplies the raw material for the analytic effort." One could also see it as being akin to Marx's ideology, especially since Schumpeter develops the notion of vision in dealing with the implications of ideology for the history of economics.

10. Schumpeter (1954, p. 90) remarks, "So true is it that, in science as elsewhere, we fight for and against not men and things as they are, but for and against the caricatures we make of them."

References

Balabkins, Nicholas W. 1987. "Value and Value-Judgements in Economics: Rugina's Contribution." *International Journal of Social Economics* 14:50–62.

Blaug, Mark. 1980. *The Methodology of Economics*. Cambridge: Cambridge University Press.

———. 1983. "The Cambridge Debate on the Theory of Capital and Distribution." In *The Crisis in Economic Theories,* edited by G. Caravale, pp. 102–30. Milan: Franco Angeli Editore.

Boulding, Kenneth. 1970. *Economics as a Science*. New York: McGraw-Hill.

Caldwell, Bruce. 1991. "Clarifying Popper." *Journal of Economic Literature* XXIX:1–33.

Heyne, Paul. 1978. "Economics and Ethics: The Problem of Dialogue." In *Belief and Ethics,* edited by Widick Schroeder and Gibson Winter. Chicago: Center for the Scientific Study of Religion.

Hume, David. [1777] 1960. *An Enquiry Concerning the Principles of Morals*. LaSalle, Illinois: The Open Court Publishing Company.

Keynes, John Neville. [1917] 1973. *The Scope and Method of Political Economy,* 4th ed. New York: Augustus M. Kelley.

Machlup, Fritz. 1965. "Why Economists Disagree." *Proceedings of the American Philosophical Society* 109:1–7.

———. 1969. "Positive and Normative Economics." In *Economic Means and Social Ends,* edited by Robert Heilbroner, pp. 99–129. Englewood Cliffs, N.J.: Prentice Hall.

Marshall, Alfred. [1920] 1982. *Principles of Economics,* 8th ed. Philadelphia: Porcupine Press.

McKenzie, Richard B. 1981. "The Necessary Normative Context of Positive Economics." *Journal of Economic Issues* 15:703–19.

Menger, Carl. 1871. *Principles of Economics,* trans. James Dingwell and Bert F. Hoselitz. New York: New York University Press.

Myrdal, Gunnar. [1954] 1984. "Implicit Values in Economics." In *The Philosophy of Economics,* edited by Daniel M. Hausman, pp. 250–59. Cambridge: Cambridge University Press.

———. 1958. "International Integration." In *Value in Social Theory: A Selection of Essays on Methodology by Gunnar Myrdal,* edited by Paul Streeten, pp. 1–8. New York: Harper and Brothers.

O'Brien, John Conway. 1981. "The Economist's Quandary: Ethical Values." *International Journal of Social Economics* 8:26–46.

Roy, Subroto. 1992. *Philosophy of Economics*. New York: Routledge.

Samuels, Warren J. 1980. "Economics as a Science and Its Relation to Policy: The Example of Free Trade." *Journal of Economic Issues* XIV:163–85.

———. 1988. "An Essay on the Nature and Significance of the Normative Nature of Economics." *Journal of Post-Keynesian Economics* 10:347–54.

Schumpeter, Joseph A. 1954. *History of Economic Analysis*. New York: Oxford University Press.

Senior, Nassau. [1836] 1965. *An Outline of the Science of Political Economy.* New York: Augustus M. Kelley.

Weber, Max. 1949. "The Meaning of 'Ethical Neutrality' in Sociology and Economics." In *Max Weber on the Methodology of the Social Sciences,* edited by Edward A. Shils and Harry A. Finch, pp. 1–47. Glencoe, Illinois: The Free Press.

Whately, Richard. [1832] 1966. *Introductory Lectures on Political Economy,* 2nd ed. New York: Augustus M. Kelley.

Wilber, Charles K., and Roland Hoksbergen. 1984. "Current Thinking on the Role of Value Judgments in Economic Science: A Survey." In *Research in the History of Economic Thought and Methodology,* Volume 2, edited by Warren J. Samuels, pp. 179–94. Greenwich, Connecticut: JAI Press, Inc.

Williams, Bernard. 1985. *Ethics and the Limits of Philosophy.* Cambridge, MA: Harvard University Press.

4.

DOES STUDYING ECONOMICS INHIBIT COOPERATION?

Robert H. Frank, Thomas Gilovich, and Dennis T. Regan

From the perspective of many economists, motives other than self-interest are peripheral to the main thrust of human endeavor, and we indulge them at our peril. In Gordon Tullock's (1976) words (as quoted by Mansbridge, 1990, p. 12), "the average human being is about 95 percent selfish in the narrow sense of the term."

In this paper we investigate whether exposure to the self-interest model commonly used in economics alters the extent to which people behave in self-interested ways. The paper is organized into two parts. In the first, we report the results of several empirical studies—some our own, some by others—that suggest economists behave in more self-interested ways. By itself, this evidence does not demonstrate that exposure to the self-interest model *causes* more self-interested behavior, since it may be that economists were simply more self-interested to begin with, and this difference was one reason they chose to study economics. In the second part of the paper, we present preliminary evidence that exposure to the self-interest model does in fact encourage self-interested behavior.

Journal of Economic Perspectives 7, no. 2 (Spring 1993): 159–71.

Do Economists Behave Differently?

Free-Rider Experiments

A study by Gerald Marwell and Ruth Ames (1981) found that first-year graduate students in economics are much more likely than others to free ride in experiments that called for private contributions to public goods. In their experiments, groups of subjects were given initial endowments of money, which they were to allocate between two accounts, one "public," the other "private." Money deposited in the subject's private account was returned dollar-for-dollar to the subject at the end of the experiment. Money deposited in the public account was pooled, multiplied by some factor greater than one, and then distributed equally among all subjects. Under these circumstances, the socially optimal behavior is for all subjects to put their entire endowment in the public account. But from an individual perspective, the most advantageous strategy is to put everything in the private account. Marwell and Ames found that economics students contributed an average of only 20 percent of their endowments to the public account, significantly less than the 49 percent average for all other subjects.

To explore the reasons for this difference, the authors asked their subjects two follow-up questions. First, what is a "fair" investment in the public good? Of the noneconomists, 75 percent answered "half or more" of the endowment, and 25 percent answered "all." Second, are you concerned about "fairness" in making your investment decision? Almost all noneconomists answered "yes." The corresponding responses of the economics graduate students were more difficult to summarize. As Marwell and Ames wrote,

> More than one-third of the economists either refused to answer the question regarding what is fair, or gave very complex, uncodable responses. It seems that the meaning of "fairness" in this context was somewhat alien for this group. Those who did respond were much more likely to say that little or no contribution was "fair." In addition, the economics graduate students were about half as likely as other subjects to indicate that they were "concerned with fairness" in making their decisions.

The Marwell and Ames study can be criticized on the grounds that their noneconomist control groups consisted of high school students and college undergraduates, who differ in a variety of ways from first-year graduate students in any discipline. Perhaps the most obvious difference is age. As we will see, however, criticism based on the age difference is blunted by our own evidence that older students generally give greater weight to social concerns like the ones that arise in free-rider experiments. It remains possible, however, that more mature students might have had a more sophisticated understanding of the nuances and ambiguities inherent in concepts like fairness, and for that reason gave less easily coded responses to the follow-up questions.

Yet another concern with the Marwell and Ames experiments is not easily dismissed. Although the authors do not report the sex composition of their group of economics graduate students, such groups are almost always preponderantly male. The authors' control groups of high school and undergraduate students, by contrast, consisted equally of males and females.[1] As our own evidence will later show, there is a sharp tendency for males to behave less cooperatively in experiments of this sort. So while the Marwell and Ames findings are suggestive, they do not clearly establish that economists behave differently.

Economists and the Ultimatum Bargaining Game

Another study of whether economists behave differently from members of other disciplines is by John Carter and Michael Irons (1991). These authors measured self-interestedness by examining behavior in an ultimatum bargaining game. This simple game has two players, an "allocator" and a "receiver." The allocator is given a sum of money (in these experiments, $10), and must then propose a division of this sum between herself and the receiver. Once the allocator makes this proposal, the receiver has two choices: (1) he may accept, in which case each player gets the amount proposed by the allocator; or (2) he may refuse, in which case each player gets zero. The game is played only once by the same partners.

Assuming the money cannot be divided into units smaller than one cent, the self-interest model unequivocally predicts that the allocator will propose $9.99 for herself and the remaining $0.01 for the receiver, and that the receiver will accept on the grounds that a penny is better than nothing. Since the game will not be repeated, there is no point in the receiver turning down a low offer in the hope of generating a better offer in the future.

Other researchers have shown that the strategy predicted by the self-interest model is almost never followed in practice: 50–50 splits are the most common proposal, and most highly one-sided offers are rejected in the name of fairness (Guth, et al., 1982; Kahneman, et al., 1986). Carter and Irons found that in both roles (allocator and receiver) economics majors performed significantly more in accord with the predictions of the self-interest model than did nonmajors.[2]

As always, questions can be raised about experimental design. In this case, for example, Carter and Irons assigned the allocator and receiver roles by choosing as allocators those who achieved higher scores on a preliminary word game.[3] Allocators trained in the marginal productivity theory of wages (that is, economics majors) might thus be more likely than others to reason that they were entitled to a greater share of the surplus on the strength of their earlier performance. But while not conclusive, the Carter and Irons results are again suggestive.

Survey Data on Charitable Giving

The free-rider hypothesis suggests that economists might be less likely than others to donate to private charities. To explore this possibility, we mailed questionnaires to 1,245 college professors randomly chosen from the professional directories of 23 disciplines, asking them to report the annual dollar amounts they gave to a variety of private charities. We received 576 responses with sufficient detail for inclusion in our study. Respondents were grouped into the following disciplines: economics ($N = 75$); other social sciences ($N = 106$); math, computer science, and engineering ($N = 48$); natural sciences ($N = 98$); humanities ($N = 94$); architecture, art, and music ($N = 68$); and professional ($N = 87$).[4] The proportion of pure free riders among economists—that is, those who reported giving no money to any charity—was 9.3 percent. By contrast, only 1.1 percent of the professional school respondents gave no money to charity, and the share of those in the other five disciplines who reported zero donations ranged between 2.9 and 4.2 percent.[5] Despite their generally higher incomes, economists were also among the least generous in terms of their median gifts to large charities like viewer-supported television and the United Way.[6]

On a number of other dimensions covered in our survey, the behavior of economists was little different from the behavior of members of other disciplines. For example, economists were only marginally less likely than members of other disciplines to report that they would take costly administrative action to prosecute a student suspected of cheating. Economists were slightly above average for the entire sample in terms of the numbers of hours they reported spending in "volunteer activities." And in terms of their reported frequency of voting in presidential elections, economists were only slightly below the sample average.[7]

		Player *X*: Cooperate	Player *X*: Defect
You	Cooperate	2 for *X* 2 for *Y*	3 for *X* 0 for *Y*
	Defect	0 for *X* 3 for *Y*	1 for *X* 1 for *Y*

Figure 4.1. Payoffs for a Prisoner's Dilemma Game

Economists and the Prisoner's Dilemma

One of the most celebrated and controversial predictions of the self-interest model is that people will always defect in a one-shot prisoner's dilemma game. Figure 4.1 shows the monetary payoffs in dollars to two players, *X* and *Y*, in a standard prisoner's dilemma. The key feature of such a game is that for each player, defection has a higher payoff irrespective of the choice made by the other player. Yet if both players follow this self-interested logic and defect, both end up with a lower payoff than if each cooperates. The game thus provides a rich opportunity to examine self-interested behavior.

We conducted a prisoner's dilemma experiment involving both economics majors and nonmajors. All groups were given an extensive briefing on the prisoner's dilemma at the start of the experiment and each subject was required to complete a questionnaire at the end to verify that he or she had indeed understood the consequences of different combinations of choices; in addition, many of our subjects were students recruited from courses in which the prisoner's dilemma is an item on the syllabus. Our subjects met in groups of three and each was told that he or she would play the game once only with each of the other two subjects. The payoff matrix, shown in figure 4.1, was the same for each play of the game. Subjects were told that the games would be played for real money, and that confidentiality would be maintained so that none of the players would learn how their partners had responded in any play of the game.

Following a period in which subjects were given an opportunity to get to know one another, each subject was taken to a separate room and asked to fill out a form indicating a response (cooperate or defect) to each of the other two players in the group. After the subjects had filled out their forms, the results were tallied and the payments disbursed. Each subject received a single payment that was the sum of three separate amounts: the payoff from the game with the first partner; the payoff from the game with the second partner; and a term that was drawn at random from a large list of positive and negative values. None of these three elements could be observed separately, only their sum. The purpose of this procedure was to prevent subjects from inferring both individual and group patterns of choice. Thus, unlike earlier prisoner's dilemma experiments,[8] ours did not enable the subject to infer what happened even when each (or neither) of the other players defected.

In one version of the experiment (the "unlimited" version), subjects were told that they could make promises not to defect during the time they were getting to know each other, but they were also told that the anonymity of their responses would render such promises unenforceable. In two other versions of the experiment (the "intermediate" and "limited" versions), subjects were not permitted to make promises about their strategies. The latter two versions differed from one another in terms of the length of pre-game interaction, with up to 30 minutes permitted for the intermediate groups and no more than 10 minutes for the limited groups.

For the sample as a whole there were a total of 267 games, which means a total of 534 choices between cooperation and defection. For these choices, the defection rate for economics majors was 60.4 percent, as compared with only 38.8 percent for nonmajors. This pattern of differences strongly supports the hypothesis that economics majors are more likely than nonmajors to behave self-interestedly ($p < .005$).[9]

One possible explanation for the observed differences between economics students and others is that economics students are more likely to be male, and males have lower cooperation rates. To control for possible influences of sex, age, and experimental condition, we performed the ordinary least squares regression reported in figure 4.2.[10] Because each subject played the game twice, the individual responses are not statistically independent. To get around this problem, we limited our sample to the 207 subjects who either cooperated with, or defected from, each of their two partners. The 60 subjects who cooperated with one partner and defected on the other were deleted from the sample. The dependent variable is the subject's choice of strategy, coded as 0 for "cooperate" and 1 for "defect." The independent variables are "econ," which takes the value 1 for economics majors, 0 for all others; "unlimited," which is 1 for subjects in the unlimited version of the experiment, 0 for all others; "intermediate," which is 1 for subjects in the intermediate version, 0 for all others; "limited," which is the reference category; "sex," coded as 1 for males, 0 for females; and "class," coded as 1 for freshmen, 2 for sophomores, 3 for juniors, and 4 for seniors.

Dependent variable: cooperate (0) or defect (1)

Variable	Coefficient	s.e.	*t*-ratio
Constant	0.579127	0.1041	5.571
Econ	0.168835	0.0780	2.16
Limited	0.00	—	—
Intermediate	−0.091189	0.0806	−1.13
Unlimited	−0.329572	0.0728	−4.53
Sex	0.239944	0.0642	3.74
Class	−0.065363	0.0303	−2.16

$R^2 = 22.2\%$ R^2(adjusted) = 20.3%
$s = 0.4402$ with 207 − 6 = 201 degrees of freedom

Source	Sum of Squares	*df*	Mean Square	*F*-ratio
Regression	11.1426	5	2.229	11.5
Residual	38.9540	201	0.193801	

Figure 4.2. Whole Sample Regression

Consistent with a variety of other findings on sex differences in cooperation,[11] we estimate that, other factors the same, the probability of a male defecting is almost 0.24 higher than the corresponding probability for a female. But even after controlling for the influence of gender, we see that the probability of an economics major defecting is almost 0.17 higher than the corresponding probability for a nonmajor.

The coefficients for the unlimited and intermediate experimental categories represent effects relative to the defection rate for the limited category. As expected, the defection rate is smaller in the intermediate category (where subjects have more time to interact than in the limited category), and falls sharply further in the unlimited category (where subjects are permitted to make promises to cooperate).[12]

Note, finally, that the overall defection rate declines significantly as students progress through school. The class coefficient is interpreted to mean that with the passage of each year the probability of defection declines, on the average, by almost 0.07. This pattern will prove important when we take up the question of whether training in economics is the cause of higher defection rates for economics majors.

For subjects in the unlimited subsample, we found that the difference between economics majors and nonmajors virtually disappears once subjects are permitted to make promises to cooperate. For this subsample, the defection rate for economics majors is 28.6 percent, compared to 25.9 percent for nonmajors. Because the higher defection rates for economics majors are largely attributable to the no-promises conditions of the experiment, the remainder of our analysis focuses on subjects in the limited and intermediate groups. The conditions encountered by these groups are of special significance, because they come closest to approximating the conditions that characterize social dilemmas encountered in practice. After all, people rarely have an opportunity to look one another in the eye and promise not to litter on deserted beaches or disconnect the smog control devices on their cars.

When the choices are pooled for the limited and intermediate groups, both economics majors and nonmajors defect more often, but the effect is considerably larger for economists. In those groups, the defection rate was 71.8 percent for economics majors and just 47.3 percent for nonmajors, levels that differ significantly at the .01 level.

As part of the exit questionnaire that tested understanding of the payoffs associated with different combinations of choices, we also asked subjects to state reasons for their choices. We hypothesized that economists would be more inclined to construe the objective of the game in self-interested terms, and therefore more likely to refer exclusively to features of the game itself, while noneconomists would be more open to alternative ways of interpreting the game, and would refer more often to their feelings about their partners, aspects of human nature, and so on. Indeed, among the sample of economics students,

31 percent referred only to features of the game itself in explaining their chosen strategies, compared with only 17 percent of the noneconomists. The probability of obtaining such divergent responses by chance is less than .05.

Another possible explanation for the economists' higher defection rates is that economists may be more likely to expect their partners to defect. The self-interest model, after all, encourages such an expectation, and we know from other experiments that most subjects defect if they are told that their partners are going to defect. To investigate this possibility, we asked students in an upper division public finance course in Cornell's economics department whether they would cooperate or defect in a one-shot prisoner's dilemma if they knew *with certainty* that their partner was going to cooperate. Most of these students were economics majors in their junior and senior years. Of the 31 students returning our questionnaires, 18 (58 percent) reported that they would defect, only 13 that they would cooperate. By contrast, just 34 percent of noneconomics Cornell undergraduates who were given the same questionnaire reported that they would defect from a partner they knew would cooperate ($p < .05$). For the same two groups of subjects, almost all respondents (30 of 31 economics students and 36 of 41 noneconomics students) said they would defect if they knew their partner would defect. From these responses, we conclude that while expectations of partner performance play a strong role in predicting behavior, defection rates would remain significantly higher for economists than for noneconomists even if both groups held identical expectations about partner performance.

Why Do Economists Behave Differently?

Economists appear to behave less cooperatively than noneconomists along a variety of dimensions. This difference in behavior might result from training in economics; alternatively, it might exist because people who chose to major in economics were different initially; or it might be some combination of these two effects. We now report evidence on whether training in economics plays a causal role.

Comparing Upperclassmen and Underclassmen

If economics training causes uncooperative behavior, then defection rates in the prisoner's dilemma should rise with exposure to training in economics, all other factors held constant. Recalling our earlier finding that defection rates for the sample as a whole fall steadily between the freshman and senior years, the question is thus whether defection rates fall to the same degree over time for economists as for noneconomists. We found that the pattern of falling defection rates holds more strongly for noneconomics majors than for economics majors in the no-promises subsample. For noneconomics underclassmen in this group (freshmen and sophomores), the defection rate is 53.7 percent, compared to only 40.2 percent of upperclassmen. By contrast, the trend toward lower defection rates is virtually absent from economics majors in the no-promises subsample (73.7 percent for underclassmen, 70.0 percent for upperclassmen). In other words, students generally show a pronounced tendency toward more cooperative behavior with movement toward graduation, but this trend is conspicuously absent for economics majors.[13]

Naturally, we are in no position to say whether the trend for noneconomists reflects something about the content of noneconomics courses. But the fact that this trend is not present for economists is at least consistent with the hypothesis that training in economics plays some causal role in the lower observed cooperation rates of economists.

Honesty Surveys

In a further attempt to assess whether training in economics inhibits cooperation, we posed a pair of ethical dilemmas to students in two introductory microeconomics courses at Cornell University and to a control group of students in an introductory astronomy course, also at Cornell. In one dilemma, the owner of a small business is shipped ten microcomputers but is billed for only nine; the question is whether the owner will inform the computer company of the error. Subjects are first asked to estimate the likelihood that the owner would point out the mistake; and then, on the same response scale, to indicate how likely *they* would be to point out the error if they were the owner. The second dilemma concerns whether a lost envelope containing $100 and bearing the owner's name and address is likely to be returned by the person who finds it. Subjects are first asked to imagine that they have lost the envelope and to estimate the likelihood that a stranger would return it. They are then asked to assume that the roles are reversed and to indicate the likelihood that they would return the money to a stranger.

Students in each class completed the questionnaire on two occasions: during the initial week of class in September, and then during the final week of class in December. For each of the four questions, each student was coded as being "more honest" if the probability checked for that question rose between September and December; "less honest" if it fell during that period; and "no change" if it remained the same.

The first introductory microeconomics instructor (instructor A) whose students we surveyed is a mainstream economist with research interests in industrial organization and game theory. In class lectures, this instructor placed heavy emphasis on the prisoner's dilemma and related illustrations of how survival imperatives often militate against cooperation. The second microeconomics instructor (instructor B) is a specialist in economic development in

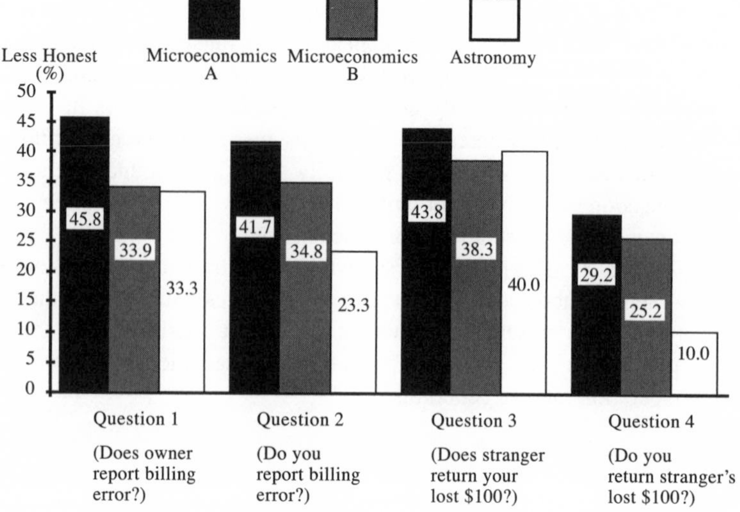

Figure 4.3. Freshmen Honesty Survey Results

Maoist China who did not emphasize such material to the same degree, but did assign a mainstream introductory text. On the basis of these differences, we expected that any observed effects of economics training should be stronger in instructor A's class than in instructor B's.

The results for these two classes, plus the class of noneconomists, are summarized in figure 4.3, which shows the proportion of each class reporting a "less honest" result at the end of the semester than at the beginning. As the figure indicates, one semester's training was accompanied by greater movement toward more cynical ("less honest") responses in instructor A's introductory economics class than in instructor B's. Subjects in instructor B's class, in turn, showed greater movement toward less honest responses than did those in our control group of introductory astronomy students.

It may seem natural to wonder whether some of the differences between the two economics classes might stem from the fact that students chose their instructors rather than being randomly assigned. Perhaps the ideological reputations of the two professors were known in advance to many students, with the result that a disproportionate number of less cynical students chose to take instructor B's course. However, the average values of the initial responses to the four questions were virtually the same for both classes. Moreover, even if students had differed across the two classes, this would not alter the interpretation of our findings, since the entries in figure 4.3 record not the *level* of cynicism but the *change* in that level between the beginning and end of the course. Even if the students in Microeconomics A were more cynical to begin with, they became still more so during the course of the semester. This finding is consistent with the hypothesis that emphasis on the self-interest model tends to inhibit cooperation.

Discussion

A variety of evidence suggests a large difference in the extent to which economists and noneconomists behave self-interestedly. We believe our survey of charitable giving and our prisoner's dilemma results lend additional support to the hypothesis that economists are more likely than others to free ride.

Both of these exercises, however, also produced evidence that economists behave in traditionally communitarian ways under at least some circumstances. For example, economists reported spending as much time as others in volunteer activities, and were only marginally less likely than others to vote in presidential elections. Moreover, in the unlimited version of our prisoner's dilemma experiments, where subjects were allowed to promise to cooperate, economists were almost as likely to cooperate as noneconomists.

We also found evidence consistent with the view that differences in cooperativeness are caused in part by training in economics. This evidence is clearly less compelling than the evidence for a difference in cooperativeness. But it would be remarkable indeed if none of the observed differences in behavior were the result of repeated and intensive exposure to a model whose unequivocal prediction is that people will defect whenever self-interest dictates.

Should we be concerned that economics training may inhibit cooperation? Some might respond that while society would benefit if more people cooperated in social dilemmas, economists cannot be faulted for pointing out the unpleasant truth that self-interest dictates defection. One difficulty with this response is that it may be wrong. Several researchers have recently suggested that the ultimate victims of noncooperative behavior may be the very people who practice it (see, for example, Akerlof, 1983; Hirshleifer, 1987; Frank, 1988; and the essays in Mansbridge, 1990). Suppose, by way of illustration, that some people always cooperate in one-shot prisoner's dilemmas while others always follow the seemingly dominant strategy of defecting. If people are free to interact with others of their own choosing, and if there are cues that distinguish cooperators from defectors, then cooperators will interact selectively with one another and earn higher payoffs than defectors. Elsewhere we have shown that even on the basis of brief encounters involving strangers, experimental subjects are adept at predicting who will cooperate and who will defect in prisoner's dilemma games (Frank, 1988, ch. 7; Frank, Gilovich, and Regan, 1992). If people are even better at predicting the behavior of people they know well—a reasonable enough presumption—then the direct pursuit of material self-interest may indeed often be self-defeating.

In an ever more interdependent world, social cooperation has become increasingly important—and yet increasingly fragile. With an eye toward both the social good and the well-being of their own students, economists may wish to stress a broader view of human motivation in their teaching.

Notes

1. This was the case, in any event, for the groups whose sex composition the authors reported.
2. Kahneman, Knetsch, and Thaler (1986) report findings similar to those of Carter and Irons: commerce students (the term used to describe business students in Canadian universities) were more likely than psychology students to make one-sided offers in ultimatum bargaining games.
3. This allocation procedure is described in a longer, unpublished version of the Carter and Irons paper (1990).
4. The "other social sciences" category includes psychology, sociology, political science, and anthropology; "natural sciences" includes physics, chemistry, biology, and geology; "humanities" includes philosophy, history, English, foreign languages, and religion; and "professional" includes education, business, and nursing.
5. Although we do not have data on the gender of each survey respondent, gender differences by discipline do not appear to account for the observed pattern of free-ridership. For example, the natural sciences, which are also preponderantly male, had only one-third as many free riders as did economics.
6. The annual median gift of economists to charities is actually slightly larger, in absolute terms, than the median for all disciplines taken as a whole. But because economists have significantly higher salaries than do the members of most other disciplines, the median gift overstates the relative generosity of economists. To correct for income differences by discipline, we proceeded as follows: First, we estimated earnings functions (salary vs. years of experience) for each discipline using data from a large private university. We then applied the estimated coefficients from these earnings functions to the experience data from our survey to impute an income for each respondent in our survey. Using these imputed income figures, together with our respondents' reports of their total charitable giving, we estimated the relationship between income and total giving. (In the latter exercise, all economists were dropped from the sample on the grounds that our object was to see whether the giving pattern of economists deviates from the pattern we see for other disciplines.) We then calculated our measure of a discipline's generosity as the ratio of the average value of gifts actually reported by members of the discipline to the average value of gifts expected on the basis of the members' imputed incomes. The computed ratio for economists was 0.91, which means that economists in our sample gave 91 percent as much as they would have been expected to give on the basis of their imputed incomes.
7. In fairness to the self-interest model, we should note that there may be

self-interested reasons for volunteering or contributing even in the case of charities like the United Way and public television. United Way campaigns, for example, are usually organized in the workplace and there is often considerable social pressure to contribute. Public television fund drives often make on-the-air announcements of donors' names and economists stand to benefit just as much as the members of any other discipline from being hailed as community-minded citizens. In the case of smaller, more personal charitable organizations, there are often even more compelling self-interested reasons for giving or volunteering. After all, failure to contribute in accordance with one's financial ability may mean outright exclusion from the substantial private benefits associated with membership in religious groups, fraternal organizations, and the like.

8. For an extensive survey, see Dawes (1980).

9. Because each subject responded twice, the 534 choices are not statistically independent, and so the most direct test of statistical significance, the chi-square test, is inappropriate for the sample as a whole. To overcome this problem, we performed a chi-square test on the number of subjects who made the same choice—cooperate or defect—in both of their games. There were 207 such subjects (78 percent of the sample). The pattern of results observed in this restricted sample is essentially the same as the one observed for the sample as a whole.

10. Because the conventional assumptions regarding the distribution of the error term are not satisfied in the case of linear models with dichotomous dependent variables, the standard ordinary least squares significance tests are not valid. In an appendix available on request from the authors, we report the results of models based on the probit and logit transformations. The statistical significance patterns shown by the coefficients from these transformed models are the same as for the ordinary least squares model. Because the coefficients of the ordinary least squares model are more easily interpreted, we report the remainder of our results in that format only.

11. See, for example, the studies cited in Gilligan (1982).

12. With the permission of subjects, we tape-recorded the conversations of several of the unlimited groups, and invariably each person promised each partner to cooperate. There would be little point, after all, in promising to defect.

13. A regression similar to the one shown in figure 4.2 confirms that this pattern continues to hold even when controlling for other factors that might influence defection rates.

References

Akerlof, George, "Loyalty Filters," *American Economic Review,* March 1983, *73*:1, 54–63.

Carter, John, and Michael Irons, "Are Economists Different, and If So, Why?" *Journal of Economic Perspectives,* Spring 1991, *5*:2, 171–77.

Carter, John, and Michael Irons, "Are Economists Different, and If So, Why?" working paper, College of the Holy Cross, December 1990.

Dawes, Robyn, "Social Dilemmas," *Annual Review of Psychology,* 1980, *31,* 163–93.

Frank, Robert H., *Passions Within Reason.* New York: W. W. Norton, 1988.

Frank, Robert H., Thomas Gilovich, and Dennis T. Regan, "The Evolution of Hardcore Cooperation." In *Ethology and Sociobiology,* forthcoming 1993.

Gilligan, Carol, *In a Different Voice.* Cambridge: Harvard University Press, 1982.

Guth, Werner, Rolf Schmittberger, and Bernd Schwarze, "An Experimental Analysis of Ultimatum Bargaining," *Journal of Economic Behavior and Organization,* December 1982, *3*:4, 367–88.

Hirshleifer, Jack, "On the Emotions as Guarantors of Threats and Promises." In Dupre, John, ed., *The Latest and the Best Essays on Evolution and Optimality.* Cambridge: The MIT Press, 1987, 307–26.

Kahneman, Daniel, Jack Knetsch, and Richard Thaler, "Fairness and the Assumptions of Economics," *Journal of Business,* Part 2, October 1986, *59,* S285–S300.

Mansbridge, Jane J., *Beyond Self-Interest.* Chicago: University of Chicago Press, 1990.

Marwell, Gerald, and Ruth Ames, "Economists Free Ride, Does Anyone Else?: Experiments on the Provision of Public Goods, IV," *Journal of Public Economics,* June 1981, *15*:3, 295–310.

Tullock, Gordon, *The Vote Motive.* London: Institute for Economic Affairs, 1976.

PART II

RATIONALITY, ETHICS, AND THE BEHAVIOR OF ECONOMIC AGENTS

All evidence indicates that economic actors (consumers, workers, firms) act out of more than calculated self-interest. Thus the assumption of rationality may be insufficient in some cases and inappropriate in others. People's behavior is influenced by many things including ethical norms. What impact does this have upon the ability of economic theory to predict outcomes of economic actions? For example, given imperfect information purely self-interested actors might be tempted into strategic behavior that results in suboptimal outcomes. Morally constrained behavior might reduce that opportunism.

The most fundamental postulate of neoclassical economics, rational actor theory, is that individual agents maximize some objective function subject to constraints. Economists and others have several reasons to be concerned with this theory. First, to the extent that economics is used as an empirical science, a faulty theory of human behavior will lead to an inability to predict and control. For example, how should government encourage people to behave in socially beneficial ways, say, to donate blood? If people are rational maximizers, government can best achieve its ends by providing a proper set of economic incentives for such behavior. But if economics misconceives the way people are motivated, incentives might fail to work. In fact, there is some evidence that blood donations decline when a system of cash payments is introduced. How could this be?

It is not clear how to account for the decline in contributions, but one possible answer relates to a second, *generative*, role for economic theory. By this is meant its role in generating behavior as opposed to merely predicting or controlling it. Economics can play this role in several possible ways. First, as the chapter by Frank, Gilovich and Regan in the previous section suggested, economics can become a sort of philosophy of life for those who study it, leading them to behave in economically rational ways. Second, and more appropriate for the blood-donation case, economically rational ways of behavior can be taught by exposure to social policies and practices that presuppose economic rationality. Thus, even those who initially behave according to social norms about giving blood may come to view blood donation as just another economic transaction, once they see people being paid for their donations. Thus, their noneconomic motives are undercut by an economic policy based solely on self-interest.

Another reason there should be concern with the validity of the assumption of economic rationality has to do with its normative role. In the previous section it was noted that the practice of neo-classical economics, despite claims of a positive/normative distinction, commits one to certain moral beliefs. For example, when economics merely identifies and describes certain behaviors as "rational," the label of rationality carries a positive connotation that may lead some to see such behavior as desirable or even morally good. (It is important to remember that the neo-classical theory of rationality is not the only possible one; Aristotle and Kant offered other definitions of rationality, which they recognized as normative in character.) Another normative role for the theory of economic rationality is as a benchmark of economic success. The use of Pareto optimality means one is measuring the success of the economic system by its satisfaction of individual preferences, as opposed to some other measure, such as, say, infant mortality or the presence of demeaning working conditions. In this "benchmark" role, the economic theory of rationality is normative because it dictates how policies and behaviors are to be judged.

Thus, there are a number of reasons why one should be concerned about whether the economic theory of rationality is a good one. How would one begin to determine the answer to that question? Certainly, with regard to the empirical role of economics, it is relevant to ask whether people actually behave according to the theory. One chapter in this section, by Robin Dawes and Richard Thaler, does just that, using experimental evidence. However, keeping in mind the generative role that theory potentially plays, one must also ask what the *consequences* are of adopting the neo-classical theory of value. Charles Wilber, in a chapter in this section, suggests, among other things, that a society constructed on the basis of pure economic rationality might face overwhelming problems of moral hazard, resulting in a kind of crisis of the moral environment. Finally, it should be noted that not all of the questions about economic rationality can be answered with purely empirical arguments; further discussion of the moral issues raised here appears later in Part V.

Several themes will appear in this section on rationality, ethics, and the behavior of economic agents. As has been seen, one of the crucial issues is the empirical validity of the neoclassical theory. Another issue is the potential consequences of adopting the theory as society's operative theory of human nature. A third issue is the question of exactly *how* people might deviate from the rational model. If people are moral agents in addition to rational maximizers, how *do* they care about the world? For example, do they simply care about the utility of other agents, or do they obey certain moral strictures—like those against lying—regardless of their effect on others' happiness? Fourth, and closely related to the previous question, is whether these moral concerns can be somehow reconciled with standard rational actor theory. All of these questions need to be answered and the articles in this section begin to address them.

Jon Elster, in his contribution, begins by arguing that there is more to human behavior than utility maximization. He rightly points out that there is much evidence readily available to support this claim, including anonymous giving and voting. He carefully and usefully distinguishes several varieties of non-maximizing behavior seen in the world, ranging from love to spite. Yet, even in light of this variety, self-interest has a certain "methodological priority," Elster argues, because it is other people's selfish interests that we take into consideration when we act out of more complicated motivations like love or spite. Elster concludes that departures from maximization can be accounted for by three factors: altruism, codes of honor and long-term self-interest.

Dawes and Thaler take on the task of empirically documenting and cataloguing moral behavior as it has been observed in experiments. They recount evidence that in experimental situations people will contribute money toward a public good, contrary to the predictions of rational actor theory. And, reminiscent of the chapter by Frank, Gilovich and Regan in the previous section, they show that groups who have studied economics contribute much less to the public good than others—an illustration of the generative role of social science. Like Elster, Dawes and Thaler attempt to separate out the possible motives for moral behavior. They find that what Elster called long-run self-interest cannot explain all the results, for example, one-shot games. They show that groups that are allowed to have discussions before they decide how to play have much lower rates of defection, which to them suggests a role for "impure altruism"—obtaining utility from doing the right thing. Finally, people seem to be more inclined to cooperate when they have been given an opportunity to develop a sense of common identity with the beneficiaries of their cooperation.

The conditions for cooperation also play an important role in the next chapter. Wilber examines the problems of organizing society, and, in particular of organizing work, in conditions of imperfect information. In those conditions, economists have demonstrated, the problem of *moral hazard* can arise. A problem arises when the payoff to one party of a contract depends upon the performance of the other party, and the performance cannot be monitored. For example, there may be a tendency to avoid work when the boss is not looking.

Such problems are surely pervasive in our complex society. Wilber believes that ethics can be part of the remedy, diminishing the tendency to shirk in such situations. He argues that alternative forms of work organization, such as co-operatives, might be effective in eliciting moral behavior under conditions of imperfect information.

In the final chapter in this section, "God and the Ghetto," Glenn Loury argues that policy makers must recognize that creating incentives based solely on the assumption of rational self-interest is doomed to failure. They need to understand that a conception of virtuous living needs to be revived in the public debate over workable policies. More surprising, coming from an economist, is his argument that virtuous living requires a spiritual motivation that is learned in the home and church. Future policy debates need to bear these behavioral issues in mind.

What the chapters in this section make clear is that there is no one form of behavior, whether self-interested or moral, that is dictated by human nature. There is abundant evidence for this. The question then becomes how the various aspects of human nature—economically rational and otherwise—can be elicited so as to create an efficient and just society.

5.

SELFISHNESS AND ALTRUISM

Jon Elster

In the state of nature, nobody cares about other people. Fortunately, we do not live in this dismal state. Sometimes we take account of other people's success and well-being, and are willing to sacrifice some of our own for their sake.[1] Or so it appears. But perhaps altruistic behavior really springs from self-interest? For instance, isn't it in my long-term self-interest to help others, so that I can receive help in return when I need it? Isn't the patron of a charity motivated by his own prestige rather than by the needs of the beneficiaries? What matters to him is that his donations be visible and publicized, not who benefits from them.[2] Some argue that people are always and everywhere motivated by self-interest, and that differences in behavior are due only to differences in their opportunities.[3] Civilized society, on this view, depends on having institutions that make it in people's rational self-interest to speak the truth, keep their promises, and help others—not on people having good motivations.

I believe this argument is plain wrong, and I'll explain why in a moment. Let us first, however, get a few things out of the way. The proposition that self-interest is fundamental could be understood in two other ways besides that just set out.[4] It could mean that all action is ultimately performed for the sake of the agent's pleasure or that self-interest has a certain methodological priority. The first view, again, is plain wrong. The second is true, but unhelpful as a guide to understanding behavior.

Consider first the view that all rational action must be self-interested be-

Beyond Self-Interest, ed. Jane J. Mansbridge (University of Chicago Press, 1990), pp. 44–52.

cause it is ultimately motivated by the pleasure it brings to the agent. An illustration could be love, often defined as taking pleasure in another person's pleasure. If I give a present to someone I love, am I not simply using that person as a means to my own satisfaction? Against this view, it is sufficient to point out that not all altruistic actions are done out of love. Some are done out of a sense of duty and need not provide any kind of pleasure. A person who is motivated solely by the warm glow that comes from having done one's duty is not acting out of duty, but engaging in narcissistic role-playing. And in any case, the means-end theory of love is inadequate. I choose the gift to satisfy the other person's desire, and my own satisfaction is simply a by-product.[5]

There is a sense, though, in which self-interest is more fundamental than altruism. The state of nature, although a thought experiment, is a logically coherent situation. But we cannot coherently imagine a world in which everyone has exclusively altruistic motivations. The goal of the altruist is to provide others with an occasion for selfish pleasures[6]—the pleasure of reading a book or drinking a bottle of wine one has received as a gift.[7] If nobody had first-order, selfish pleasures, nobody could have higher-order, altruistic motives either. Some of the excesses of the Chinese cultural revolution illustrate the absurdity of universal altruism. All Chinese citizens were told to sacrifice their selfish interests for the interests of the people—as if the people were something over and above the totality of Chinese citizens. The point is just a logical one. If some are to be altruistic, others must be selfish, at least some of the time, but everybody *could* be selfish all the time. The assumption that all behavior is selfish is the most parsimonious we can make, and scientists always like to explain much with little. But we cannot conclude, neither in general nor on any given occasion, that selfishness is the more widespread motivation.[8] Sometimes the world is messy, and the most parsimonious explanation is wrong.

The idea that self-interest makes the world go round is refuted by a few familiar facts. Some forms of helping behavior are not reciprocated and so cannot be explained by long-term self-interest. Parents have a selfish interest in helping their children, assuming that children will care for parents in their old age—but it is not in the selfish interest of children to provide such care.[9] And still many do. Some contributors to charities give anonymously and hence cannot be motivated by prestige.[10] Some forms of income redistribution are perhaps in the interest of the rich. If they don't give to the poor, the poor might kill them. But nobody was ever killed by a quadriplegic.[11] From a self-interested point of view, the cost of voting in a national election is much larger than the expected benefit. I might get a tax break of a few hundred dollars if my candidate wins, but that gain has to be multiplied by the very small probability that my vote will be decisive—much smaller than the chance that I'll be killed in a car accident on my way to voting. And still large numbers of people vote. Many people report their taxable income and tax-free deductions correctly, even when tax evasion would be almost riskless.

Some of these examples invite a counterargument. It *is* in children's rational self-interest to help their parents, because if they don't their friends would criticize and perhaps desert them. It *is* selfishly rational to vote, because if one doesn't one will be the target of informal social sanctions, ranging from raised eyebrows to social ostracism. Against this, I would simply like to make two points. It is not clear that it is in the rational self-interest of other people to impose these sanctions. And in any case the argument does not apply to behavior that cannot be observed by others. Anonymous contributions fall in this category, as does voting in many electoral systems.

Pure nonselfish behavior is represented by anonymous contributions to impersonal charities. Gifts to specific persons could be explained (although I don't really think so) by the donor's pleasure in giving pleasure. Publicly visible gifts could be explained by the prestige of donating or by the social sanctions imposed on nondonors. Only gifts from unknown to unknown—voluntary donation of blood is perhaps the purest example—are unambiguously nonselfish. On average, such transfers amount to about one percent of people's income—not quite enough to make the world go around, but not negligible either if there are few recipients. When we add abstention from riskless tax evasion the amount increases. Ambiguously nonselfish transfers are quite large. Since, in my opinion, the ambiguity can often be resolved in favor of the nonselfish interpretation, this makes the amount even bigger.

Let us look at the fine grain of altruistic motivation. Helping or giving out of love is instrumental behavior, that is, concerned with outcomes. If I help my child, I seek the best means to make that child happy. (Behavior can be rational and instrumental and not yet be selfish, contrary to a widespread but vulgar view that equates rationality with selfishness.) The concept of duty is more ambiguous: it can be instrumental or squarely noninstrumental. To begin with the latter, consider Kant's "categorical imperative" which, roughly speaking, corresponds to the question, But what if everyone did that? What if everyone cheated on their taxes? What if everyone stayed home on voting day or refused to help the poor? This powerful appeal is not concerned with actual outcomes, with what would happen if *I* took a certain course of action. It is concerned with what would happen, hypothetically, if everyone took it. Suppose I am moved by the categorical imperative and try to decide how much I should contribute to charity. I decide on the total amount of charitable contributions that is needed, divide by the number of potential donors, and donate the sum that comes out. If everyone did that, things would be just fine.

In the real world, however, not everyone is going to do that. Many people give nothing. Knowing that, some would argue that it is their duty to give more than what would be needed if everyone did the same. They are motivated by actual outcomes of action under actual circumstances, not by outcomes under hypothetical circumstances. Because they are sensitive to outcomes and to circumstances, they give more the less others give. Conversely, if others give much, they reduce their contribution. To see why, it is sufficient to invoke the decreasing marginal utility of money. If many have already given much, the recipients have a relatively high income, at which a further dollar adds less to their welfare than it does at lower levels. If one is concerned with the instrumental efficacy of giving, the motivation to give is reduced.

Kantians are concerned neither with outcomes nor with circumstances. The people discussed in the last paragraph—they are often called utilitarians—are concerned with both. A third category of people is concerned with circumstances, but not with outcomes. They look at what others are doing and follow the majority. If others give little, they follow suit, and similarly if others give much. The underlying motivation is a norm of *fairness*. One should do one's share, but only if others are doing theirs. This motivation is insensitive to outcomes, as shown by the fact that it leads to exactly the opposite pattern of outcome-oriented utilitarianism. Suppose that we have had a big party and that next morning there is a lot of cleaning up to be done. Everyone joins in, although the kitchen is small and we are tripping over each other's feet, so that the work is actually done less efficiently than it would be if some of us went instead to sit on the back porch. But the norm of fairness forbids free riding, even when everyone would benefit from it.[12]

Giving and helping are supposed to be in the interest of the recipients or beneficiaries. But how do we tell what is in their interest? The answer seems obvious: we find out by asking them. Sometimes, however, they cannot answer. Small children and mentally incompetent persons cannot tell us whether they want our help. We have to rely on some notion of objective interest, and usually that is not too difficult. Hard cases arise when people's expressed interest differs from what we, the donors, believe to be their real interest. The expressed interest might reflect an excessive preoccupation with the present, whereas we, the donors, want to improve their life as a whole. Such *paternalism* is relatively easy to justify when the relation is literally that of parent to child, but harder when the recipients are adults with full civic rights, including the right to vote. Giving food stamps instead of money is an example. If the recipients had voted for this mode of transfer, it would be an unobjectionable form of self-paternalism, but that is not how these decisions are made. They are taken by the welfare bureaucracy.

Paternalistic decisions should not be taken lightly. For one thing, the opportunity to choose—including the right to make the wrong choices—is a valuable, in fact, indispensable, means to self-improvement. For another, there is a presumption that people are the best judges of their own interest. From the point of view of a middle-class welfare official the values and priorities of the poor may look crazy, but that is not really any of his business. His lifestyle probably appears the same way to them. Paternalism is appropriate only when freedom to choose is likely to be severely self-destructive, especially when it will also harm other people.

Paternalism, even when misguided, is concerned with the well-being of the recipient. Gift giving can also, however, be a technique of domination and manipulation. It can serve the interests of the donor, against—and not through—the interests of the recipients. I can do no better here than to quote at some length from Colin Turnbull's account of gifts and sacrifices among the Ik:

> These are not expressions of the foolish belief that altruism is both possible and desirable: they are weapons, sharp and aggressive, which can be put to diverse uses. But the purpose for which the gift is designed can be thwarted by the non-acceptance of it, and much Icien ingenuity goes into thwarting the would-be thwarter. The object, of course, is to build up a whole series of obligations so that in times of crisis you have a number of debts you can recall, and with luck one of them may be repaid. To this end, in the circumstances of Ik life, considerable sacrifice would be justified, to the very limits of the minimal survival level. But a sacrifice that can be rejected is useless, and so you have the odd phenomenon of these otherwise singularly self-interested people going out of their way to "help" each other. In point of fact they are helping themselves and their help may very well be resented in the extreme, but it is done in such a way that it cannot be refused, for it has already been given. Someone, quite unasked, may hoe another's field in his absence, or rebuild his stockade, or join in the building of a house that could easily be done by the man and his wife alone. At one time I have seen so many men thatching a roof that the whole roof was in serious danger of collapsing, and the protests of the owner were of no avail. The work done was a debt incurred. It was another good reason for being wary of one's neighbors. [One particular individual] always made himself unpopular by accepting such help and by paying for it on the spot with food (which the cunning old fox knew they could not resist), which immediately negated the debt. (1972, 146)

Now, it would not be possible to manipulate the norm of reciprocity unless it had a grip on people, since otherwise there would be nothing to manipulate. Turnbull's account demonstrates both the fragility of altruism and its robustness.

Selfishness has a bad name, but compared to some other motivations it can look positively altruistic. When people are motivated by envy, spite, and jealousy, they have an incentive to reduce other people's welfare. The hard way to doing better than others is to improve one's own performance. The easy way is to trip up the competition. Taking pleasure in other people's misfortune is probably more frequent than actively promoting it, but sometimes people do go out of their way to harm others at no direct gain to themselves. When a good—such as custody of a child—cannot be divided between the claimants, one response is, "If I can't have it, nobody shall." A depressing fact about many peasant societies is that people who do better than others are often accused of witchcraft and thus pulled down to, or indeed below, the level of others. Against this background, ruthless selfishness can have a liberating effect.

To have this effect, however, selfishness must be restrained. Traditional societies governed by envy and the principle of not sticking one's neck out can be suffocating, but the state of nature in which short-term self-interest dictates every decision is just as bad. Consider a firm that has reached a wage agreement with its workers. If wages are paid at the end of the production period, the following game arises. At the beginning of the period, workers have the choice between working and not working. If they decide to work, the firm has the choice, at the end of the period, between paying them the agreed-upon wage and not paying them. If this were all there was to the story, it is clear that a rational, selfish management would decide not to pay them and that rational workers, anticipating nonpayment, would decide not to work. Any promise of payment that the firm might make would lack credibility. As a consequence, both the firm and the workers would end up worse off than if the promise of payment had been credible.

One restraining principle could be codes of honor. If people pursue their selfish ends subject to the constraint of not telling lies or breaking promises, more cooperation can be achieved than if lies are made and promises broken whenever it seems expedient. This is not altruism, although it may have similar effects. Rather, being honest when it does not pay to do so is a form of irrationality. This characterization may seem to offend common sense. The same argument can, however, be made with respect to threats. . . . When a person vows to exact revenge if others act against his interest, the question arises whether the threat is credible. Avenging oneself when it does not pay to do so is a form of irrationality. Rational persons let bygones be bygones. But if the person is irrational, his threats command greater respect. If this conclusion is accepted, the parallel argument with respect to honesty may seem more acceptable. (A fuller discussion of similarities and differences between threats and promises is found in the appendix.)

In some cases, unilateral honesty ensures gains for both parties. The example of wage payment illustrates this case: if the management is known to be honest, it is in the self-interest of the workers to come to work. In other cases, both parties have to be honest. Figure 5.1 illustrates this case.

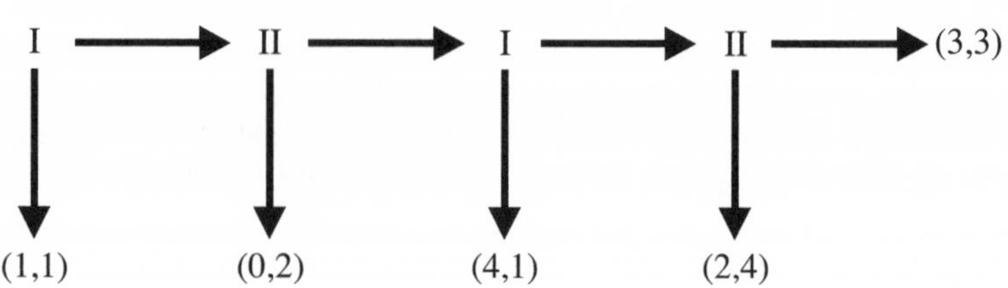

Figure 5.1. The wage-payment game.

In this game, the parties take turns moving. If they choose to move "down," the game ends. If they move "across," the game continues up to the last node, at which player II has a choice between terminating the game by either moving down or across. When the game is terminated, the players receive payoffs as indicated, the first number being the payoff accruing to I and the second that of II. In this game, both parties must believe each other to be honest for a cooperative outcome to be realized. (At least, I shall tell a story in which this is a plausible conclusion.) Suppose first that I is honest but that II is rational rather than a man of honor. In that case I could move across at the first node and promise to move across at the third node, knowing that II will then move down at the last node. But if I is a man of honor, he may resist being taken advantage of in this way. Rather than accept the unequal outcome (2,4) he moves down at the first node. Suppose next that II is honest but believes I to be rational. II will then anticipate that at the penultimate node I will play down rather than across, even if II has made a credible promise to play across at the last node. Knowing this, II will play down at the second node. Knowing this, I will play down at the first node.

Note that honesty is not the same as altruism. In the game of figure 5.1, assume that I is an altruist in the sense of always maximizing the sum of the two rewards but that II is purely selfish. Neither is honest, that is, neither can be counted on to keep a promise unless it is in his (altruistic or selfish) interest to do so. This will ensure the outcome (2,4). II will know that at the penultimate mode, I will play across to ensure a joint gain of six rather than five. Knowing this, II will play across at the second node. Knowing this, I will play across at the first node. Altruism may yield socially desirable outcomes even in the absence of honesty.

Conversely, cut-throat competitiveness in the market may coexist with stable norms of honesty, if the agents are motivated by self-interest without guile. For instance, this has always been considered the ideal form of capitalism. Cut-throat competitiveness without honesty, that is, self-interest with guile or opportunism, is a much uglier creature. Superficially, most societies would seem to exhibit more honest behavior than what the opportunistic model would predict. Yet we must be wary in inferring from the fact that observed behavior is consistent with norms of honesty that it is actually *sustained* by these norms. It could also be sustained by a motivation neglected up to this point in the argument, namely, long-term self-interest.

Consider again the wage payment problem. If there is a single period of production and wages are paid at the end of that period, the promise to pay will not be credible. If, however, there are many periods and wages are paid at the end of each of them, the promise can be sustained even if managers are known to be dishonest. They will know, namely, that if they don't pay the workers, the latter will not come to work in the next week. More precisely, workers can follow the rule "Always work in the first week. In later weeks, work if and only if wages were paid at the end of the preceding week." Against this "Tit-for-

Tat" strategy the rational response of management usually is to pay wages.[13] Long-term self-interest can mimic the norm of honesty.

Why, then, are we not in the state of nature? There is no general answer to this question. Altruism, codes of honor, and long-term self-interest all enter into the explanation. What seems clear is that self-interest cannot be the whole story.

Appendix

To bring out the formal similarity between threats and promises, consider the decision tree in figure 5.2. In threats as well as promises, the payoffs to Eve are constrained by $a > c$ and $a > d$. The threat or promise is intended to induce Adam to move left so that she can ensure for herself a gain that is greater than what she would get if he moved right. Suppose first that $a > b > c > d$. Then Eve can threaten to move right if Adam moves left. But this threat is not credible. He knows she will not cut off her nose to spite her face by moving right; hence he moves right, knowing she will move left. The outcome will be worse for Eve and better for Adam than it would have been if the threat had been credible. Suppose next that $b > a > d > c$. Then Eve can promise to move left if Adam moves left. Once again, however, this promise is not credible. Adam knows that once he has moved left it will be in her self-interest to move right. As a result he will move left and Eve will move right, leaving them both worse off than if her promise had been credible. Suppose finally that $b > a > c > d$. Here Eve can brandish both the carrot and the stick, promising to move left if he moves left and threatening to move right if he moves right. Neither communication is credible; Adam moves right, Eve moves left; he is better off and she is worse off than if the promise/threat had been credible.

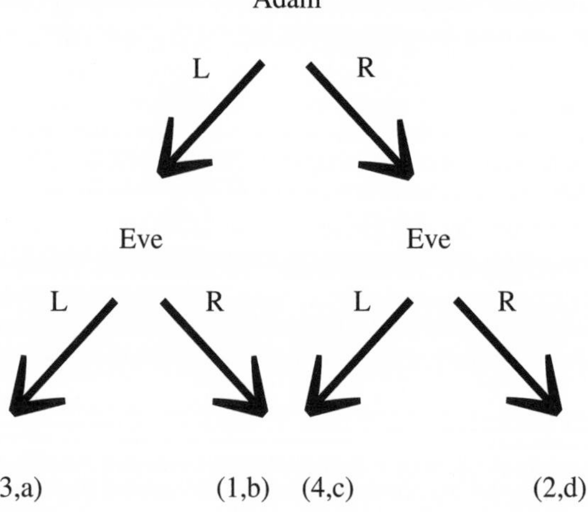

Figure 5.2. Decision tree.

Notes

This chapter was adapted from Jon Elster, *Nuts and Bolts for the Social Sciences* (Cambridge: Cambridge University Press, 1989), and Jon Elster, *The Cement of Society* (Cambridge: Cambridge University Press, 1989).

1. The second part of this sentence adds something to the first. I might take account of other people's interest only in the choice between two actions that serve my interest equally well.

2. Indeed, sometimes the motivating force seems to be the desire to give, and to be known as giving, *more than other donors*. I was first struck by this motivation in the Art Institute of Chicago, where the size of the plaques honoring the donors is carefully adjusted to the size of the donation. What looks like altruistic behavior toward the public may in fact spring from emulation and envy of other donors.

3. Actually, we might observe differences in behavior when both institutions and motivations are similar, namely, when the situation has multiple equilibria. History and accidents will then determine which of them is realized.

4. In addition there is the view that altruistic motivations can be explained in terms of "selfish genes," for example, because it pays a gene to have its bearer sacrifice itself for the sake of close relatives who are also bearers of the gene.

5. Love is not the true converse of spite. A spiteful person acts to frustrate other people's desires because their frustration makes him feel good. Their suffering is instrumental to his welfare. The true converse of this attitude is the person who helps others because he likes to see happy faces around him.

6. This need not be true. A person may help his grandchild, to whom he feels indifferent, in order to give (nonselfish) pleasure to his child. But that presupposes that the child derives pleasure from the selfish pleasure of the grandchild.

7. When a small child buys a gift for her parents, they are often more touched by the act of giving than pleased by the gift—but they are touched only because they know the child was trying to please them rather than to touch them.

8. One might need only one selfish person, and all others could get all their pleasure from watching him and each other.

9. I am referring here to societies in which parents cannot disinherit their children.

10. Many, no doubt, would most like to have their cake and eat it too: to be well known as an anonymous donor.

11. And even when income redistribution is in the interest of the donors, it need not be motivated by that interest.

12. I am assuming, for simplicity, that we have no intrinsic pleasure just in being together.

13. For long-term self-interest to induce the firm to pay out wages, it must not be too myopic. In fact, a myopic firm will be doubly tempted to defect. In the first place a myopic bargainer is at a disadvantage. By his impatience he will be forced to concede more than he would otherwise have done. If the workers are less impatient, they may claim and get high wages. The combination of high wages and myopia may then, in the second place, induce the firm to defect at the end of the first period.

6.

COOPERATION

Robyn M. Dawes and Richard H. Thaler

Economics can be distinguished from other social sciences by the belief that most (all?) behavior can be explained by assuming that agents have stable, well-defined preferences and make rational choices consistent with those preferences in markets that (eventually) clear. An empirical result qualifies as an anomaly if it is difficult to "rationalize," or if implausible assumptions are necessary to explain it within the paradigm. This column will present a series of such anomalies.

Introduction

Much economic analysis—and virtually all game theory—starts with the assumption that people are both rational and selfish. For example, predictions that players will defect in the prisoner's dilemma game and free ride in public goods environments are based on both assumptions. People are assumed to be clever enough to figure out that defection or free riding is the dominant strategy, and are assumed to care nothing for outcomes to other players; moreover, people are assumed to have no qualms about their failure to do "the right thing."[1]

The predictions derived from this assumption of rational selfishness are, however, violated in many familiar contexts. Public television successfully raises enough money from viewers to continue to broadcast. The United Way

Journal of Economic Perspectives 2, no. 3 (Summer 1988): 187-97.

and other charities receive contributions from many if not most citizens. Even when dining at a restaurant away from home in a place never likely to be visited again, most patrons tip the server. And people vote in presidential elections where the chance that a single vote will alter the outcome is vanishingly small. As summarized by Jack Hirshleifer (1985, p. 55), "... the analytically uncomfortable (though humanly gratifying) fact remains: from the most primitive to the most advanced societies, a higher degree of cooperation takes place than can be explained as a merely pragmatic strategy for egoistic man." But why?

In this chapter, ... the evidence from laboratory experiments is examined to see what has been learned about when and why humans cooperate. This chapter considers the particularly important case of cooperation vs. free riding in the context of public good provision.

Single Trial Public Goods Experiments

To investigate why people cooperate, it is necessary to examine behavior in both single play and multiple play environments. Does cooperation evolve, for instance, only as individuals repeatedly interacting with each other find it in their interests to cooperate? A typical public goods experiment uses the following procedures. A group of subjects (most often students but sometimes other adult members of the community) is brought to the laboratory. Groups vary in size, but experiments usually have between 4 and 10 subjects. Each subject is given a sum of money, for example, \$5. The money can either be kept and taken home, or some or all of the money can be invested in a public good, often called a "group exchange." Money invested in the group exchange for the n participants is multiplied by some factor k, where k is greater than 1.0 but less than n. The money invested, with its returns, is distributed equally among all group members. Thus, while the entire group's monetary resources are increased by each contribution (because $k > 1$), each individual's share of one such contribution is less than the amount she or he invests (because $k < n$). Suppose $k = 2$ and $n = 4$. Then if everyone contributes all \$5 to the public good, each ends up with \$10. This is the unique Pareto efficient allocation: no other solution can make everyone better off. But the dominant Nash strategy is to contribute nothing, because in exchange for a player's \$5 contribution, that player receives only \$2.50, while the rest of the payoff (\$7.50) goes to the other players. The rational selfish strategy is to contribute nothing and hope that the other players decide to invest their money in the group exchange. If one player contributes nothing while all the others contribute \$5, then that player will end up with \$12.50, while the other players end up with \$7.50. These conditions constitute a true social dilemma played with real money.

What does economic theory predict will happen in such a game? One prediction, called the *strong free rider hypothesis*, is that everyone will choose the dominant strategy, that is, nothing will be contributed to the public good. This is surely the outcome predicted by the selfish rational model. A less extreme prediction, called the *weak free rider hypothesis*, is that some people will free ride while others will not, yielding a suboptimal level of the public good, though not necessarily zero. The weak free rider hypothesis obviously does not yield very precise predictions.

The results of single play ("one shot") public goods experiments lend little support to the strong free rider hypothesis. While not everyone contributes, there is a substantial number of contributors, and the public good is typically provided at 40–60 percent of the optimal quantity. That is, on average, the subjects contribute 40–60 percent of their stake to the public good. In a study by Marwell and Ames (1981), these results held in many conditions: for subjects playing the game for the first time, or after a previous experience; for subjects who believed they were playing in groups of 4 or 80; and for subjects playing for a range of monetary stakes.[2] Indeed, Marwell and Ames found only one notable exception to this 40–60 percent contribution rate. When the subjects were a group of University of Wisconsin economics graduate students, the contribution rate fell to 20 percent, leading them to title their article "Economists Free Ride: Does Anyone Else?"[3] (Interestingly, economists told about the experiments predicted on the average a rate of about 20 percent—but for all participants, not just their students.)

Multiple Trial Experiments

A natural question to ask about the surprisingly high level of cooperation observed by Marwell and Ames is what would happen if the same players repeated the game several times. This question has been investigated by Kim and Walker (1984); Isaac, Walker, and Thomas (1984); and Isaac, McCue, and Plott (1985). The experimental design in these papers is similar to Marwell and Ames, except that there are usually ten repetitions of the game. Two major conclusions emerge from these papers. First, on the initial trial, cooperation is observed at rates similar to those obtained by Marwell and Ames. For example, across nine different experiments with varying designs, Isaac, McCue and Plott obtained a 53 percent contribution rate to the public good. Second, within a few repetitions, cooperation declines sharply. After five trials, the contributions to the public good were only 16 percent of the optimum. The experiments by Isaac, Walker and Thomas also obtained a decline in the contribution rate over time, though the decline was not as abrupt.[4]

Why does the contribution rate decline with repetition? One reasonable conjecture is that subjects learn something during the experiment that induces them to adopt the dominant strategy of free riding. Perhaps the subjects did not understand the game in the first trial and only learned that free riding was dominant over time. This possibility, however, appears unlikely in light of other experimental evidence. For example, the usual cooperation rates of roughly 50 percent are observed in trial one even for *experienced* subjects, that is, subjects who have participated in other multiple trial public goods experiments (e.g., Isaac and Walker, forthcoming). Also, Andreoni (1987a) has investigated the learning hypothesis directly, using the simple procedure of restarting the experiment. Subjects were told they would play a ten-period public goods game. When the ten periods were completed, the subjects were told they would play again for another ten rounds with the same other players. In the first ten trials Andreoni replicated the decaying contribution rate found by previous investigators, but upon restarting the game contributions went back up to virtually the same contribution rates observed on the initial trial in the first game (44 percent on trial one of the second game vs. 48 percent in the first). Such results seem to rule out any explanation of cooperation based on subjects' misunderstanding the task.[5]

Reciprocal Altruism

One currently popular explanation of why we observe so much cooperation in and outside of the laboratory invokes reciprocal altruism as the mechanism. This explanation, most explicitly developed by Axelrod (1984), is based on the observation that people tend to reciprocate—kindness with kindness, cooperation with cooperation, hostility with hostility and defection with defection. Thus, being a free rider may actually be a less fruitful strategy when the chooser takes account of the probable future response of others to his or her cooperation or defection. A cooperative act itself—or a reputation for being a cooperative person—may with high probability be reciprocated with cooperation, to the ultimate benefit of the cooperator.

The most systematic strategy based on the principle of reciprocal altruism is a Tit-for-Tat one first suggested by Anatol Rapoport, in which a player begins by cooperating and then chooses on trial t the same response the other player has made on trial $t - 1$. The real strength of this explanation lies in demonstrating, both analytically and by computer tournaments of interacting players (programs) in iterated social dilemmas, that any person or small group of people practicing such reciprocal altruism will have a statistical tendency to receive higher payoffs "in the long run" than those who don't practice it. In fact, Tit-for-Tat "won" two computer tournaments Axelrod conducted in which game theorists proposed various strategies that were compared against each other in pairwise encounters with repeated plays. Because evolution is concerned with such long run probabilistic phenomena, it can be inferred that reciprocating people have greater "inclusive fitness" than do non-reciprocating ones. Hence, to the degree to which such a tendency has some genetic basis, it should evolve as an adaptation to the social world.

An implication of reciprocal altruism is that individuals will be uncooperative in dilemma situations when there is no possibility of future reciprocity from others, as in situations of anonymity or interacting with people on a "one-shot" basis. Yet we observe 50 percent cooperation rates even in single trial experiments, so reciprocal altruism cannot be used directly to explain the experimental results described so far. Also, of course, it is very difficult to play Tit-for-Tat, or any other strategy based on reciprocal altruism, when more than two people are involved in the repeated dilemma situation. If some members of a group cooperate on trial *t* while others defect, what should a player attempting to implement a Tit-for-Tat type strategy choose on the subsequent trial?

A related hypothesis that appears consistent with the decaying contribution rates observed in the multiple trial experiments is suggested by the theoretical work of Kreps, Milgrom, Roberts, and Wilson (1982). They investigate the optimal strategy in a repeated prisoner's dilemma game with a finite number of trials. If both players are rational, then the dominant strategy for both is to defect on every trial. While Tit-for-Tat has been shown to be effective in infinitely repeated prisoner's dilemma games (or equivalently, games with a constant small probability of ending after any given trial), games with a known end point are different. In any finite game both players know that they should defect on the last trial, so there is no point in cooperating on the penultimate trial, and by backward induction, it is never in one's best interest to cooperate. What Kreps et al. show is that if you are playing against an opponent whom you think may be irrational (i.e., might play Tit-for-Tat even in a game with finite trials), then it may be rational to cooperate early in the game (to induce your irrational opponent to cooperate too). Since the public goods games have a similar structure, it could be argued that players are behaving rationally in the Kreps et al. sense. Once again, however, the data rule out this explanation. Cooperation never falls to zero, even in one-trial games or in the last period of multi-trial games when it can never be selfishly rational to cooperate.

Additional evidence against the reciprocity hypothesis comes from another experiment designed by Andreoni. One group of 15 subjects played repeated trials in groups of 5 as described above. Another group of 20 subjects played the same game in groups of 5, but the composition of the group varied on each trial. Moreover, the subjects did not know which 4 of the other 19 subjects would constitute their group in any given round of the game. In this condition, there can be no strategic advantage to cooperation, since the players in the next round will be, in essence, strangers. If cooperation in early rounds of these experiments is observed, strategic cooperation can be ruled out. Indeed, Andreoni found that cooperation was actually a bit higher in the stranger condition than in a comparable condition where the groups remained intact. (This effect was statistically significant, though slight.)

One conclusion which emerges from these experiments is that people have a tendency to cooperate until experience shows that those with whom they are interacting are taking advantage of them. This "norm of cooperation" will resemble reciprocal altruism in infinitely repeated games; but the behavior, as we have seen, is also observed in cases when reciprocal altruism would be inappropriate. One explanation for this type of behavior is offered by Robert Frank (1987). Frank argues that people who adopt a norm of cooperation will do well by eliciting cooperation from others, and attracting interaction with other cooperators. The key to Frank's argument is that one cannot successfully fake being cooperative for an extended period of time—just as one cannot be successful getting people to believe too many lies.[6] Furthermore, because cooperators are, by assumption, able to identify one another, they are able to interact selectively and exclude defectors.

Altruism

There are other explanations of why people cooperate in both the lab and the field. One is that people are motivated by "taking pleasure in others' pleasure." Termed *pure altruism,*[7] this motive has been eloquently stated by Adam Smith, in *The Theory of Moral Sentiments* (1759; 1976): "how selfish soever man may be supposed to be, there are evidently some principles in his nature, which interest him in the fate of others, and render their happiness necessary to him, though he derive nothing from it, except the pleasure of seeing it." While the pleasure involved in seeing it may be considered "selfish" (following the sophomoric argument that altruism is by definition impossible, because people do what they "want" to do), the passage captures the idea that people are motivated by positive payoffs for others as well as for themselves. Consequently, they may be motivated to produce such results through a cooperative act. One problem with postulating such pure altruism as a reason for contributing to public goods is that such contributions cannot be explained purely in terms of their effects. If they could, for example, then governmental contributions to the same goal should "crowd out" private contributions on a dollar-for-dollar basis, since the results are identical no matter where the funding comes from. Such crowding out does not appear to be nearly complete. In fact, econometric studies indicate that an increase in governmental contribution to such activities is associated with a decrease in private contribution of only 5 to 28 percent (Abrams and Schmitz, 1978, 1984; Clotfelter, 1985).

Another type of altruism that has been postulated to explain cooperation is that involved in the act of cooperating itself, as opposed to its results. "Doing the right (good, honorable, . . .) thing" is clearly a motive for many people. Sometimes termed *impure altruism*, it generally is described as satisfaction of conscience, or of noninstrumental ethical mandates.

The roles of pure and impure altruism and other causes for cooperation (or the lack thereof) have been investigated over the last decade by the team of Robyn Dawes, John Orbell and Alphons van de Kragt. In one set of experiments (Dawes et al., 1986), they examined the motives for free riding. The game used for these experiments had the following rules. Seven strangers were given $5 each. If enough people contributed their stake to the public good (either 3 or 5 depending on the experiment), then every person in the group would receive a $10 bonus whether or not they contributed. Thus, if enough subjects contribute, each contributor would leave with $10 and each non-contributor would leave with $15. If too few contributed, then non-contributors would keep their $5 while contributors would leave with nothing. Subjects were not permitted to talk to one another (though this was modified in subsequent experiments). In this context two reasons for not contributing can be identified. First, subjects may be afraid that they will contribute but not enough others will, so their contribution will be futile. This motive for defecting was termed "fear." Second, subjects may hope that enough others will contribute and hope to receive $15 instead of $10. This motive was called "greed." The relative importance of fear and greed was examined by manipulating the rules of the game. In the "no greed" condition, payoffs were changed so that all subjects would receive $10 if the number of contributors was sufficient (rather than $10 for contributors and $15 for free riders). In the "no fear" condition contributors were given a "money back guarantee": if a subject contributed and not enough others did, the subject would receive the money back. (However, in this condition if the public good was provided, contributors would receive only $10 while free riders would get $15.) The results suggested that greed was more important than fear in causing free riding. In the standard game contribution rates averaged 51 percent. In the no fear (money back) game contributions rose to 58 percent, but in the no greed game contributions were 87 percent.[8]

Another possible interpretation is that the no greed game condition can produce a stable equilibrium, while the no fear cannot. If subjects in the no greed condition believe that the mechanism of truncating payoffs works to motivate others to contribute, their motive will be enhanced as well, because the only negative result of contributing occurs if enough others *don't* contribute. In contrast, subjects in the no fear condition who conclude that the conditions will encourage others to contribute will be tempted to free ride themselves, leading to the conclusion that others will be tempted as well, leading to the conclusion that they should themselves contribute, etc.—an infinite loop.

One of the most powerful methods for inducing cooperation in these games is to permit the subjects to talk to one another. Twelve groups were run with the same payoffs described earlier, but under conditions in which discussions were allowed. The effect of this discussion was remarkable (van de Kragt, et al., 1983). Every group used the discussion period to specify a group of people who were designated to cooperate. The most common means of making the distributional decision was by lottery, though volunteering was also observed. One group attempted interpersonal utility comparisons to determine relative "need." Whatever methods the groups used, they worked. All 12 groups provided the public good, and in 3 of the groups more than the required number of subjects contributed. These results are consistent with the earlier ones. Subjects designated as contributors cannot greedily expect more from free riding, because their contributions are (believed to be) crucial for their obtaining the bonus (and were in all but 3 groups). Moreover, belief that others in the designated set of contributors will be motivated to contribute by the designated contributor mechanism will enhance—rather than diminish—each designated contributor's motive to contribute.

One possible explanation for the value of discussion is that it "triggers" ethical concerns that yield a utility for doing the "right" thing (i.e., impure altruism). Elster (1986), for example, has argued that group discussions in such situations yield arguments for group-regarding behavior (it is hard to argue for selfishness), and that such arguments have an effect not only on the listener but on the person making them as well. To test this hypothesis, a new set of experiments was conducted (Orbell, van de Kragt and Dawes, forthcoming). In this set of experiments all 7 subjects were given $6 each. They could either keep the money or contribute it to the public good in which case it would be worth $12 to the other 6 members of the group. In this case, keeping the $6 is a dominant strategy because the person who does so receives both that $6 and $2 from each of the other 6 group members who gave away the money.

Subjects first met in groups of 14 in a waiting room in which they were not allowed to talk; they were then divided into the two groups on a clearly random basis. Half of these subgroups were allowed to talk about the decision, half not. The experimenters told half of the groups that the $12 given away would go to the other six people in their own group, while the other half of the groups were told that the money would go to six people in the other group. There are thus four conditions—discussion or no discussion crossed with money goes to own group or other group. If discussion simply makes individuals' egoistic payoffs clear, then it should not increase cooperation rate in any of these conditions since free riding is dominant. If, however, discussion increases utility for the act of cooperation per se, then discussion should be equally effective whether the money given away goes to members of their own group or to the other group—which consists, after all, of very similar people who were indistinguishable prior to the random drawing (usually college students or poorer members of the community).

The results were clear. In the absence of discussion, only about 30 percent of the subjects gave away the money, and those who did so indicated that their motive was to "do the right thing" irrespective of the financial payoffs.[9] Discussion raises the cooperation rate to 70 percent, but only when the subjects believe the money is going to members of their own groups; otherwise, it is usually less than 30 percent. Indeed, in such groups it was common to hear comments that the "best" possible outcome would be for all group members to keep their money while those in the other group gave it away (again, people from whom the subjects have been randomly separated about 10 minutes earlier).

Thus, group identity appears to be a crucial factor in eschewing the dominating strategy. That result is compatible with previous social-psychological research on the "minimal group" paradigm (e.g. Tajfel and Turner, 1979; the papers contained in Turner and Giles, 1981), which has repeatedly demonstrated that allocative decisions can be sharply altered by manipulations substantially weaker than 10 minutes of discussion. For example, a "common fate" group identity—where groups received differing levels of payoffs depending on a coin toss—led subjects to attempt to "compensate" for non-cooperators in their own group by increasing cooperation rates, while simultaneously decreasing cooperation when the non-cooperators were believed to be in the other group, even when the identities of the people involved were unknown (Kramer and Brewer, 1986).

In the groups in which discussion was permitted, it was very common for people to make promises to contribute. In a second series of experiments, Orbell, van de Kragt and Dawes investigated whether these promises were important in generating cooperation. Perhaps people feel bound by their promises—or believe they will receive a "satisfactory" payoff if they give away the money when others promise to do so because others will be bound by such promises. The main result was that promise making was related to cooperation only when every member of the group promised to cooperate. In such groups with universal promising, the rate of cooperation was substantially higher than in other groups. In groups in which promising was not universal, there was no relationship between each subject's choice to cooperate or defect and (1) whether or not a subject made a promise to cooperate, or (2) the number of other people who promised to cooperate. Consequently, the number of promises made in the entire group and the group cooperation rate were unrelated. These data are consistent with the importance of group identity if (as seems reasonable) universal promising creates—or reflects—group identity.

Commentary

In the rural areas around Ithaca it is common for farmers to put some fresh produce on a table by the road. There is a cash box on the table, and customers are expected to put money in the box in return for the vegetables they take. The box has just a small slit, so money can only be put in, not taken out. Also, the box is attached to the table, so no one can (easily) make off with the money.

We think that the farmers who use this system have just about the right model of human nature. They feel that enough people will volunteer to pay for the fresh corn to make it worthwhile to put it out there. The farmers also know that if it were easy enough to take the money, someone would do so.

In contrast to these farmers, economists either avoid judgments of human nature, or make assumptions that appear excessively harsh. It is certainly true that there is a "free rider problem." Not all people can be expected to contribute voluntarily to a good cause, and any voluntary system is likely to produce too little of the public good (or too much of the public bad in the case of externalities). On the other hand, the strong free rider prediction is clearly wrong—not everyone free rides all of the time.

There is a big territory between universal free riding and universal contributing at the optimal rate. To understand the problems presented by public goods and other dilemmas it is important to begin to explore some issues that are normally ignored in economics. For example, what factors determine the rate of cooperation? It is encouraging to note that cooperation is positively related to the investment return on the public good. The more the group has to gain through cooperation, the more cooperation is observed—the supply of cooperation is upward sloping. The results involving the role of discussion and the establishment of group identity are, however, more difficult to incorporate into traditional economic analyses. (One economist attempting to do so proposed that group discussion simply confuses subjects to the point that they no longer understand it is in their best interests to be defectors.)

More generally, the role of selfish rationality in economic models needs careful scrutiny. Amartya Sen (1977) has described people who are always selfishly rational as "rational fools," because mutual choices based only on egoistic payoffs consistently lead to suboptimal outcomes for all involved. Perhaps we need to give more attention to "sensible cooperators."

Notes

We wish to thank James Andreoni, Linnda Caporael, Mark Isaac, and John Orbell for helpful comments on an earlier draft.

1. For a modern treatment of the theory of public goods, see Bergstrom, Blume, and Varian (1986).

2. In the experiments with the highest stakes, contribution rates were somewhat lower, in the 28–35 percent range.

3. This result has never been replicated, and so should be treated as preliminary. We wonder, however, whether economists *are* different. Do economists as a group donate less to charity than other similar groups? Are they less likely to leave tips in out-of-town restaurants?

4. For experiments with a high return to contributing to the public good, the initial contribution rate was 52 percent, which fell to 32 percent on trial 10. In

versions with low returns to contributing, the initial rate was 40 percent and the final rate was 8 percent.

5. A similar conclusion is reached by Goetze and Orbell (forthcoming).

6. As the late Senator Sam Ervin said: "The problem with lying is that you have to have a perfect memory for what you said." None of us do. It's easier to remember what actually happened, although that is not easy either.

7. The terms pure and impure altruism are introduced by Andreoni (1987b).

8. Notice that contributing could be selfishly rational if a subject thought that the probability his or her contribution would be critical (i.e., exactly $M-1$ others will contribute) was greater than one-half. However, subjects who contributed did not generally believe that their contribution was necessary. Virtually no contributors believed they were critical to obtaining the public good with a probability greater than 0.50. In fact, pooling across all conditions, 67 percent of the contributors believed so many others would contribute that their own contributions would be redundant.

9. In a similar—but simulated—one-shot experiment Hofstadter (1983) had discovered a roughly identical cooperation rate among his eminent friends. Most defect, but some cooperate, and for reasons of impure altruism. As one cooperator, Professor Daniel C. Dennett of Tufts, put it: "I would rather be the person who bought the Brooklyn bridge than the person who sold it. Similarly, I feel better spending $3 gained by cooperation than $10 gained by defection." (Hofstadter terms that a "wrong reason" for cooperating in a dilemma situation; yet it is the one often given by the subjects who cooperate without discussion in the experiments described above, and similar ones.)

References

Abrams, Burtran A., and Mark A. Schmitz, "The Crowding Out Effect of Government Transfers on Private Charitable Contributions," *Public Choice*, 1978, *33*, 29–39.

Abrams, Burtran A., and Mark A. Schmitz, "The Crowding Out Effect of Government Transfers on Private Charitable Contributions: Cross Sectional Evidence," *National Tax Journal*, 1984, *37*, 563–568.

Andreoni, James, "Why Free Ride? Strategies and Learning in Public Goods Experiments," unpublished, University of Wisconsin, Department of Economics, 1987a.

Andreoni, James, "Impure Altruism and Donations to Public Goods: A Theory of Warm-Glow Giving," unpublished, University of Wisconsin, Department of Economics, 1987b.

Axelrod, Robert, *The Evolution of Cooperation*, New York: Basic Books, 1984.

Bergstrom, Theodore, Lawrence E. Blume, and Hal Varian, "On the Private Provision of Public Goods," *Journal of Public Economics*, 1986, *29*, 25–49.

Clotfelter, Charles T., *Federal Tax Policy and Charitable Giving*, Chicago: The University of Chicago Press, 1985.

Dawes, Robyn M., John M. Orbell, Randy T. Simmons, and Alphons J. C. van de Kragt, "Organizing Groups for Collective Action," *American Political Science Review,* 1986, *80,* 1171–1185.

Elster, Jon, "The Market and the Forum: Three Varieties of Political Theory." In Jon Elster and Aanund Hylland, eds., *Foundations of Social Choice Theory: Studies in Rationality and Social Change,* Cambridge: Cambridge University Press, 1986, pp.103–132.

Frank, Robert, "If *Homo Economicus* Could Choose His Own Utility Function, Would He Want One with a Conscience?" *American Economic Review,* September 1987, *77,* 593–605.

Goetze, David, and John M. Orbell, "Understanding and Cooperation," *Public Choice,* forthcoming.

Hirshleifer, Jack, "The Expanding Domain of Economics," *American Economic Review,* December 1985, *75, Number 6,* 53–70.

Hofstadter, Douglas, "Metamagical Themas," *Scientific American,* 1983, *248,* 14–28.

Isaac, R. Mark, Kenneth F. McCue, and Charles Plott, "Public Goods Provision in an Experimental Environment," *Journal of Public Economics,* 1985, *26,* 51–74.

Isaac, R. Mark, James M. Walker, and Susan H. Thomas, "Divergent Evidence on Free Riding: An Experimental Examination of Possible Explanations," *Public Choice,* 1984, *43,* 113–149.

Isaac, R. Mark, and James M. Walker, "Group Size Effects in Public Goods Provision: The Voluntary Contributions Mechanism," *Quarterly Journal of Economics,* forthcoming.

Kim, Oliver, and Mark Walker, "The Free Rider Problem: Experimental Evidence," *Public Choice,* 1984, *43,* 3–24.

Kramer, R. M., and Marilyn Brewer, "Social Group Identity and the Emergence of Cooperation in Resource Conservative Dilemmas." In H. Wilke, D. Messick, and C. Rutte, eds., *Psychology of Decision and Conflict. Vol. 3. Experimental Social Dilemmas,* Frankfurt Am Main: Verlag Peter Lang, 1986, pp. 205–230.

Kreps, David, Paul Milgrom, John Roberts, and Robert Wilson, "Rational Cooperation in Finitely Repeated Prisoners' Dilemmas," *Journal of Economic Theory,* 1982, *27,* 245–252.

Marwell, Gerald, and Ruth Ames, "Economists Free Ride, Does Anyone Else?" *Journal of Public Economics,* 1981, *15,* 295–310.

Orbell, John M., Robyn M. Dawes, and Alphons J. C. van de Kragt, "Explaining Discussion Induced Cooperation," *Journal of Personality and Social Psychology,* forthcoming.

Sen, Amartya K., "Rational Fools: A Critique of the Behavioral Foundations of Economic Theory," *Journal of Philosophy and Public Affairs,* 1977, *6,* 317–344.

Smith, Adam, *The Theory of Moral Sentiments.* Oxford: Clarendon Press, 1976. (Originally published in 1759.)

Tajfel, Henri, and John C. Turner, "An Integrative Theory of Intergroup Conflict." In W. Austin and S. Worchel, eds., *The Social Psychology of Intergroup Relations,* Monterey, CA: Brooks/Cole, 1979, pp. 33–47.

Turner, John C., and Howard Giles, *Intergroup Behavior,* Chicago: University of Chicago Press, 1981.

van de Kragt, Alphons J. C., John M. Orbell, and Robyn M. Dawes, "The Minimal Contributing Set as a Solution to Public Goods Problems," *American Political Science Review,* 1983, *77,* 112–122.

7.

TRUST, MORAL HAZARDS, AND SOCIAL ECONOMICS: INCENTIVES AND THE ORGANIZATION OF WORK

Charles K. Wilber

A central concern of economics is how an economy allocates its resources—its raw materials, capital, and labor—among competing uses. Economists can often be classified by which of three mechanisms they emphasize in determining this allocation: markets, bureaucratic administration, or moral values. Under a system of allocation by markets, individuals pursue their own self-interest and the market coordinates their decisions, resulting in society's resource allocation. In a bureaucratic control system, individual self-interest is again the motivating force but it is limited to a greater or lesser degree because citizens accept societal constraints, fear the consequences if they do not, or simply have a tradition of acceptance. In a system of allocation by moral values, individual self-interest is limited and cooperation encouraged by a set of widely accepted moral values which in some way transcend the narrow self-interest of one individual.

Free market economists place almost complete reliance on markets, and a central thrust of their policies has been to extend the market allocation mechanism into all possible areas, from school lunches to the environment to civil

---

On the Condition of Labor and the Social Question One Hundred Years Later: Commemorating the 100th Anniversary of Rerum Novarum *and the Fiftieth Anniversary of the Association for Social Economics,* ed. Thomas O. Nitsch, Joseph M. Phillips Jr., and Edward L. Fitzsimmons, vol. 69 of *Toronto Studies in Theology* (Edwin Mellen Press, 1994).

rights. There are exceptions, of course. The Reagan administration's social agenda of limiting abortion and punishing drug use, for example, generated many bureaucratic interferences in the market that were inconsistent with a libertarian stance. Also in an area like defense, free market advocates accept bureaucratic controls as unavoidable. Only at the level of the family is allocation by moral values feasible or desirable. Of course such values are important for the society, but they should be left to charitable impulses of individual decision makers. Efforts to encourage allocation by moral values are seen as self-defeating.

Liberal economists also give markets a central role in resource allocation. However, they find numerous areas in which bureaucratic control is necessary to improve the functioning of markets. Pollution, occupational hazards, and discrimination all result if markets operate unfettered, so government must play a role. In addition the political process empowers government to place limits on self-interested behavior and bureaucratic allocation must be used to combat poverty, to prevent corporate wrongdoing, and to provide the many public goods the market will not. They do not place much emphasis on allocation by moral values.

Social economists argue that sole reliance on any one of these mechanisms is misguided, for each has flaws which prevent it from being completely successful in solving our economic problems. The use of markets and government intervention must be supplemented with the encouragement of moral values.

I argue in this chapter that subordination of short-run interests to long-run interests and moral behavior which constrains free riding, in addition to being good in themselves, are essential for the efficient operation of the economy. Traditional economists are wrong when they claim that individual self-interest and bureaucratic controls are sufficient to achieve efficient market outcomes. The next section of the chapter outlines the theory underlying this claim. The remainder of the chapter applies the theory to the organization of work.

I. Imperfect Information, Interdependence and Moral Hazards

The importance of this combined approach to creating a better functioning economy and society can be illustrated by recent scholarly work in economics (see Akerlof 1984; Boulding 1973; Hirsch 1978; Hirschman 1970; Schotter 1985; Schmid 1978) that demonstrates that, under conditions of interdependence and imperfect information, rational self-interest frequently leads to socially irrational results. Traditional economic theory assumes independence of economic actors and perfect information. However, the more realistic assumptions that one person's behavior affects another's and that each has less than perfect knowledge of the other's likely behavior, give rise to strategic behavior, or what game theorists call "moral hazards." An example will be helpful.

A classic example of moral hazard, known as "The Parable of Distrust" is the situation where both the employer and worker suspect that the other one can not be trusted to honor their explicit or implicit contract. For example, the employer thinks the worker will take too many coffee breaks, spend too much time talking with other workers, and generally work less than the employer thinks is owed. The worker, on the other hand, thinks the employer will try to speed up the pace of work, fire him unjustly if given the chance, and generally behave arbitrarily. When this is the case the worker will tend to shirk and the employer will increase supervision to stop the expected shirking. If the worker would self-supervise, production costs would be lower. Thus this distrust between employer and worker reduces efficiency.

In this case the pursuit of individual self-interest results in the worker and the employer as individuals and as a group becoming worse off than if they had been able to cooperate, i.e., not shirk and not supervise. The problem is simple and common. The employer and worker are interdependent and do not have perfect knowledge of what the other will do, and the resulting lack of trust leads to behavior that is self-defeating. This outcome is made worse if distrust is accompanied with feelings of injustice. For example, if the worker feels that the contract is unfair (low wages, poor grievance machinery, etc.), the tendency to shirk will be increased.

There are numerous other cases, for example inflation. A labor union fights for a wage increase only to find that others also have done so and thus the wage increase is offset by rising consumer prices. No one union alone can restrain its wage demands and maintain the support of its members. Business firms are caught in the same dilemma. They raise prices to compensate for increased labor and other costs only to discover that costs have increased again. Distrust among unions, among firms, and between unions and firms makes impossible a cooperative agreement on price and wage increases.

The case of recession is similar. As aggregate demand in the economy declines, each company attempts to cope with its resulting cash flow difficulties through employee layoffs. However, if all companies pursue this strategy, aggregate demand will decline further, making more layoffs necessary. Most companies agree that the result is undesirable for each company and for the whole economy, but no one company on its own can maintain its workforce. In effect each company says it will not lay off its employees if all the others also do not lay off their employees. Yet, again, no agreement is concluded.

These cases have two things in common. They all have a group (in these cases, workers and their employers) with a common interest in the outcome of a particular situation. And, second, while each attempts to choose the best available course of action, the result is not what any member of the group desires. In these cases the individual motives lead to undesired social and individual results. Adam Smith's "invisible hand" not only fails to yield the common good, but in fact works malevolently.

Why is it so difficult for the individuals involved to cooperate and make an agreement? The reason is that exit is cheap, but voice is expensive (Hirschman 1970, 1986). Exit means to withdraw from a situation, person, or organization and depends on the availability of choice, competition, and well-functioning markets. It is usually inexpensive and easy to buy or not, sell or not, hire or fire, and quit or shirk on your own. Voice means to communicate explicitly your concern to another individual or organization. The cost to an individual in time and effort to persuade, argue, and negotiate will often exceed any prospective individual benefit.[1]

In addition, the potential success of voice depends on the possibility of all members joining for collective action. But then there arises the "free rider" problem. If someone cannot be excluded from the benefits of collective action, she has no incentive to join the group agreement. Self-interest will tempt people to take the benefits without paying the costs; i.e., watching educational television without becoming a subscriber. This free riding explains why union organizing is next to impossible in states that prohibit union shops (where a majority of the workers voting for a union means all workers must join and pay dues).

The problem is further complicated by the possibility that what started simply as a self-interested or even benevolent relationship will become malevolent. Face-to-face strategic bargaining may irritate the parties involved if the other side is perceived as violating the spirit of fair play. This can result in a response of hatred rather than mere selfishness. Collective action is even more unlikely if the members of the group are hateful and distrustful of one another.

These moral hazards are situations where there is some act under the individual's unilateral control that promises to produce a welfare improvement for that individual that is not consistent with what individuals who share a common preference want to obtain as a long-run result. The alternative line of action that would be consistent with the more preferred long-run result requires cooperation with others; thus no matter how hard the individual tries, alone she can produce no net benefits or fewer than in the unilateral activity. So the moral hazard exists because the alternative line of action requires some level of trust which can lead all to engage in the process necessary to reach group agreement.

A common consciousness of one's interdependence with others is required for an individual or organization to overcome moral hazards. Collective action requires a degree of mutual trust. If malevolence arises, the moral hazard will be strengthened. In addition, morally constrained behavior is necessary to control free riding. Thus self-interested individualism fails, for moral hazards are ubiquitous in our economy.

Could not a traditional economist construct an "enriched" notion of self-interested behavior that would overcome moral hazards without the need for moral values? I think the answer is a qualified yes. An enriched concept of self-interest could encompass the foregoing of short-run interests for long-run interests, but moral commitment makes this much easier. Furthermore, this would leave the free rider problem unresolved.

The argument might proceed like this. A self-interested person, recognizing the reality of interdependencies and imperfect information, is willing to cooperate with others if it increases his personal welfare. Thus cooperation becomes one more means to maximize one's self-interest.

However, the flaw in the argument is the failure to account for the likelihood of cooperative behavior based only on self-interest to degenerate into individuals cheating on the collective agreement. Free riding must be accounted for. Pushed to its logical extreme, individual self-interest suggests that faced with interdependence and imperfect information, it is usually in the interest of an individual to evade the rules by which other players are guided.

This problem can be illustrated by the case of OPEC. The member countries can be considered to be acting out of enlightened self-interest. They have many fundamental differences—political, economic, religious, geopolitical. At times two of the members—Iran and Iraq—have been in such disagreement as to be in a declared state of war. Nevertheless, OPEC has survived because each member realizes that its own well-being is closely connected with that of the others. OPEC tries to maintain high prices and profit levels by setting production quotas. However, since 1973, their biggest problem has been evasion of the quotas by individual member countries. Enlightened economic actors do cheat. Each member country has an incentive to cheat on the cooperative agreement because, with the production quota holding up prices, if one member expands its output it makes even greater profits. However, if one country violates the agreement, the others usually follow. The result is that the increased output from all the member countries drives down the price and every member is worse off than before. Thus, enlightened self-interest results in a cooperation that is inherently unstable.

Traditional economists could respond with the claim that establishing enforcement mechanisms is the answer to cheating on collective agreements. As an example, OPEC sets up committees to determine production quotas and verification groups to ensure compliance. However, even with a great amount of resources expended on collective enforcement, cheating continues. The recent invasion of Kuwait by Iraq has its origin in the former's production above their quota which had the effect of lowering revenues to Iraq. Not only is cheating a major problem for OPEC, but the costs of policing collective agreements is substantially more than the costs of maintaining those agreements through internalized moral commitments.

How then can we overcome the moral hazards generated by interdependence and imperfect information? The resolution of the problem is not easy, for they are persistent and intractable. There are at least three possibilities:

government intervention; group self-regulation; and institutional reinforcement of those moral values that constrain self-interested behavior.

Market failures such as pollution or monopoly have generally been seen as warrants for government intervention. However, there are ubiquitous market failures of the moral hazard variety in everyday economic life. In these cases private economic actors can also benefit from government measures for their protection, because interdependence and imperfect information generate distrust and lead the parties to self-defeating behavior. Certain kinds of government regulation—from truth-in-advertising to food-and-drug laws—can reduce distrust and thus economic inefficiency, providing gains for all concerned. However, government regulation has its limits. Where the regulated have concentrated power (i.e., electric companies), the regulators may end up serving the industry more than the public. In addition, there are clearly situations in which government operates to serve the self-interest of the members of its bureaucratic apparatus. Free market economists would have us believe that such is always the case. This is an exaggeration. Government can serve the common good, but it has clear limits. One major limitation on the ability of government to regulate is the willingness of people to be regulated.

The Kennedy administration's wage-price guidelines were a partially successful attempt to control inflation through public encouragement of labor and management cooperation to limit wage increases to productivity increases. The cooperation broke down because of the growing struggle among social classes and occupational groups for larger shares of GNP. More formal cooperation between labor and management, monitored by government, might reduce the distrust that cripples their relationship. In order to do so government would have to be accepted by all sides as above the fray and willing to encourage agreements that would benefit society. The experience of the 1970s in which government activity delivered less than it promised, and of the 1980s when it was used to serve the agenda of bureaucrats and to facilitate the goals of the powerful, both imply a diminished capacity of government to play this role.

The second way to overcome moral hazards is self-regulation. Sellers could voluntarily discipline themselves not to exploit their superior information. This is the basis of professional ethics. Surgeons, for example, take on the obligation, as a condition for the exercise of their profession, to avoid performing unnecessary operations, placing the interest of the patient first. The danger is that their professional association will end up protecting its members at the expense of others.

This leads us to the final possibility—developing institutions to heighten group consciousness and reinforce moral values that constrain self-interested behavior so that the pursuit of short-run rewards and free riding can be controlled. Is it possible to rebuild institutional mechanisms so that long-run interests and moral values become more important in directing economic behavior? Yes, but we must re-think our view of people as simply self-interested maximizers. Economists have made a major mistake in treating love, benevolence, and particularly public spirit as scarce resources that must be economized lest they be depleted. This is a faulty analogy because, unlike material factors of production, the supply of love, benevolence, and public spirit is not fixed or limited. These are resources whose supply may increase rather than decrease through use. Also they do not remain intact if they stay unused (Hirschman 1986, p. 155). These moral resources respond positively to practice, in a learning-by-doing manner, and negatively to nonpractice. Obviously if overused they become ineffective.

A good example is a comparison of the system of blood collection for medical purposes in the United States and in England (Richard M. Titmuss 1970). In the United States we gradually replaced donated blood with purchased blood. As the campaigns for donated blood declined, because purchased blood was sufficient, the amount of donations declined. In effect, our internalized benevolence towards those unknown to us, who need blood, began to atrophy from nonuse. In contrast, blood donations remained high in England where each citizen's obligation to others was constantly emphasized.

People learn their values from their families, from their religious faith, and from their society. In fact a principle objective of publicly proclaimed laws and regulations is to stigmatize certain types of behavior and to reward others, thereby influencing individual values and behavior codes. Aristotle understood this: "Lawgivers make the citizen good by inculcating habits in them, and this is the aim of every lawgiver; if he does not succeed in doing that, his legislation is a failure. It is in this that a good constitution differs from a bad one" (Nicomachean Ethics, 1103b).

Habits of benevolence and civic spirit, in addition to heightened group consciousness, can be furthered by bringing groups together to solve common problems. Growth of worker participation in management, consultation between local communities and business firms to negotiate plant closings and relocations, establishment of advisory boards on employment policy that represent labor, business, and the public, all are steps toward a recognition that individual self-interest alone is insufficient, that mutual responsibilities are necessary in a world where interdependence and imperfect information generate distrust and tempt individuals into strategic behavior that, in turn, results in sub-optimal outcomes.

The key point is that competitive situations generate strategic behavior and, in turn, distrust. In an environment of distrust, behavior based on individual self-interest leads to sub-optimal outcomes. Changing the environment from a competitive one to a cooperative one might provide the trust necessary for people to alter their behavior. This is not a call for altruism but is an argument that it is possible to change the environment so that people will realize that their long-term interests require foregoing their short-term interests.

We conclude that no one allocative mechanism can successfully enable our economy to attain the three goals of basic material needs, self-esteem, and freedom. The market, bureaucratic control, and social values all have their advantages and disadvantages as mechanisms for directing society's resources toward those ends. So some combination must be incorporated in any policies that are undertaken to build a new social consensus. In addition, they must be complemented by an environment that encourages cooperative behavior.

II. The Organization of Work

Distrust between workers and employers leads to inefficient results, if neither side trusts the other to live up to the contract. As a result the worker has an incentive to shirk and the employer has to increase supervision costs to counter the possibility. If somehow workers would self-supervise, i.e., not shirk, productivity would be higher and all could benefit.

Changing the institutional environment from a purely competitive one by adding cooperative mechanisms might enable the trust to grow that is necessary for people to alter their behavior. The most likely approach is encouragement of workers' self-management and worker ownership. Of course, most firms and their managers believe that efficiency and discipline require one absolute center of control over work—their control. Nevertheless, in some cases, managers are exploring ways to change the organization of production to increase their workers' job satisfaction. Quality-control circles and profit sharing are becoming common management responses to encourage employees to make their work contribution through the social group in the factory (Michael J. Piore, 1986, pp. 48–54).

The reason for these new management initiatives is clear—under the old system, many workers expressed their boredom, anger and despair by working as slowly as possible, by appearing at work irregularly, by doing poor quality work, by occasional acts of sabotage, and by frequent job changes. The "efficient" system of authoritarian discipline and minute division of labor has been a contributing factor to lagging productivity in the U.S. economy. These managers see profit sharing and other worker participation devices as a means of establishing the more cooperative relationship with their employees that is necessary to compete in the economic world aborning.

It is useful to look at some ways workers have tried to gain control over their work situations. I summarize a particular form of cooperation, worker management, and two specific instances, the Employee Stock Ownership Plan (ESOP) at Weirton Steel in the United States and the industrial cooperatives of Mondragon in the Basque region of Spain.

A. Worker Management

Worker-owned and managed firms are relatively new on the national scene in the United States, though some have existed at the local level for many years.[2] They have become important for several reasons. It is becoming clear that profitable plants are being closed, not just unprofitable ones, and this is more common when the plant is a small part of a conglomerate holding company. The plant may be closed because higher profits can be earned if it is moved to a lower wage area, for a tax write-off, or for a variety of other non-production related reasons (Barry Bluestone and Bennett Harrison 1982). In these situations, purchase of the plant by the present employees preserves jobs, which makes it an attractive possibility. In addition, there is now a legal mechanism, Employee Stock Ownership Plan (ESOP), to facilitate employee ownership, and it provides significant tax incentives to firms (U.S. Congress, Joint Economic Committee 1976).

There is increasing evidence that worker-owned firms incorporating employee participation and workplace democracy have rates of productivity at least as high and frequently higher than traditional firms (see Henry M. Levin 1982; R. Oakeshott 1978; K. Friden 1980). Thus worker-owned firms have been used to maintain employment at plants that otherwise would have closed *and* have been used to maintain and improve productivity as well as the quality of work life. In fact, they all appear to be linked. As employees become owners and managers, the old distrust that led to shirking and excessive supervision can often be reduced. The new environment enables workers to see that the short-run advantage of shirking is outweighed by the negative impact on long-run productivity and profits that they share in. Free riding is still possible, of course, if the employees never develop the moral commitments to coalesce as a group (B. Thurston 1980, pp. 19–20).

A 1988 report[3] published in England indicates that stock ownership and profit sharing schemes actually stimulate worker performance. It analyzed the results of 414 companies in the period 1977–1985 and showed that those with such programs did consistently, and in some cases spectacularly, better than the others. Also, the smaller the firm, the more direct was the impact.

B. Weirton Steel

An interesting case in the United States is Weirton Steel. Since 1984, some 8,400 employees have owned the company under an ESOP and have operated the plant profitably. Management and labor attribute this success—under the previous ownership of National Steel the company was on the edge of bankruptcy—to the implementation of the ESOP. In the face of general decline in the steel industry, Weirton has expanded its employment from 7,800 when the ESOP began to 8,400. The company has paid out about one-third of its profits each year—$15–20 million—while reinvesting the remainder in plant modernization. R. Alan Prosswimmer, company Vice-President and chief financial officer, attributes the company's turnaround to the ESOP: "Over $10 million in savings last year alone were attributable to our employee programs." Walter Bish, President of the Independent Steelworkers Union, added that the workers, since becoming owners, "are much more aware of the fact that quality is important." Rank and file workers speak similarly saying that the ESOP has resulted in "a lot of attitude changes," because previously workers "were working for National Steel and the profits went there. Now the profits are staying here" (Pete Sheehan 1987).

C. Mondragón

Of particular interest as a model for employee-owned and managed firms are the industrial cooperatives of Mondragón in the Basque region of Spain (see Levin 1983a; William Whyte and Kathleen Whyte 1988). Their achievements are quite impressive. The first of the Mondragón cooperatives was established in 1958. Twenty years later the 100 cooperatives together had sales close to $1 billion, one-fifth of which was exported to other countries. Among the many goods produced are refrigerators and other home appliances, heavy machinery, hydraulic presses, steel, semi-conductors, and selenium rectifiers. Among the cooperatives are the largest refrigerator manufacturer in Spain, a bank with over $500 million in assets, a technological research center, a technical high school and engineering college, and an extensive social security system with health clinics and other social services.

The ownership and management structure of the Mondragón cooperatives are of particular interest. Every new member must invest a specified amount in the firm where they are employed. At the end of each year a portion of the firms' surplus or profit is allocated to each worker's capital account in proportion to the number of hours worked and the job rating. The job rating schedule allows for a quite narrow 3:1 ratio between the highest and lowest paid workers. The result is a pay scale quite different from that prevailing in private industry. In comparison lower paid workers earn more in the cooperatives, middle level workers and managers earn the same, and top managers earn considerably less. Each cooperative's board of directors is selected by all the members and, in turn, the board appoints the managers. There is a social council made up of elected representatives of the lowest paid workers which negotiates with the board over worker grievances and other issues of interest.

The purely economic results are impressive. When both capital and labor inputs are accounted for, the Mondragón cooperatives are far more productive in their use of resources than private firms in Spain. One comparison with the 500 largest firms in Spain found that in the 1970s the average cooperative used only 25 percent as much capital equipment per worker but worker productivity reached 80 percent of that in private industry (Levin 1983b).

How might we explain this highly efficient labor force in the Mondragón cooperatives? Clearly worker motivation plays a major part. As workers became owners and participated in management decisions the incentives to shirk were lessened. The structural environment made it easier for trust to develop. Thus strategic behavior declined as workers saw that their short-term individual interests could conflict with their long-term interests. Shirking might benefit them here and now but productivity would benefit them over the long haul.

The free rider problem was controlled by moral commitment to group solidarity. Basque nationalism clearly has been the foundation for this moral commitment, which makes it difficult to transfer the Mondragón experience whole. However, this may be a chicken-egg problem. Must the moral commitment to group solidarity exist first or will the experience of ownership and management help create it? I do not know, but the continued deterioration of our industrial structure is creating the conditions for worker buyouts.

Other factors also inhibit the transferability of the Mondragón experiment. Ties with local communities and limited labor mobility appear important to the success of the cooperatives. In the United States, where there is more labor mobility and weaker ties of community, the moral commitment to group solidarity may be more difficult to generate.

Fostering subordination of short-run interests to long-run interests and moral constraints to free riding are our most important challenges. Thus building institutional mechanisms, such as worker management structures, that overcome moral hazards and create trust is essential to provide the necessary incentives.

Notes

1. Exit is more difficult in Japan where the Confucian tradition is much more binding. As a result, with much greater emphasis on harmony and consensus at all levels, voice is more appreciated and cultivated.

2. The best known and most studied of these firms are the plywood cooperatives in Oregon and Washington. See K. Berman (1967).

3. The report *Profit Sharing and Profitability* (1988) was reported on in the *Sunday Times* (1989).

References

Akerlof, George A. *An Economist's Book of Tales,* Cambridge: Cambridge University Press, 1984.

Berman, K. *Worker-Owned Plywood Companies,* Pullman, WA: Washington State University Press, 1967.

Bluestone, Barry and Harrison, Bennett. *The Deindustrialization of America,* New York: Basic Books, Inc., 1982.

Boulding, Kenneth E. *The Economy of Love and Fear,* Belmont, CA: Wadsworth Publishing Co., 1973.

Friden, K. *Workplace Democracy and Productivity,* Washington, DC: National Center for Economic Alternatives, 1980.

Hirsch, Fred. *Social Limits to Growth,* Cambridge, MA: Harvard University Press, 1978.

Hirschman, Albert O. *Exit, Voice, and Loyalty: Responses to Decline in Firms, Organizations, and States,* Cambridge, MA: Harvard University Press, 1970.

"Letting Workers in on the Share-Out," *The Sunday Times,* January 22, 1989, E1.

———. *Rival Views of Market Society,* New York: Viking, 1986.

Levin, Henry M. "Issues in Assessing the Comparative Productivity of Worker-Managed and Participatory Firms in Capitalist Societies," in D. Jones and J. Svejnar (eds.), *Participatory and Self-Managed Firms,* Lexington, MA: D.C. Heath, 1982.

———. (1983a). "The Workplace: Employment and Business Intervention," in E. Seidman (ed.), *Handbook of Social Intervention,* Beverly Hills, CA: Sage Publications, 1983.

———. (1983b). "Raising Employment and Productivity with Producer Co-operatives," in P. Streeten and H. Maier (eds.), *Human Resources, Employment and Development, Vol. II,* New York: St. Martin's Press, 1983.

Oakeshott, R. *The Case for Workers' Coops,* London: Routledge & Kegan Paul, 1978.

Piore, Michael J. "A Critique of Reagan's Labor Policy," *Challenge,* March/April 1986, (*29*), 48–54.

Profit Sharing and Profitability, London: Kogan Page/IPM, 1988.

Schmid, A. Allan. *Property, Power, and Public Choice: An Inquiry into Law and Economics*, New York: Praeger, 1978.

Schotter, Andrew. *Free Market Economics: A Critical Appraisal,* New York: St. Martin's Press, 1985.

Sheehan, Pete. "A New Model of Economic Democracy: The Workers of Weirton Steel," *New Oxford Review,* December 1987, (*54*), 13–17.

Thomas, H. and Logan, C. *Mondragon: An Economic Analysis,* Boston: George Allen & Unwin, 1982.

Thurston, B. "South Bend Lathe, E.S.O.P. on Strike against Itself?" *Self-Management,* Fall 1980, (*8*), 19–20.

Titmuss, Richard M. *The Gift Relationship,* London: Allen and Unwin, 1970.
U.S. Congress, Joint Economic Committee, *Broadening the Ownership of New Capital: ESOPs and Other Alternatives,* 94th Congress, 2nd session, Washington, DC: Government Printing Office, 1976.
Whyte, William and Whyte, Kathleen. *Making Mondragon: The Growth and Dynamics of the Worker Co-operative Complex,* Cornell: ILR Press, 1988.

8.

GOD AND THE GHETTO

Glenn C. Loury

It is now twenty-five years since the National Advisory Commission on Civil Disorders, popularly known as the Kerner Commission, issued its scathing report on the urban riots of the 1960s. The commission blamed white racism for the riots and concluded famously that "our nation is moving toward two societies, one black, one white—separate and unequal."

Much has changed in the intervening years. Indeed, many of the commission's recommended reforms have been adopted. Yet the problems of our inner cities seem as intractable as ever. This raises troubling questions about the Kerner Commission's conclusions, and forces us to think again about what must be done.

President Johnson created the commission after a spate of violent disturbances in cities across the country during the summer of 1967 left the nation in crisis. He ordered former Illinois Governor Otto Kerner and his associates to determine exactly what had happened in these riots, why it had happened, and what should be done to prevent it from happening again.

Less than eight months later the commission issued its findings, declaring that the rage, alienation, and hopelessness of the ghetto were the consequence of racial isolation, inferior education, limited economic opportunity, and an attitude of indifference, if not hostility, toward blacks from the white majority. "What white Americans have never fully understood—but what the Negro can never forget—is that white society is deeply implicated in the

Wall Street Journal, 25 February 1993.

ghetto. White institutions created it, white institutions maintain it, and white society condones it."

Much Has Changed

In the quarter century since the appearance of this landmark document, much has changed. Federal programs of employment training, educational subsidy, housing assistance and welfare reform have been enacted. The courts and Congress have expanded civil rights protections. Employment opportunities for blacks as a whole have improved markedly, as have incomes and educational attainment. Blacks wield vastly more political clout today, at all levels of government, than was the case in 1968.

Yet it is arguable that conditions in some big city neighborhoods are worse now than in the late 1960s. The human tragedy that so moved the commission—drugs, gangs, violence, unemployment, failed schools, broken families, teen pregnancies, disease, despair, alienation—are still to be observed in the black ghettos of the 1990s.

The reality is that the conditions of black ghettos today reveal as much about the disintegration of urban black society as they do about the indifference, hostility or racism of white society. Institutional barriers to black participation in American life still exist, but they have come down considerably and everybody knows it. Everybody also knows that other barriers have grown up within the urban black milieu in these last decades that are profoundly debilitating.

The effects are manifest in patterns of behavior involving criminality, unwed childbearing, low academic achievement, drug use and gratuitous violence. These behaviors, which destroy a person's ability to seize existing opportunity, must be changed if progress is to come.

Here our social scientists, and our politicians, have failed us. For the longest time it was forbidden to speak of the unraveling social fabric of ghetto life. This has changed in the past decade, with the discovery of the black underclass, but the former conspiracy of silence has not been replaced with a meaningful discourse on how this broken world will be mended.

Liberals, like the sociologist William Julius Wilson, have now acknowledged that behavioral problems are fundamental, but insist that these problems derive ultimately from a lack of economic opportunities and will abate once "good jobs at good wages" are at hand. Conservatives, such as the political scientist Charles Murray, see the tragic developments in the inner cities as the unintended legacy of a misconceived welfare state. If the government would stop underwriting irresponsible behavior, they argue, poor people would be forced to discover the virtues of self-restraint.

These polar positions have something in common. They both implicitly assume that economic factors lie behind the behavioral problems, even behaviors involving sexuality, marriage, childbearing and parenting. Both points of view suggest that behavioral problems in the ghetto can be cured from without, by changing government policy, by getting the incentives right. Both smack of a mechanistic determinism, wherein the mysteries of human motivation are susceptible to calculated intervention. Both have difficulty explaining why some poor minority communities show a much lower incidence of these behavioral problems than others, and are apparently less influenced by the same economic forces.

Ultimately, such sterile debates over policy fail to engage the fundamental questions of personal morality, of character and values. We do not give public voice to the judgments that it is wrong to abuse drugs, to be sexually promiscuous, to be indolent and without discipline, to be disrespectful of legitimate authority, to be unreliable, untruthful, unfaithful.

The advocacy of a conception of virtuous living has vanished from American public discourse, especially in the discussion of race and social policy. For example, the institution of marriage has virtually disappeared from inner city black communities. The vast majority of poor black children are raised by a mother alone. But who will say that black men and women should get together and stay together more than they now do, for the sake of their children? Who will say that young people of any race should abstain from sexual intimacy until their relationships have been consecrated by marriage?

These are, in our secular age, not matters for public policy. Government, it would appear, must confine itself to dealing with the consequences of these matters not having been taken up elsewhere.

Luckily, government is not the only source of authority. In every community there are agencies of moral and cultural development that seek to shape the ways in which individuals conceive of their duties to themselves, their obligations to each other, and their responsibilities before God.

The family and the church are primary among these. These institutions have too often broken down in the inner city; they have been overwhelmed by an array of forces from within and without. Yet these are the natural sources of legitimate moral teaching—indeed, the only sources. If those institutions are not restored, the behavioral problems of the ghetto will not be overcome. Such a restoration obviously cannot be the object of programmatic intervention by public agencies. Rather, it must be led from within the communities in question, by the moral and political leaders of those communities.

The mention of God may seem quaint, but it is clear that the behavioral problems of the ghetto (and not only there) involve spiritual issues. A man's spiritual commitments influence his understanding of his parental responsibilities. No economist can devise an incentive scheme for eliciting parental involvement in a child's development that is as effective as the motivations of conscience deriving from the parents' understanding that they are God's stewards in the lives of their children.

The Power of Faith

One cannot imagine effectively teaching sexual abstinence, or the eschewal of violence, without an appeal to spiritual concepts. The most effective substance-abuse recovery programs are built around spiritual principles. The reports of successful efforts at reconstruction in ghetto communities invariably reveal a religious institution, or a set of devout believers, at the center of the effort.

To evoke the issue of spirituality is not to deny the relevance of public action. There are great needs among the inner city poor, of the sort identified in the Kerner Commission's report, toward which public efforts should be directed. But if we do not want to be marking the 50th anniversary of that report's release with a reflection on the wretched condition of America's ghettos, then we must be willing to cautiously and sensitively expand our discourse about this problem beyond a recitation of the crimes of white racism and public neglect. Some of the work that needs doing involves giving support to the decent and virtuous people in these communities whose lives are a testimony to the power of faith.

PART III

ETHICAL THEORIES AND THEORIES OF JUSTICE

The two previous sections of this book have examined how the relationship between ethics and economics is important both for the construction of theory and for understanding the behavior of economic agents. This section begins the examination of the third question—how to assess the differential impact of economic institutions and policies. That is, to answer the question of whether outcomes are desirable, ethical evaluations must be applied in addition to economic evaluations. This requires some understanding of available moral theories, along with the main arguments for and against them. A moral theory is needed to provide a framework for responding to some of the questions that will be raised later in the book. For example, if one determines that value-free economics is impossible, which moral values should inform the discipline? If people do not behave simply as rational maximizers, what moral theories might guide their actions? What moral theory should be used to answer applied policy questions? And finally, if individual preference sovereignty is rejected as the overriding goal of the economic system, what moral benchmarks or objectives should take its place? All of these issues cannot be even understood, much less resolved, without some sort of a moral theory as a guide.

In addition, moral theory may be of help in answering some questions that have been only hinted at so far. First of all, in a free market society, in which firms have strong incentives to act in their own interests, is there a place for morality, or a kind of business ethics? Do firms have any obligations other than to earn money for their stockholders?

Consider a recent regulatory case. It was recently discovered that a particular model of automobile was susceptible to catching on fire in an accident, leading to unnecessary deaths and injuries. The costs of recalling all the vehicles involved and fixing each one would have been high. Finally, the producers of the car agreed to a settlement with regulators in which they would not be forced to fix the defect, but promised to undertake other safety measures that would save as many lives, but at lower cost.

What moral issues are at stake here? If the company knew of the problem before it sold the cars, did it act improperly in selling them? Once the problem became apparent, did the firm have a duty to fix the defect at any reasonable expense? Did the firm relieve itself of any such responsibility when it agreed to alternative actions that would save as many lives? Trying to answer such questions without a moral theory is like trying to send a rocket into space without physical theory. Several of the many candidates for this theoretical role will be examined in this section of the book.

In addition to issues of business ethics, another new issue introduced in this section is distributive justice. While ethical theory tends to focus on actions and persons, theories of distributive justice focus on institutions. It answers questions about how the goods of society are to be given out.

These issues have been at the center of political debate in the United States in recent years. The United States has experienced a vitriolic debate about its welfare system. In a wealthy society, are the poor entitled to some kind of governmental help? Are they entitled to have their needs met? If so, should this help be unconditional, or should certain obligations be attached to government support? One could go further and ask: Are gross inequalities intolerable even if everyone's basic needs are met? There is a theoretical literature that seeks to answer such questions, and this section covers it.

The first chapter in this section, by W. David Solomon, explains the three main types of moral theories: consequentialist ethics, deontological ethics, and virtue ethics. Consequentialism holds that the right action is the one that results in the best outcomes. One type of consequentialism, utilitarianism, is dominant in economic theory and asserts that the outcomes that matter are utility or preference satisfaction.

Implementing utilitarianism presents certain problems. How does one measure welfare or preference satisfaction, particularly when different individuals must be compared? Do consequences count if they are not expected in advance? Does the welfare of future generations matter? What of animals? How does one compare two different states of affairs in which population levels differ? How does an individual make ethical decisions when quantifying utility is difficult, if not impossible?

Despite these difficulties, it is argued by many that utility is the only intrinsically good thing. Others argue that utilitarianism is justified on the basis of equal respect among persons. There has been a recent resurgence in the popularity of consequentialism and many economists find it appealing because of its apparent compatibility with neo-classical economic theory.

In deontological ethics, in contrast to consequentialist ethics, moral duties or rights sometimes take precedence over outcomes, because those duties or rights are morally valuable in themselves. The deontological position is intuitively appealing as can be seen by means of an example: assume a situation in which you must choose between killing one innocent person yourself and allowing two others to be murdered by another person. The consequences, in terms of the number of lives lost, are not as bad if you commit the murder. But to do so violates the moral obligation not to kill.

Virtue theory traces its roots to Aristotle. Among the most prominent present-day proponents of virtue theory is Alasdair MacIntyre. Happiness plays a central role in virtue theory, just as in utilitarianism, but virtue theorists mean something different when they refer to happiness. Aristotle used the term to refer to activity in accordance with virtue. Virtues, in turn, are the personal qualities that enable us to do the things that good people do. To use an analogy, a good watch is one that tells time well, looks stylish, and has other such virtues. Of course, the qualities of a good person are more complicated than those of a good watch, and require some kind of agreement on the proper ends of humankind. MacIntyre has argued that an important feature of modern societies is their inability to reach agreement on such matters. But most people would agree that the human virtues include truthfulness, courage, and so on. These virtues come into play in different human *practices*, or spheres of endeavor, each of which has distinct goods and virtues. Thus the main goods of play writing may include witty wordplay, while the goods of news writing may prominently include being informative and concise, and the virtues of the practitioners of each of these fields vary accordingly.

Virtue theory might have much to teach modern business people. Businesses might perform better if they concentrated on developing virtues or excellences like quality, rather than focusing exclusively on the bottom line. Richard P. Nielsen's chapter on the "manager as Eichmann, Richard III, Faust, or Institution Citizen" can be profitably discussed in terms of virtue theory.

Amitai Etzioni, in the second essay, suggests a way in which deontological considerations might be used to augment neo-classical economics. The essence of the deontological, or Kantian, approach, he says, is that while the utilitarian views the person as a unified bundle of preferences, the Kantian sees the self as bifurcated. Each person has a set of desires as well as a separate aspect of the self that judges those preferences in light of moral considerations. The ultimate choices of the individual are the product of both aspects of the self. This notion, as Etzioni points out, is consistent with the work of those economists who have introduced "meta-preferences," a secondary set of preferences over the domain of all possible preferences. In addition to the fact that preferences have this dual nature, Etzioni points out that they respond to experience, and thus are endogenous in an important way.

Although Etzioni argues for the incorporation of the moral aspects of the individual into economic theory, he argues against seeing the moral aspects of the world as a limited and distinct area in which special rules apply. Morality interpenetrates all of economic life; its implications are sweeping and do not apply only to certain areas. For example, in considering work life, the moral value of work, and not just preferences, Etzioni says, must be taken into account. Moreover, moral behavior undergirds all of the economy, which would quickly disintegrate if large numbers of people attempted to cheat one another or failed to honor their contracts. Thus, moral considerations demand a radical rethinking of all of economics.

Virginia Held addresses another approach to ethics: Is there such a thing as a feminist ethics? Carol Gilligan was one of the first to study this issue. Her work was framed as a criticism of Lawrence Kohlberg, who apparently had found that moral development among girls was less advanced than among boys. Gilligan tried to document that what appears to be a lack of moral development is rather a distinctively "female" form of moral thought, which is shared by many girls and women, as well as some young boys. Men tend to have what Held calls a "justice perspective" on morality. This form of morality emphasizes rules and individual conscience. In contrast, women have a "care perspective," which centers on meeting others' needs and maintaining relationships, rather than rigid adherence to moral rules.

Following the general lines of Gilligan's approach, Held argues that women tend to share certain ways of thinking, acting and feeling about moral problems. These distinctive forms of female moral experience are in part the product of the activities that women have historically been involved in, especially mothering. To the extent that moral theory is based upon moral experience, Held argues women's distinctive experiences should be included. Held believes that this is especially the case because the experience of mothering is so central and important to human life, compared with the realm of public affairs, which provides the inspiration for many "male" forms of moral thinking.

Held enumerates several aspects of women's morality. First, it is attentive to the needs of "particular others," in contrast to all other people in general. That is, it emphasizes the special obligations we have to those who are close to us, as opposed to other people as such. Second, a feminist morality deemphasizes, but does not discard, moral rules and principles. Third, there is more to morality than just knowledge; equally important are the associated feelings and motivations. Fourth, one of the most important female experiences providing inspiration for feminist morality is the process of giving birth; the pain of bearing a child inspires the commitment of the mother, who does not want her suffering to have been in vain. Fifth, a feminist morality emphasizes the survival of children and relations of care and concern. Finally, Held argues that while much of what feminists say about morality has been said before, as some critics have alleged, the important thing is that many problems and experiences specific to women have been largely ignored.

Richard P. Nielsen takes on a more applied issue: business or organizational ethics. The chief concern of this article is the possible conflict between obeying orders and honoring one's individual conscience. One of the most important reasons for being concerned with this conflict is the potential and actual harm institutions can inflict upon people. Consumers suffer serious injuries from unsafe products every year. Employees are harmed by unsafe working conditions; over 4,000 die each year from work related causes. In addition, air and water pollution harm millions as do cancer inducing products and working conditions.

An organization can encourage its managers to become institution citizens by providing an environment which cultivates the habit of thinking and judging independently as the basis for acting civically with others—employees, customers, suppliers, owners, civic representatives—and resisting the immoral behaviors and phenomena of the Eichmann, Richard III, and Faust managerial types.

James Sterba, the final author in this section, concentrates entirely on issues of justice. One way of looking at justice is to see it as a virtue of institutions or societies, rather than of individuals. It deals with the way goods are distributed among individuals. Goods here are broadly defined, and could, for example, be economic, as when the tax system is considered; or political, as when the electoral system is at issue; or legal, when it is being determined what rights citizens should have.

How does one possibly determine what institutions are just? John Rawls, who was strongly influenced by Kant, has one of the most famous modern answers to this question. He argues that just institutions are those that would be rationally agreed to by representative members of society in a hypothetical situation called the original position. In the original position, agents would be subject to what Rawls calls a veil of ignorance, meaning that they would not know their abilities or status in society, among other things. Also, they would not know their own conceptions of the good, or value systems. They would be asked to come up with a contract that specified the rights and rewards that are attached to various positions in society. Thus, Rawls's line of argument asks us to consider questions of the following type: What salary structure would you support for the medical sector, if you thought you could become either a doctor or a nurse's assistant?

Rawls argues that people in such a situation would choose a system that (1) granted the individual the maximum level of liberties consistent with the same liberties for everyone else and (2) made the worst-off person as well-off as possible. Thus, supposing that the worst-paid people in society were nurse's aides, we would pay them as much as doctors, unless we knew that paying doctors more made everyone—including nurse's aides—better off.

In addition to Rawls's contractarian position, Sterba outlines several other approaches to justice. One is an approach that Rawls strongly rejected: utilitarianism. According to utilitarianism, the requirements of justice are met by maximizing the total or average utility of society. This school of thought was introduced above while discussing consequentialist ethics. Some of the main utilitarians were John Stuart Mill and Jeremy Bentham.

Both deontological and consequentialist ethics have their analogues in theories of justice: Rawls's theory has a deontological form and utilitarianism, of course, is a form of consequentialism. So, too, does virtue theory, which also goes by the name communitarianism. An early communitarian critic of Rawls was Michael Sandel, whose argument—somewhat surprisingly, perhaps—was that Rawls adhered to an incorrect theory of what a person was. Sandel argued that in order to claim, as Rawls does, that justice is the primary virtue of societies, one had to hold a certain theory of the person. Not only was this theory of the self incorrect, Sandel argued, but it was also inconsistent with some of Rawls's main claims, in particular that the poor were entitled to some of the wealth currently held by the rich.

Another approach is libertarianism. For the proponents of this doctrine, freedom is the primary consideration in issues of justice. Freedom here refers to the freedom to be left alone, as opposed to the freedom to do specific things. Thus, government activity—especially in its redistributive role—is to be kept to a minimum. One major contemporary representative of the libertarian school is John Hospers.

Representing perhaps the diametric opposite of libertarianism on the spectrum of justice theories is socialism. Equality is the main value. As Sterba points out, Marx made perhaps the strongest possible statement of this commitment to egalitarianism when he called for the abolition of private property in the *Communist Manifesto*. In the *Critique of the Gotha Program*, one of Marx's later writings, he used the now well-known phrase, "From each according to his abilities, to each according to his needs."

Perhaps the most recent approach to justice is that of feminism. One writer in this school, Susan Okin, argues that the Rawlsian approach is in some ways consistent with feminist concerns, though Rawls himself mainly ignored such potential feminist applications of his theory. For example, we can imagine being in an original position situation in which we did not know whether we would be a man or a woman, and had to decide on institutions relating to gender. Okin believes that such thinking leads one to the conclusion that gender itself—the assignment of duties and rights according to sex—is unjust and should be abolished.

What is Sterba's view on all of these approaches? One might be tempted to survey the wide range of existing theories and throw up one's hands. But Sterba's view is that despite their differences, the various approaches, when properly interpreted, in fact lead to very similar policy prescriptions. For example, Sterba claims that even the libertarian ideal of negative freedom can be used to justify an egalitarian program. So, there is less disagreement here than it might at first appear.

Economic problems are inextricably bound up with moral ones, both as issues of individual ethics and issues of social justice. This section presents the main theoretical approaches that philosophers have used to address these topics. If this body of thought can be incorporated into economics, the field will be enriched.

9.

NORMATIVE ETHICAL THEORIES

W. David Solomon

G. E. Moore's classic proposal for the structure of ethics distinguished three key questions: (1) What particular things are good? (2) What kinds of things are good? and (3) What is the meaning of "good"? (Moore, 1903). The first question is the central question of casuistry, while the second question falls within normative ethics, and the third, within metaethics (although Moore used neither the term "metaethics" nor "normative ethics" in his early work). Normative ethics as a field of inquiry, then, is positioned somewhat precariously between the detail of casuistry and the abstractness of metaethics.

The character of normative ethics was also strongly influenced in the first half of the twentieth century by the almost universal acceptance of the principle of moral neutrality. This principle, accepted by virtually all mainstream Anglo-American moral philosophers from the 1930s to the 1960s, asserted that the results of metaethical investigations were logically independent of normative ethics. When coupled with the original understanding of metaethics as an account of the meaning of key ethical terms, it implied that such semantic investigations were logically irrelevant to inquiries about how to live. Under the influence of this principle, normative ethics was largely abandoned by Anglo-American moral philosophers in favor of a single-minded pursuit of metaethical inquiry. And since the metaethical views most in favor during this period were various forms of noncognitivism (e.g., emotivism and prescriptivism), it was regularly asserted that normative ethics should be relegated to preachers, novelists, and other nonphilosophers.

This sharp distinction between metaethical and normative inquiry, however, together with the relegation of normative ethics to nonphilosophical inquiry, was too unstable to last. Philosophers increasingly recognized that the principle of moral neutrality was not a theoretically neutral presupposition of ethical inquiry but rather drew a considerable amount of its support from the prevailing noncognitivist view. When these noncognitivist views were severely challenged in the late 1950s and 1960s (by, among others, Philippa Foot, Kurt Baier, Stephen Toulmin, and Alan Gewirth), the sharp distinction between metaethics and normative ethics was blunted; this opened the way to a resurgence of interest in normative ethics, expressed by new attempts to reformulate and to defend classical ethical views. Classical Kantian theory was developed in a creative and persuasive manner by John Rawls and his student, Thomas Nagel, along with Alan Donagan, Alan Gewirth, and others. Utilitarianism received new attention from, among others, Richard Hare and his students Derek Parfit and Peter Singer. The classical Aristotelian/Thomist view was reformulated and defended by Elizabeth Anscombe, Peter Geach, Alasdair MacIntyre, and like-minded moral philosophers.

What was revived under the label "normative ethics," however, was not identical to what had previously been neglected by moral philosophers as normative ethics. The watershed in ethical theory in the 1960s changed not only the interests of moral philosophers but also their conception of their discipline. Normative ethics came to be understood as that pole of ethical theory that stood closest to practice. Whereas previously the distinction that most clearly structured ethical inquiry was the distinction between metaethics and normative ethics, the crucial distinction increasingly came to be that between ethical theory and applied ethics.

Ethical theory was distinguished from applied ethics by being both more general and more abstract, and also by being less driven by a concern that its results would have some immediate consequences for action or policy. Ethical theory inquired into the epistemological and metaphysical features of ethics as well as into the most general truths about how we should live. Also, the new conception of ethical theory held that these two kinds of inquiry were continuous—it was not possible to pursue either kind without attending to its implications for the other. Ethical theory had become a seamless web with areas of greater or less practical relevance, roughly corresponding to those areas earlier distinguished as the normative and the metaethical.

There are certain common assumptions about the nature of normative ethics, as well as a widely shared taxonomy of the varieties of normative theory. The common assumptions include the claim that the central task of normative ethics is to define and to defend an adequate theory for guiding conduct. The received taxonomy divides normative theories into three basic types: virtue theories, deontological theories, and consequentialist theories. The following section will examine these three types of normative theory with the aim of exploring their distinctive features.

Types of Normative Theory

The basis for distinguishing the three types of normative theory lies in three universal features of human actions. This recourse to the features of actions should not be surprising, since the aim of normative theory is to guide action. Every human action involves (1) an agent who performs (2) some action that has (3) particular consequences. These three features may be set out as follows:

P	-------	++++++++++
Agent	Action	Consequences

If Jones tells a lie to Smith that causes Smith to miss his train, then Jones is the agent, his telling a lie is the action, and Smith's missing the train is one of the consequences of the action. Difficulties arise, of course, in many cases in determining whether someone is an agent in a particular case (e.g., if Jones is insane when he shoots the president, is he really the agent of any action?); or the nature of the particular action performed (e.g., if Jones is cutting down a tree, believing reasonably that he is the only one in the forest, but Smith wanders by and the tree falls on him, causing his death, does a killing take place or merely a death?); or what the consequences of a particular action may be (e.g., if Jones tells Smith "Take the stuff," but Smith understands him to say "Take the snuff," with the consequence that he takes the snuff and due to a hitherto undiscovered allergy becomes ill, is his illness a consequence of Jones's action in saying "Take the stuff"?). These are difficult questions, of course, and they have been much discussed in contemporary action theory in philosophy. In the typical case of human action, however, agent, action, and consequences can be identified, and the typical case provides the basis for the widely shared taxonomy of normative theories.

Ethical or broadly evaluative judgments can also be classified using a taxonomy drawing on these features of human action. Some ethical judgments are primarily evaluations of agents, such as "Jones is a compassionate doctor" or "Smith is a conscientious nurse." In these cases the object evaluated is a particular person, and he or she is evaluated as a possible or actual agent of an action. Some other ethical judgments are primarily about actions in the narrow sense, such as "Jones has a duty to tell the patient the truth about the diagnosis" or "The direct killing of the innocent is always wrong." In these cases, the primary object of ethical evaluation is an action—the thing done or to be done. This action may be characterized either as required ("X must be done") or as permitted ("X would be right to do") or as forbidden ("A would be wrong to do"). More concrete characterizations of actions are also possible, such as "X was a vicious action" or "X was a heroic action." In all of the cases, however, the action is the primary object of evaluation.

A third class of ethical judgments is primarily about states of affairs or objects that are neither agents nor actions, such as "Health is more important than money" or "Human suffering is a terrible thing." Ethical judgments like these do not, directly at least, evaluate either agents or actions. However, the objects evaluated in them, may be, and frequently are, the possible consequences of actions. Thus, this last class of judgments can also be matched to one of the three basic features of human action.

Normative theories may have any of three basic structures, and the differences among these structures are determined by which of the three kinds of practical judgments is taken as basic by a particular theory. Virtue theories take judgments of agents or persons as most basic; deontological theories take judgments of actions as most basic; and consequentialist theories take judgments of the possible consequences of an action as more basic. The sense in which a theory takes a judgment of a certain kind as most basic will become clear in the discussion of each type of theory.

Virtue Theories

Normative theories that regard judgments of agents or of character as most basic are called virtue theories because of the central role played in them by the notion of a virtue. In the context of these theories, a virtue is understood as a state of a thing "in virtue of which" it performs well or appropriately. In this broad understanding of virtue not only human beings possess virtues but also certain inanimate objects—a virtue of a knife, for example, will be a sharp blade. Indeed, anything that can be said to have a function or role attached to it because of the kind of thing it is may be said to possess virtues, at least potentially.

A virtue theory takes judgments of character or of agents as basic in that it regards the fundamental task of normative theory as depicting an ideal of human character. The ethical task of each person, correspondingly, is to become a person who has certain dispositions to respond in a characteristic way to situations in the world. Differences among persons may be of quite different kinds. Some people are shorter or fatter than others, some more or less intelligent, some better or worse at particular tasks, and some more courageous, just, or honest than others. These differences can be classified in various ways: physical versus mental differences, differences in ability versus differences in performance, and so on. Those features of human beings on which virtue theories concentrate in depicting the ideal human being are states of character. Such theories typically issue in a list of virtues for human beings. These virtues are states of character that human beings must possess to be successful as human beings.

Typically, a virtue theory has three goals:

1. to develop and to defend some conception of the ideal person

2. to develop and to defend some list of virtues necessary for being a person of that type
3. to defend some view of how persons can come to possess the appropriate virtues.

Virtually all ancient moral philosophers developed normative ethical theories of this sort. The ethical theories of Plato and Aristotle, in particular, provide models of this kind of normative ethical theory. As a consequence, the particular disputes that occurred among ancient philosophers centered on questions that one would expect to arise within a virtue perspective. What are human virtues? How are they acquired? Are they essentially states of knowledge? Can one know that a certain trait of character is a virtue without possessing it? Is it possible to have one, or a few, of the virtues without possessing all of them? Are all human virtues of the same type or are there fundamentally different kinds? Are human virtues a matter of nature or of convention? And, most important of all, what is the correct list of moral virtues? Much of the discussion of ethics in ancient Greece centered on a particular short list of virtues—justice, temperance, courage, and wisdom—that came to be called the *cardinal virtues*. After the introduction of Christianity into Europe, these four virtues were joined by faith, hope, and charity—the so-called *Christian virtues*—to form the seven virtues; these, together with the seven deadly vices, dominated medieval thinking about ethics.

One can also see how questions of human character are basic according to virtue theories by seeing how questions about (1) which actions one ought to perform and (2) which consequences one ought to bring about are subordinated to questions of human character. For a virtue theory the question "Which actions ought one to perform?" receives the response "Those actions that would be performed by a perfectly virtuous agent." Similarly, those states of affairs one is required to bring about in the world as a consequence of one's actions are those states of affairs valued by a perfectly virtuous person. Of course, particular actions may also be required by one's particular virtues. For example, someone who possesses the virtue of honesty may be required by the virtue itself to tell the truth in certain cases. Or someone may be required to pursue certain consequences by certain virtues. For example, an agent who has the virtue of benevolence may be required to pursue the happiness or well-being of others. But these requirements are derivative from the virtues, and the fundamental ethical question thus remains a question about the correct set of virtues for human beings.

Deontological Theories

Deontological normative theories take moral judgments of action as basic, and they regard the fundamental ethical task for persons as one of doing the right thing—or, perhaps more commonly, of avoiding doing the wrong thing. While virtue theories guide action by producing a picture of ideal human character and a list of virtues constitutive of that character, deontological theories characteristically guide action with a set of moral principles or moral rules. These rules may refer to particular circumstances and have the following form:

> Actions of type T are never (always) to be performed in circumstance C.

Or, they may be absolute in that they forbid certain actions in all circumstances and have the following form:

> Actions of type T′ are never to be performed.

The essential task of a deontological theory, then, is twofold:

1. to formulate and to defend a particular set of moral rules
2. to develop and to defend some method of determining what to do when the relevant moral rules come into conflict.

One must qualify, however, the claim that deontological theories make rules fundamental in ethics. What is fundamental, in fact, are actions themselves and their moral properties. This emphasis on actions can take either of two forms: A normative theory may guide action by requiring agents to perform certain kinds of action that can be specified by a rule or other general action guide. Alternatively, one might regard normative theories as requiring particular actions that in their "particularity" elude specification by a rule. This difference has led some moral philosophers to distinguish two forms of deontological normative theories: *rule deontological* theories, which guide action in the first manner, and *act deontological* theories, which guide action in the second. Virtually all influential deontological theories, however, have taken a rule form, and for this reason, this discussion will continue to emphasize the centrality of rules.

Just as a virtue theory subordinates judgments of actions and consequences in a characteristic way, a deontological theory subordinates judgments of character and consequence. The state of character ethically most important in a deontological view is conscientiousness—that state of character that disposes persons to follow rules punctiliously, whatever the temptations may be to make an exception in a particular case. Conscientiousness does not have value in itself, but it has value derivatively because it is the most important state of character for ensuring that persons follow rules and, hence, that they do what is right. In a similar way, the consequences of actions that deontologists are most concerned with are the consequences of particular rule-followings. Not all of an agent's practical life, however, need be reduced to rule-following. An agent may have certain personal ideals or particular projects that exist apart from moral rules. These personal ideals or personal projects may be pursued, according to the deontologist, but their pursuit is permitted only if it does not violate the moral rules. Moral rules define the limits of practical pursuits and projects. They are the moral framework within which nonmoral matters can go on. And this is the sense in which moral rules with their emphasis on judgments of actions are basic, according to the deontological view.

Just as virtue theory has its historical roots in the moral philosophy of ancient Greece, deontological theories have affinities with legalistic modes of thought characteristic of Judaic and later Roman thought. The Decalogue (Ten Commandments), although it functions in a religious context, provides a model of a set of rules of conduct that are basic in much the same way rules function in a deontological theory. One is required to follow the rules in the Decalogue because they are the commandments of God, and reasons can be given why it is appropriate to do what God tells one to do. When a deontological theory is deployed in a secular context, however, this reason for rule-following is necessarily absent. Nor can deontologists require that rules be followed because doing so is necessary to become persons of a certain sort or because doing so is necessary to bring about certain consequences. If they took the first route, their view would become a virtue theory; if they took the second route, it would become a consequentialist theory. For a view to be genuinely deontological, it must claim that an agent's fundamental ethical task is to perform certain actions and that the value of this task cannot be dependent on the value of either virtues or consequences.

The most profound attempt to defend this view was anticipated in ancient moral philosophy by the Stoics and was developed in its most persuasive form by the modern German philosopher Immanuel Kant. The Stoics claimed that moral rules are expressions in the human realm of laws of nature and that rational creatures are required to follow these rules because, as creatures, they are parts of nature and, as such, obligated to bring their action in line with natural forces. Human beings differ from other objects of nature by possessing both freedom and reason. Since they are free, they may act against nature; since they have reason, however, they can understand natural laws and choose to bring their action in line with such forces. Kant's view agrees with the Stoic view in broad outline, but he develops the notions of freedom and reason far beyond the Stoic view. Kant's ultimate answer to questions about how we discover the correct set of moral rules is that only by following the dictates of reason can we be genuinely free.

Consequentialist Theories

Consequentialist normative theories take judgments of the value of the consequences of actions as most basic. According to these theories, one's crucial ethical task is to act so that one will bring about as much as possible of whatever the theory designates as most valuable. If a particular consequentialist theory designates, for example, that pleasure is the only thing valuable in itself, then one should act so as to bring as much pleasure as possible. The goals of a consequentialist theory itself are threefold:

1. to specify and to defend some thing or list of things that are good in themselves
2. to provide some technique for measuring and comparing quantities of these intrinsically good things
3. to defend some practical policy for those cases where one is unable to determine which of a number of alternative actions will maximize the good thing or things.

Like deontological theories, consequentialist theories can be divided into act and rule varieties. *Act consequentialism* requires agents to perform the particular action that in a particular situation is most likely to maximize good consequences. *Rule consequentialism* requires agents to follow those moral rules the observance of which will maximize good consequences. The difference between these two forms of consequentialism, however, is not as straightforward as it may at first seem. It is particularly difficult to precisely characterize rule consequentialism. Is the agent supposed to follow those rules that, if followed by everyone, would maximize good consequences, or rather those rules that will maximize goodness, regardless of how other agents act? There are a number of similar difficulties in characterizing rule consequentialism, and these difficulties have led some moral philosophers to deny that there is a genuine distinction here at all. They have argued, indeed, that when any form of rule consequentialism is rigorously characterized, it will be found to degenerate into a form of act consequentialism.

For consequentialists, the distinction between *instrumentally* good things and *intrinsically* good things is also of special importance. Instrumentally good things are good only insofar as they play some role in bringing about intrinsically good things. If, in a particular case, some thing that is ordinarily instrumentally good does not stand in the appropriate relation to an intrinsically good object, then its goodness evaporates. Its goodness is merely dependent. Intrinsically good things, on the contrary, are good not because of any relation in which they may stand to other things. Their goodness is independent because it is constituted by the kind of thing the good thing is. Thus, a particular consequentialist theory may hold that only pleasure is intrinsically good, but that other things, including types of action and states of character, are instrumentally good. The virtue of honesty, for example, might be regarded as instrumentally good by such a theory since honesty is likely to contribute to maximizing human happiness. Even if honesty is typically instrumentally good, however, situations may arise in which one could maximize pleasure by acting deviously rather than honestly. In such cases, a consequentialist theory (complications about rule versions of the theory aside) would hold that one should perform the devious action. According to this view, there is nothing about honesty in itself that is good.

Consequentialist theories find their fullest expression in modern thought, especially in the thought of the British utilitarians Jeremy Bentham, John Stuart Mill, and Henry Sidgwick. Drawing on earlier work in the British empiricist tradition, the classic utilitarians claimed that the only intrinsically good thing is human happiness, which they understood as constituted by pleasure and the absence of pain. The utilitarian maxim, "Act always in such a way as to promote the greatest happiness to the greatest number," has been the paradigmatic consequentialist moral principle and has inspired many more recent consequentialists.

There was much disagreement among classical utilitarians, however, about the details of their view. Can pleasures be distinguished qualitatively as well as quantitatively? What role should rules and virtues play within the practical thought of a utilitarian? How can the flavor of the absolute prohibitions associated with justice and the inviolability of the person be preserved within a utilitarian framework? These questions, along with other similar ones, were answered differently by different utilitarians. They were at one, however, in aspiring to formulate and defend a particular version of consequentialism.

The distinction above between the instrumentally and intrinsically good makes it possible to specify more clearly what a consequentialist theory is and to overcome certain difficulties of definition that may creep in. If a consequentialist theory is characterized as one that specifies some object, state of affairs, or property that should be maximized, one might ask whether the object or state of affairs referred to in this definition might be either a state of character or the performance of certain actions. If so, then the distinctions between a consequentialist theory, on the one hand, and a deontological theory or a virtue theory, on the other, seems to be in jeopardy. If the intrinsically valuable things specified by a consequentialist theory can include actions or states of character, then virtue theories and deontological theories would seem to be mere species of consequentialism, distinguished from other forms of consequentialism by the type of thing they specify as intrinsically valuable. Virtue theories would be consequentialist theories that specify states of character as intrinsically valuable; deontological theories would be consequentialist theories that specify the performance of certain actions as valuable. If deontological and virtue theories are merely varieties of consequentialism, however, there are not three basic structures but rather one basic structure with a number of varieties.

One might deal with this difficulty by defining a consequentialist theory as one that specifies what is intrinsically good but includes neither states of affairs nor actions, but this seems arbitrary. In addition, although this solution no longer allows that deontological theories and virtue theories are varieties of consequentialism, it does not make it possible to understand how these three types of theory exhibit different structures. One can see that there are different structures here, however, by looking more closely at the differences among these theories. Suppose that a particular consequentialist theory specifies certain virtues as the only intrinsically valuable things. Suppose, more specifically, that a particular consequentialist theory, C, specifies that the virtue of justice is the only intrinsically valuable thing. One can also suppose that a virtue theory, V, specifies the good for human beings such that it is constituted solely by the virtue of justice. Are these two theories practically equivalent? If virtue theories are a mere variety of consequentialism, they should be. If they are not, then virtue theories are not a mere variety of consequentialist theory.

One can see that these two theories are not practically equivalent by considering the practical requirements each imposes on an agent. C requires that an agent act in such a way that he or she will maximize the number of just persons. Since consequentialist theories require that agents maximize whatever is intrinsically valuable, and since the only intrinsically valuable thing according to C is the virtue of justice, agents are required by this theory to maximize justice. V, however, need not have this consequence. What V requires of an agent is that he or she develop those virtues that are constitutive of being a good human being. V requires, then, merely that an agent develop justice. There is nothing in V itself that requires an agent to try to bring about justness in others. A virtue theory more complicated than V may include a virtue—perhaps benevolence—that requires agents to promote the well-being of others as well as themselves. But this requirement to maximize the number of people who possess virtues is not a requirement derived from the nature of a virtue theory itself. It can be derived only from some particular virtue that may—or may not—be a component of a particular virtue theory.

One can arrive at this same point by considering an agent who finds herself in a situation where she can maximize the number of just persons only by becoming herself unjust. In order to make others just, she must become unjust. One example of such a case might be a politician who believes that the best way to make the citizens of her country just is to acquire political power and to exercise it in ways that only she can succeed in doing. Also, suppose she knows that only by renouncing justice herself, by being prepared to act unjustly, can she acquire political power. Thus it is only by becoming unjust that she can most efficiently make others just.

What do C and V have to say to this agent? It is clear that C would approve the renunciation of justice on her part if that would maximize the number of persons who possess justice. The loss of this particular agent's own justice to the sum of justice in the world is more than offset by the gain in the number of persons who are just. The sacrifice is worth it. But what would V require? It is equally clear that V does not require the agent to sacrifice her own justice.

Virtue theories hold that an agent's own character plays a special role in his or her practical thinking that it does not play in a consequentialist theory. A virtue theory gives agents reasons to act because it is supposed that each person wants to be a flourishing and fulfilled human being. An agent's own life and character then will have a certain primacy according to a virtue theory. Virtues are not just intrinsically valuable things that should be inculcated in as many agents as possible. They are states of character that each agent must acquire in order to succeed as a human being. Thus, V will not necessarily require that this agent become unjust even if this would maximize the amount of justice in the world.

Similar conclusions follow with regard to a comparison between consequentialist theories and deontological theories. Consider a particular consequentialist teleological theory, C′, that specifies that the only intrinsically valuable things are acts of truth-telling, and a particular deontological theory, D, that specifies that the only moral rule is one that enjoins truth-telling in all cases. Are these two theories practically equivalent? Again it is useful to consider a case in which maximizing a particular good requires the renunciation of it by an agent. Suppose that an agent finds himself in a situation in which he can most efficiently produce the maximum ratio of truth-tellings to lyings by himself telling a lie. Perhaps he has discovered that, by telling others that whenever they tell a lie their life is shortened by three weeks, he can most efficiently promote truth-telling. But he also knows that this is a lie. What should he do?

It seems clear that C′ would require him to act in whatever way will maximize the number of truth-tellings, and, if this requires him to lie, so be it. Although his lie may be intrinsically bad, its badness will be more than outweighed by the intrinsically good states of affairs it brings about. The person who accepts D, however, believes that there is a moral rule enjoining everyone always to tell the truth. This rule gives him a reason to act, because he is committed to doing the right thing. He is not committed primarily to bringing about as many right or dutiful actions as possible; rather, he is committed to doing the right thing. Just as a virtue theory holds that an agent stands in a more intimate relation to his own character than he does to the characters of other persons, a deontological theory holds that an agent stands in a more intimate relation to his own actions than he does to the actions of others. The action of an agent who follows a moral rule will have a different moral significance for a deontologist than the action of an agent who brings it about that someone else follows a moral rule. For a deontologist, it is not as important that there be rule-followings as that he or she follow moral rules. D need not then require, or even permit, that the agent tell a lie if this is necessary to maximize truth-telling, and hence C′ and D, like C and V, are not practically equivalent. If they are not practically equivalent, however, then deontological normative theories, like virtue theories, are not mere varieties of consequentialism.

Deeper Differences among Normative Theories

This comparison of virtue, deontological, and consequentialist normative theories suggests that the differences among them are deeper than might at first appear. Indeed it suggests that while they certainly differ with regard to which of the three kinds of practical judgments they take as most basic, there are other, and more fundamental, differences among them. To accept one of these normative theories is to accept a particular attitude toward the relation of an agent to his or her character and actions. If one adopts a virtue theory, one's own character comes to have an especially important place in one's practical thinking. It is of the first importance that one become a person of a certain sort. This view need not imply, as it may seem to, that one is committed to an egoistic or selfish life. One may be guided by a virtue theory to pursue a life dominated by generosity and concern for others. One may, indeed, strive to become completely selfless in the sense of always putting the needs of others ahead of one's own needs. But even if this is one's goal, it is also true that one's own character forms the primary focus of one's practical life. The apparent combination here of concern for self and concern for others may appear paradoxical, but it is surely not incoherent. Some of the greatest moral heroes—for example, Gandhi, Jesus, and Albert Schweitzer—seem to have combined these two concerns in their lives.

In a similar way, if one adopts a deontological theory, one's own actions come to play an especially important role in one's practical thinking. It makes a difference to one that one's actions are wrong. It is more important practically to an agent that he or she has told a lie than that a lie has been told. In cases where one's telling a single lie will prevent three others from telling lies, one will not decide what to do by simple arithmetic. Of course, a deontologist will not expect that others will have the same concern for her lie as she will have for it. She may recognize that for someone else, his telling a lie will have a different practical significance for him than her telling a lie will have for him. And just as she may not be prepared to tell one lie to prevent him from telling two, she will not expect him to tell one lie to prevent her from telling two. Indeed, she will recognize that from his point of view, his telling one lie is worse in an important sense than her telling two, just as from her point of view her telling one lie is worse than his telling two.

The special significance given to one's actions by a deontological theory need not imply that a deontologist is egoistic or, in the ordinary sense of the term, self-centered. In this way the deontologist is in a situation similar to that of the virtue theorist. The particular moral rules that one is required to follow may give the needs and interests of others parity with one's own, or, more likely, they may require one to put others ahead of oneself. What they cannot require is that one take up a particular attitude toward the rules themselves. The rules cannot, as it were, define their own condition of application—nor can they specify how they relate to one's faculty of practical decision making at the deepest level.

To a consequentialist, giving this special significance to one's character or one's actions may seem confused and possibly morally corrupt. Of course, consequentialists may be concerned with questions of character, but character cannot be their central normative focus. According to consequentialism, what is of primary ethical importance is that the amount of the intrinsically valuable be maximized. Determining the most effective means for maximization involves straightforward questions of efficiency. These questions may be neither simple nor easily answered, but structurally they are straightforward: Which of the possible courses of action will most likely maximize the amount of goodness in the world? In canvassing the possible means to this end, the consequentialist requires an agent to throw his own character and actions into the same category with other possible means. The kind of character one should develop depends upon the kind of character that will contribute most to the relevant goal. The actions one should perform depend similarly on con sequentialist goals. For a consequentialist, one must put a certain distance between oneself—considered as the agent who must make practical choices—and one's own character and actions. One's character and actions have the same role in one's practical thinking as would any other possible means—one's wealth, for example, or influence—that are in a more usual sense external. More important, one's own character and actions have no more special role in practical thinking than do the character and actions of others. All are regarded as possible means to maximize intrinsically good things, and one's own actions and character may have special significance only insofar as they may be more easily—because more directly—manipulated by oneself.

One might think, however, that one feature of the agent's character cannot be treated as a mere means, even by a consequentialist. For any consequentialist theory, it will surely be important that persons have those states of character that dispose them to pursue or to favor intrinsically good things. It might be argued that this state of character cannot be treated by the theory as a mere means. But this argument underestimates the resources within consequentialism for distancing an agent from his or her character. Suppose an agent holds a consequentialist normative theory, C″, according to which the only intrinsically good things are states of human pleasure. Suppose also that this agent has a character such that he is disposed always to act in ways he believes will maximize human pleasure. This argument suggests that this agent will not be prepared to sacrifice for the goal of maximal pleasure his own disposition to pursue this goal. But why should this be the case? One might think that a case could never arise in which an agent could contribute most to maximizing pleasure by changing his character to that of someone unconcerned with maximizing pleasure. But this view is surely wrong. Suppose the agent discovers an empirical law according to which human pleasure is maximized only if agents are disposed not to pursue human pleasure but to pursue knowledge. But if this is true—and it is surely possibly true—the agent should act to change as many persons' characters as possible from pleasure-seeking to knowledge-seeking characters. Nor is there any reason why, on consequentialist grounds, this agent should make an exception in his or her own case. So even those features of human character that lead an agent to pursue the maximization of intrinsically good things are not given a special place by consequentialists. Every feature of the character of an agent may be regarded as a possible means to the maximization of the relevant goal.

This feature of consequentialist theories was first emphasized by Henry Sidgwick, the greatest of modern utilitarians. Sidgwick was convinced that if the utilitarian goal of human happiness was to be maximized, then it was necessary that most persons not be utilitarians. Indeed, he thought that what was probably required was that most persons hold deontological views and have their character shaped in accordance with such views. He proposed then, for utilitarian reasons, that utilitarianism be propagated as an esoteric view, and that only a few of the most able and intelligent members of society have their characters shaped in accord with it (Sidgwick, 1907). These bearers of the esoteric view, in turn, would mold the characters of those less able and enlightened in accord with a deontological perspective. Had Sidgwick's enlightened few become convinced that maximal human happiness required that they, too, acquire "deontological characters," simple consistency would have required them to change their own characters appropriately. In this way, consequentialism might require that agents strive to bring about a world in which no one, not even oneself, has the kind of character that would dispose one to strive at the most basic practical level for consequentialist goods.

Justifying Normative Theories

The question of how, if at all, one can rationally choose among these three normative theories is a question taken up under the topic of moral epistemology. It is important to note here, however, that these normative theories emerge in Western thought as components in comprehensive philosophical theories developed by Plato, Aristotle, Aquinas, Kant, Mill, and other major philosophers. They are embedded in rich and complex worldviews in ways that make it difficult to discuss them in isolation from their theoretical and historical settings.

The tendency within contemporary ethical theory is to discuss the merits of these views in purely ethical terms and to ignore to a large extent their larger theoretical settings. Thus, consequentialism is frequently attacked because it is alleged to countenance the judicial punishment of the innocent if that is required for achieving some good end. In arguments like this one, the alleged ethical implications of a normative theory are appealed to in order to evaluate the theory. Similarly, deontologists may be criticized for holding that certain actions are morally forbidden even if performing them in a particular case might prevent an enormous tragedy. It is now a matter of record that these arguments have been unsuccessful in producing agreement within normative ethics. Nevertheless, the same slightly tired arguments continue to be made.

The lesson from the history of these views would seem to be, however, that if any of them is to be adequately defended, or successfully criticized, its theoretical setting must be taken into account. Each of these theories has complex relations with particular philosophical accounts of rationality, explanation, nature, intention, the law, the passions, and other topics of central philosophical interest. A more adequate account of them, if possible here, would have to take these theoretical entanglements into account. Certainly any serious attempt to choose rationally among them would have to locate them in this larger theoretical setting.

Normative Ethics and Practice

The raison d'être for normative ethics, as we have seen, is to guide action, and the theories explored above have been developed with such guidance in mind. There is general disagreement, however, about exactly how these normative theories are to relate to the resolution of particular normative problems. It is not easy to demonstrate how the debate between consequentialists and deontologists is related to more concrete disagreements about surrogate motherhood or consideration of future generations. Part of the difficulty arises from the fact that each of the three normative theories embodies a particular conception of how it relates to concrete normative problems. There is no theory-independent criterion of how normative theories are to guide action, since each theory embodies a view about its own application. In this way normative theories double back on themselves with regard to their action-guiding function.

An illustration of this doubling-back phenomenon is found in current debates about the relation of virtue theories to practice. Virtue theories are frequently criticized because they do not yield concrete action guides in the way that consequentialist and deontological theories appear to do. The moral advice to "Be just" lacks the action-guiding bite of either a moral rule that requires an agent to perform certain actions or a consequentialist conception that specifies some good to be maximized. But this objection fails to take account of the distinctive way in which virtue theories purport to guide action. A central claim of virtue theories is that the action-guiding function of a normative theory is not to resolve concrete puzzles about action. Edmond Pincoffs, a leading contemporary virtue theorist, coined the useful term "quandary ethics" precisely to designate what virtue theories are against: a conception of normative ethics as guiding action by giving a particular solution to quandaries about action. If one supposes that the only way in which a normative theory can guide action is by resolving particular moral quandaries, then one is unlikely to take virtue theories seriously.

Virtue theories offer, however, an alternative account of the action-guiding function of normative theories. They claim that an adequate normative theory will prescribe something like a training program to make agents ethically "fit." This program may not specify exactly how one is to act in particular cases, because these decisions are best left to the prudential decisions of a "morally fit" agent in the concrete decision-making situation. Thus, virtue theories double back on themselves and specify how they are to relate to practice. Both deontological and consequentialist theories also contain such self-referential accounts of their own application.

An important implication of this doubling-back phenomenon is that one cannot assess the adequacy of normative theories by invoking a well-defined criterion for "successful" action-guiding without begging the question. To have such a well-defined criterion is already to have taken a position on some of the fundamental questions in normative ethics.

This difficulty is actually even more serious than this first point suggests. It is not just that each of the three normative theories embodies a well-defined criterion of how normative theory should relate to practice. Also, there are a number of different models of how general ethical thinking should relate to concrete practice. Some of these models have loose affinities with some of the normative theories, but there is not a fixed or necessary connection between them. Indeed, the conflicts among the normative theories cut across, in complex ways, the conflicts among these models for relating normative theory to practice. A representative collection of these models would include (1) deductivism, (2) dialectical models, (3) principlism, (4) casuistical models, and (5) situation ethics. These models have been for the most part badly defined in the current literature, and the differences among them and their relations to traditional normative theories tend to be matters of dispute.

Deductivism

The deductivist model regards the action-guiding function of ethical theory to be the development of highly abstract and general first principles that, together with some factual description of a particular morally problematic situation, will entail concrete action guides. According to this model, moral principles developed and defended within normative ethical theory will play the role of premises in deductive arguments for ethical judgments about particular cases. This model of application is particularly attractive to some deontologists and consequentialists. It is related to more general accounts of justification in contemporary epistemology that suggest that all justification must come from some set of foundational claims in the area in question. It also makes large demands on the justificatory resources of a normative theory, since all of the justification for the principles must come from the theory itself. There is no "bottom up" justification from particular moral beliefs to general principles, as will be found in some of the other models.

Dialectical Models

Partly because of worries about the foundationalist character of deductivism, some moral theorists understand the relation between normative theory and practice in a dialectical way. Instead of supposing that justification is exclusively "top down," they suppose that there is dialectical interplay between the principles in a normative theory and particular moral judgments. Normative principles may be modified if they fail to fit our deeply held particular moral beliefs, just as our particular beliefs may be modified in order to fit principles. Whether agents modify principles or particular judgments will depend upon their degree of commitment to each and to the other beliefs they might hold. Just as the deductivist model has affinities with foundationalist theories in epistemology, the dialectical model is inspired by coherentist epistemological theories, which suggest that justification in general is to be understood as a function of how large sets of propositions "hang together" or cohere. The most influential form of the dialectical model is John Rawls's "method of reflective equilibrium," which he uses to support his deontological normative theory.

Principlism

Some philosophers have wanted to downplay the importance of normative theory for resolving concrete ethical problems. They emphasize, for example, that consequentialist and deontological normative theories in most cases mandate the same actions, and that it is only in exceptional cases that differences seem to emerge. And they add that the exceptional cases are likely to be so difficult to resolve that both consequentialists and deontologists disagree among themselves about what normative theory requires. They conclude that general ethical reflection should focus on what they call "middle-level" principles, that is, not the most general principles in any normative theory but those that are likely to be acceptable to adherents of different normative theories. They hope that agreement may be easier to achieve in practical matters if the premises for practical arguments are not sought at the deepest level of normative theory. This model has been especially influential in bioethics and has been developed and defended by Tom Beauchamp and James Childress (1989). The middle-level principles they propose are labeled autonomy, beneficence, nonmaleficence, and justice. Their claim is that these principles, when suitably refined, are likely to be acceptable to both rule consequentialists and deontologists.

Casuistical Model

Some philosophers have understood genuinely practical and action-guiding thinking in a way that makes it even more remote from the disputes among the classical normative theories. They propose that the appropriate model for practical reflection is found in the case-based approach popular in late medieval and early modern moral thought. According to this approach, ethical reflection should focus on certain paradigm cases of morally good action or morally bad action. Arguments from these paradigm cases to more problematic cases may be made by exploring similarities and differences between the two. This approach rejects attempts to formulate the goodness or badness of paradigm cases in abstract and general principles, and emphasizes analogical as opposed to deductive reasoning. Albert Jonsen and Stephen Toulmin (1988) have been the leading advocates of this model in recent normative ethics.

Situation Ethics

Some might suggest that situation ethics is not so much a model for practical thinking as a rejection of any model. It claims that one should approach the resolution of particular moral problems by eschewing all general action guides in favor of concentrated attention to the details of the particular situation. In some of its versions it may look a bit like the casuistical model; but in its most radical formulations it would mandate that even paradigm cases should play no central role in particular reflection because they could deflect the agent's attention from the particular features of the case under consideration. Among contemporary thinkers, Joseph Fletcher has been the most prominent advocate of this view, although his early commitment to situation ethics developed later into a more general commitment to consequentialism. In his formulation of situation ethics, he suggests that reflection on particular cases should be guided by the general principle, "Do the loving thing!" However, he is insistent that this principle does not play the role of a premise in any deductive practical argument.

These five models represent different ways of thinking about how ethical reflection might be brought to bear on particular moral problems. They range from deductivism, in which successful ethical reflection requires premises drawn from an adequate normative theory, to situation ethics, which eschews any dependence on normative theory. The other three theories occupy the middle ground between these two extremes. In contemporary ethics there is no consensus on which of these models is most adequate. Each has its defenders and its critics, and there is a lively discussion in the contemporary literature about their respective merits.

When this disagreement about the correct approach to concrete ethical reflection is added to the disagreement among classical normative theories, it is easy to see why contemporary applied ethics involves conflicts of such depth and complexity. One is confronted not only with competing normative theories, but also with competing conceptions of how such theories would relate to concrete ethical problems. These two different levels of disagreement indeed tend to reinforce one another, since particular disagreements at each level tend to be tied to particular disagreements at the other.

References

Anscombe, G. E. M. 1958. "Modern Moral Philosophy." *Philosophy* 33:1–19. An influential attack on deontological and consequentialist normative theories and defense of a virtue approach to normative ethics.

Beauchamp, Tom L., and Childress, James F. 1989. *Principles and Biomedical Ethics*. 3d ed. New York: Oxford University Press. The most discussed contemporary defense of principlism.

Brandt, Richard. 1979. *A Theory of the Good and the Right*. Oxford: At the Clarendon Press. A defense of ideal rule utilitarianism.

Broad, Charlie D. 1930. *Five Types of Ethical Theory*. London: Routledge & Kegan Paul. An early attempt to develop a taxonomy of normative ethical theories.

Donagan, Alan. 1977. *The Theory of Morality*. Chicago: University of Chicago Press. A defense of a comprehensive deontological normative theory.

Fletcher, Joseph. 1966. *Situation Ethics: The New Morality*. Philadelphia: Westminster. The classic statement and defense of situation ethics.

Foot, Philippa. 1978. *Virtues and Vices; And Other Essays in Moral Philosophy*. Berkeley: University of California Press. A collection of influential articles defending a virtue approach to normative theory.

Frankena, William K. 1973. *Ethics*. 2d ed. Englewood Cliffs, N.J.: Prentice-Hall. An influential discussion of the taxonomy of normative theories.

Jonsen, Albert R., and Toulmin, Stephen E. 1988. *The Abuse of Casuistry: A History of Moral Reasoning*. Berkeley: University of California Press. The most important recent discussion of the casuistical model.

Kittay, Eva Feder, and Meyers, Diana T., eds. 1987. *Women and Moral Theory*. Totowa, N.J.: Rowman and Littlefield. A useful recent collection of articles developing the feminist critique of moral theory.

MacIntyre, Alasdair C. 1981. *After Virtue: A Study in Moral Theory*. Notre Dame, Ind.: University of Notre Dame Press. The most important recent restatement and defense of an Aristotelian virtue theory.

Moore, G. E. 1903. *Principia Ethica*. Cambridge: At the University Press.

Nagel, Thomas. 1970. *The Possibility of Altruism*. Oxford: At the Clarendon Press. An important defense of a deontological theory.

Parfit, Derek. 1984. *Reasons and Persons*. Oxford: At the Clarendon Press. The most sophisticated recent defense of utilitarianism.

Rawls, John. 1971. *A Theory of Justice*. Cambridge, Mass.: Harvard University Press. The most influential recent statement and defense of a Kantian deontological theory and a dialectical model for the justification of normative principles.

Ross, W. D. 1930. *The Right and The Good*. Oxford: At the Clarendon Press. An enormously influential statement and defense of a deontological normative theory. It also contains important criticisms of consequentialism.

Scheffler, Samuel, ed. 1998. *Consequentialism and Its Critics*. Oxford: Oxford University Press. A useful recent collection of articles exploring consequentialism.

Sidgwick, Henry. 1907. *The Methods of Ethics*. 7th ed. London: Macmillan.

Smart, John Jameson Carswell, and Williams, Bernard A. 1973. *Utilitarianism: For and Against*. Cambridge: At the University Press. An important exchange between a prominent consequentialist and a critic of consequentialism.

Williams, Bernard A. 1985. *Ethics and the Limits of Philosophy*. Cambridge, Mass.: Harvard University Press. A recent criticism of the very idea of a normative theory.

10.

TOWARD A KANTIAN SOCIO-ECONOMICS

Amitai Etzioni

Relevant Kantian Positions

In recent years, under the impact of John Rawls' *Theory of Justice,* Michael J. Sandel's *Liberalism and the Limits of Justice* and other such works, utilitarianism has come under renewed criticism, and elements of Kant's political philosophy and ethics have gained new support. Implications of these developments for a new paradigm for the study of economic behavior—one that integrates economics and other social sciences—is the main subject of this chapter. Before this is attempted, the specific Kantian positions that have such implications are briefly outlined.

At issue is the status of individual rights and of moral tenets. Utilitarians base their moral position on the general welfare. The government should not impose a moral tenet on individuals because such interventions reduce the total sum of human happiness, and because each person is the best judge of his or her preferences. (This position is part and parcel of the core assumptions of neoclassical economics.) Kantians challenge the position that all human desires have an equal standing, that none can be judged by over-arching criteria as more worthy than others. They also question whether utilitarianism provides a sound defense of individual rights. As Sandel put it: "If enough cheering Romans pack the Coliseum to watch the lions devour the Christians, the

Review of Social Economy 45, no. 1 (April 1987): 37–47.

collective pleasure of the Romans will surely outweigh the pain of the Christians, intense though it be." In contrast, Kantians emphasize that each person is endowed with basic rights, founded on justice, an inviolate moral imperative which cannot be traded off for the sake of enhancing the total welfare. To make this point, Kantians draw on a distinct realm of rights and obligations, of moral values, set apart from that of satisfactions and goods, the foci of utilitarianism and the neoclassical concept of utility.

All this leads to a critical difference in the view of self: by the utilitarians, the person is a unified bundle of desires, of preferences; by Kantians, the self is divided, one part standing over the other, judging it and deciding whether or not to yield to any particular desire. Indeed, this ability of self is viewed as an essential quality that distinguishes humans from animals. Also, while judgments might be based on many values (for example, aesthetic ones), at issue here is the significant role of moral values in human judgment.

Kant took numerous other positions, and those cited here are intertwined in his work with extensive metaphysical assumptions. Many of those are either irrelevant to the issue at hand or may be rejected without losing the important observations we draw upon. In the following discussion, reference to Kant is strictly limited to questions of the human ability to judge and the role of moral values in such judgments.

Toward a Bi-Utility Conception

Paralleling the renewed interest in Kant is a movement, encompassing some economists and some members of other social sciences who study economic behavior, which questions one of the cornerstones of neoclassical economies—the assumption that individuals seek but one ultimate utility to which all specific desires can be reduced. Everyday observations and empirical evidence have led many scholars to question the empirical validity of the assumption that actors seek to maximize one utility, the person's desires. One line of response to such challenges has been to stretch the concept of utility and of satisfaction to include living up to one's moral obligations, such as benevolent acts and service to the community. Margolis, after observing that "in recent years efforts to incorporate altruistic preferences within the conventional framework have become fairly common," adds:

> We have no more need to distinguish between the bread Smith buys to give to the poor and that which he buys for his own consumption, than to distinguish his neighbor's demand for sugar to make cookies from his demand for sugar to make gin in the cellar. (1982, p. 11)

This approach ignores the crucial difference between acting and judging an act, and the deep substantive differences between satisfaction resulting out of pleasure and out of living up to a moral obligation.[1]

The difference is most evident in the numerous situations in which the two sources of satisfaction conflict rather than in the relatively few situations in which the two are compatible, in which the person's desires are also ways of discharging the moral obligations of the same person. Thus, if one is keen on the money in the till but refrains from pocketing it when chances seem favorable that the money will not be missed because one feels that it is not right to steal, the resulting satisfaction is quite different from that generated when one does pocket the cash.

Conceptually stretching the concept of utility to encompass self-love and love for others destroys the central thesis of Adam Smith, at least the Adam Smith of *The Wealth of Nations*, that economic relations thrive on self-interest. If there is no difference in principle between love for self and for others, there is no need for an invisible hand, and the difference between market and family relations pales; indeed, so does the distinction between profit and loss. After all, one man's loss is another man's gain.

Similar signs of theoretical strain in the mono-utility conception appear in discussions of preferences, the elements of which jointly make up the utility. Thomas Schelling (1984) provides a long list of examples that trouble the economist's assumption of uni-vocal, unencumbered preferences. One example will have to stand for the many: a guest asks his host to keep his car keys if he becomes intoxicated. Puzzle: What is the guest's preference? To have his keys? Then why ask the host to refuse? To be prevented from driving while under the influence? Then why ask for the keys?

What ties the Kantian recognition of the distinct standing and special significance of the human capacity to render judgment to the car keys of a prospective drunk? A major reason the preferences of people are encumbered is their moral judgments. Schelling's potential drunk, for example, experiences simultaneously the urge to drink and a moral commitment not to endanger the lives of others.

Economists have responded to these observations in several ways. Some continue to seek to establish that there are no moral factors, merely moral pretenses (see below). Others have increasingly recognized that there is a second set (a side basket) of preferences that affect behavior, preferences which reflect concern for others and the community or a commitment to moral values. Of those, John Harsanyi (1982), Howard Margolis (1982), and Richard Thaler and H. M. Shefrin (1981) have attempted to show that this second set of preferences can be accommodated within neoclassical economics by assuming a supra-preference that ties moral and non-moral preferences into one utility.

Others have come closer to making the break. They recognize, in varying degrees, the power of moral obligations. Sen (1977) goes part of the way in explicating the concept of commitment, although he does not see it as necessarily concerning moral obligations. Goodin (1980) sees a close association between the notion of a commitment and the sense of setting aside an important realm as a "sacred" one, to use Durkheim's term. People treat moral principles as important and do so by setting them aside as a *differentiated* set of considerations. Okun refers to these areas as "the domain of rights" (1975, p. 100). Walzer (1983, p. 97) lists fourteen major areas of "blocked exchanges," including basic freedoms (one has a claim on them without paying for them), marriage (licenses for polygamy are not sold) and divine grace.

One characteristic of such considerations, Goodin suggests, is to repudiate the instrumental rationality of considerations of costs and benefits. A person feels obligated to save a life, make a donation, and so on, without such calculations. *Only after these commitments are violated* do people enter into a second realm of decisions in which moral considerations are weighed against others and calculations enter. This, by the way, explains why people *sometimes* calculate how much to give or, if they give X, what it will do for their reputation. This should not be used, however, to argue that they do not have *other*, "sacred," non-negotiable, moral commitments. In short, morality affects their choices twice.

Hirschman (1984, pp. 12–14) uses the terms "preferences" and "meta-preferences" to conceptualize the judgment involved. He adds that if these two levels of preferences always coincided, the meta-preferences would be merely shadows of the preferences and would have no significance. The same would hold if they always conflicted, because this would suggest the meta-preferences are powerless. As Hirschman put it, they would not only be dismissed as wholly ineffectual, but doubt would arise as to whether they existed at all. The fruitfulness of the assumption lies in the frequently observed behavior of either choices that are blocked by moral judgments or choices followed that lead to regret, guilt, and so on, that have behavioral consequences (Etzioni, 1986).

All this points to a new philosophical and ethical base for a different paradigm for the study of economic behavior, for a socio-economics that recognizes at least two utilities, the traditional one and that of living up to one's moral values. Each provides inherent and different satisfactions, fundamentally divergent sources of value. Probably the most promising starting point for such an endeavor is to explore what lies behind the preferences.

Opening the Preferences

Neoclassical economics holds that preferences not only reflect one overarching utility but that they are given. "Given" is interpreted to mean that they are studied by other disciplines, such as psychology and sociology.

However, if all that was at issue was a matter of division of labor, then in order to understand economic behavior one would have to take from these other disciplines their findings on the factors that shape preferences and incorporate them into joint models. This is, in effect, what many applied economists do, on an ad hoc basis, in defiance of orthodoxy (McKean and Keller, 1983). This practice indicates the merit of a conceptual adaptation.

Other economists imply that the forces that shape preferences are irrational and hence are not subject to scientific study. Stigler and Becker (1977) go a step further and assert that all such explanations are "not illuminating," and thus preferences should be assumed to be constant and explanations for variations in behavior should be sought within neoclassical economics, in differences in income and in constraints. Sociologists and psychologists, however, have known for many decades that behavior which is considered irrational from the viewpoint of the observer is not random, is not exempt from scientific laws. Stigler and Becker's attempts to conceptualize behavior such as music appreciation and drug addiction (in which one changes his preferences as he gets into the act) as constituting an investment of scarce capital rather than as changing preferences require numerous far-fetched assumptions (Blaug, 1976) and are but one more indication of how strained the mono-utility theory has become.

Beyond attempts to shore up the paradigm of a discipline lies an ethical issue. Neoclassical economists' objections to opening up preferences to an empirical study of their dynamics and the factors that shape them are rooted in utilitarian individualism. If preferences are individually set and fixed, general welfare can, at least in principle, be calculated. However, once one recognizes that choices by individuals are deeply influenced by social processes, power holders and persuasive advertising, one must develop a conception of who guides the social processes, who is in power and whose values advertising promotes. Otherwise, the factors that affect preferences, and through them economic behavior, are not accounted for.

Neoclassical economists often seem, in effect, to argue that by not admitting that preferences are malleable in their theory they protect the individual's rights in reality. This is simply a case of a misplaced level of analysis: the theory will not change reality; it merely refuses to take in on the conceptual level what there is.[2] Indeed, one may go a step further and suggest that by refusing to deal with the forces that affect individual preferences one also neglects the study of the factors that shore up individual liberties, factors that are themselves to a significant extent social, political, moral and not intra-individual. Socio-economics encompasses the study of these factors. The decisions of criminals, for example, are viewed as *both* influenced by considerations of costs and benefits (as economists have stressed in recent years) *and* as affected by the extent of their moral upbringing and the values promoted by the peer groups they join (Wilson, 1985).

De-Colonization Is Not Enough

Economists may suggest that part of the difficulty their discipline has run into along the lines indicated so far is the result of the application of neoclassical economics in recent decades to non-economic behavior such as decisions to have children (treated as "durable consumer goods"), religious commitments (viewed as a quest for "after-life consumption") and the intra-personal development of music appreciation and drug addiction. These analyses share one feature: the application of neoclassical economics to areas in which exchange relations do not exist, and hence prices must be imputed. These raise very difficult technical problems that need not concern us here other than to raise the question: How far can one stretch the assumptions, the interpretation of the data and the regression analyses without violating not merely the validity of the conclusions but also the ethics of science? That economists are concerned about these matters is reflected in articles such as "Let's Take the *Con* Out of Econometrics" (Leamer, 1983, italic provided; Black, 1982).

Beyond the ethical issues raised by the methodology are the questions raised by the assumptions. We saw that people set aside certain areas of their lives as having a special claim, as "sacred," and that one of the main ways these are characterized is by objecting to calculating costs and benefits in these matters. To assume that people will normally trade those is more than technical error ("prices" here would be much higher than is imputed from areas in which trade is normal precisely because taboos are violated). To introduce cost/benefit analysis into our "temples" is to diminish their values, to violate their taboos (Kelman, 1981). For example, the notion that it is inefficient to prevent hijacking (Landes, 1978) or that it is efficient to form a market for babies available for adoption (Posner, 1977) disregards the effects such markets have on sanctity of life, on the treatment of the aged and the handicapped and on parenthood. The same holds true for the argument that duels are an efficient way to settle conflicts (Schwartz, et al. 1984).

In private conversations, many neoclassical economists admit that these analyses, often referred to as imperialistic intrusions into other disciplines, "go too far" or "are a bit silly" and suggest that economists should stick to the study of economic behavior. Behind these statements is an assumption that the social world is compartmentalized into some divisions that are governed by market mechanisms and some that are not. However, we suggest that non-market factors strongly affect *economic* behavior. For instance, relations among employers and employees, incentive schemes, labor markets and productivity cannot be adequately conceptualized without taking into account the intrinsic value of work for the identity of many workers (those who internalize certain values), the role of work ethics, the effects of team spirit, the value put on cooperation and so on.

The same holds for relations among businesses. Neoclassical economic models treat the market as if it were self-sustaining. Lists of the conditions for perfect competition vary, but the following elements are often included: the largest firm in any given industry is to make no more than a small fraction of the industry's sales (or purchases); the firms are to act independently of one another; actors have complete knowledge of offers to buy or sell; the commodity (sold or bought in the market) is divisible; and the resources are movable among users (Stigler, 1968, pp. 181–182).[3] This is but a more formal conceptualization of the notion that self-interests are automatically compatible with one another and require no external factors to advance their harmonization or limit their conflicts. Markets, however, are embedded in societies that provide both the rules which competition requires and the institutional framework without which it cannot be sustained.

Moral factors are but one step removed. The rules, and the institutions that embody them, such as the courts, the SEC and corporate charters, are not the result of deliberate rational negotiations but are the product of historical, societal and cultural evolution. Part and parcel of these evolutions are the sets of general and particular values, embodied in behavioral rules and in institutions.

While it has been stated numerous times (Hirsch, 1976), and the evidence is abundant, it seems one still must repeat the basic observation that rules and institutions cannot rest on deterrence because there are not enough policemen, inspectors and auditors for it to be effective, and the guardians themselves need guarding. Rules and institutions hence must rely, to a significant extent, on internalized moral commitments. Deterrence functions as a secondary mechanism that deals with those who violate these commitments, and thus backs up but cannot replace moral commitments.

Hence, a theory of *economic* behavior, of markets, must account for the factors that enhance rather than weaken the rules of the game, that affect the strength and reach of the relevant moral commitments. For instance, private property and limited liability, two cornerstones of capitalism, are nothing but two moral concepts defining the rights and obligations of owners. While economists tend to treat these concepts as given and as static, they are in flux in the sense that their legitimating power changes over time. For example, the extensive introduction of social regulation in the sixties and early seventies in effect constituted a diminution in the power of these concepts because the government increasingly limited the autonomous use of private assets and incorporated capital, and specified the ways they had to be employed. The forces that led to the rise of social regulation (and later, to its decline) include economic, technological and political developments (Tolchin and Tolchin, 1983). However, among them, changes in the moral conceptions of a society play an important role. For instance, the question of whether employers are free to hire, fire and promote as they see fit or whether they must favor minorities and women is in part a moral issue. Moral issues also loom in statements such as "the business of business is business," or that business should shoulder certain social responsibilities; for example, not to invest in South Africa.

The role of ethical factors is also evident in the attitudes toward fraud in transactions. Most business transactions are conducted by word of mouth. To write down all agreements, to have them reviewed by lawyers and to rely on enforcement by courts would bring the economy to a near standstill. Mutual trust is essential. True, in part trust is based on self-interest; those who violate it are likely to lose future business. However, in many situations in which the relations are transient, a major factor that sustains trust is the internalization of values by those involved, who feel that violating one's commitment is highly immoral (Phelps, 1975).

Similarly, moral attitudes affect the level of savings and personal as well as public debt. Until the 1950s, Americans considered being in debt a serious moral transgression and most of them did not violate the taboo. Personal debt rose significantly only after these attitudes changed (Longman, 1985; Maital, 1982). Simultaneously, until the public grew relatively more tolerant of deficits, legislators did not run up the public debt (Buchanan, 1985). More than half the people entitled to welfare do not avail themselves of the opportunity, in part because of the stigma attached (Moffitt, 1983).

The notion that people will free ride and hence need both "side"-payments (Olson, 1965) and close supervision (Ehrenberg and Smith, 1982; Williamson, 1975) in order to carry their share of the load rather than to "shirk" is not backed up by the evidence for collective action (in service of public goods such as voting) or in studies of work in private settings. Experiment after experiment has shown that most people, given a chance, will not free ride (Marwell and Ames, 1981). Indeed, this finding is so widely supported that designers of experiments found it dull and focused on a subsidiary question: whether or not the contributions to the group that are made match the *size* of contributions economists calculated are the proper contributions. Studies of voting were unable to sustain the notion that self-interest propels citizens to exert themselves. (The studies seek to understand why people vote if there is nothing in it for them, personally, directly and specifically.) Researchers found two reasons to account for voting: the act is expressive in that the effort itself is satisfying (Barry, 1978), and the act discharges a moral obligation. These findings significantly improve the predictive power of the models. Following the interdependent utility notion, some neoclassical economists and political scientists see in these expressive and moral acts nothing but self-interest but, as indicated above, this approach blurs the issue that needs clarifying. Other evidence strongly suggests that *close* supervision, especially of work that requires initiative, responsibility or attention to quality, is counter-productive, while, in many situations, involving the workers in the work process enhances productivity.

In short, it is not enough for neoclassical economics to give up its imperialism, its attempts to understand non-economic behavior in rationalist, egotist terms. The role of moral commitments and the factors that shape them must be taken into account in studying economic behavior, including subjects such as saving, incentives to work, behavior of markets and productivity. An integrated paradigm of social factors (among which only moral ones were explored here) and economic factors is to be tested by the same criteria by which neoclassical economics is judged: the ability to predict and to explain, parsimony, and the ethical implications of the paradigms for those who view the world through its framework.

Notes

1. The question has been raised if discharging one's moral obligations ought to be considered a source of satisfaction, of feeling, or whether this constitutes too much a concession to the utilitarian psychology. I side with those who assume that obligations do require a psychic force or "handle" to be effective, however, one that is radically different in nature from satisfying a desire. The distinction is completely familiar from elementary introspection. On the other hand, I agree that references to moral values as a second source of utility stretch the term; it might be better to refer to two ultimate sources of valuation rather than to utility.

2. I am indebted to Mike McPherson for this point.

3. For a formal discussion of the Walrasian model and related points, see Malinvaud, 1972, pp. 138–143; Bohm, 1973, pp. 128–142.

References

Barry, Brian. *Sociologists, Economists and Democracy,* Chicago, IL, 1978.

Black, Fischer. "The Trouble with Econometric Models," *Financial Analysts Journal, 35,* 1982, pp. 3–11.

Blaug, Mark. "The Empirical Status of Human Capital Theory: A Slightly Jaundiced Survey," *Journal of Economic Literature, 14,* September 1976, pp. 837–855.

Bohm, Peter. "Estimating Demands for a Public Good: An Experiment," *European Economic Review, 3,* 1972, pp. 111–130.

Buchanan, James M. *Liberty, Market and State: Political Economy in the 1980s,* Wheatsheaf Press, forthcoming.

Ehrenberg, Ronald G. and Robert S. Smith. *Modern Labor Economics: Theory and Public Policy,* Glenview, IL, 1982.

Etzioni, Amitai. "The Case for a Multiple Utility Conception," *Economics and Philosophy, 2,* 1986, pp. 159–183.

Goodin, Robert E. "Making Moral Incentives Pay," *Policy Sciences, 12,* August 1980, pp. 131–145.

Harsanyi, John C. "Cardinal Welfare, Individualistic Ethics, and International Comparisons of Utility," *Journal of Political Economy, 63,* 1955, pp. 309–321.

Hirsch, Fred. *Social Limits to Growth,* Cambridge, MA, 1976.

Hirschman, Albert O. "Against Parsimony: Three Easy Ways of Complicating Some Categories of Economic Discourse," *Bulletin: The American Academy of Arts and Sciences, 37,* 8, May 1984, pp. 11–28.

Kelman, Steven. "Cost-Benefit Analysis: An Ethical Critique," *Regulation,* January/February 1981, pp. 33–40.

Landes, William. "An Economic Study of U.S. Aircraft Hijacking, 1961–1976," *The Journal of Law and Economics, 21,* 1978, pp. 1–31.

Leamer, Edward E. "Let's Take the 'Con' Out of Econometrics," *American Economic Review, 73,* 1, March/April 1983, pp. 3–11.

Longman, Phillip. "The Fall of the Idea of Thrift: How the Economists Came to Label Virtue a Vice," *The Washington Monthly,* January 1985.

Maital, Shlomo. *Minds, Markets, and Money,* New York, 1982.

Malinvaud, E. *Lectures on Microeconomic Theory,* Amsterdam, 1972.

Margolis, Howard. *Selfishness, Altruism and Rationality: A Theory of Social Choice,* Cambridge, MA, 1982.

Marwell, Gerald and Ruth E. Ames. "Economists Free Ride, Does Anyone Else?" *Journal of Public Economics, 13,* 1981, pp. 295–310.

McKean, John R. and Robert R. Keller. "The Shaping of Tastes, Pareto Efficiency and Economic Policy," *Journal of Behavioral Economics, 12,* Summer 1983, pp. 23–41.

Moffitt, R. "An Economic Model of Welfare Stigma," *American Economic Review, 73,* 1983, pp. 1023–1035.

Okun, Arthur. *Equality and Efficiency: The Big Tradeoff,* Washington, DC, 1975.

Olson, Mancur. *The Logic of Collective Action,* Cambridge, MA, 1965.

Phelps, Edmund S. "Introduction," *Altruism, Morality, and Economic Theory,* New York, 1985, pp. 1–9.

Posner, Richard A. *Economic Analysis of Law,* 2nd ed., Boston, 1977.

Rawls, John. *A Theory of Justice,* Cambridge, MA, 1981.

Sandel, Michael J. *Liberalism and the Limits of Justice,* Cambridge, MA, 1980.

Schelling, Thomas C. "Self-Command in Practice, in Policy, and in a Theory of Rational Choice," *American Economic Review, 74,* 2, May 1984, pp. 1–11.

Schwartz, Warren, Keith Baxter and David Ryan. "The Duel: Can These Gentlemen Be Acting Efficiently?" *The Journal of Legal Studies, 13,* 1984, pp. 321–355.

Sen, Amartya. "Rational Fools," *Philosophy and Public Affairs, 6,* 1977, pp. 317–344.

Smith, Adam. *The Wealth of Nations,* New York, 1937.

Stigler, George J. "Competition," in the *International Encyclopedia of Social Science, 3,* New York, 1968, pp. 181–182.

Stigler, George J. and Gary S. Becker. "De Gustibus Non Est Disputandum," *American Economic Review, 67,* 2, March 1977, pp. 76–90.

Thaler, Richard and H. M. Shefrin. "An Economic Theory of Self Control," *Journal of Political Economy, 89,* 1981, pp. 392–406.

Tolchin, Susan and Martin Tolchin. *Dismantling America: The Rush to Deregulate,* Boston, 1983.

Walzer, Michael. *Spheres of Justice,* New York, 1983.

Williamson, Oliver E. *Markets and Hierarchies: Analysis and Antitrust Implications,* New York, 1975.

Wilson, James Q. *Thinking about Crime,* New York, 1985.

11.

FEMINIST TRANSFORMATIONS OF MORAL THEORY

Virginia Held

The history of philosophy, including the history of ethics, has been constructed from male points of view, and has been built on assumptions and concepts that are by no means gender-neutral.[1] Feminists characteristically begin with different concerns and give different emphases to the issues we consider than do non-feminist approaches. And, as Lorraine Code expresses it, "starting points and focal points shape the impact of theoretical discussion."[2] Within philosophy, feminists often start with, and focus on, quite different issues than those found in standard philosophy and ethics, however "standard" is understood. Far from providing mere additional insights which can be incorporated into traditional theory, feminist explorations often require radical transformations of existing fields of inquiry and theory.[3] From a feminist point of view, moral theory along with almost all theory will have to be transformed to take adequate account of the experience of women.

I shall in this paper begin with a brief examination of how various fundamental aspects of the history of ethics have not been gender-neutral. And I shall discuss three issues where feminist rethinking is transforming moral concepts and theories.

Philosophy and Phenomenological Research 1, supplement (Fall 1990): 321–44.

The History of Ethics

Consider the ideals embodied in the phrase "the man of reason." As Genevieve Lloyd has told the story, what has been taken to characterize the man of reason may have changed from historical period to historical period, but in each, the character ideal of the man of reason has been constructed in conjunction with a rejection of whatever has been taken to be characteristic of the feminine. "Rationality," Lloyd writes, "has been conceived as transcendence of the 'feminine,' and the 'feminine' itself has been partly constituted by its occurrence within this structure."[4]

This has of course fundamentally affected the history of philosophy and of ethics. The split between reason and emotion is one of the most familiar of philosophical conceptions. And the advocacy of reason "controlling" unruly emotion, of rationality guiding responsible human action against the blindness of passion, has a long and highly influential history, almost as familiar to nonphilosophers as to philosophers. We should certainly now be alert to the ways in which reason has been associated with male endeavor, emotion with female weakness, and the ways in which this is of course not an accidental association. As Lloyd writes, "From the beginnings of philosophical thought, femaleness was symbolically associated with what Reason supposedly left behind—the dark powers of the earth goddesses, immersion in unknown forces associated with mysterious female powers. The early Greeks saw women's capacity to conceive as connecting them with the fertility of Nature. As Plato later expressed the thought, women 'imitate the earth.' "[5]

Reason, in asserting its claims and winning its status in human history, was thought to have to conquer the female forces of Unreason. Reason and clarity of thought were early associated with maleness, and as Lloyd notes, "what had to be shed in developing culturally prized rationality was, from the start, symbolically associated with femaleness."[6] In later Greek philosophical thought, the form/matter distinction was articulated, and with a similar hierarchical and gendered association. Maleness was aligned with active, determinate, and defining form; femaleness with mere passive, indeterminate, and inferior matter. Plato, in the *Timaeus,* compared the defining aspect of form with the father, and indefinite matter with the mother; Aristotle also compared the form/matter distinction with the male/female distinction. To quote Lloyd again, "This comparison . . . meant that the very nature of knowledge was implicitly associated with the extrusion of what was symbolically associated with the feminine."[7]

The associations between Reason, form, knowledge, and maleness have persisted in various guises, and have permeated what has been thought to be moral knowledge as well as what has been thought to be scientific knowledge, and what has been thought to be the practice of morality. The associations between the philosophical concepts and gender cannot be merely dropped, and the concepts retained regardless of gender, because gender has been built into them in such a way that without it, they will have to be different concepts. As feminists repeatedly show, if the concept of "human" were built on what we think about "woman" rather than what we think about "man," it would be a very different concept. Ethics, thus, has not been a search for universal, or truly human guidance, but a gender-biased enterprise.

Other distinctions and associations have supplemented and reinforced the identification of reason with maleness, and of the irrational with the female; on this and other grounds "man" has been associated with the human, "woman" with the natural. Prominent among distinctions reinforcing the latter view has been that between the public and the private, because of the way they have been interpreted. Again, these provide as familiar and entrenched a framework as do reason and emotion, and they have been as influential for non-philosophers as for philosophers. It has been supposed that in the public realm, man transcends his animal nature and creates human history. As citizen, he creates government and law; as warrior, he protects society by his willingness to risk death; and as artist or philosopher, he overcomes his human mortality. Here, in the public realm, morality should guide human decision. In the household, in contrast, it has been supposed that women merely "reproduce" life as natural, biological matter. Within the household, the "natural" needs of man for food and shelter are served, and new instances of the biological creature that man is are brought into being. But what is distinctively human, and what transcends any given level of development to create human progress, are thought to occur elsewhere.

This contrast was made highly explicit in Aristotle's conceptions of polis and household; it has continued to affect the basic assumptions of a remarkably broad swath of thought ever since. In ancient Athens, women were confined to the household; the public sphere was literally a male domain. In more recent history, though women have been permitted to venture into public space, the associations of the public, historically male sphere with the distinctively human, and of the household, historically a female sphere, with the merely natural and repetitious, have persisted. These associations have deeply affected moral theory, which has often supposed the transcendent, public domain to be relevant to the foundations of morality in ways that the natural behavior of women in the household could not be. To take some recent and representative examples, David Heyd, in his discussion of supererogation, dismisses a mother's sacrifice for her child as an example of the supererogatory because it belongs, in his view, to "the sphere of natural relationships and instinctive feelings (which lie outside morality)."[8] J. O. Urmson had earlier taken a similar position. In his discussion of supererogation, Urmson said, "Let us be clear that we are not now considering cases of natural affection, such as the sacrifice made by a mother for her child; such cases may be said with some justice not to fall under the concept of morality . . ."[9] And in a recent article called "Distrusting Economics," Alan Ryan argues persuasively about the questionableness of economics and other branches of the social sciences built on the assumption that human beings are rational, self-interested calculators; he discusses various examples of non self-interested behavior, such as of men in wartime, which show the assumption to be false, but nowhere in the article is there any mention of the activity of mothering, which would seem to be a fertile locus for doubts about the usual picture of rational man.[10] Although Ryan does not provide the kind of explicit reason offered by Heyd and Urmson for omitting the context of mothering from consideration as relevant to his discussion, it is difficult to understand the omission without a comparable assumption being implicit here, as it so often is elsewhere. Without feminist insistence on the relevance for morality of the experience in mothering, this context is largely ignored by moral theorists. And yet, from a gender-neutral point of view, how can this vast and fundamental domain of human experience possibly be imagined to lie "outside morality"?

The result of the public/private distinction, as usually formulated, has been to privilege the points of view of men in the public domains of state and law, and later in the marketplace, and to discount the experience of women. Mothering has been conceptualized as a primarily biological activity, even when performed by humans, and virtually no moral theory in the history of ethics has taken mothering, as experienced by women, seriously as a source of moral insight, until feminists in recent years have begun to.[11] Women have been seen as emotional rather than as rational beings, and thus as incapable of full moral personhood. Women's behavior has been interpreted as either "natural" and driven by instinct, and thus as irrelevant to morality and to the construction of moral principles, or it has been interpreted as, at best, in need of instruction and supervision by males better able to know what morality requires and better able to live up to its demands.

The Hobbesian conception of reason is very different from the Platonic or Aristotelian conceptions before it, and from the conceptions of Rousseau or Kant or Hegel later; all have in common that they ignore and disparage the experience and reality of women. Consider Hobbes's account of man in the state of nature contracting with other men to establish society. These men hypothetically come into existence fully formed and independent of one another, and decide on entering or staying outside of civil society. As Christine Di Stefano writes, "What we find in Hobbes's account of human nature and political order is a vital concern with the survival of a self conceived in masculine terms . . . This masculine dimension of Hobbes's atomistic egoism is powerfully underscored in his state of nature, which is effectively built on the foundation of denied maternity."[12] In *The Citizen*, where Hobbes gave his first systematic exposition of the state of nature, he asks us to "consider men as if but even now sprung out of the earth, and suddenly, like mushrooms, come to full maturity, without all kind of engagement with each other."[13] As Di Stefano says, it is a most incredible and problematic feature of Hobbes's state of nature that the men in it "are not born of, much less nurtured by, women, or anyone else."[14] To abstract from the complex web of human reality an abstract man for rational perusal, Hobbes has, Di Stefano continues, "expunged human reproduction and early nurturance, two of the most basic and typically female-identified features of distinctively human life, from his account of basic human nature. Such a strategy ensures that he can present a thoroughly atomistic subject . . ."[15] From the point of view of women's experience, such a subject or self is unbelievable and misleading, even as a theoretical construct. The Leviathan, Di Stefano writes, "is effectively comprised of a body politic of orphans who have reared themselves, whose desires are situated within and reflect nothing but independently generated movement . . . These essential elements are natural human beings conceived along masculine lines."[16]

Rousseau, and Kant, and Hegel paid homage to the emotional power, the aesthetic sensibility, and the familial concerns, respectively, of women. But since in their views morality must be based on rational principle, and women were incapable of full rationality, or a degree or kind of rationality comparable to that of men, women were deemed, in the view of these moralists, to be inherently wanting in morality. For Rousseau, women must be trained from childhood to submit to the will of men lest their sexual power lead both men and women to disaster. For Kant, women were thought incapable of achieving full moral personhood, and women lose all charm if they try to behave like men by engaging in rational pursuits. For Hegel, women's moral concern for their families could be admirable in its proper place, but is a threat to the more universal aims to which men, as members of the state, should aspire.[17]

These images, of the feminine as what must be overcome if knowledge and morality are to be achieved, of female experience as naturally irrelevant to morality, and of women as inherently deficient moral creatures, are built into the history of ethics. Feminists examine these images and see that they are not the incidental or merely idiosyncratic suppositions of a few philosophers whose views on many topics depart far from the ordinary anyway. Such views are the nearly uniform reflection in philosophical and ethical theory of patriarchal attitudes pervasive throughout human history. Or they are exaggerations even of ordinary male experience, which exaggerations then reinforce rather than temper other patriarchal conceptions and institutions. They distort the actual experience and aspirations of many men as well as of women. Annette Baier recently speculated about why it is that moral philosophy has so seriously overlooked the trust between human beings that in her view is an utterly central aspect of moral life. She noted that "the great moral theorists in our tradition not only are all men, they are mostly men who had minimal adult dealings with (and so were then minimally influenced by) women."[18] They were for the most part "clerics, misogynists, and puritan bachelors," and thus it is not surprising that they focus their philosophical attention "so single-mindedly on cool, distanced relations between more or less free and equal adult strangers . . ."[19]

As feminists, we deplore the patriarchal attitudes that so much of philosophy and moral theory reflect. But we recognize that the problem is more serious even than changing those attitudes. For moral theory as so far developed is incapable of correcting itself without an almost total transformation. It cannot simply absorb the gender that has been "left behind," even if both genders would want it to. To continue to build morality on rational principles opposed to the emotions and to include women among the rational will leave no one to reflect the promptings of the heart, which promptings can be moral rather than merely instinctive. To simply bring women into the public and male domain of the polis will leave no one to speak for the household. Its values have been hitherto unrecognized, but they are often moral values. Or to continue to seek contractual restraints on the pursuits of self-interest by atomistic individuals, and to have women join men in devotion to these pursuits, will leave no one involved in the nurturance of children and cultivation of social relations, which nurturance and cultivation can be of greatest moral import.

There are very good reasons for women not to want simply to be accorded entry as equals into the enterprise of morality as so far developed. In a recent survey of types of feminist moral theory, Kathryn Morgan notes that "many women who engage in philosophical reflection are acutely aware of the masculine nature of the profession and tradition, and feel their own moral concerns as women silenced or trivialized in virtually all the official settings that define the practice."[20] Women should clearly not agree, as the price of admission to the masculine realm of traditional morality, to abandon our own moral concerns as women.

And so we are groping to shape new moral theory. Understandably, we do not yet have fully worked out feminist moral theories to offer. But we can suggest some directions our project of developing such theories is taking. As Kathryn Morgan points out, there is not likely to be a "star" feminist moral theorist on the order of a Rawls or Nozick: "There will be no individual singled out for two reasons. One reason is that vital moral and theoretical conversations are taking place on a large dialectical scale as the feminist community struggles to develop a feminist ethic. The second reason is that this community of feminist theoreticians is calling into question the very model of the individualized autonomous self presupposed by a star-centered male-dominated tradition. . . . We experience it as a common labour, a common task."[21]

The dialogues that are enabling feminist approaches to moral theory to develop are proceeding. As Alison Jaggar makes clear in her useful overview of them, there is no unitary view of ethics that can be identified as "feminist ethics." Feminist approaches to ethics share a commitment to "rethinking ethics with a view to correcting whatever forms of male bias it may contain."[22] While those who develop these approaches are "united by a shared project, they diverge widely in their views as to how this project is to be accomplished."[23]

Not all feminists, by any means, agree that there are distinctive feminist virtues or values. Some are especially skeptical of the attempt to give positive value to such traditional "feminine virtues" as a willingness to nurture, or an affinity with caring, or reluctance to seek independence. They see this approach as playing into the hands of those who would confine women to traditional roles.[24] Other feminists are skeptical of all claims about women as such, emphasizing that women are divided by class and race and sexual orientation in ways that make any conclusions drawn from "women's experience" dubious.[25]

Still, it is possible, I think, to discern various important focal points evident in current feminist attempts to transform ethics into a theoretical and practical activity that could be acceptable from a feminist point of view. In the glimpse I have presented of bias in the history of ethics, I focused on what, from a feminist point of view, are three of its most questionable aspects: (1) the split between reason and emotion and the devaluation of emotion; (2) the public/private distinction and the relegation of the private to the natural; and (3) the concept of the self as constructed from a male point of view. In the remainder of this chapter, I shall consider further how some feminists are exploring these topics. We are showing how their previous treatment has been distorted, and we are trying to reenvision the realities and recommendations with which these aspects of moral theorizing do and should try to deal.

I. Reason and Emotion

In the area of moral theory in the modern era, the priority accorded to reason has taken two major forms. On the one hand has been the Kantian, or Kantian-inspired search for very general, abstract, deontological, universal moral principles by which rational beings should be guided. Kant's Categorical Imperative is a foremost example: it suggests that all moral problems can be handled by applying an impartial, pure, rational principle to particular cases. It requires that we try to see what the general features of the problem before us are, and that we apply an abstract principle, or rules derivable from it, to this problem. On this view, this procedure should be adequate for all moral decisions. We should thus be able to act as reason recommends, and resist yielding to emotional inclinations and desires in conflict with our rational wills.

On the other hand, the priority accorded to reason in the modern era has taken a Utilitarian form. The Utilitarian approach, reflected in rational choice theory, recognizes that persons have desires and interests, and suggests rules of rational choice for maximizing the satisfaction of these. While some philosophers in this tradition espouse egoism, especially of an intelligent and long-term kind, many do not. They begin, however, with assumptions that what are morally relevant are gains and losses of utility to theoretically isolatable individuals, and that the outcome at which morality should aim is the maximization of the utility of individuals. Rational calculation about such an outcome will, in this view, provide moral recommendations to guide all our choices. As with the Kantian approach, the Utilitarian approach relies on abstract general principles or rules to be applied to particular cases. And it holds that although emotion is, in fact, the source of our desires for certain objectives, the task of morality should be to instruct us on how to pursue those objectives most rationally. Emotional attitudes toward moral issues themselves interfere with rationality and should be disregarded. Among the questions Utilitarians can ask can be questions about which emotions to cultivate, and which desires to try to change, but these questions are to be handled in the terms of rational calculation, not of what our feelings suggest.

Although the conceptions of what the judgments of morality should be based on, and of how reason should guide moral decision, are different in Kantian and in Utilitarian approaches, both share a reliance on a highly abstract, universal principle as the appropriate source of moral guidance, and both share the view that moral problems are to be solved by the application of such an abstract principle to particular cases. Both share an admiration for the rules of reason to be appealed to in moral contexts, and both denigrate emotional responses to moral issues.

Many feminist philosophers have questioned whether the reliance on abstract rules, rather than the adoption of more context-respectful approaches, can possibly be adequate for dealing with moral problems, especially as women experience them.[26] Though Kantians may hold that complex rules can be elaborated for specific contexts, there is nevertheless an assumption in this approach that the more abstract the reasoning applied to a moral problem, the more satisfactory. And Utilitarians suppose that one highly abstract principle, The Principle of Utility, can be applied to every moral problem no matter what the context.

A genuinely universal or gender-neutral moral theory would be one which would take account of the experience and concerns of women as fully as it would take account of the experience and concerns of men. When we focus on the experience of women, however, we seem to be able to see a set of moral concerns becoming salient that differs from those of traditional or standard moral theory. Women's experience of moral problems seems to lead us to be especially concerned with actual relationships between embodied persons, and with what these relationships seem to require. Women are often inclined to attend to rather than to dismiss the particularities of the context in which a moral problem arises. And we often pay attention to feelings of empathy and caring to suggest what we ought to do rather than relying as fully as possible on abstract rules of reason.

Margaret Walker, for instance, contrasts feminist moral "understanding" with traditional moral "knowledge." She sees the components of the former as involving "attention, contextual and narrative appreciation, and communication in the event of moral deliberation."[27] This alternative moral epistemology holds that "the adequacy of moral understanding decreases as its form approaches generality through abstraction."[28]

The work of psychologists such as Carol Gilligan and others has led to a clarification of what may be thought of as tendencies among women to approach moral issues differently. Rather than interpreting moral problems in terms of what could be handled by applying abstract rules of justice to particular cases, many of the women studied by Gilligan tended to be more concerned with preserving actual human relationships, and with expressing care for those for whom they felt responsible. Their moral reasoning was typically more embedded in a context of particular others than was the reasoning of a comparable group of men.[29] One should not equate tendencies women in fact display with feminist views, since the former may well be the result of the sexist, oppressive conditions in which women's lives have been lived. But many feminists see our own consciously considered experience as lending confirmation to the view that what has come to be called "an ethic of care" needs to be developed. Some think it should supercede "the ethic of justice" of traditional or standard moral theory. Others think it should be integrated with the ethic of justice and rules.

In any case, feminist philosophers are in the process of reevaluating the place of emotion in morality in at least two respects. First, many think morality requires the development of the moral emotions, in contrast to moral theories emphasizing the primacy of reason. As Annette Baier notes, the rationalism typical of traditional moral theory will be challenged when we pay attention to the role of parent. "It might be important," she writes, "for father figures to have rational control over their violent urges to beat to death the children whose screams enrage them, but more than control of such nasty passions seems needed in the mother or primary parent, or parent-substitute, by most psychological theories. They need to love their children, not just to control their irritation."[30] So the emphasis in many traditional theories on rational control over the emotions, "rather than on cultivating desirable forms of emotion,"[31] is challenged by feminist approaches to ethics.

Secondly, emotion will be respected rather than dismissed by many feminist moral philosophers in the process of gaining moral understanding. The experience and practice out of which feminist moral theory can be expected to be developed will include embodied feeling as well as thought. In a recent overview of a vast amount of writing, Kathryn Morgan states that "feminist theorists begin ethical theorizing with embodied, gendered subjects who have particular histories, particular communities, particular allegiances, and particular visions of human flourishing. The starting point involves valorizing what has frequently been most mistrusted and despised in the western philosophical tradition . . ."[32] Among the elements being reevaluated are feminine emotions.

The "care" of the alternative feminist approach to morality appreciates rather than rejects emotion. The caring relationships important to feminist morality cannot be understood in terms of abstract rules or moral reasoning. And the "weighing" so often needed between the conflicting claims of some relationships and others cannot be settled by deduction or rational calculation. A feminist ethic will not just acknowledge emotion, as do Utilitarians, as giving us the objectives toward which moral rationality can direct us. It will embrace emotion as providing at least a partial basis for morality itself, and for moral understanding.

Annette Baier stresses the centrality of trust for an adequate morality.[33] Achieving and maintaining trusting, caring relationships is quite different from acting in accord with rational principles, or satisfying the individual desires of either self or other. Caring, empathy, feeling with others, being sensitive to each other's feelings, all may be better guides to what morality requires in actual contexts than may abstract rules of reason, or rational calculation, or at least they may be necessary components of an adequate morality.

The fear that a feminist ethic will be a relativistic "situation ethic" is misplaced. Some feelings can be as widely shared as are rational beliefs, and feminists do not see their views as reducible to "just another attitude."[34] In her discussion of the differences between feminist medical ethics and non-feminist medical ethics, Susan Sherwin gives an example of how feminists reject the mere case by case approach that has come to predominate in nonfeminist medical ethics. The latter also rejects the excessive reliance on abstract rules characteristic of standard ethics, and in this way resembles feminist ethics. But the very focus on cases in isolation from one another deprives this approach from attending to general features in the institutions and practices of medicine that, among other faults, systematically contribute to the oppression of women.[35] The difference of approach can be seen in the treatment of issues in the new reproductive technologies, where feminists consider how the new technologies may further decrease the control of women over reproduction.

This difference might be thought to be one of substance rather than of method, but Sherwin shows the implications for method also. With respect to reproductive technologies one can see especially clearly the deficiencies of the case by case approach: what needs to be considered is not only choice in the purely individualistic interpretation of the case by case approach, but control at a more general level and how it affects the structure of gender in society. Thus, a feminist perspective does not always counsel attention to specific case vs. appeal to general considerations, as some sort of methodological rule. But the general considerations are often not the purely abstract ones of traditional and standard moral theory, they are the general features and judgments to be made about cases in actual (which means, so far, patriarchal) societies. A feminist evaluation of a moral problem should never omit the political elements involved; and it is likely to recognize that political issues cannot be dealt with adequately in purely abstract terms any more than can moral issues.

The liberal tradition in social and moral philosophy argues that in pluralistic society and even more clearly in a pluralistic world, we cannot agree on our visions of the good life, on what is the best kind of life for humans, but we can hope to agree on the minimal conditions for justice, for coexistence within a framework allowing us to pursue our visions of the good life.[36] Many feminists contend that the commitment to justice needed for agreement *in actual conditions* on even minimal requirements of justice is as likely to demand relational feelings as a rational recognition of abstract principles. Human beings can and do care, and are capable of caring far more than at present, about the sufferings of children quite distant from them, about the prospects for future generations, and about the well-being of the globe. The liberal tradition's mutually disinterested rational individualists would seem unlikely to care enough to take the actions needed to achieve moral decency at a global level, or environmental sanity for decades hence, as they would seem unable to represent caring relationships within the family and among friends. As Annette Baier puts it, "A moral theory, it can plausibly be claimed, cannot regard concern for new and future persons as an optional charity left for those with a taste for it. If the morality the theory endorses is to sustain itself, it must provide for its own containers, not just take out a loan on a carefully encouraged maternal instinct or on the enthusiasm of a self-selected group of environmentalists, who make it their business or hobby to be concerned with what we are doing to mother earth."[37]

The possibilities as well as the problems (and we are well aware of some of them) in a feminist reenvisioning of emotion and reason need to be further developed, but we can already see that the views of nonfeminist moral theory are unsatisfactory.

II. The Public and the Private

The second questionable aspect of the history of ethics on which I focused was its conception of the distinction between the public and the private. As with the split between reason and emotion, feminists are showing how gender-bias has distorted previous conceptions of these spheres, and we are trying to offer more appropriate understandings of "private" morality and "public" life.

Part of what feminists have criticized has been the way the distinction has been accompanied by a supposition that what occurs in the household occurs as if on an island beyond politics, whereas the personal is highly affected by the political power beyond, from legislation about abortion to the greater earning power of men, to the interconnected division of labor by gender both within and beyond the household, to the lack of adequate social protection for women against domestic violence.[38] Of course we recognize that the family is not identical to the state, and we need concepts for thinking about the private or personal, and the public or political. But they will have to be very different from the traditional concepts.

Feminists have also criticized deeper assumptions about what is distinctively human and what is "natural" in the public and private aspects of human life, and what is meant by "natural" in connection with women.[39] Consider the associations that have traditionally been built up: the public realm is seen as the distinctively human realm in which man transcends his animal nature, while the private realm of the household is seen as the natural region in which women merely reproduce the species.[40] These associations are extraordinarily pervasive in standard concepts and theories, in art and thought and cultural ideals, and especially in politics.

Dominant patterns of thought have seen women as primarily mothers, and mothering as the performance of a primarily biological function. Then it has been supposed that while engaging in political life is a specifically human activity, women are engaged in an activity which is not specifically human. Women accordingly have been thought to be closer to nature than men,[41] to be enmeshed in a biological function involving processes more like those in which other animals are involved than like the rational discussion of the citizen in the polis, or the glorious battles of noble soldiers, or the trading and rational contracting of "economic man." The total or relative exclusion of women from the domain of public life has then been seen as either inevitable or appropriate.

The view that women are more determined by biology than are men is still extraordinarily prevalent. It is as questionable from a feminist perspective as many other traditional misinterpretations of women's experience. Human mothering is an extremely different activity from the mothering engaged in by other animals. The work and speech of men is recognized as very different from what might be thought of as the "work" and "speech" of other animals. Human mothering is fully as different from animal mothering. Of course all human beings are animal as well as human. But to whatever extent it is appropriate to recognize a difference between "man" and other animals, so would it be appropriate to recognize a comparable difference between "woman" and other animals, and between the activities—including mothering—engaged in by women and the behavior of other animals.

Human mothering shapes language and culture, it forms human social personhood, it develops morality. Animal behavior can be highly impressive and complex, but it does not have built into it any of the consciously chosen aims of morality. In creating human social persons, human mothering is different in kind from merely propagating a species. And human mothering can be fully as creative an activity as those activities traditionally thought of as distinctively human, because to create *new* persons, and new types of *persons*, can surely be as creative as to make new objects, products, or institutions. *Human* mothering is no more "natural" or "primarily biological" than is any other human activity.

Consider nursing an infant, often thought of as the epitome of a biological process with which mothering is associated and women are identified. There is no reason to think of human nursing as any more simply biological than there is to think of, say, a businessmen's lunch this way. Eating is a biological process, but what and how and with whom we eat are thoroughly cultural. Whether and how long and with whom a woman nurses an infant, are also human, cultural matters. If men transcend the natural by conquering new territory and trading with their neighbors and making deals over lunch to do so, women can transcend the natural by choosing not to nurse their children when they could, or choosing to nurse them when their culture tells them not to, or singing songs to their infants as they nurse, or nursing in restaurants to overcome the prejudices against doing so, or thinking human thoughts as they nurse, and so forth. Human culture surrounds and characterizes the activity of nursing as it does the activities of eating, or governing, or writing, or thinking.

We are continually being presented with images of the humanly new and creative as occurring in the public realm of the polis, or the realms of marketplace or of art and science outside the household. The very term "reproduction" suggests mere repetition, the "natural" bringing into existence of repeated instances of the same human animal. But human reproduction is not repetition.[42] This is not to suggest that bringing up children in the interstices of patriarchal society, in society structured by institutions supporting male dominance, can achieve the potential of transformation latent in the activity of human mothering. But the activity of creating new social persons and new kinds of persons is potentially the most transformative human activity of all. And it suggests that morality should concern itself first of all with this activity, with what its norms and practices ought to be, and with how the institutions and arrangements throughout society and the world ought to be structured to facilitate the right kinds of development of the best kinds of new persons. The flourishing of children ought to be at the very center of moral and social and political and economic and legal thought, rather than, as at present, at the periphery, if attended to at all.

Revised conceptions of public and private have significant implications for our conceptions of human beings and relationships between them. Some feminists suggest that instead of seeing human relationships in terms of the impersonal ones of the "public" sphere, as standard political and moral theory has so often done, we might consider seeing human relationships in terms of those experienced in the sphere of the "private," or of what these relationships could be imagined to be like in post-patriarchal society.[43] The traditional approach is illustrated by those who generalize, to other regions of human life than the economic, assumptions about "economic man" in contractual relations with other men. It sees such impersonal, contractual relations as paradigmatic, even, on some views, for moral theory. Many feminists, in contrast, consider the realm of what has been misconstrued as the "private" as offering guidance to what humans beings and their relationships should be like even in regions beyond those of family and friendship. Sara Ruddick looks at the implications of the practice of mothering for the conduct of peace politics.[44] Marilyn Friedman and Lorraine Code consider friendship, especially as women understand it, as a possible model for human relationships.[45] Others see society as non-contractual rather than as contractual.

Clearly, a reconceptualization is needed of the ways in which every human life is entwined with personal and with social components. Feminist theorists are contributing imaginative work to this project.

III. The Concept of Self

Let me turn now to the third aspect of the history of ethics which I discussed and which feminists are re-envisioning: the concept of self. One of the most important emphases in a feminist approach to morality is the recognition that more attention must be paid to the domain between, on the one hand, the self as ego, as self-interested individual, and, on the other hand, the universal, everyone, others in general.[46] Traditionally, ethics has dealt with these poles of individual self and universal all. Usually, it has called for impartiality against the partiality of the egoistic self; sometimes it has defended egoism against claims for a universal perspective. But most standard moral theory has hardly noticed as morally significant the intermediate realm of family relations and relations of friendship, of group ties and neighborhood concerns, especially from the point of view of women. When it has noticed this intermediate realm it has often seen its attachments as threatening to the aspirations of the Man of Reason, or as subversive of "true" morality. In seeing the problems of ethics as problems of reconciling the interests of the self with what would be right or best for "everyone," standard ethics has neglected the moral aspects of the concern and sympathy which people actually feel for particular others, and what moral experience in this intermediate realm suggests for an adequate morality.

The region of "particular others" is a distinct domain, where what can be seen to be artificial and problematic are the very egoistic "self" and the universal "all others" of standard moral theory. In the domain of particular others, the self is already constituted to an important degree by relations with others, and these relations may be much more salient and significant than the interests of any individual self in isolation.[47] The "others" in the picture, however, are not the "all others," or "everyone," of traditional moral theory; they are not what a universal point of view or a view from nowhere could provide.[48] They are, characteristically, actual flesh and blood other human beings for whom we have actual feelings and with whom we have real ties.

From the point of view of much feminist theory, the individualistic assumptions of liberal theory and of most standard moral theory are suspect. Even if we would be freed from the debilitating aspects of dominating male power to "be ourselves" and to pursue our own interests, we would, as persons, still have ties to other persons, and we would at least in part be constituted by such ties. Such ties would be part of what we inherently are. We are, for instance, the daughter or son of given parents, or the mother or father of given children, and we carry with us at least some ties to the racial or ethnic or national group within which we developed into the persons we are.

If we look, for instance, at the realities of the relation between mothering person (who can be female or male) and child, we can see that what we value in the relation cannot be broken down into individual gains and losses for the individual members in the relation. Nor can it be understood in universalistic terms. Self-development apart from the relation may be much less important than the satisfactory development of the relation. What matters may often be the health and growth of and the development of the relation-and-its-members in ways that cannot be understood in the individualistic terms of standard moral theories designed to maximize the satisfaction of self-interest. The universalistic terms of moral theories grounded in what would be right for "all rational beings" or "everyone" cannot handle, either, what has moral value in the relation between mothering person and child.

Feminism is of course not the only locus of criticism of the individualistic and abstractly universalistic features of liberalism and of standard moral theory. Marxists and communitarians also see the self as constituted by its social relations. But in their usual form, Marxist and communitarian criticisms pay no more attention than liberalism and standard moral theory to the experience of women, to the context of mothering, or to friendship as women experience it.[49] Some recent nonfeminist criticisms, such as offered by Bernard Williams, of the impartiality required by standard moral theory, stress how a person's identity may be formed by personal projects in ways that do not satisfy universal norms, yet ought to be admired. Such views still interpret morality from the point of view of an individual and his project, not a social relationship such as that between mothering person and child. And recent nonfeminist criticisms in terms of traditional communities and their moral practices, as seen for instance in the work of Stuart Hampshire and Alasdair MacIntyre, often take traditional gender roles as given, or provide no basis for a radical critique of them.[50] There is no substitute, then, for feminist exploration of the area between ego and universal, as women experience this area, or for the development of a refocused concept of relational self that could be acceptable from a feminist point of view.

Relationships can be evaluated as trusting or mistrustful, mutually considerate or selfish, harmonious or stressful, and so forth. Where trust and consideration are appropriate, which is not always, we can find ways to foster them. But understanding and evaluating relationships, and encouraging them to be what they can be at their best, require us to look at relationships between actual persons, and to see what both standard moral theories and their nonfeminist critics often miss. To be adequate, moral theories must pay attention to the neglected realm of particular others in the actual relationships and actual contexts of women's experience. In doing so, problems of individual self-interest vs. universal rules may recede to a region more like background, out-of-focus insolubility or relative unimportance. The salient problems may then be seen to be how we ought best to guide or to maintain or to reshape the relationships, both close and more distant, that we have, or might have, with actual other human beings. Particular others can be actual children in need in distant continents, or the anticipated children of generations not yet even close to being born. But they are not "all rational beings" or "the greatest number," and the self that is in relationships with particular others and is composed to a significant degree by such relations is not a self whose ego must be pitted against abstract, universal claims. Developing the needed guidance for maintaining and reshaping relationships presents enormous problems, but a first step is to recognize how traditional and nonfeminist moral theory of both an individualistic and communitarian kind falls short in providing it.

The concept of the relational self which is evolving within feminist thought is leading to interesting inquiry in many fields. An example is the work being done at the Stone Center at Wellesley College.[51] Psychologists there have posited a self-in-relation theory and are conducting empirical inquiries to try to establish how the female self develops. They are working with a theory that a female relational self develops through a mutually empathetic mother-daughter bond.

The work has been influenced by Jean Baker Miller's reevaluation of women's psychological qualities as strengths rather than weaknesses. In her book *Toward a New Psychology of Women*, published in 1976, Miller identified women's "great desire for affiliation" as one such strength.[52] Nancy Chodorow's *The Reproduction of Mothering,* published in 1978, has also had a significant influence on the work done at the Stone Center, as it has on much feminist inquiry.[53] Chodorow argued that a female affiliative self is reproduced by a structure of parenting in which mothers are the primary caretakers, and sons and daughters develop differently in relation to a parent of the same sex, or a parent of different sex, as primary caretaker. Daughters develop a sense of self by identifying themselves with the mother; they come to define themselves as connected to or in relation with others. Sons, in contrast, develop a sense of self by differentiating themselves from the mother; they come to define themselves as separate from or unconnected to others. An implication often drawn from Chodorow's work is that parenting should be shared equally by fathers and mothers so that children of either sex can develop with caretakers of both same and different sex.

In 1982, Carol Gilligan, building on both Miller and Chodorow, offered her view of the "different voice" with which girls and women express their understanding of moral problems.[54] Like Miller and Chodorow, Gilligan valued tendencies found especially in women to affiliate with others and to interpret their moral responsibilities in terms of their relationships with others. In all, the valuing of autonomy and individual independence over care and concern for relationships, was seen as an expression of male bias. The Stone Center has tried to elaborate and to study a feminist conception of the relational self. In a series of Working Papers, researchers and clinicians have explored the implications of this conception for various issues in women's psychology (e.g., power, anger, work inhibitions, violence, eating patterns) and for therapy.

The self as conceptualized in these studies is seen as having both a need for recognition and a need to understand the other, and these needs are seen as compatible. They are created in the context of mother-child interaction, and are satisfied in a mutually empathetic relationship. This does not require a loss of self, but a relationship of mutuality in which self and other both express intersubjectivity. Both give and take in a way that not only contributes to the satisfaction of their needs as individuals, but also affirms the "larger relational unit" they compose.[55] Maintaining this larger relational unit then becomes a goal, and maturity is seen not in terms of individual autonomy but in terms of competence in creating and sustaining relations of empathy and mutual intersubjectivity.

The Stone Center psychologists contend that the goal of mutuality is rarely achieved in adult male-female relationships because of the traditional gender system. The gender system leads men to seek autonomy and power over others, and to undervalue the caring and relational connectedness that is expected of women. Women rarely receive the nurturing and empathetic support they provide. Accordingly, these psychologists look to the interaction that occurs in mother-daughter relationships as the best source of insight into the promotion of the healthy, relational self. This research provides an example of exploration into a refocused, feminist conception of the self, and into empirical questions about its development and implications.

In a quite different field, that of legal theory, a refocused concept of self is leading to reexaminations of such concepts as property and autonomy and the role these have played in political theory and in constitutional law. For instance, the legal theorist Jennifer Nedelsky questions the imagery that is dominant in constitutional law and in our conceptions of property: the imagery of a bounded self, a self contained within boundaries and having rights to property within a wall allowing it to exclude others and to exclude government. The boundary metaphor, she argues, obscures and distorts our thinking about human relationships and what is valuable in them. "The boundedness of selves," Nedelsky writes, "may seem to be a self-evident truth, but I think it is a wrong-headed and destructive way of conceiving of the human creatures law and government are created for."[56] In the domain of the self's relation to the state, the central problem, she argues, is not "maintaining a sphere into which the state cannot penetrate, but fostering autonomy when people are already within the sphere of state control or responsibility."[57] What we can from a feminist perspective think of as the male "separative self" seems on an endless quest for security behind such walls of protection as those of property. Property focuses the quest for security "in ways that are paradigmatic of the efforts of separative selves to protect themselves through boundaries . . ."[58] But of course property is a social construction, not a thing; it requires the involvement of the state to define what it is and to defend it. What will provide what it seeks to offer will not be boundaries and exclusions, but constructive relationships.

In an article on autonomy, Nedelsky examines the deficiencies in the concept of self with which so much of our political and legal thinking about autonomy has been developed. She well recognizes that of course feminists are centrally concerned with freedom and autonomy, with enabling women to live our own lives. But we need a language with which to express these concerns which will also reflect "the equally important feminist precept that any good theorizing will start with people in their social contexts. And the notion of social context must take seriously its constitutive quality; social context cannot simply mean that individuals will, of course, encounter one another."[59] The problem, then, is how to combine the claim of the constitutiveness of social relations with the value of self-determination. Liberalism has been the source of our language of freedom and self-determination, but it lacks the ability to express comprehension of "the reality we know: the centrality of relationships in constituting the self."[60]

In developing a new conception of autonomy that avoids positing self-sufficient and thus highly artificial individuals, Nedelsky points out first that "the capacity to find one's own law can develop only in the context of relations with others (both intimate and more broadly social) that nurture this capacity, and second, that the 'content' of one's own law is comprehensible only with reference to shared social norms, values, and concepts."[61] She sees the traditional liberal view of the self as implying that the most perfectly autonomous man is the most perfectly isolated, and finds this pathological.

Instead of developing autonomy through images of walls around one's property, as does the Western liberal tradition and as does U.S. constitutional law, Nedelsky suggests that "the most promising model, symbol, or metaphor for autonomy is not property, but childrearing. There we have encapsulated the emergence of autonomy through relationship with others . . . Interdependence [is] a constant component of autonomy."[62] And she goes on to examine how law and bureaucracies can foster autonomy within relationships between citizen and government. This does not entail extrapolating from intimate relations to large-scale ones; rather, the insights gained from experience with the context of childrearing allow us to recognize the relational aspects of autonomy. In work such as Nedelsky's we can see how feminist reconceptualizations of the self can lead to the rethinking of fundamental concepts even in terrains such as law, thought by many to be quite distant from such disturbances.

To argue for a view of the self as relational does not mean that women need to remain enmeshed in the ties by which they are constituted. In recent decades, especially, women have been breaking free of relationships with parents, with the communities in which they grew up, and with men, relationships in which they defined themselves through the traditional and often stifling expectations of others.[63] These quests for self have often involved wrenching instability and painful insecurity. But the quest has been for a new and more satisfactory relational self, not for the self-sufficient individual of liberal theory. Many might share the concerns expressed by Alison Jaggar that disconnecting ourselves from particular others, as ideals of individual autonomy seem to presuppose we should, might make us *in*capable of morality, rather than capable of it, if, as so many feminists think, "an ineliminable part of morality consists in responding emotionally to particular others."[64]

I have examined three topics on which feminist philosophers and feminists in other fields are thinking anew about where we should start and how we should focus our attention in ethics. Feminist reconceptualizations and recommendations concerning the relation between reason and emotion, the distinction between public and private, and the concept of the self, are providing insights deeply challenging to standard moral theory. The implications of this work are that we need an almost total reconstruction of social and political and economic and legal theory in all their traditional forms as well as a reconstruction of moral theory and practice at more comprehensive, or fundamental, levels.

Notes

This chapter is based in part on my Truax Lectures on "The Prospect of Feminist Morality" at Hamilton College on November 2 and 9, 1989. Early versions were also presented at Colgate University; at Queens University in Kingston, Ontario; at the University of Kentucky; and at the New School for Social Research. I am grateful to all who made possible these occasions and commented on the chapter at these times, and to Alison Jaggar, Laura Purdy, and Sara Ruddick for additional discussion.

1. See e.g. Cheshire Calhoun, "Justice, Care, Gender Bias," *The Journal of Philosophy* 85 (September, 1988): 451–63.

2. Lorraine Code, "Second Persons," in *Science, Morality and Feminist Theory,* ed. Marsha Hanen and Kai Nielsen (Calgary: University of Calgary Press, 1987), p. 360.

3. See e.g. *Revolutions in Knowledge: Feminism in the Social Sciences,* ed. Sue Rosenberg Zalk and Janice Gordon-Kelter (Boulder: Westview Press, forthcoming).

4. Genevieve Lloyd, *The Man of Reason: 'Male' and 'Female' in Western Philosophy* (Minneapolis: University of Minnesota Press, 1984), p. 104.

5. Ibid., p. 2.

6. Ibid., p. 3.

7. Ibid., p. 4. For a feminist view of how reason and emotion in the search for knowledge might be reevaluated, see Alison M. Jaggar, "Love and Knowledge: Emotion in Feminist Epistemology," *Inquiry* 32 (June, 1989): 151–76.

8. David Heyd, *Supererogation: Its Status in Ethical Theory* (New York: Cambridge University Press, 1982), p. 134.

9. J. O. Urmson, "Saints and Heroes," in *Essays in Moral Philosophy,* ed. A. I. Melden (Seattle: University of Washington Press, 1958), p. 202. I am indebted to Marcia Baron for pointing out this and the previous example in her "Kantian Ethics and Supererogation," *The Journal of Philosophy* 84 (May, 1987): 237–62.

10. Alan Ryan, "Distrusting Economics," *New York Review of Books* (May 18, 1989): 25–27. For a different treatment, see *Beyond Self-Interest,* ed. Jane Mansbridge (Chicago: University of Chicago Press, 1990).

11. See especially *Mothering: Essays in Feminist Theory,* ed. Joyce Trebilcot (Totowa, New Jersey: Rowman and Allanheld, 1984); and Sara Ruddick, *Maternal Thinking: Toward a Politics of Peace* (Boston: Beacon Press, 1989).

12. Christine Di Stefano, "Masculinity as Ideology in Political Theory: Hobbesian Man Considered," *Women's Studies International Forum* (Special Issue: *Hypatia*), Vol. 6, No. 6 (1983): 633–44, p. 637.

13. Thomas Hobbes, *The Citizen: Philosophical Rudiments Concerning Government and Society,* ed. B. Gert (Garden City, New York: Doubleday, 1972 [1651]), p. 205.

14. Di Stefano, op. cit., p. 638.

15. Ibid.

16. Ibid., p. 639.

17. For examples of relevant passages, see *Philosophy of Woman: Classical to Current Concepts,* ed. Mary Mahowald (Indianapolis: Hackett, 1978); and *Visions of Women,* ed. Linda Bell (Clifton, New Jersey: Humana, 1985). For discussion, see Susan Moller Okin, *Women in Western Political Thought* (Princeton, New Jersey: Princeton University Press, 1979); and Lorenne Clark and Lynda Lange, eds., *The Sexism of Social and Political Theory* (Toronto: University of Toronto Press, 1979).

18. Annette Baier, "Trust and Anti-Trust," *Ethics* 96 (1986): 231–60, pp. 247–48.

19. Ibid.

20. Kathryn Pauly Morgan, "Strangers in a Strange Land: Feminists Visit Relativists," in *Perspectives on Relativism,* ed. D. Odegaard and Carole Stewart (Toronto: Agathon Press, 1990).

21. Kathryn Morgan, "Women and Moral Madness," in *Science, Morality and Feminist Theory*, ed. Hanen and Nielsen, p. 223.

22. Alison M. Jaggar, "Feminist Ethics: Some Issues for the Nineties," *Journal of Social Philosophy* 20 (Spring/Fall, 1989), p. 91.

23. Ibid.

24. One well-argued statement of this position is Barbara Houston, "Rescuing Womanly Virtues: Some Dangers of Moral Reclamation," in *Science, Morality and Feminist Theory,* ed. Hanen and Nielsen.

25. See e.g. Elizabeth V. Spelman, *Inessential Woman: Problems of Exclusion in Feminist Thought* (Boston: Beacon Press, 1988). See also Sarah Lucia Hoagland, *Lesbian Ethics: Toward New Value* (Palo Alto, California: Institute of Lesbian Studies, 1989); and Katie Geneva Cannon, *Black Womanist Ethics* (Atlanta, Georgia: Scholars Press, 1988).

26. For an approach to social and political as well as moral issues that attempts to be context-respectful, see Virginia Held, *Rights and Goods: Justifying Social Action* (Chicago: University of Chicago Press, 1989).

27. Margaret Urban Walker, "Moral Understandings: Alternative 'Epistemology' for a Feminist Ethics," *Hypatia* 4 (Summer, 1989): 15–28, p. 19.

28. Ibid., p. 20. See also Iris Marion Young, "Impartiality and the Civic Public. Some Implications of Feminist Critiques of Moral and Political Theory," in Seyla Benhabib and Drucilla Cornell, *Feminism as Critique* (Minneapolis: University of Minnesota Press, 1987).

29. See especially Carol Gilligan, *In a Different Voice: Psychological Theory and Women's Development* (Cambridge, Massachusetts: Harvard University Press, 1988); and Eva Feder Kittay and Diana T. Meyers, eds., *Women and Moral Theory* (Totowa, New Jersey: Rowman and Allanheld, 1987).

30. Annette Baier, "The Need for More Than Justice," in *Science, Morality and Feminist Theory,* ed. Hanen and Nielsen, p. 55.

31. Ibid.

32. Kathryn Pauly Morgan, "Strangers in a Strange Land . . . ," p. 2.

33. Annette Baier, "Trust and Anti-Trust."

34. See especially Kathryn Pauly Morgan, "Strangers in a Strange Land . . ."

35. Susan Sherwin, "Feminist and Medical Ethics: Two Different Approaches to Contextual Ethics," *Hypatia* 4 (Summer, 1989): 57–72.

36. See especially the work of John Rawls and Ronald Dworkin; see also Charles Larmore, *Patterns of Moral Complexity* (Cambridge: Cambridge University Press, 1987).

37. Annette Baier, "The Need for More Than Justice," pp. 53–54.

38. See e.g. Linda Nicholson, *Gender and History: The Limits of Social Theory in the Age of the Family* (New York: Columbia University Press, 1986); and Jean Bethke Elshtain, *Public Man, Private Woman* (Princeton, New Jersey: Princeton University Press, 1981). See also Carole Pateman, *The Sexual Contract* (Stanford, California: Stanford University Press, 1988).

39. See e.g. Susan Moller Okin, *Women in Western Political Thought.* See also Alison M. Jaggar, *Feminist Politics and Human Nature* (Totowa, New Jersey): Rowman and Allanheld, 1983).

40. So entrenched in this way of thinking that it was even reflected in Simone de Beauvoir's pathbreaking feminist text *The Second Sex,* published in 1949. Here, as elsewhere, feminists have had to transcend our own early searches for our own perspectives.

41. See e.g. Sherry B. Ortner, "Is Female to Male as Nature Is to Culture?" in *Woman, Culture, and Society,* ed. Michelle Z. Rosaldo and Louis Lamphere (Stanford: Stanford University Press, 1974).

42. For further discussion and an examination of surrounding associations, see Virginia Held, "Birth and Death," in *Ethics* 99 (January, 1989): 362–88.

43. See e.g., Virginia Held, "Non-Contractual Society: A Feminist View," in *Science, Morality and Feminist Theory,* ed. Hanen and Nielsen.

44. Sara Ruddick, *Maternal Thinking.*

45. See Marilyn Friedman, "Feminism and Modern Friendship: Dislocating the Community," *Ethics* 99 (January, 1989): 275–90; and Lorraine Code, "Second Persons."

46. See Virginia Held, "Feminism and Moral Theory," in *Women and Moral Theory,* ed. Kittay and Meyers.

47. See Seyla Benhabib, "The Generalized and the Concrete Other: The Kohlberg-Gilligan Controversy and Moral Theory," in *Women and Moral Theory,* ed. Kittay and Meyers. See also Caroline Whitbeck, "Feminist Ontology: A Different Reality," in *Beyond Domination,* ed. Carol Gould (Totowa, New Jersey: Rowman and Allanheld, 1983).

48. See Thomas Nagel, *The View from Nowhere* (New York: Oxford University Press, 1986). For a feminist critique, see Susan Bordo, "Feminism, Postmodernism, and Gender-Skepticism," in *Feminism/Postmodernism,* ed. Linda Nicholson (New York: Routledge, 1989).

49. On Marxist theory, see e.g. *Women and Revolution,* ed. Lydia Sargent (Boston: South End Press, 1981); Alison Jaggar, *Feminist Politics and Human Nature;* and Ann Ferguson, *Blood at the Root: Motherhood, Sexuality and Male Dominance* (London: Pandora, 1989). On communitarian theory, see Marilyn Friedman, "Feminism and Modern Friendship . . . ," and also her paper "The Social Self and the Partiality Debates," presented at the Society for Women in Philosophy meeting in New Orleans, April 1990.

50. Bernard Williams, *Moral Luck* (Cambridge: Cambridge University Press, 1981); *Public and Private Morality,* ed. Stuart Hampshire (Cambridge: Cambridge University Press, 1978); and Alasdair MacIntyre, *After Virtue: A Study in Moral Theory* (Notre Dame, Indiana: University of Notre Dame Press, 1981). For discussion see Susan Moller Okin, *Justice, Gender, and the Family* (New York: Basic Books, 1989).

51. On the Stone Center concept of the self see especially Jean Baker Miller, "The Development of Women's Sense of Self," Wellesley, Massachusetts: Stone Center Working Paper No. 12; Janet Surrey, "The 'Self-in-Relation': A Theory of Women's Development" (Wellesley, Massachusetts: Stone Center Working Paper No. 13); and Judith Jordan, "The Meaning of Mutuality" (Wellesley, Massachusetts: Stone Center Working Paper No. 23). For a feminist but critical view of this work, see Marcia Westkott, "Female Re-

lationality and the Idealized Self," *American Journal of Psychoanalysis* 49 (September, 1989): 239–50.

52. Jean Baker Miller, *Toward a New Psychology of Women* (Boston: Beacon Press, 1976).

53. Nancy Chodorow, *The Reproduction of Mothering: Psychoanalysis and the Sociology of Gender* (Berkeley: University of California Press, 1978).

54. Carol Gilligan, *In a Different Voice*.

55. J. V. Jordan, "The Meaning of Mutuality," p. 2.

56. Jennifer Nedelsky, "Law, Boundaries, and the Bounded Self," *Representations* 30 (Spring, 1990): 162–89, at 167.

57. Ibid., p. 169.

58. Ibid., p. 181.

59. Jennifer Nedelsky, "Reconceiving Autonomy: Sources, Thoughts and Possibilities," *Yale Journal of Law and Feminism* 1 (Spring, 1989): 7–36, p. 9. See also Diana T. Meyers, *Self, Society, and Personal Choice* (New York: Columbia University Press, 1989).

60. Ibid.

61. Ibid., p. 11.

62. Ibid., p. 12. See also Mari J. Matsuda, "Liberal Jurisprudence and Abstracted Visions of Human Nature," *New Mexico Law Review* 16 (Fall, 1986): 613–30.

63. See e.g. *Women's Ways of Knowing. The Development of Self, Voice, and Mind,* by Mary Field Belenky, Blyth McVicker Clinchy, Nancy Rule Goldberger, and Jill Mattuck Tarule (New York: Basic Books, 1986).

64. Alison M. Jaggar, "Feminist Ethics: Some Issues for the Nineties," p. 11.

12.

ARENDT'S ACTION PHILOSOPHY AND THE MANAGER AS EICHMANN, RICHARD III, FAUST, OR INSTITUTION CITIZEN

Richard P. Nielsen

Hannah Arendt was a respected and controversial philosopher and political theorist who died in 1975. Her most noted work was *Eichmann in Jerusalem: A Report on the Banality of Evil* (1963). Originally commissioned by and published in *The New Yorker,* it was later expanded into book form. It is considered something of a modern classic due to its thought provoking analytic power. Arendt's philosophy of action and her analysis of Eichmann as a person and of his organizational situation can be an important aid in helping us manage both effectively and morally under pressure in turbulent times.

Arendt was concerned with the relationship between thinking and acting, between philosophy and politics. Many managers know that conflicts can exist between institutional requirements to obey orders and individual conscience, that institutions can harm people, and that responsibility for institution behavior that harms people is shared at different organizational levels. While literally thousands of articles and books have been published about managing under stress from a psychological perspective, relatively little has been published from a philosophical perspective.

Before considering how Arendt's action philosophy can be useful for man-

California Management Review 26, no. 3: 191–201.

agement, it is necessary to consider similarities between the conditions Arendt was addressing and modern institutional conditions.

Institutional Factors Related to Arendt's Action Philosophy

Institutional Requirements to Obey Orders vs. Individual Conscience

Part of Arendt's work is concerned with totalitarian environments where obeying orders is required. We might like to think that with respect to the importance and force of institutional requirements to obey orders versus individual conscience, things are very different in modern institutions. However, there are some similarities. As Robert E. Wood of Sears, Roebuck has observed:

> We stress the advantages of the free enterprise system, we complain about the totalitarian state, but in our individual organizations we have created more or less a totalitarian system in industry, particularly in large industry.[1]

Lawrence Blades has observed that, as far as legal protection of employees from arbitrary institutional power, the law states that for the most part employers

> may dismiss their employees at will . . . for good cause, for no cause, or even for cause morally wrong, without being thereby guilty of legal wrong.[2]

David W. Ewing, Managing Editor of the *Harvard Business Review,* concludes that

> there is very little protection in industry for employees who object to carrying out immoral, unethical or illegal orders from their superiors. If the employee doesn't like what he or she is asked to do, the remedy is to pack up and leave. This remedy seems to presuppose an ideal economy, where there is another company down the street with openings for jobs just like the one the employee left.[3]

Charles W. Summers in a *Harvard Business Review* article states that

> corporate executives may argue that . . . they recognize and protect . . . against arbitrary termination through their own internal procedures. The simple fact is that most companies have not recognized and protected that right.[4]

What frequently results from the lack of protection for those who resist orders that are immoral and/or illegal is that they either have to leave their organization, accept punishment, or conform. Many others who see what happens to those who try to resist, conform without resisting. Ewing observes:

> It [pressure to obey immoral or illegal orders] is probably most dangerous, however, as a low-level infection. When it slowly bleeds the individual conscience dry and metastasizes insidiously, it is most difficult to defend against. There are no spectacular firings or purges in the ranks. There are no epic blunders. Under constant and insistent pressure, employees simply give in and conform. They become good "organization people."[5]

Institutional Harm

Do institutions harm people? One of the most important reasons for considering the conflict between pressures to obey immoral or illegal institutional orders versus individual conscience is the potential and actual harm institutions can inflict upon people.

According to the Consumer Product Safety Commission, 30,000 people in the United States received serious injuries from unsafe products in 1976. It is estimated that each year more than 20 million Americans are injured seriously enough in consumer product related incidents to require medical treatment, or to be absent from work a day or more.[6]

Employees also are harmed by unsafe working conditions. The Occupational Safety and Health Administration reports that in 1976, 4,500 employees died and one out of 11 employees received serious injuries from work related causes in the United States. These large numbers do not include estimates for the number of people harmed in such areas as water and air pollution, or the long-term effects of such things as products and working conditions that cause cancer.[7]

There are also many problem-specific types of harm caused by institutions. For example, consider the multinational business manager who manages the movement of a manufacturing facility from one country to another because the first country's laws consider a particular manufacturing process to cause cancer among employees or people living around the plant. The plant is moved to another country where the employee safety and pollution control laws are not so rigorous and the country may think that it needs to be more concerned with economic development than with health and safety. Instead of people being harmed in one country, they are harmed in another country. This situation is not unusual today and many modern industrial countries are involved.

There are some factories operating in the United States today where federal health analysts estimate that employees handling certain chemicals for more than five years have a higher than 80 percent probability of getting cancer.

Consider the situation of a manager in a nuclear power plant who is required as a condition of employment not to release information about potential or actual dangers in a plant for fear of media and political distortion. These are examples of institutions that can and do harm employees, consumers, and the public.[8]

Managerial Distance from Physical Harm

Numbers and types of harm are only part of the picture. Another important factor is how close the manager is to an overt act that harms people. For example, Eichmann, the Nazi who helped organize the mass murder of civilians, was separated by a significant organizational distance from the point where the organization harmed people. In his own words, Eichmann was guilty only of "aiding and abetting" in the commission of crimes. According to Arendt[9] and the Israeli Court, it was never proved that Eichmann ever committed an overt act.

So also in the modern institution, the degree of responsibility tends to increase as we draw further away from the worker or the foreman who has the closest contact with the citizen, consumer, or employee harmed by organization behavior. The inadequacy of a defense based solely on the distance from the interface between the organization and the harmed person was reaffirmed in the June 1975 landmark case of United States vs. Park, where the Supreme Court ruled 6 to 3 that John R. Park, the President of Acme Markets, was criminally liable for conduct far down in the corporate hierarchy.[10]

In principle, as in the Eichmann case, distance by itself is not an adequate defense in U.S. business. However, in practice, the greater distance of top managers relative to middle managers appears to protect them more than the middle distance of middle managers.[11] Is this better than the Nuremberg situation where the reverse was the case with respect to convictions and penalties?

"Ideal Types" of Managerial Morality

The German sociologist Max Weber constructed "ideal types" (models) of human behavior that were designed to serve as characterizations that reveal essential features of human behavior. Weber's most well-known "ideal type," the protestant capitalist, was presented in his *Protestant Ethic and the Spirit of Capitalism.*[12] While Weber recognized that there were Catholic Florentines and Venetians who were capitalists long before there was such a thing as a Protestant, the "ideal type" Protestant Ethic was used to illuminate certain key aspects of capitalist behavior. The "ideal type" is used in the sense of illuminating a particularly important characteristic of a behavior rather than as mutually exclusive categories that all or even any people can be neatly placed into.

The "ideal types" of Eichmann, Richard III, Faust, and Institution Citizen are used in this Weberian sense to try to illuminate several different and key aspects of managerial morality under pressure as a basis for considering the appropriateness and usefulness of Arendt's action philosophy.

Eichmann as Manager

From Arendt we learn that Eichmann was an upper middle-level manager in a Nazi institution engaged in, as Arendt phrased it, the "administrative massacre" of millions of people. Eichmann never belonged to the higher Party circles. He managed in an institutional environment where obeying orders was required. According to Arendt, Eichmann believed that he was practicing the virtue of obedience when he was aiding his institution. Hitler ordered Goering, Goering ordered Himmler, Himmler ordered Heydrich, Heydrich ordered Eichmann, and Eichmann carried out the orders. Arendt explains what she thinks Eichmann thought.

> His guilt came from his obedience, and obedience is praised as a virtue. His virtue had been abused by the Nazi leaders. But he was not one of the ruling clique, he was a victim, and only the leaders deserved punishment.[13]

Arendt concludes her analysis of Eichmann and his organizational situation with the judgment that Eichmann was guilty, but instead of being an insane or monstrously evil person, Eichmann was, perhaps more horribly, well within the range of sanity and normality—he was neither abnormal nor a monster. Eichmann was a "thoughtless" and "banal" man who did not understand what was right or wrong about his role as a manager in an organization that harmed people. He was not able to distinguish right from wrong in his organizational context because he did not think about what he was doing and cooperating with. Arendt explains:

> Despite all the efforts of the prosecution, everybody could see that this man was not a monster. . . . he certainly would never have murdered his superior in order to inherit his post. He merely, to put the matter colloquially, never realized what he was doing. . . . He was not stupid. It was sheer thoughtlessness—something by no means identical with stupidity.[14]

Eichmann was capable of being both a good technical manager and ignorant of the evil role he was playing as a manager in an institution. He was very narrow, and this narrowness contributed to his evil behavior. According to Arendt, Eichmann was "ignorant of everything that was not directly, technically and bureaucratically connected with his job."

Despite the extreme evil his organization committed, Eichmann as a Weberian "ideal type," as well as the individual person Eichmann, as a thoughtless man, brings into serious question the validity of assuming that all managers naturally understand what is right or wrong in organizational contexts where obeying orders is at a very high premium. As Arendt explains:

> The judges did not believe him, because they were . . . perhaps too conscious of the very foundations of their profession to admit that an average, "normal" person neither feeble-minded nor indoctrinated nor cynical, could be perfectly incapable of telling right from wrong. They . . . missed the greatest moral and even legal challenge of the whole case. Their case rested on the assumption that the defendant, like all "normal persons," must have been aware of the criminal nature of his acts. . . . However, under the conditions of the Third Reich only "exceptions" could be expected to react normally.[15]

Ewing's book describes several cases where managers were severely punished for not doing what was illegal or what they thought was morally wrong.[16] Ewing also found such courageous managers to be exceptions. Not thinking about illegal or immoral behavior while working hard and creatively for organizational goals is frequently both encouraged and rewarded. The key "ideal type" characteristic illuminated by Eichmann and his organizational situation is thoughtlessness, and as Arendt phrased it, the banality of evil.

Richard III as Manager

In her analysis of Eichmann, Arendt recognized that in contrast to the Eichmann "ideal type," people could act from base motives.[17] She referred to "calculated wickedness" and distinguished it from banal or thoughtless evil. The "ideal type" she used to refer to "calculated wickedness" was Richard III, who in Shakespeare's play says to himself "Evil be thou my good."[18] In contrast to the Eichmann "ideal type," the Richard III "ideal type" can tell the difference between good and evil. The Richard III knows a behavior is evil and decides to do it for personal gain. Both the Eichmann and the Richard III types are guilty according to Arendt. The key difference is that the Richard III type knows exactly that what he is doing is evil.

As mentioned earlier, administrative harm—unsafe products, working conditions, environmental effects, etc.—is an example of how organizations can harm people. A Richard III type manager might intentionally produce and market products that he knows to be unsafe in order to increase sales and profits and advance in the institution. Similarly, such a manager might produce and market unsafe products so as not to oppose what he thinks is wrong in order to maintain his position and not "rock the boat." Such cooperation with administrative harm can be done for greater personal gain or out of a desire not to lose what a manager already has in terms of employment, position, influence, benefits, etc.

Faust as Manager

In Goethe's *Faust*, Faust exchanges his soul for what he considers higher goods:

> *FAUST:* I am too old to treat it as a jest,
> Too young to have given up the game
> What satisfaction can this world bestow? . . .
> Poor devil. What hath thou to give?
> *MEPHISTOPHELES:* . . . One day you'll want to sit
> O'er some good thing . . .
> *FAUST:* If e'er I cry to the passing hour
> "Thou are so beautiful; Oh, linger, yet" . . .
> Then I will go down gladly to the pit.[19]

The higher goods offered by Mephistopheles and accepted by Faust were knowledge and love of another person. Faust believed that to make a pact with a devil was wrong; however, he also believed that what he considered higher goods, knowledge and the love of another person, were worth doing wrong for.

Unlike the Richard III "ideal type" Faust's ends were not base. Knowledge and love are good for Faust and the world. For Faust, exchanging his soul was reasonable. The higher ends justified the bad means.

This is not an uncommon phenomenon. A manager may identify so closely with the mission of his institution that he is willing to act illegally and immorally for the higher good of the institution or the institution's mission. For example, a manager may decide that it is "worth it" to have a few employees die of cancer from working in a factory producing a chemical or drug that can improve the lives of thousands of people. A manager might allow a product to be manufactured and marketed that he knows will harm people because to recall the products, redesign them, and remarket them might be so expensive as to seriously damage the financial health of the institution. For this manager the higher good of the financial health or perhaps survivability of the institution might be more important than the lives or injuries of a few consumers.

Curiously, Arendt did not refer to this Faust "ideal type." However, she did refer to a related phenomenon, the situation where a policy maker is willing to act a lesser evil rather than a greater evil. She found three problems with this approach. First, she found it morally wrong because the people hurt by the lesser evil behavior are not consulted and do not agree to be hurt. Second, she thought that those who use "lesser evil" means are slowly or quickly transformed into the "larger evil" they think they are fighting against or resisting. Third, she lacked confidence in our ability to correctly predict the actuality of greater future evils that we might exchange for present and certain lesser evils.[20]

Arendt's Action Philosophy and the Manager as Institution Citizen

Arendt's use of the "ideal type" technique was learned from her teacher and friend Karl Jaspers, who in turn learned about it from his teacher and friend Max Weber.[21] Jaspers used Weber's "ideal type" technique for his *Psychology of World Views*. Jaspers tried to distinguish basic types of "world views" and illuminate the consequences for human behavior. This work also marked Jaspers' change in work and career from psychology to philosophy.[22]

However, Jaspers found that in addition to understanding a "world view" it was also necessary to understand why a person adopts a "world view" and what causes people to think, act, and make concrete choices in relation to alternative "world views." Jaspers was interested in how a person lives and acts his own "world view," and philosophy, as is explained in his *Philosophy*.[23] Arendt continued and advanced this work.

Unlike most modern social and political philosophers since Marx, Arendt and Jaspers do not so much tell us what to believe or what specific actions to take, as they offer us an orientation and examples of how to think and act in difficult situations. Arendt's philosophical orientation integrates three key concepts:

- the importance of the habit of independent thinking and judgment;
- the need to understand and resist individual and organizational phenomena of the evil "ideal types"; and,
- the need to act civically, i.e. as a citizen, with others.

According to M. A. Hill:

> The . . . paradigmatic quality of her thinking is rooted in the way she understood the task of the thinker. . . . She believed that it is up to the actors themselves to judge how to act, and to persuade each other on the best course to follow. . . . She did not believe there was any . . . theory that could eliminate the need for judgment by offering in its place a certain knowledge of the consequences of different courses of action. . . . For Hannah Arendt, thinking was an ongoing activity . . . an end in itself. . . . For her the justification for thinking was not the knowledge it confers, but the possibility of meaning that it holds out. . . . She offered an understanding of what it means to act and what it means to think, as activities that are viewed without the help of prior assumptions, "without bannisters," as she once put it.[24]

Arendt thought that we need to learn more about thinking, judging, and acting without historical theoretical or ideological bannisters. This was in large part because of the "ideal type" phenomena of totalitarianism, the Eichmann, Richard III, and Faust as reflected in both individual and organizational principles. Arendt felt that previous Western social and political philosophy did not adequately include these phenomena, and she also thought that the content of the traditional philosophies could not include the phenomena of totalitarianism and Eichmann.[25]

Arendt explains how her action philosophy is related to the Eichmann "ideal type":

> Factually, my preoccupation with mental activities has two rather different origins. The immediate impulse came from my attending the Eichmann trial in Jerusalem. In my report of it I spoke of "the banality of evil." Behind that phrase, I held no thesis or doctrine, although I was dimly aware of the fact that it went counter to our tradition of thought—literary, theological, or philosophic—about the phenomenon of evil. . . . The question that imposed itself was: Could the activity of thinking as such, the habit of examining whatever happens to come to pass or to attract attention, regardless of results and specific content, could this activity be among the conditions that make men abstain from evil-doing or even actually "condition" them against it? . . . Second, . . . I had been concerned with the problem of Action. . . . If, as I suggested before, the ability to tell right from wrong should turn out to have anything to do with the ability to think, then we must be able to "demand" its exercise from every sane person, no matter how erudite or ignorant, intelligent or stupid, he may happen to be . . . absence of thought is not stupidity; it can be found in highly intelligent people, and a wicked heart is not its cause; it is probably the other way round, that wickedness may be caused by absence of thought. In any event, the matter can no longer be left to "specialists" as though thinking, like higher mathematics, were the monopoly of a specialized discipline.[26]

Arendt also believed that while thinking must be an individual and independent, habitual activity it was also necessary to understand important principles of institutional totalitarianism and act civically with others, i.e. as a citizen of a country or an institution, to resist immoral behavior and phenomena.[27] Arendt's concerns were to be both with oneself, to which the activity of thinking corresponds, and to be together with others, from which flows action. She was concerned with the relationship between thinking and acting, between philosophy and politics. Arendt made a distinction between a "good man" and a "good citizen," between a moral stance and a political action. This distinction was important because in order for action to be effective it generally has to come from people acting together.

Arendt argued that this acting with others was crucial for several key reasons.[28] One reason revolved around the idea of a public space. That is, people need to be able to have a space to interact with others in order to discuss and persuade each other on important issues. People need to act with others so as not to be atomized and isolated from the institution they are trying to serve;

otherwise there is a strong tendency to be concerned only with private security and private interests. This not only makes people ineffective as citizens but also makes them more susceptible to explicit and implicit coercion, immoral ideologies, and immoral "ideal type" behaviors. The act of working with others helps establish a place in the institution, a political space which makes opinions significant and actions effective.

Arendt also understood that institutional civil liberties could be important as encouragement and protection of responsible institutional citizenship.

> All other differences between the institutions of democratic and totalitarian countries can be shown to be secondary and side issues. This is not a conflict between socialism and capitalism, or state-capitalism and free enterprise, or a class-ridden and classless society. It is a conflict between . . . civil liberties and the . . . abolition of civil liberties.[29]

In her view, institutions, without provisions for civil liberties were more totalitarian than not. In order for the manager to serve as a citizen in an institution, it is important to have protected civil liberties. This is also the theme of David Ewing's book, *Freedom Inside the Organization: Bringing Civil Liberties to the Workplace,* quoted earlier.

In summary, the manager as institution citizen cultivates the habit of thinking and judging independently as a basis for acting civically with others and resisting the immoral "ideal type" behaviors and phenomena of totalitarianism—the Eichmann, Richard III, and Faust which are not uncommon within countries, institutions, and individuals. In addition, Arendt believed that institutional systems with protected civil liberties and "citizen" actions were almost the antithesis of the totalitarian phenomenon. She also recognized that totalitarian systems are both evil and strong. Therefore, in order to effectively combat such systems as well as the cancerous growths of totalitarianism within countries, institutions, and individuals, very tough-minded habits of independent thinking and judging by managers as well as civic action protected by institutional civil liberties are necessary. A large part of manager civic responsibility is for the manager as a citizen of an institution to develop the habit of thinking and judging independently as a basis for discussing and acting with others to build and preserve the good characteristics and behaviors of institutions while resisting the immoral "ideal type" behaviors and characteristics.

Arendt's Action Philosophy as an Aid to Managing under Pressure

Many, but certainly not all and perhaps not even most, managers are familiar with how institutions can harm people, how there can be conflicts between organizational requirements to obey orders and individual conscience, and how responsibility for organization behavior that harms people is shared at different organizational levels. Arendt's action philosophy as illuminated in the "ideal type" of manager as Institution Citizen is useful to the manager for five main reasons.

First, Arendt's analysis and action philosophy can help us better understand the severe pressures managers sometimes encounter and that such pressures are not new. Second, it can help us better understand the range of "ideal type" responses that we can choose among as well as be on guard against. That there are alternative types of responses can help us think about and perhaps make better judgments and decisions about which type is better for us individually and collectively. Third, Arendt's action philosophy of the manager as Institution Citizen can provide an effective orientation and guide for dealing with pressures associated with moral issues. Fourth, Arendt's action philosophy is for the most part free of the political-economic, corporate, and even religious ideologies that so many managers have found inadequate for dealing with modern moral issues within institutional contexts. Fifth, philosophy can serve as a more powerful approach, or at least supplement to a psychological approach to stress management, which frequently ignores the more fundamental moral and philosophical issues.

As Goethe observed, "The world only goes forward because of those who oppose it." The same is true of institutions and the managers who serve as loyal opposition and Institution Citizen.[30]

Notes

1. David W. Ewing, *Freedom Inside the Organization: Bringing Civil Liberties to the Workplace* (New York, NY: McGraw Hill, 1977), p. 21.
2. Lawrence E. Blades, "Employment at Will vs. Individual Freedom: On Limiting the Abusive Exercise of Employer Power," *Columbia Law Review* 67 (1967): 1405–1406.
3. Ewing, op. cit., pp. 8, 21.
4. Charles W. Summers, "Protecting All Employees against Unjust Dismissal," *Harvard Business Review* 58 (1980): 132, 139.
5. Ewing, op. cit., pp. 216–217.
6. Richard P. Nielsen, "Should Executives Be Jailed for Consumer and Employee Health and Safety Violations?" *The Journal of Consumer Affairs* 13 (1979): 128–134. (Data and quotations for this article were obtained through telephone interviews while the author was serving as free-lance reporter/researcher for *The New York Times*. The data and quotations are used with permission of *The New York Times*.)
7. Ibid.
8. Ibid. See also, Ewing, op. cit.

9. Hannah Arendt, *Eichmann in Jerusalem: A Report on the Banality of Evil* (New York, NY: Viking Press, 1963; revised and enlarged edition, 1964), pp. 214–215.

10. Richard P. Nielsen, "Criminal Executives," *Business and Society Review* (1977), p. 73.

11. Nielsen, op. cit., 1979; and Ewing, op. cit.

12. Max Weber, *The Protestant Ethic and the Spirit of Capitalism,* trans. Talcott Parsons with Forward by R. H. Tawney (New York, NY: Charles Scribner's Sons, 1904, 1930).

13. Hannah Arendt, op. cit., p. 247.

14. Ibid., p. 287.

15. Ibid., pp. 26–27.

16. Ewing, op. cit.

17. Arendt, op. cit., p. 287; also, Hannah Arendt, *The Life of the Mind,* two volumes of an uncompleted work, published posthumously, Mary McCarthy, ed. (New York, NY: Harcourt Brace Jovanovich, 1978), pp. 3–9.

18. E. Young Bruehl, *Hannah Arendt: For Love of the World* (New Haven, CT: Yale University Press, 1982), p. 369.

19. Thomas Mann, ed., *The Permanent Goethe* (New York, NY: The Dial Press, 1948), pp. 69, 72.

20. Arendt, op. cit., 1978.

21. Young-Bruehl, op. cit., pp. 63–70.

22. Ibid., p. 63.

23. Karl Jaspers, *Philosophy* (Heidelberg-Berlin: Springer-Verlag, 1948).

24. M. A. Hill, ed. *Hannah Arendt: The Recovery of the Public World* (New York, NY: St. Martin's Press, 1979), p. x.

25. Arendt, op. cit., 1978.

26. Ibid., pp. 3, 5, 13.

27. Hannah Arendt, *The Human Condition* (Chicago, IL: University of Chicago Press, 1958); Hannah Arendt, *The Origins of Totalitarianism* (New York, NY: Schocken Books, 1951; second enlarged edition, New York, NY: World Publishing Co., 1958; third edition with new prefaces, New York, NY: Harcourt Brace & World, 1966).

28. Arendt, op. cit., 1958, 1978.

29. Young-Bruehl, op. cit., p. 206.

30. Richard P. Nielsen, "A Politics of Markets and a Market of Politics," *Journal of Marketing* 48 (1984): 101–103; Richard P. Nielsen, "Strategic Planning and Consensus Building for External Relations," *Long Range Planning* 16 (1983): 74–81; Richard P. Nielsen, "Toward a Method for Building Consensus with Internal Constituencies during Strategic Planning," *Sloan Management Review* 22 (1981): 29–40; Richard P. Nielsen, "Stages in Moving Toward Cooperative Problem Solving Employee Relations Projects," *Human Resources Management* 18 (1979): 2–8; Richard P. Nielsen, "Industrial Policy: Reviews and Historical Perspective," *Public Administration Review* 43 (1983): 471–475.

13.

SOCIAL JUSTICE

James P. Sterba

Virtually all of us become involved at some time or another in disputes about justice. Sometimes our involvement in such disputes is rooted in the fact that we believe ourselves to be victims of some form of injustice, such as job discrimination; sometimes our involvement is rooted in the fact that others believe us to be the perpetrators or at least the beneficiaries of some form of injustice affecting them, such as unfair taxing policies. Sometimes the injustice at issue seems to require for its elimination a drastic reform, or even a revolutionary change in the political system, such as took place in the Soviet Union, Eastern Europe and South Africa. Sometimes it seems to require for its elimination only some electoral pressure or administrative decision such as may be required in ending a war, such as the Vietnam War. Whatever the origin and whatever the practical effect, such disputes about justice are difficult to avoid, especially when dealing with issues, like the distribution of employment opportunities, the distribution of income, the structure of political institutions, and the use of the war-making capabilities of a nation that have widespread social effects.

But if we can hardly avoid getting involved in disputes about justice, how can we resolve such disputes in a reasonable way? A reasonable resolution of such disputes requires a critical evaluation of the alternative conceptions of justice available to us. We need to carefully consider whatever reasons have been, or might be, advanced in favor of the alternative conceptions of justice that are available to us. Hopefully, through such a process of critical evaluation, one of these conceptions will begin to emerge as the most defensible—maybe it will even be the conception we initially endorsed.

In any case, the importance of having a defensible conception of justice can hardly be denied. According to contemporary philosopher John Rawls, whose book *A Theory of Justice* has been translated into every major European language as well as Chinese, Japanese and Korean:

> Justice is the first virtue of social institutions, as truth is of systems of thought. A theory however elegant and economical must be rejected or revised if it is untrue; likewise laws and institutions no matter how efficient and well-arranged must be reformed or abolished if they are unjust.[1]

So it is difficult to overestimate the need to critically evaluate the alternative conceptions of justice that are available to us.

In philosophical debate at the end of the twentieth century, five major conceptions of justice are defended. First, there is a Libertarian Conception of Justice. In recent elections, libertarian party candidates have not done very well. But Ronald Reagan, George Bush, and Margaret Thatcher, whose views on economic issues are close to a Libertarian Conception of Justice, were politically successful and did succeed in refashioning the economies of their respective nations. According to this conception of justice, liberty is the ultimate political ideal. Thus all assignments of rights and duties are ultimately to be justified in terms of an ideal of liberty.

Second, there is a Socialist Conception of Justice. In the United States there has never been a viable socialist presidential candidate, but elsewhere there have been many successful socialist candidates. For example, the late Olof Palme led the Social Democrats back to power in Sweden and François Mitterrand, a socialist, has been for some time president of France. According to a Socialist Conception of Justice, equality is the ultimate political ideal. Thus all assignments of rights and duties are ultimately to be justified in terms of an ideal of equality.

Third, there is a Welfare Liberal Conception of Justice. This is the conception of justice endorsed, for example, by the left wing of the Democratic party in the United States, whose leaders have been Jesse Jackson and Ted Kennedy. According to this conception of justice, the ultimate political ideal is a blend of liberty and equality, and this blend can be characterized as contractual fairness or maximal utility. Thus all assignments of rights and duties are ultimately to be justified in terms of an ideal of contractual fairness or maximal utility.

Fourth, there is a Communitarian Conception of Justice. This conception is somewhat difficult to associate with any particular political group, but it does seem to be reflected in a wide range of Supreme Court decisions in the United States today, and has its roots in the republicanism of Madison and Jefferson. According to this Communitarian Conception of Justice, the common good is proclaimed to be the ultimate political ideal, and this ideal is said to support a virtue-based conception of human flourishing.

Last, there is a Feminist Conception of Justice. This is the conception endorsed by the National Organization of Women (NOW) and by numerous other women's organizations in the United States and elsewhere. According to a Feminist Conception of Justice, the ultimate political ideal is a gender-free society. Thus all assignments of rights and duties are ultimately to be justified in terms of a gender-free society.

All of these conceptions of justice have certain features in common. Each regards its requirements as belonging to the domain of obligation rather than to the domain of charity; they simply disagree about where to draw the line between these two domains. Each is also concerned to give people what they deserve or should rightfully possess; they simply disagree about what it is that people deserve or rightfully possess. These common features constitute a generally accepted core definition of justice. What we need to do, however, is examine that part of each of these conceptions of justice over which there is serious disagreement in order to determine which conception, if any, is most defensible.

Libertarian Justice

Libertarians frequently cite the novelist/philosopher Ayn Rand as an intellectual source of their view.[2] Ayn Rand, whose given name was Alice Rosenbaum, was born in St. Petersburg in 1905. She received a degree in history from the University of Petrograd and found work as a tour guide. In 1926, she came to the United States at the invitation of relatives in Chicago. In 1929, she married Francis O'Connor. She is probably best known for her novels such as *The Fountainhead,* published in 1943, and *Atlas Shrugged*, published in 1957 both of which sold millions of copies, but she also published a number of works of nonfiction such as *The Virtue of Selfishness* in 1964 and *Capitalism: The Unknown Ideal* in 1966. She died in New York in 1982.

Ayn Rand defends a particular conception of human rights which regards individuals as ends in themselves and society as a means to the peaceful and orderly *voluntary* co-existence of individuals. Rand claims:

> The principle of man's individual rights represented the extension of morality into the social system—as a limitation of the power of the state, as man's protection against the brute force of the collective, as the subordination of *might to right*.[3]

This conception is contrasted with an altruistic-collectivist ethics which regards each individual as a sacrificial means to the ends of others and society as an end in itself. According to Rand, the conception of human rights she defends is required for a free society, and until recently characterized the political system of the United States. She writes:

> The United States held that man's life is his by right (which means: by moral principle and by nature), that a right is the property of an individual, that society as such has no rights, and that the only moral purpose of a government is the protection of individual rights.[4]

In basic sympathy with Rand, contemporary libertarians such as John Hospers take liberty to be the ultimate moral and political ideal and typically define "liberty" as "the state of being unconstrained by other persons from doing what one wants." This definition limits the scope of liberty in two ways. First, not all constraints, whatever the source, count as a restriction on liberty; the constraints must come from other persons. For example, people who are constrained by natural forces from getting to the top of Mount Everest do not lack liberty in this regard. Second, the constraints must run counter to people's wants. Thus, people who do not want to hear Beethoven's Fifth Symphony do not have their liberty restricted when other people forbid its performance, even though the proscription does in fact constrain what they are able to do.

Given this definition of liberty, libertarians go on to characterize their moral and political ideal as requiring that each person should have the greatest amount of liberty commensurate with the same liberty for all. According to Hospers, who taught for many years at USC and was the Libertarian party's first presidential candidate:

> The political philosophy that is libertarianism . . . is the doctrine that every person is the owner of his own life, and that no one is the owner of anyone else's life; and that consequently every human being has a right to act in accordance with his own choices, unless those actions infringe on the equal liberty of other human beings to act in accordance with their choices.[5]

From this ideal, libertarians claim that a number of more specific requirements, in particular a right to life, a right to freedom of speech, press, and assembly, and a right to property can be derived.

It is important to note that the libertarian's right to life is not a right to receive from others the goods and resources necessary for preserving one's life; it is simply a right not to be killed. So understood, the right to life is not a right to receive welfare. In fact, there are no welfare rights in the libertarian view. Accordingly, the libertarian's understanding of the right to property is not a right to receive from others the goods and resources necessary for one's welfare, but rather a right to acquire goods and resources either by initial acquisition or by voluntary agreement.

Obviously, by defending rights such as these, libertarians can only support a limited role for government. That role is simply to prevent and punish initial acts of coercion—the only wrongful actions for libertarians. This government should be limited to a minimal or night watchman state.

Libertarians do not deny that it is a good thing for people to have sufficient goods and resources to meet at least their basic nutritional needs, but libertarians do deny that government has a duty to provide for such needs. Some good things, such as the provision of welfare to the needy, are requirements of charity rather than justice, libertarians claim. Accordingly, failure to make such provisions is neither blameworthy nor punishable.

Yet I have argued that the libertarian's own ideal of liberty, when correctly interpreted, actually supports the rights of a welfare state rather than those of a minimal or night watchman state. As I have put my argument elsewhere:

> [A]s long as libertarians think of themselves as putting forth a moral resolution for cases of severe conflict of interest, they cannot allow that it would be unreasonable *both* to require the rich to sacrifice the liberty to meet some of their luxury needs in order to benefit the poor and to require the poor to sacrifice the liberty to meet their basic needs in order to benefit the rich. But I submit that if one of these requirements is to be judged reasonable, then, by any neutral assessment, it must be the requirement that the rich sacrifice the liberty to meet some of their luxury needs so that the poor can have the liberty to meet their basic needs; there is no other plausible resolution if libertarians intend to be putting forth a moral resolution.[6]

On this account, I claim that the libertarian's own ideal of liberty supports a right to welfare, but a right to welfare that is conditional upon the poor doing all that they can legitimately do to meet their own needs.

Libertarian philosopher Tibor Machan responds to my critique by accepting its theoretical thrust but rejecting its practical significance. He grants that if the type of conflict cases I describe between the rich and the poor actually obtained, the poor would have action welfare rights. But he then denies that the type of conflict cases I describe—in which the poor have done all that they legitimately can to satisfy their basic needs in a libertarian society—actually does obtain. Machan argues:

> [O]n some occasions there can be people who, with no responsibility for their situation, are highly unlikely to survive without disregarding the rights of others and taking from them what they need. But are such cases typical? . . . The typical conflict situation in society involves people who wish to take shortcuts to earning their living (and a lot more) by attacking others, not those who lack any other alternative to attacking others so as

> to reach the same goal. . . . Normally persons do not lack the opportunities and resources to satisfy their basic needs.[7]

This response actually narrows the gap between Machan's and my views. Theoretically nothing divides them. Their only difference is a practical one. Machan thinks that virtually all of the poor have sufficient opportunities and resources to satisfy their basic needs and that, therefore, welfare rights are not justified. I think that many of the poor do not have sufficient opportunities and resources to satisfy their basic needs and that, therefore, welfare rights are justified. Obviously, if a convincing case could be made as to what are the actual opportunities of the poor, this practical dispute could be resolved.

Socialist Justice

In contrast with libertarians, socialists take equality to be the ultimate political ideal. In the *Communist Manifesto,* Karl Marx and Friedrich Engels maintain that the abolition of private property is a necessary first requirement for building a society that accords with the political ideal of equality.

Karl Marx was born in Trier in the Rhineland, then part of Prussia in 1818. His father, a well-known lawyer, became a Christian to avoid the disabilities then being placed on Jews in Germany. In 1835, Marx went to the University of Bonn to study law, transferred first to Berlin and then to Jena from which he received a doctorate for his thesis on the ancient Greek atomists. Barred from a university position by his liberal political views, Marx became an editor for a newspaper in Cologne which was soon suppressed by the Prussian government. In 1842, he married Jenny von Westphen who he had courted for several years and in whose honor he had written three volumes of poetry. In 1843, Marx moved to Paris to edit a new journal, and there he began his lifelong collaboration with Frederich Engels.

Engels was born in 1820 in Barmen, a village in the Rhineland. Family financial reversals required that he interpret his liberal education, and take a position in one of his father's commercial firms in England. In 1844, Engels visited Paris and contributed two articles to the journal Marx was editing in Paris.

Working together, Marx and Engels completed the *German Ideology* in 1846, and they published the *Communist Manifesto* in 1848. After the 1848 Revolution, Marx was forced to leave Paris, and went to London which was to be home for the rest of his life. Marx's financial situation in London was desperate for many years. He had no regular source of income except what Engels was able to provide. By 1856, three of Marx's six children had died. In 1867, Marx published the first volume of *Capital.* Marx's *Critique of the Gotha*

Program was published by Engels in 1891. In 1883, Marx died and was buried next to his wife, who had died two years earlier. Engels died in 1895.

In the *Communist Manifesto,* in which they recommend the abolition of private property, Marx and Engels write:

> You are horrified at our intending to do away with private property. But in your existing society, private property is already done away with for nine-tenths of the population; its existence for the few is solely due to its non-existence in the hands of those nine-tenths. You reproach us, therefore, with intending to do away with a form of property, the necessary condition for whose existence is the non-existence of any property for the immense majority of society.[8]

In the *Critique of the Gotha Program,* Marx provides a much more positive account of what is required to build a society based upon the political ideal of equality. In such a society, Marx contends that the distribution of social goods must conform, at least initially, to the principle from each according to his ability, to each according to his contribution. But when the highest stage of communist society has been reached, Marx claims,

> only then can the narrow horizon of bourgeois right be fully left behind and society inscribe on its banners: from each according to his ability, to each according to his needs![9]

At first hearing, this socialist conception of justice might sound ridiculous to someone brought up in a capitalist society. The obvious objection is, how can you get persons to contribute according to their ability if income is distributed on the basis of their needs and not on the basis of their contributions? The answer, according to a socialist conception of justice, is to make the work that must be done in a society as much as possible enjoyable in itself. According to socialists Edward Nell and Onora O'Neill,

> Marx . . . held that labor could be more than a means; it could also be an end of life. . . . Each man works at what he wants to work at. He works because that is his need.[10]

As a result, people will want to do the work they are capable of doing because they find it intrinsically rewarding. For a start, socialists might try to get people to accept presently existing, intrinsically rewarding jobs at lower salaries—top executives, for example, to work for $300,000, rather than $900,000, a year. Yet ultimately, socialists hope to make all jobs as intrinsically rewarding as possible, so that after people are no longer working primarily for external rewards, when making their best contributions to society, distribution can proceed on the basis of need.

Socialists propose to implement their ideal of equality by giving workers democratic control over the workplace. They believe that if workers have more to say about how they do their work, they will find their work intrinsically more rewarding. As a consequence, they will be more motivated to work, because their work itself will be meeting their needs. Socialists believe that extending democracy to the workplace will necessarily lead to socialization of the means of production and the end of private property. Socialists, of course, do not deny that civil disobedience or even revolutionary action may be needed to overcome opposition to extending democracy to the workplace.

However, even with democratic control of the workplace, some jobs, such as collecting garbage or changing bedpans, probably cannot be made intrinsically rewarding. Socialists propose to divide such jobs up in some equitable manner. Some people might, for example, collect garbage one day a week, and then work at intrinsically rewarding jobs for the rest of the week. Others would change bedpans or do some other slop job one day a week, and then work at an intrinsically rewarding job the other days of the week. By making jobs intrinsically as rewarding as possible, in part through democratic control of the workplace and an equitable assignment of unrewarding tasks, socialists believe people will contribute according to their ability even when distribution proceeds according to need.

Another difficulty raised concerning the socialist conception of justice involves the proclaimed necessity of abolishing private property and socializing the means of production. Against this view, I have argued that

> [i]t seems perfectly possible to give workers more control over their workplace while the means of production remain privately owned. Of course, private ownership would have a somewhat different character in a society with democratic control of the workplace, but it need not cease to be private ownership. After all, private ownership would also have a somewhat different character in a society where private holdings, and hence bargaining power, were distributed more equally than they are in most capitalist societies, yet it would not cease to be private ownership. Accordingly, we could imagine a society where the means of production are privately owned but where—because ownership is so widely dispersed throughout the society (e.g., nearly everyone owns ten shares of major industrial stock and no one more than twenty shares) and because of the degree of democratic control of the workplace—many of the criticisms socialists make of existing capitalist societies would no longer apply.[11]

Contemporary libertarian philosopher Robert Nozick illustrates another argument often used against a socialist conception of justice—that it is opposed to liberty. Nozick asks us to imagine that we are in a society that has just distributed income according to some ideal pattern, possibly a pattern of equality. He writes:

> Now suppose that Wilt Chamberlain is greatly in demand by basketball teams, being a great gate attraction. (Also suppose contracts run only for a year, with players being free agents.) He signs the following sort of contract with a team: In each home game, twenty-five cents from the price of each ticket of admission goes to him. (We ignore the question of whether he is "gouging" the owners, letting them look out for themselves.) The season starts, and people cheerfully attend his team's games; they buy their tickets, each dropping a separate twenty-five cents of their admission price into a special box with Chamberlain's name on it. They are excited about seeing him play; it is worth the total admission price to them. Let us suppose that in one season one million persons attend his home games, and Wilt Chamberlain winds up with $250,000, a much larger sum than the average income and larger even than anyone else has. Is he entitled to this income?[12]

Since such an income would surely upset the initial pattern of income distribution, whatever that happened to be, Nozick contends that this illustrates how an ideal of liberty upsets the patterns required by other political ideals and hence calls for their rejection.

Nozick's critique, however, only applies to political ideals that require an absolute equality of income. Yet for many political ideals, the inequalities of income generated in Nozick's example would be objectionable only if they deprived people of something to which they had a right, such as equal opportunity. And whether people were so deprived would depend on to what uses the Wilt Chamberlains of the world put their greater income. But clearly there is no necessity for those who have legitimately acquired greater income to use it in ways that violate the rights of others.

Finally, it is important to note that the socialist ideal of equality does not accord with what existed, until recently, in the republics of the former Soviet Union and Eastern Europe. Judging the acceptability of the socialist ideal of equality by what took place in those countries would be as unfair as judging the acceptability of the libertarian ideal of liberty by what takes place in countries like Guatemala or South Korea, where citizens are arrested and imprisoned without cause. By analogy, it would be like judging the merits of college football by the way Vanderbilt's or Columbia's teams play rather than by the way Alabama's or Notre Dame's teams play. Actually, a fairer comparison would be to judge the socialist ideal of equality by what takes place in countries like Sweden and to judge the libertarian ideal of liberty by what takes place in the United States. Even these comparisons, however, are not wholly appropriate because none of these countries fully conforms to those ideals.

Welfare Liberal Justice: The Contractarian Perspective

Finding merit in both the libertarian's ideal of liberty and the socialist's ideal of equality, welfare liberals attempt to combine both liberty and equality into one political ideal that can be characterized as contractual fairness or maximal utility. A classical example of the contractual approach to welfare liberal justice is found in the political works of eighteenth-century German philosopher Immanuel Kant.

Immanuel Kant was born in 1724 in Konigsberg, East Prussia (now called Kaliningrad, and part of Russia) and he never journeyed more than forty miles from the city. Kant appears to have seriously entertained the possibility of marriage at least twice during his life. On one occasion he was in the process of assessing his financial situation to determine whether to propose to a young widow when the woman accepted a marriage proposal from someone else. On another occasion, a Westphalian visitor to Konigsberg, in whom Kant was interested, left town with her employer before Kant could make up his mind.

Kant was educated in Leibniz's philosophy, but later was profoundly influenced by Hume and Rousseau. By Kant's own admission, Hume awakened him from his dogmatic slumbers. However, Rousseau seemed to have had an even stronger influence on him. When he received a copy of Rousseau's *Emile* in 1762, his rigid schedule (rising, drinking coffee, writing, lecturing, dining, walking, each at a set time) was thrown out of kilter for two whole days while he read the book.

Kant's most important work, his *Critique of Pure Reason,* was published in 1781. After that his other famous writings followed in quick succession. In 1783 he published *Prologomena to Any Future Metaphysics;* in 1785, *Foundations of a Metaphysics of Morals;* in 1786, *Metaphysical First Principles of Natural Science;* in 1787, the second edition of *Critique of Pure Reason;* in 1788, *Critique of Practical Reason;* in 1790, *Critique of Judgment;* in 1792, *Theory and Practice;* in 1793, *Religion within the Bounds of Reason Alone;* in 1795, *Perpetual Peace;* and in 1797, *Metaphysics of Morals*.

Only once did Kant come into collision with political authority. That was in connection with his *Religion within the Bounds of Reason Alone*. The work was approved by the theological faculty of Konigsberg in 1793. But in 1794, the work was censured by Frederick William II, and Kant was forbidden to write or lecture on any religious subject. Kant accepted this censure, an act for which he was widely criticized.

Kant died in 1804. He was already fifty-seven years old when he published his *Critique of Pure Reason*. Consequently, his literary production from 1781 to the time of his death constitutes a remarkable performance. He was working on a restatement of his philosophy at the time of his death.

In *Theory and Practice,* Kant sets out his social contract justification of a civil state. Kant claims that a civil state ought to be founded on an original contract satisfying the requirements of freedom (the freedom to seek happiness in whatever way one sees fit as long as one does not infringe upon the freedom of others to pursue a similar end), equality (the equal right of each person to restrict others from using his or her freedom in ways that deny equal freedom to all), and independence (that independence of each person that is necessarily presupposed by the free agreement of the original contract).

According to Kant,

> An original contract by means of which a civil and thus completely lawful constitution and commonwealth can alone be established . . . [does not have to be assumed to] actually exist as a fact. . . . Such an assumption would mean that we would first have to prove from history that some nation, whose rights and obligations have been passed down to us, did in fact perform such a [contract] and handed down some authentic record or legal instrument, orally or in writing, before we could regard ourselves as bound by a pre-existing civil constitution.[13]

Kant argues that it suffices that the laws of a civil state are such that people would agree to them under conditions in which the requirements of freedom, equality, and independence obtain. Laws that accord with this original contract would then, Kant claims, give all members of society the right to reach any degree of rank that they could earn through their labor, industry, and good fortune. Thus, the equality demanded by the original contract would not, in Kant's view, exclude a considerable amount of economic liberty.

The Kantian ideal of a hypothetical contract as the moral foundation for a welfare liberal conception of justice has been further developed by John Rawls in his book *A Theory of Justice*. Rawls, like Kant, argues that

> principles of justice . . . are the principles that free and rational persons who are concerned to advance their own interests would accept in an initial position of equality.[14]

Yet Rawls goes beyond Kant by interpreting the conditions of his "original position" to explicitly require a "veil of ignorance." He writes:

> Among the essential features of this situation is that no one knows his place in society, his class position or social status, nor does any one know his fortune in the distribution of natural assets and abilities, his intelligence, strength and the like. I shall even assume that the parties do not know their conceptions of the good or their special psychological propensities.[15]

This veil of ignorance, Rawls claims, has the effect of depriving persons in the original position of the knowledge they would need to advance their own interests in ways that are morally arbitrary.

According to Rawls, the principles of justice that would be derived in the original position are the following:

I. A special conception of justice with a principle of equal political liberty, a principle of equal opportunity, and a principle requiring that the distribution of economic goods works to the greatest advantage of the least advantaged.

II. A general conception of justice with a principle requiring that the distribution of all social goods works to the greatest advantage of the least advantaged.

Rawls's general conception of justice differs from his special conception of justice by allowing trade-offs between political liberty and other social goods. According to Rawls, persons in the original position would want the special conception of justice to be applied in place of the general conception of justice whenever social conditions allow all representative persons to benefit from the exercise of their political liberties.

Rawls holds that these principles of justice would be chosen in the original position because persons so situated would find it reasonable to try to secure for themselves the highest minimum payoff. In effect, they would want to follow the conservative dictates of the "maximin strategy" and *max*imize the *min*imin payoff. Rawls describes their reasoning as follows:

> Now looking at the situation from the standpoint of one person selected arbitrarily, there is no way for him to win special advantages for himself. Nor, on the other hand, are there grounds for his acquiescing in special disadvantages. Since it is not reasonable for him to expect more than an equal share in the division of social goods, and since it is not rational for him to agree to less, the sensible thing for him to do is to acknowledge as the first principle of justice one requiring an equal distribution.[16]

Rawls goes on to argue:

> Thus, the parties start with a principle establishing equal liberty for all, including equality of opportunity, as well as an equal distribution of income and wealth. But there is no reason why this acknowledgment should be final. If there are inequalities . . . that work to make everyone better off in comparison with the benchmark of initial equality, why not permit them The immediate gain which a greater inequality might allow can be regarded as intelligently invested in view of its future return. If, for example, these inequalities set up various incentives which succeed in eliciting more productive efforts, a person in the original position may look upon them as necessary to cover the costs of training and to encourage effective performance.[17]

Rawls's defense of a welfare liberal conception of justice has been challenged in a variety of ways. Some critics have endorsed Rawls's contractual approach while disagreeing with Rawls over what principles of justice would be derived from it. These critics usually attempt to undermine the use of a maximin strategy in the original position. Other critics, however, have found fault with the contractual approach itself. One such critic is Oxford philosopher Ronald Dworkin.

Dworkin argues that hypothetical agreements, such as the agreement persons would make in the original position, do not (unlike actual agreements) provide independent arguments for the fairness of those agreements. He writes:

> [Rawls's] contract is hypothetical, and hypothetical contracts do not supply an independent argument for the fairness of enforcing their terms. A hypothetical contract is not simply a pale form of an actual contract; it is no contract at all.[18]

Dworkin asks us to consider the following example:

> Suppose I did not know the value of my painting on Monday; if you had offered me $100 for it then I would have accepted. On Tuesday I discover it was [more] valuable. You cannot argue that it would be fair for the courts to make me sell it to you for $100 on Wednesday. It may be my good fortune that you did not ask me on Monday, but that does not justify coercion against me later.[19]

Dworkin contends that the fact that on Monday he would have accepted your offer of $100 for a painting he owned, because he did not know the value of the painting, in no way shows that it would be fair to force him to sell the painting to you for $100 after he subsequently learns that the painting is valuable. Accordingly, Dworkin holds that the fact that persons would hypothetically agree to do something in the original position does not provide an independent argument for abiding by that agreement in everyday life.

But while it seems correct to argue, as Dworkin does, that the hypothetical agreement in the painting case does not support a demand that I presently sell you the painting for $100, it is not clear how this undermines the relevance of the hypothetical agreement that emerges from Rawls's original position. For surely Rawls need not endorse the view that *all* hypothetical agreements are morally binding. Nor could Dworkin reasonably argue that this example and the few others that he gives support the conclusion that *no* hypothetical agreements are morally binding. Because if that were the case, we could argue by analogy from the fact that *some* actual agreements are not binding (such as an agreement to commit murder), to the conclusions that *no* actual agreement is morally binding, which, of course, is absurd. Consequently, Dworkin would have to provide some further argument to show that the specific agreement that would result from the original position is not morally binding. He can't derive that conclusion simply from the premise that *some* hypothetical agreements (e.g. the one concerning the picture) is not morally binding.

Philosopher Richard Miller raises another challenge to Rawls's contractual approach. However, he does so from the point of view of Marxist social theory. Miller maintains that if certain elements of Marxist social theory are correct then neither Rawls's principles of justice nor any other candidates for "morally acceptable principles" would emerge from the original position.

Miller cites the following elements of Marxist social theory:

> no social arrangement that is acceptable to the best-off class is acceptable to the worst-off class; the best-off class is a ruling class, that is, a class whose interests are served by the major political and ideological institutions; and the need for wealth and power typical of the best-off class is much more acute than what is typical of the rest of society.[20]

What Miller is claiming is that if persons in the original position accepted these elements of Marxist social theory (and persons in the original position are presumed to have access to all available general information), then they would not choose Rawls's principles of justice nor any other "morally acceptable principles" you like.

Let us suppose, however, that the needs and interests of a society are in extreme conflict, and that the conflict has the form of what Marx calls "class conflict." Let us consider the case in which the opposing classes are the rich, propertied capitalist class and the poor, relatively propertyless proletariat class. No doubt persons in the original position would know that in such a society compliance with almost any principles of conflict resolution could be achieved only by means of a stringent enforcement system. But why should that fact keep them from choosing any principles of social cooperation whatsoever? Surely, persons in the original position would still have reason to provide for the basic needs of the members of the poor, relatively propertyless proletariat class because they may turn out to be in that class, and thus would be inclined to favor a basic needs social minimum.

Of course, the members of the capitalist class who have developed special needs for wealth and power could claim that they would suffer acutely in any transition to a society with a basic needs social minimum. Yet persons in the original position, imagining themselves to be ignorant of whether they belong to the capitalist or the proletariat class, would have grounds to discount such considerations in deciding upon principles of social cooperation. They would realize that members of the capitalist class are not "compelled" to pursue their interest by depriving the members of the proletariat class of an acceptable minimum of social goods. They act as they do, depriving others of an acceptable social minimum, simply to acquire more social goods for themselves. Unlike members of the proletariat class, the members of the capitalist class could be reasonably expected to act otherwise. Accordingly, persons in the original position would recognize this and require whatever sacrifice from the members of the capitalist class would be necessary to restore to the members of the proletariat class the benefits of a basic needs social minimum. In this way, it would be possible to derive from Rawls's original position acceptable results, even assuming conditions of class conflict.

Welfare Liberal Justice: The Utilitarian Perspective

One way to avoid the challenges that have been directed at a contractarian defense of welfare liberal justice is to find some alternative way of defending welfare liberal justice. Historically, utilitarianism has been thought to provide such an alternative defense, and John Stuart Mill is one of the classical defenders of this view.

John Stuart Mill was born in London in 1806. He was educated at home by his father, a prominent economist, and Jeremy Bentham, who were eager for a subject on whom to test out their educational theories. At age three, Mill learned Greek; at six, Latin. All the while, he was treated to an intensive regimen of mathematics and logic. Later, when he was twenty, Mill experienced a deep depression. He came to recognize that his education had provided him with little opportunity for emotional development, and he turned to Wordsworth and Coleridge, the great Romantic poets, and in other ways tried to compensate for this lack.

In 1823, Mill became a clerk with the East India Company and rose to the office of Chief Examiner. In 1830, he was introduced to Harriet Taylor, then married and mother of two children. She became his closest friend and confidant, and Mill credits her with inspiring much of his own thinking and writing. This unconventional relationship, lasting twenty years, estranged Mill from his family and most of their friends. In 1851, they were married, two years after her husband had died. Seven years later, Harriet herself died from tuberculosis, probably contracted from Mill, who was suffering from the disease. In 1865, Mill was elected to Parliament, despite his refusal to campaign, and served one term.

Mill published *On Liberty* in 1859, claiming that, more than anything else he wrote, this book was a joint production with Harriet Taylor. In 1863, he published *Utilitarianism,* and in 1869, *The Subjection of Women.* Cared for in his last years by his stepdaughter Helen, Mill died in Avignon in 1873 and was buried alongside Harriet.

In *Utilitarianism,* Mill argues that

> actions are right in proportion as they tend to promote happiness: wrong as they tend to produce the reverse of happiness.[21]

By happiness, Mill means pleasure and the absence of pain: by unhappiness, pain and the privation of pleasure. Mill differs from Bentham in maintaining that pleasures can be evaluated in terms of quality as well as quantity. According to Mill, the more desirable pleasures are those that would be preferred by competent judges who have experienced the alternatives. Applying this standard for evaluating pleasures, Mill contends:

> It is better to be a human being dissatisfied than a pig satisfied. . . . And if . . . the pig[s] are of a different opinion, it is because they only know their own side of the question.[22]

Now while most people tend to share Mill's preference for being human here, it is not clear how that preference could be supported by a competent judge who had experienced both alternatives. Experiencing what it is like to be a pig is not the same as imagining what it is like to be a human trapped in a pig's body!

In chapter 5 of *Utilitarianism*, Mill surveys various types of actions and situations that are ordinarily described as just or unjust, and concludes that justice simply denotes a certain class of very important rules, the adherence to which is essential for maximizing social utility. Mill writes:

> While I dispute the pretensions of any theory which sets up an imaginary standard of justice not grounded on utility, I account the justice which is grounded on utility to be the chief part, and incomparably the most sacred and binding part, of all morality.[23]

Thus, Mill rejects the idea that justice and social utility are ultimately distinct ideals, maintaining instead that justice is in fact derivable from the ideal of social utility. In this way, it is claimed that a Welfare Liberal Conception of Justice can be given a utilitarian foundation.

Nevertheless, a serious problem remains for this utilitarian defense of welfare liberal justice. There would appear to be ways of maximizing social utility overall that do an injustice to particular individuals. Think of the Roman practice of throwing Christians to the lions for the enjoyment of all those in the Colosseum. Didn't this unjust practice maximize social utility overall?

John Rawls makes the same point somewhat differently. He criticizes utilitarianism for thinking of society as a whole, as if it were just one person, and thereby treating the desires and satisfactions of separate persons as if they were the desires and satisfactions of just one person. He describes the utilitarian perspective as follows:

> Just as the well-being of a person is constructed from the series of satisfactions that are experienced at different moments in the course of his life, so in very much the same way the well-being of society is to be constructed from the fulfillment of the systems of desires of the many individuals who belong to it. Since the principle for an individual is to advance as far as possible his own welfare, his own system of desires, the principle for society is to advance as far as possible the welfare of the group, to realize to the greatest extent the comprehensive system of desire arrived at from the desires of its members.[24]

In just this way, Rawls claims, utilitarianism fails to preserve the distinction between persons. But is Rawls right? It may well be that a proper assessment of the relative merits of the contractual and utilitarian approaches to welfare liberal justice will turn on this very issue.

Communitarian Justice

Another prominent political ideal defended by contemporary philosophers is the communitarian ideal of the common good. As one might expect, many contemporary defenders of a communitarian conception of justice regard their conception as rooted in Aristotelian moral theory.

Aristotle was born in 384 B.C. in the northern Greek city of Stagira in Macedonia. His father, Nicomachus, held the post of physician to Amnytas II, King of Macedonia and the father of Philip the Great. When Aristotle was eighteen, he entered Plato's Academy, where he studied and taught for approximately twenty years. Plato is said to have considered him "the mind of the school." Nevertheless, after Plato's death, Aristotle was not named to head the Academy, and he decided to leave Athens. He went to Assos in Asia Minor where he married Pythias. They had a daughter, but after Pythias died, Aristotle took Herpyllis as a mistress and had a son by her, Nicomachus. In 343 B.C., Philip of Macedon invited Aristotle to tutor his thirteen-year-old son, Alexander, who would become Alexander the Great. During this period, Aristotle renewed his interest in politics, collecting and studying constitutions from around the world. Soon after the death of Philip, Aristotle returned to Athens and began his own school, the Lyceum. In adjacent buildings, Aristotle assembled a large library and a museum of natural history with the help of a grant of money from Alexander and specimens that Alexander had sent in from around his empire. There Aristotle worked for twelve or thirteen years, producing most of the works that survive to this day in the form of lecture notes. In response to the anti-Macedonian feeling that swept through Greece after the death of Alexander, Aristotle left Athens, lest, as he is said to have put it, the Athenians sin twice against philosophy. He died in Chalis one year later, in

322 B.C., at the age of sixty-two, leaving behind a will in which he provided for Herpyllis, their son, and his daughter by Pythias, and for the emancipation of his four slaves and their children. He also requested to be buried beside his wife Pythias.

In the *Nicomachean Ethics* (named after his son who is supposed to have edited these notes), Aristotle distinguishes between different varieties of justice. He points out:

> In one sense we apply the word "just" to things which produce and preserve happiness, and the things that form part of happiness for the community. And the law prescribes certain conduct; the conduct of a brave man (for instance, not to desert one's post, not to run away in battle, not to throw down one's arms); and that of a self-controlled man (for instance, not to commit adultery or violent assault); that of a good-tempered man (for instance, not to strike a person or to use abusive language) and similarly as to all the other forms of virtue—some acts the law enjoins and others it forbids, rightly if the law has been rightly framed and not so well if it has been drafted carelessly. . . . Justice thus understood therefore is not a part of virtue, but the whole of it, and its opposite, injustice, is not a part of vice, but the whole.[25]

Aristotle contrasts this sense of justice in which justice is understood as the whole of virtue, with justice as a particular part of virtue, in which justice is understood as what is fair or equal, and the just person is the person who takes only a proper share.

Aristotle focuses his discussion on justice in the latter sense, which further divides into distributive justice, corrective justice, and justice in exchange. Each of these varieties of justice can be understood to be concerned with achieving equality. For distributive justice it is equality between equals; for corrective justice it is equality between punishment and the crime; and for justice in exchange it is equality between whatever goods are exchanged. Aristotle also claims that justice has both its natural and conventional aspects: this twofold character of justice seems to be behind Aristotle's discussion of equity, in which equity, which is a natural standard, is described as a corrective to legal justice, which is a conventional standard.

Note that few of the distinctions Aristotle makes here seem tied to the acceptance of any particular conception of justice. One could, for example, accept the view that justice requires formal equality, but then specify the equality that is required in different ways. Even the ideal of justice as giving people what they deserve, which has its roots in Aristotle's account of distributive justice, is also subject to various interpretations. For an analysis of the concept of desert would show that there is no conceptual difficulty with claiming, for example, that everyone deserves to have his or her needs satisfied or that everyone deserves an equal share of the goods distributed by his or her society.

Consequently, Aristotle's account is primarily helpful for getting clear about the distinctions belonging to the concept of justice—distinctions that are common to all conceptions of justice.

If we turn to contemporary communitarians we find that rather than determining the particular requirements of their conception of justice, they have frequently chosen to defend their conception by attacking other conceptions of justice, and, by and large, they have focused their attacks on the welfare liberal conception of justice.

One of the best-known attacks of this sort has been put forth by political scientist Michael J. Sandel. Sandel claims that a welfare liberal conception of justice is founded on an inadequate conception of the nature of persons, according to which none of the particular wants, interests, or ends that we happen to have at any given time constitute who we are essentially. According to this conception, we are independent of and prior to all such wants, interests, or ends.

Sandel claims that this conception of the nature of persons is inadequate because

> we cannot regard ourselves as independent in this way without great cost to those loyalties and convictions whose moral force consists partly in the fact that living by them is inseparable from understanding ourselves as the particular persons we are—as members of this family or community or nation or people, as bearers of this history, as sons and daughters of that revolution, as citizens of this republic. Allegiances such as these are more than values I happen to have or aims I "espouse at any given time." They go beyond the obligations I voluntarily incur and the "natural duties" I owe to human beings as such. They allow that to some I owe more than justice requires or even permits, not by reason of agreements I have made but instead in virtue of those more or less enduring attachments and commitments which taken together partly define the person I am.[26]

Thus, according to Sandel, the conception of the nature of persons required by a welfare liberal conception of justice is inadequate because it fails to take into account the fact that some of our wants, interests, and ends are at least in part constitutive of who we are essentially. Without these desires, interests, and ends, we would not be the same persons we presently happen to be.

Sandel contends that welfare liberals are led to rely on this inadequate conception of persons for reasons that are fundamental to the conception of justice they want to defend. Specifically, welfare liberals want to maintain the priority of justice and, more generally, the priority of the right over the good. For example, according to Rawls:

> The principles of right and so of justice put limits on which satisfactions have value; they impose restrictions on what are reasonable conceptions

> of one's good. We can express this by saying that in justice as fairness the concept of right is prior to that of the good.[27]

To support these priorities, Sandel argues that welfare liberals endorse this inadequate conception of the nature of persons. For example, Rawls states that

> It is not our aims that primarily reveal our nature but rather the principles that we would acknowledge to govern the background conditions under which these aims are to be found and the manner in which they are to be pursued. *For the self is prior to the ends which are affirmed by it;* even a dominant end must be chosen from among numerous possibilities. . . . We should therefore reverse the relation between the right and the good . . . and view the right as prior.[28]

What this passage shows, according to Sandel, is that welfare liberals like Rawls believe that the priority of justice and the priority of the right are grounded in the priority of the self to its ends.

At first glance, Sandel's case against welfare liberalism looks particularly strong. After all, Rawls actually does say that "the self is prior to the ends which are affirmed by it," and this claim seems to express just the inadequate conception of the nature of persons that Sandel contends underlies a Welfare Liberal Conception of Justice. Nevertheless, Sandel's case against welfare liberalism presupposes that there is no other plausible interpretation that can be given to Rawls's claim than the one that Sandel favors. But there is another interpretation according to which to say that persons are prior to their ends simply means that they are morally prior to those ends, that is, that they are morally responsible for those ends to the degree that they can or could have changed them. Of course, the degree to which people can or could have changed their ends varies, but it is that which determines the degree to which we are morally responsible for those ends and, hence, morally prior to them.

Nor does this interpretation deny that certain ends may in fact be constitutive of the persons we are, so that if those ends were to change we would become different persons. We can see, therefore, that nothing in this interpretation of Rawls's claim presupposes a self that exists prior to all its ends. Rather, the picture we are given is that of a self that is responsible for its ends insofar as its ends can or could have been revised. Such a self may well be constituted by at least some of its ends, but it is only responsible for those ends to the degree to which they can or could have been revised. So the sense in which a self is prior to its ends is simply moral: insofar as its ends can or could have been revised, a self may be called upon to change them or compensate others for their effects when they turn out to be morally objectionable. Clearly, this interpretation of Rawls's claim avoids any commitment to the inadequate conception of the nature of persons which Sandel contends underlies a Welfare Liberal Conception of Justice. Of course, this does not show that a Communitarian Conception of

Justice might not in the end be the most morally defensible conception of justice. It only shows that this particular communitarian attack on a Welfare Liberal Conception of Justice is not successful.

Another communitarian attack on welfare liberalism has been put forward by Alasdair MacIntyre. In a recent article, MacIntyre argues that virtually all forms of liberalism attempt to separate rules defining right action from conceptions of the human good. He writes:

> This socially embodied divorce between rules defining right action on the one hand and conceptions of the human good on the other is one of those aspects of such societies in virtue of which they are entitled to be called liberal.[29]

MacIntyre contends that these forms of liberalism not only fail but have to fail because the rules defining right action cannot be adequately grounded apart from a conception of the good. According to MacIntyre,

> Adequate knowledge of moral rules is inseparable from and cannot be had without genuine knowledge of the human good.[30]

For this reason, MacIntyre claims, only some refurbished Aristotelian theory that grounds rules supporting right action in a complete conception of the good can ever hope to be adequate. MacIntyre's critique relates to the way that the contrast between liberals and their communitarian critics is usually formulated. Usually, liberals are said to defend the view that society should be neutral with respect to conceptions of the good, while communitarians are usually said to defend the view that society should enforce a particular conception of the good. For example, according to Ronald Dworkin,

> liberalism takes, as its constitutive political morality, that theory of equality [which holds that] political decisions must be, so far as possible, independent of any particular conception of the good life, or of what gives value to life.[31]

By contrast, MacIntyre contends that

> Any political society . . . which possesses a shared stock of adequately determinate and rationally defensible moral rules, publicly recognized to be the rules to which characteristically and generally unproblematic appeals may be made, will therefore, implicitly or explicitly, be committed to an adequately determinate and rationally justifiable conception of the human good.[32]

But this way of putting the contrast—liberals favoring neutrality with respect to conceptions of the good, and communitarians favoring commitment to a particular conception of the good—has bred only confusion. What it suggests is that liberals are attempting to be value neutral when they clearly are not. Liberals, like their communitarian critics, are committed to a substantive conception of the good. The relevant difference between liberals and communitarians is that liberals are only committed to a partial conception of the good whereas communitarians aspire to a relatively complete conception of the good. So it would be best to view most forms of liberalism as attempting to ground moral rules on part of a conception of the good—specifically, that part of a conception of the good that is more easily recognized, and needs to be publicly recognized, as good. For Rawls, for example, this partial conception of the good is a conception of fairness, according to which no one deserves his or her native abilities nor his or her initial starting place in society. Given this interpretation of liberalism, then, in order to properly evaluate the debate between liberals and communitarians, we would need to do a comparative analysis of their conceptions of the good with their practical requirements. However, since the conception of the good so far specified and defended by communitarians, like Sandel and MacIntyre, has few, if any, practical requirements when compared with the conceptions developed by liberal theorists, it is difficult to know if, where, and to what extent communitarianism and liberalism actually differ in their practical requirements.

Feminist Justice

Defenders of a feminist conception of justice present a distinctive challenging critique to defenders of other conceptions of justice. In his *The Subjection of Women* published in 1864, John Stuart Mill, one of the earliest male defenders of women's liberation, argues that the subjection of women was never justified but was imposed upon women because they were physically weaker than men. According to Mill,

> [T]his system of inequality . . . arose simply from the fact that from the very earliest twilight of human society, every woman (owing to the value attached to her by men, combined with her inferiority in muscular strength) was found in a state of bondage to some man. Laws and systems of polity always begin by recognizing the relations they find already existing between individuals. They convert what was a mere physical fact into a legal right, give it the sanction of society, and principally aim at the substitution of public and organized means of asserting and protecting these rights, instead of the irregular and lawless conflict of physical strength. Those who had already been compelled to obedience became in this manner legally bound to it.[33]

Mill argues that society must remove the legal restrictions that deny women the same opportunities enjoyed by men. However, Mill does not consider whether because of past discrimination against women it may be necessary to do more than simply remove legal restrictions: he does not consider whether positive assistance may also be required.

Usually, however, it is not enough simply to remove unequal restrictions to make a competition fair among those who have been participating. Positive assistance to those who have been disadvantaged in the past may also be required, as would be the case in a race where some were unfairly impeded by having to carry ten-pound weights for part of the race. To render the outcome of such a race fair, we might want to transfer the ten-pound weights to the other runners in the race, and thereby advantage the previously disadvantaged runners for an equal period of time. Similarly, positive assistance, such as affirmative action programs, may be necessary if women who have been disadvantaged in the past are now going to be able to compete fairly with men.

In his book *The Subjection of Women,* Mill also does not see any need to compensate women for the work they do in the home, whereas Harriet Taylor in her *Enfranchisement of Women* does see such a need. She writes:

> The truly horrible effects of the present state of the law among the lowest of the working population, is exhibited in those cases of hideous maltreatment of their wives by working men, with which every newspaper, every police report teems. Wretches unfit to have the smallest authority over any living thing, have a helpless woman for their household slave. These excesses could not exist if women both earned, and had the right to possess part of the income of family.[34]

In this work, Taylor also speaks out more strongly in favor of married women having a life and career of their own. In these respects, Taylor is clearly more in accord with present-day feminism than Mill is.

In her book *Justice, Gender and the Family,* contemporary political scientist Susan Okin argues, in basic agreement with Mill and Taylor, for the feminist ideal of a gender-free society. A gender-free society is a society where basic rights and duties are not assigned on the basis of a person's biological sex. In such a society, being male or female is not the grounds for determining what basic rights and duties a person has. Since a conception of justice is usually thought to provide the ultimate grounds for the assignment of rights and duties, we can refer to this ideal of a gender-free society as "feminist justice."

Okin goes on to consider whether John Rawls's welfare liberal conception of justice can support the ideal of a gender-free society. Noting Rawls's failure to apply his original position-type thinking to the institution of the family, Okin is skeptical about the possibility of using a welfare liberal ideal of fairness to support feminist justice. She contends that in a gender-structured society like our own, male philosophers cannot achieve the sympathetic imagination required to see things from the standpoint of women. In a gender-structured society, Okin claims, male philosophers cannot do the original position-type thinking required by the welfare liberal ideal of fairness because they lack the ability to put themselves in the position of women. As Okin puts it,

> For if principles of justice are to be adopted unanimously by representative human beings ignorant of their particular characteristics and positions in society, they must be persons whose psychological and moral development is in all essentials identical. This means that the social factors influencing the differences presently found between the sexes—from female parenting to all the manifestations of female subordination and dependence—would have to be replaced by genderless institutions and customs.[35]

So, according to Okin, original position-type thinking can only really be achieved in a gender-free society.

Yet at the same time that Okin despairs of doing original position-type thinking in a gender-structured society, like our own, she herself purportedly does a considerable amount of just that type of thinking. For example, she claims:

> Rawls's principles of justice would seem to require a radical rethinking not only of the division of labor within families but also of all the non-family institutions that assume it.[36]

She also claims that the abolition of gender seems essential for the fulfillment of Rawls's criterion of political justice. More specifically, she contends that

> if those in the original position did not know whether they were to be men or women, they would surely be concerned to establish a thoroughgoing social and economic equality between the sexes that would protect either sex from the need to pander to or servilely provide for the pleasures of the other. They would emphasize the importance of girls' and boys' growing up with an equal sense of respect for themselves and equal expectations of self-definition and development. They would be highly motivated, too, to find a means of regulating pornography that did not seriously compromise freedom of speech. In general, they would be unlikely to tolerate basic social institutions that asymmetrically either forced or gave strong incentives to members of one sex to serve as sex objects for the other.[37]

But which is it? Can we or can we not do the original position-type thinking required by a welfare liberal ideal of fairness? Okin's own work seems to demonstrate that we can do such thinking and that her reasons for thinking that we cannot are not persuasive. For to do original position-type thinking, it is not necessary that everyone be able to put themselves imaginatively in the position of everyone else. All that is necessary is that some people be able to do so. For some people may not be able to do original position-type thinking because they have been deprived of a proper moral education. Others may be able to do original position-type thinking only after they have been forced to mend their ways and live morally for a period of time.

Moreover, in putting oneself imaginatively in the place of others, one need not completely replicate the experience of others, for example, one need not actually feel what it is like to be a murderer to adequately take into account the murderer's perspective. Original position-type thinking with respect to a particular issue only requires a general appreciation of the benefits and burdens accruing to people affected by that issue. So with respect to feminist justice, we need to be able to generally appreciate what women and men stand to gain and lose when moving from a gendered society to a gender-free society.

Of course, even among men and women in our gendered society who are in a broad sense capable of a sense of justice, some may not presently be able to do such original position-type thinking with respect to the proper relationships between men and women; these men and women may only be able to do so after the laws and social practices in our society have significantly shifted toward a more gender-free society. But this inability of some to do original position-type thinking does not render it impossible for others, who have effectively used the opportunities for moral development available to them to achieve the sympathetic imagination necessary for original position-type thinking with respect to the proper relationships between men and women. In this way, Rawls's welfare liberal ideal of fairness can be used to support the ideal of a gender-free society.

Like Susan Okin, I also endorse a gender-free society, but I claim that to identify feminist justice with a gender-free society is to characterize the ideal only negatively. I maintain that the ideal so characterized tells us what we need to get rid of, not what we need to put in its place. A more positive characterization is provided by the ideal of androgyny. Putting the ideal of feminist justice more positively in terms of the ideal of androgyny also helps bring out why men should be attracted to feminist justice.[38]

I further maintain that the ideal of androgyny requires that traits that are truly desirable in society be equally available to both women and men, or in the case of virtues, equally expected of both women and men.[39] I contend that support for this ideal of androgyny can be derived both from a right to equal opportunity that is a central requirement of a Welfare Liberal Conception of Justice and from an equal right of self-development that is a central requirement of a Socialist Conception of Justice. This ideal requires that

> First, all children irrespective of their sex must be given the same type of upbringing consistent with their native capabilities. Second, mothers and

> fathers must also have the same opportunities for education and employment consistent with their native capabilities.[40]

And I go on to consider how achieving equal opportunity for women and men requires vastly improved day care facilities and flexible (usually part-time) work schedules for both women and men. Christina Sommers has criticized feminist philosophers, like Okin and myself, for what she considers to be an attack on the traditional family structures. She distinguishes liberal feminists from radical feminists. She contends that liberal feminists, like herself, want equal opportunity in the workplace and politics, but would leave marriage and motherhood "untouched and unimpugned." By contrast, Sommers contends that radical feminists are committed to an assimilationist or androgynous ideal that would destroy the (traditional) family and deny most women what they want. She writes:

> By denigrating conventional feminine roles and holding to an assimulationist ideal of social policy, the feminist movement has lost its natural constituency. The actual concerns, beliefs, and aspirations of the majority of women are not taken seriously except as illustrations of bad faith, false consciousness, and successful brainwashing.[41]

Sommers, however, never explains how it is possible to secure for women equal opportunity in the workplace and politics while rejecting androgyny in favor of traditional gender roles. For example, how could women be passive, submissive, dependent, indecisive and weak and still enjoy the same opportunities in the workplace and politics that are enjoyed by men who are aggressive, dominant, independent, decisive and strong?

Marilyn Friedman does not challenge Sommers's contention that radical feminists are committed to an assimilationist or androgynous ideal. Friedman does, however, question whether what Sommers supports is really what most women want. She writes:

> In one . . . study, 63 percent of women surveyed expressed preferences for nontraditional family arrangements.[42]

She also points out:

> The so-called "traditional family"—a nuclear family consisting of a legally married heterosexual couple and their children, in which the man is the sole breadwinner and "head" of the household, and the woman does the domestic work and childcare—comprises only 16 percent of U.S. households in 1977 according to the U.S. Census Bureau.[43]

In responding to Friedman, Sommers explains that what she means by a traditional family is one that consists of two heterosexual parents and one or more children in which the mother plays a distinctive gender role in caring for the children. This definition obviously broadens the class of families to which Sommers is referring. But in her response, Sommers goes on to renounce any attempt to be promoting the traditional family, even as she defines it. She writes:

> Friedman would have you believe that I am promoting (that is her word) the traditional family, promoting motherhood, promoting femininity. As a liberal feminist all I do promote is the right and liberty to live under the arrangement of one's choice.[44]

According to Sommers, if people want to live in nontraditional families, they should be free to do so.

Friedman further disagrees with Sommers's contention that what Rhett Butler is doing in *Gone with the Wind* when he forcefully carries Scarlett O'Hara up the stairs is raping her. In a subsequent response to Sommers, Friedman, noting that Scarlett O'Hara, although initially unwilling, later appears to be a willing sexual partner, defines "rape" as "any very intimate sexual contact which is *initiated* forcefully or against the will of the recipient." Friedman allows that others might want to define such activity as sexual domination rather than rape, but under either definition, Friedman condemns it, whereas Sommers does not. In her response, Sommers cites approvingly the following passage from Helen Taylor's book *Scarlett's Women: Gone with the Wind and Its Female Fans*. Helen Taylor writes:

> [T]he majority of my correspondents (and I agree) recognize the ambiguous nature of the encounter and interpret it as a scene of mutually pleasurable rough sex. . . . By far the majority of women who responded to me saw the episode as erotically exciting, emotionally stirring and profoundly memorable. Few of them referred to it as "rape."[45]

Yet however one assesses this debate between Sommers and Friedman, it seems clear that if feminist justice can, in fact, be shown to be compatible or required by the ideals of libertarian justice, welfare liberal justice, socialist justice and communitarian justice which many people hold dear, then the case for feminist justice would be strengthened immeasurably. In fact, it would make the practical requirements of feminist justice virtually inescapable.

Conclusion

In searching for a way of reasonably resolving the disputes about justice in which we are all involved, we have noted that five major conceptions of justice—libertarian justice with its ideal of liberty, welfare liberal justice with its ideal of contractual fairness or maximal utility, socialist justice with its ideal of equality, communitarian justice with its ideal of the common good, and feminist justice with its ideal of a gender-free society—when correctly interpreted, may not be all that different in their practical requirements. If this is the case, then to reasonably resolve disputes about justice, all we would have to do is get clear about what are the shared practical requirements of these conceptions of justice and then simply act upon them. But we have also noted that there is a need to broaden the application of these conceptions of justice to include distant peoples, future generations, and even the whole biotic community. Hopefully, this too can be done in a way that produces agreement on practical requirements.

Notes

1. John Rawls, *A Theory of Justice* (Cambridge: Harvard University Press, 1971), p. 3.
2. John Hospers, *Libertarianism* (Los Angeles: Nash, 1971); Douglas Den Uyl and Douglas Rasmussen, *The Philosophic Thought of Ayn Rand* (Chicago: University of Illinois Press, 1984).
3. Ayn Rand, *The Virtue of Selfishness* (New York: New American Library, 1963), p. 93.
4. Ibid.
5. John Hospers, "What Libertarianism Is," in *The Libertarian Alternative,* edited by Tibor Machan (Chicago: Nelson-Hall Inc., 1974), p. 3.
6. James P. Sterba, "A Libertarian Justification for a Welfare State," *Social Theory and Practice* (1985), pp. 291–2.
7. Tibor Machan, *Individuals and Their Rights* (La Salle: Open Court, 1989), pp. 104–7.
8. Karl Marx and Friedrich Engels, *Communist Manifesto* (London, 1888).
9. Karl Marx, *Critique of the Gotha Program,* edited by C. P. Dutt (New York: International Publishers, 1966), p. 10.
10. Edward Nell and Onora O'Neill, "Justice under Socialism," *Dissent* (1972), pp. 483–91.
11. James P. Sterba, *Morality in Practice,* 4th ed. (Belmont: Wadsworth Publishing Co., 1993), p. 18.
12. Robert Nozick, *State Anarchy and Utopia* (New York: Basic Books, 1974), p. 161.
13. Hans Reiss, ed., *Kant's Political Writings* (Cambridge: Cambridge University Press, 1970), p. 79.
14. Rawls, op. cit., p. 11.
15. Ibid.
16. Ibid., p. 150.
17. Ibid., p. 151.
18. Ronald Dworkin, "The Original Position," *University of Chicago Law Review* 40 (1973).

19. Ibid.
20. Richard Miller, "Rawls and Marxism," *Philosophy and Public Affairs* (1974), pp. 167–80.
21. John Stuart Mill, *Utilitarianism* (Indianapolis: Hackett Publishing Co., 1979), p. 7.
22. Ibid., p. 10.
23. Ibid., p. 58.
24. Rawls, op. cit., p. 22.
25. Aristotle, *Aristotle's Ethics for English Readers,* trans. H. Rackham (Oxford: Basil Blackwell, 1943), pp. 88–9.
26. Michael J. Sandel, *Liberalism and the Limits of Justice* (Cambridge University Press, 1982), p. 179.
27. John Rawls, *A Theory of Justice* (Harvard University Press, 1971), p. 31.
28. Ibid., p. 560.
29. Alasdair MacIntyre, "Privatization of the Good," *Review of Politics* (1990).
30. Ibid.
31. Dworkin, op. cit., p. 127.
32. MacIntyre, op. cit.
33. John Stuart Mill, *The Subjection of Women* (1869).
34. Harriet Taylor, *The Enfranchisement of Women* (1851).
35. Susan Okin, *Justice, Gender and the Family* (New York, 1989), p. 107.
36. Ibid., p. 104.
37. Ibid., pp. 104–5.
38. James P. Sterba, "Feminist Justice and the Pursuit of Peace," *Hypatia* (1994).
39. James P. Sterba, "Feminist Justice and the Family," in *Perspectives on the Family,* ed. Robert Moffat, Joseph Grcic and Michael Baylis (1990).
40. Ibid.
41. Christina Sommers, "Philosophers against the Family," in *Person to Person,* ed. George Graham and Hugh Lafollette (Philadelphia: Temple University Press, 1989).
42. Marilyn Friedman, "They Lived Happily Ever After: Sommers on Women and Marriage," *The Journal of Social Philosophy* (1991).
43. Ibid.
44. Christina Sommers, "Do These Feminists Like Women?" *The Journal of Social Philosophy* (1991).
45. Ibid.

PART IV

ECONOMIC INSTITUTIONS AND ETHICS

Institutions—such as markets and property rights—affect people's welfare in ways that need to be evaluated both in economic and ethical terms. Some economists may believe that the market is to be judged only on its efficiency in meeting wants, but Elizabeth Anderson, in two chapters, shows that moral concerns should play a part in our evaluations of the market. Some suggest that cost-benefit analysis is unproblematic, but how, Paul Streeten asks, are the interests of future people to be accounted for? Again, moral questions arise to complicate the issue. Explaining discrimination may be a matter of competing metaphors, Steven Shulman says, but how does one evaluate the moral content of the metaphors? Economic development may be simply a matter of finding the best means to economic growth, but what of non-economic considerations such as educating the population or the role of women, David Crocker asks?

It is often proposed that markets should be used to allocate goods and services wherever possible because they are more efficient than the alternatives. How can one evaluate such proposals? Elizabeth Anderson, in "The Ethical Limitations of the Market," suggests an answer. She argues that when we allocate a good or service through a certain institution such as the market, we treat it in accordance with the norms of that institution. Those norms may allow us to realize some values, but fail to realize—or even undermine—others. Thus, a good is properly traded on the market if its value is successfully realized by the norms of the market. Also, an institution like the market, together with its associated norms, embodies certain interpretations or ideals, while possibly denying or ignoring other ideals. To determine whether a good is appropriately distributed by the market, one can examine the rival ideals at stake. The way people value things when they are allocated through the market is what Anderson calls *use*. When we *use* something, we treat it in accordance with certain norms of the market:

> First, market relations are impersonal ones. Second, the market is understood to be a sphere in which one is free, within the bounds of the law, to pursue one's personal advantage unrestrained by any consideration of the advantage of others. Third, the goods traded on the market are exclusive and rivals in consumption. Fourth, the market is purely want-regarding: from its standpoint all matters of value are simply matters of personal taste. Finally, dissatisfaction with a commodity or market relation is expressed primarily by "exit," not "voice." (p. 182)

To determine whether a good should be traded on the market, according to Anderson, one should consult this list of market norms to see if they are compatible with the full realization of its values.

To illustrate the application of this theory, consider Anderson's treatment of the good of personal relationships. Anderson says that the practice of modern relationships is informed by the ideals of intimacy and commitment, as opposed to the ideal of market freedom embodied in the market. This means that the goods of personal relationships are, to a significant extent, shared ones. So, each partner enjoys those goods and knows that the other also enjoys them. And the goods at stake must be provided in the spirit of a gift, rather than out of narrow self-interest, meaning for Anderson that they must express a cognizance of and appreciation for the personal characteristics of the recipient.

All of this conflicts with the market norm of *impersonality*, which requires that goods be provided without regard to any characteristics of the buyer other than his or her willingness to pay. Also, the goods of personal relationships cannot be attained if they are given for base motives, like economic gain. Thus, Anderson argues, we can see that sexuality is not appropriately traded on the market. A prostitute is motivated by monetary gain and, in providing her sexual "services," does not respond to the personal qualities of his or her customer. Furthermore, the goods of personal relationships can be seen as "higher" than those of the market. By implicitly equating the personal goods of the prostitute with the money of the client, a lower good, prostitution degrades the prostitute. For these and other reasons cited by Anderson, prostitution does not realize the goods of love; thus, we should not distribute sex on the market.

Paul Streeten's chapter can also be seen as examining a moral limitation of market structures. Streeten asks what kind of consideration is owed the interests of future generations in making decisions today. Of course, the market in most cases is blind to such considerations, since it is oriented to the purchasing power of those who are alive today. If it is determined that future generations indeed should have some sort of moral standing in our deliberations, then we have a failure of the market and some kind of government intervention on their behalf may be needed. In instances when government intervention is already taken for granted, as in cases in which cost-benefit analysis is being used to evaluate a project, the interests or needs of the future represent at least an additional factor to be added to the analysis.

Streeten begins his essay by posing the paradox that while both growth advocates and environmental advocates seem concerned about the future, they strongly disagree on how the interests of future persons can best be served. Streeten points out that, of course, the paradox is resolved once one recognizes that the proponents of growth and the environmentalists have different factual and evaluative premises. For example, the latter see a greater likelihood of a sudden environmental turn for the worse in the future. Streeten discusses the possibility of reconciling the concerns of the growth advocates with those of the environmentalists by using a different measure of GNP that more accurately reflects the well-being of the population. For example, this measure might include social costs in addition to private ones, while excluding goods that were produced in order to alleviate problems that were generated by the economy in the first place.

Assuming that one decides to take into account the interests of future generations and that one decides to do so in a quantified, utilitarian way, one question that arises is whether and by how much costs and benefits in the future should be discounted. Streeten considers several arguments for discounting and rejects all of them, coming to the conclusion that discounting is not appropriate.

Streeten considers various practical issues raised by concerns about the future. He argues that such concerns are valid even when some members of the community have pressing needs right now, since both problems can be addressed at the same time. The author also says that some environmental problems require the kind of international cooperation possible only by granting power to some kind of international governmental authority.

Steven Shulman raises the issue of how racial discrimination can be explained and what role metaphors might play in such an explanation. While Shulman agrees economics is essentially metaphorical, he argues that the metaphors of economics are substantive, and not merely rhetorical. They have empirical content and suggest certain moral judgments. This is a crucial point, because it allows an opening for some possibility of evaluating alternative metaphors. Shulman illustrates this possibility by assessing the validity of two widely known metaphors for discrimination, those of the Nobel Laureates Gunnar Myrdal and Gary Becker.

In Becker's work, the operative metaphor for discrimination is the commodity. Racism amounts to a "taste for discrimination," which is represented as an argument in an agent's utility function, just like any other commodity. This interpretation, Shulman points out, suggests that racism is not unique in American society, but is rather on a par with a multitude of other such tastes.

Moreover, it suggests that racism might eventually be eliminated by competition, because the employer who has such tastes cannot operate as efficiently as the more open-minded one.

For Myrdal, on the other hand, it is the metaphor of the vicious circle that is central. There are three main factors at work, and they are mutually reinforcing. The three keys factors are economic conditions, black standards and manners of living, and discrimination. Myrdal, unlike Becker, emphasizes the uniqueness of discrimination as a social problem in America. He argues that a dilemma exists in the United States because racism is at odds with American democratic values.

Shulman considers the content of these models of discrimination and finds that they are empirically unsatisfactory, since they cannot explain why the unemployment gap between blacks and whites has increased in recent years, while the wage gap has diminished. Shulman's solution to this empirical problem is a model that combines elements of both Becker's and Myrdal's metaphors. In that model, employers weigh various costs and benefits of discrimination in deciding whether to discriminate; recent changes in costs and benefits of different kinds of discrimination have made employment discrimination relatively more advantageous for employers than wage discrimination.

The next selection is a second piece by Elizabeth Anderson. In this chapter, she applies her theory of what goods are properly traded on the market to the case of commercial surrogate mothering. In keeping with the approach developed in the first chapter in this section, Anderson asks if the goods of women's labor are best realized when they are treated as commodities. She argues that they are not, for two sets of reasons, one relating to the commodification of the mother's "services" and another centering on the commodification of the children themselves.

We focus here on the argument regarding the commodification of children. At issue once again in this case are several rival modes of valuation. Anderson argues that the values involved are best served when children are valued according to the norms of parental love, rather than those of the market. These norms require that parents act in the interests of children, or in the family's shared interests; on the other hand, surrogate mothers must give up the children involved for private gain, without taking into account the interests of the child. Also, the norms of parental love dictate that the parents love their child unconditionally, and not on the basis of any particular characteristics of the child. The parents who acquire the child from a surrogate mother violate this norm, because they choose the mother based partly on IQ and other characteristics, so as to ensure the "quality of the product." Finally, like the surrogate mother, the surrogacy agency acts solely in the interests of the couple who pay the fee, for example, by doing everything in its power to pry the child free from the birth mother. All of these violations of parental norms amount to treating the child as a commodity, which is degrading to the child. It is easy to dismiss such effects as merely symbolic, but children in general may be hurt by the degradation, if, for example, they come to fear being sold themselves.

In the final chapter in this section, David Crocker documents the recent emergence of the field of developmental ethics and attempts to suggest some of the factors behind this emergence. He points out that the seminal works on development ethics were written in the early 1960s. He describes a diverse group of scholars and practitioners—from both the developing and developed world—who have taken up the cause since that time.

There are five considerations, according to Crocker, that support the need for this kind of work. The first is that moral questions and dilemmas come up every day in the practice of development. For example, when the exigencies of economic development threaten the integrity of local cultures, how should the conflict be resolved? The second consideration is changes that have taken place in theories of development and underdevelopment. Many authors in the development area have recently seen the need to consider the ultimate purpose of development. This raises the issue of what constitutes true development. These issues are important and cannot be separated from more instrumental issues. A third factor that has encouraged the consideration of ethical issues in development is the author's notion of a "theory-practice." This concept represents an attempt to avoid a specious dichotomy between pure and applied fields.

A fourth impetus for the rise of development ethics is the end of another dichotomy—the fact-value distinction, which is the subject of a separate section of this book. The notion of a "value-free" social science has been under fierce attack from many quarters for a long time. If critics are right, and the distinction is fallacious, then we have no reason to keep moral considerations separate from empirical ones, and the way is cleared for a morally informed development field. Finally, Crocker argues that recent trends in, and problems with, Anglo-American philosophy are one source of the interest in the ethics of development. Anglo-American philosophy has taken a greater interest in practical issues in recent years. Crocker argues that both philosophers and development people have much to learn from one another. However, Anglo-American philosophy cannot be simply adopted wholesale by the development field; it must change and grow to fill its new role. The most obvious example is that philosophers must become informed about the developing world.

These are but a few of the possible examples of ethical concerns that emerge from a consideration of the impact of the market as an economic institution.

14.

THE ETHICAL LIMITATIONS OF THE MARKET

Elizabeth Anderson

A distinctive feature of modern capitalist societies is the tendency of the market to take over the production, maintenance, and distribution of goods that were previously produced, maintained, and distributed by nonmarket means. Yet, there is a wide range of disagreement regarding the proper extent of the market in providing many goods. Labor has been treated as a commodity since the advent of capitalism, but not without significant and continuing challenges to this arrangement. Other goods whose production for and distribution on the market are currently the subject of dispute include sexual intercourse, human blood, and human body parts such as kidneys. How can we determine which goods are properly subjects of market transactions and which are not? The purpose of this article is to propose a theory of what makes economic goods differ from other kinds of goods, which can help to answer this question.

I propose that we think of economic goods as those goods whose dimensions of value are best realized within market relations. The market, like any other social institution, embodies norms regulating the production, exchange, and enjoyment of goods that are sensitive to some qualitative distinctions among values and insensitive to others. These norms also foster and sustain certain shared understandings of the interactions and relations of the participants and thereby promote particular ideals of self and society. The ethical limitations of the market (or any other system of social relations) can thus be explored in part by seeking the answers to three questions.

Economics and Philosophy 6, no. 2 (1990): 179–205.

First, what dimensions of value in things, relationships, and persons are acknowledged and successfully realized, or ignored and undermined, by the norms of the market? Second, what are the ideals of self and society that the market attempts to embody? Do market institutions embody an adequate interpretation of these ideals, or do they fail to realize the ideals to which they aim to give expression? Third, does the extension of the market to a certain realm undermine the realization of other ideals?

This chapter has four parts. In the first part, I explore the ideals and social relations of the market. In the next two parts, I contrast economic values with the values of personal relationships and of social democracy. For each of these other two spheres of life, several cases will be examined in which values are undermined when the norms of the market come to govern them. In the final section, I draw some general conclusions about the limitations of the market and of welfare economics as a theory of value.

The Ideals and Social Relations of the Modern Market

We can understand the nature of economic goods by investigating the ways we value commodities; the social relations within which we produce, distribute, and enjoy them; and the ideals which these relations are supposed to embody.[1] The most important ideal that the modern market attempts to embody is a particular conception of freedom. On this view, freedom is primarily exercised in the choice and consumption of commodities in private life. It consists in having a large menu of choices in the marketplace and in exclusive power to use and dispose of things and services in the private sphere without having to ask permission from anyone else.[2]

The economic ideal of freedom is closely linked with the way we value commodities. I call this mode of valuation "use" and contrast it in three ways with other modes of valuation that demand constraints on use. First, I follow Kant in contrasting "use" with higher forms of regard, such as respect. To merely use something is to subordinate it to one's own ends, without regard for whatever intrinsic value it might have. For example, several years ago certain owners of David Smith sculptures stripped the paint off of these works because Smith's unpainted works were selling for more money than his painted works were. These owners treated Smith's art as a mere commodity, since they disregarded its intrinsic aesthetic worth in favor of its mere usefulness for their independently defined ends. Second, use is an impersonal mode of valuation. It is contrasted with valuing something for its personal or sentimental attachments to oneself, as when one cherishes an heirloom. A mere commodity is something one regards as interchangeable with any other item of the same kind and quality and something that one is prepared to trade with equanimity for any other commodity at some price. But a cherished item is viewed as unique and irreplaceable. Since it is valued for its special connections to the self, it is sold only under duress, and its loss is felt as a personal one (Simmel, 1978, pp. 123, 404, 407). Finally, use values may be contrasted with shared values, whose value for oneself is dependent on other people also enjoying them. Such values cannot be realized in private acts of use, but rather reside in a shared public understanding of the meanings of the goods. For example, certain sites of historical events may be valued as parts of a national heritage or the layout of a neighborhood valued as the locus of a particular community. Again, the preservation of these values requires constraints on use. For instance, zoning laws may be required to preserve the architectural integrity of a city or rent control required to enable a community's residents to remain living together as members of a community.

The market ideal of freedom has a special connection with the mode of valuation of commodities known as use. For the freedom that the market gives us is the freedom to use commodities without the constraints implied by other modes of valuation. The realization of the noneconomic values that inhere in things often requires constraints on use and, hence, constraints on the degree to which these things are treated as commodities. But to explore these points, we must achieve a fuller understanding of the distinctive character of economic goods. This requires an investigation into the social relations of the market.

Five features of the social norms and relations of the market are particularly important for understanding the distinctive character of economic values. First, market relations are impersonal ones. Second, the market is understood to be a sphere in which one is free, within the limits of the law, to pursue one's personal advantage unrestrained by any consideration for the advantage of others. Third, the goods traded on the market are exclusive and rivals in consumption. Fourth, the market is purely want-regarding: from its standpoint all matters of value are simply matters of personal taste. Finally, dissatisfaction with a commodity or market relation is expressed primarily by "exit," not "voice." That is, one simply drops out of the market relationship rather than sticking with it and trying to reform it from within. Actual market practices often deviate in significant ways from the patterns described here. But these patterns are still characteristic of the market. They express a shared understanding of the purpose and meaning of market relations that I believe every experienced participant in the modern market will recognize. Let us examine each of these features in more detail.

Perhaps the most characteristic feature of market relations is their impersonality. The producers and consumers of economic goods are typically strangers. Each party to a market transaction views one's relation to the other as merely a means to the satisfaction of ends defined independently of the relationship and of the other party's ends. The parties have no precontractual obligations to provide one another with the goods they exchange. They deal with one another on an explicit basis of exchange, in which each good that changes hands has its equivalent in return. The explicit basis of exchange serves to guarantee mobility. If each transaction between buyer and seller can be completed to the reciprocal advantage of each, leaving no unpaid debts on either side, then nothing ties the parties together over time. They are free to change their trading partners at any time.

The impersonality of market relations thus defines a sphere of freedom from personal ties and obligations. There is another side to this impersonal freedom: one need not exhibit any specific personal characteristics or invoke any special relationships to gain access to the goods traded on the market. The market is open to all indifferently, as long as they have the money to pay for the goods. Money income—not one's personal status, characteristics, or relationships—is what determines one's access to the realm of commodity values.[3]

The impersonality of the market leaves its participants free to pursue their individual interests unrestrained by any consideration of other people's advantage. Each party to a market transaction is expected to take care of himself and not to depend on the other to look after his own interests. Every extension of the market thus represents an extension of the sphere of egoism. Indeed, the market would not be economically efficient if each party to a transaction tried to satisfy the other's preferences at his own expense. The success of a commercial transaction, its bringing benefit to both parties, depends on the possibility of drawing sharp lines between the interests of the negotiators. One must be able to define and satisfy one's interests independently of the other. This is why the market is a domain for the expression of individualism—one cannot function successfully in it without drawing a clear distinction between self and other.

Individuals' interests are independently definable and satisfiable only with respect to a certain class of goods. Such goods have the properties of exclusivity and rivalry in consumption. A good is exclusive if access to its benefits can be limited to the purchaser. If there is no means of excluding people from enjoying a good, it is impossible to charge a price for it. A good is a rival in consumption if the amount that one person consumes reduces the total amount of it available to others (Fisher, 1981, p. 175). The value that can be obtained from commodities is rival, since it is typically realized through personal appropriation and use. Insofar as another person with distinct ends gains control over it, I lose such control and consequently lose the use value of the good. The value of a rival good cannot be given to another without losing it oneself. But many goods are not rival—I do not lose, but rather enhance my knowledge, or my pleasure in a joke, by conveying these goods to others.

A further feature of the market is that it is a want-regarding institution. What it responds to is "effective demand," that is, desires backed up by money or the willingness to pay for things. Commodities are exchanged without regard for the reasons people have in wanting them. This fact has two implications. First, it means that the market does not respond to needs as such and does not draw any distinction between urgent needs and intense desires. Second, the market does not draw any distinction between reflective desires, which can be backed up by reasons or principles, and mere matters of taste. Since it provides no means for discriminating among the reasons people have for wanting or providing things, it cannot function as a forum for the expression of principles about the things traded on it. The market conception of personal autonomy reflects this fact. The market provides individual freedom from the value judgments of others. It does not regard any one individual's preferences as less worthy of satisfaction than anyone else's, as long as one can pay for one's own satisfaction. But it provides this freedom at the cost of reducing preferences, from the market's point of view, to mere matters of taste, about which it is pointless to dispute (Sheffrin, 1978).

A final feature of economic relations is that an individual's influence on the provision and exchange of commodities is primarily exercised through "exit," not "voice" (Hirschman, 1970). The counterpart to the customer's freedom to stop purchasing a particular product or to stop patronizing a particular retail outlet is the producer's freedom to say "take it or leave it." The customer has no voice—that is, no right to directly participate in the design of the product or to determine how it is marketed.

In the light of this account of the norms of the market, we can offer a more precise account of an economic good. A thing is an economic good if its production, distribution, and enjoyment is properly governed by these five norms, and its value can be fully realized through use. These criteria allow us to anticipate the shape of arguments that certain goods should not be treated as commodities. There may be certain values that are realized only if the exchange of particular goods is responsive to personal characteristics or takes place on a nonexplicit basis of exchange. Our ability to realize other goods may be impaired if we view them as exclusive and rival, rather than as shared. In the next section, I show how many of the goods of personal relationships have these characteristics. Some ideals may be realized only if the provision of certain goods is responsive to the needs of others or reflects shared principles and not just individual matters of taste. And the realization of a good as shared, or as reflecting principles, may require that its distribution be regulated through institutions of voice rather than exit. In the third section of this chapter, I show how many of the goods of social democracy are of this kind.

Since these arguments are based on comparisons of ideal types, some observations about the limitations of ideal typical analysis is in order. Any particular social institution or practice is apt to diverge from its ideal type in multifarious and complex ways and to include mixtures of norms more prominently associated with institutions and practices in other spheres of life. And the norms that presently govern our actual practices often inadequately express the ideals these practices are supposed to embody. The arguments I present are intended to highlight evaluative considerations that find little place in the standard models for criticizing market and other institutions—that is, in welfare economics and in most liberal theories of justice. The standard models highlight other evaluative considerations, such as efficiency, that are also important. Hence, any move from a relative evaluation of ideal types to a relative evaluation of actual practices must be informed by a detailed empirical investigation of the actual norms they embody, an evaluation of how well they combine norms from different spheres, how well these norms express the ideals in terms of which they are justified, and how well the practices fare by other criteria such as justice and efficiency. Since I obviously cannot provide such details here, the cases I discuss should be taken as illustrations of the kinds of arguments I wish to endorse and not as comprehensive evaluations of the practices in question.

The Values of Personal Relationships and the Market

The sphere of personal relationships is in many ways the polar opposite to that of market relationships. For, as we shall see, the ideals of personal relationships are embodied in norms of exchange that directly conflict with market norms. Two of many ideals central to the personal sphere of life are intimacy and commitment. Living on intimate terms with another person involves a mutual revelation of private concerns and sharing of cherished emotions that are responsive to the other's personal characteristics. This is the romantic side of personal relations, which involves passion, affection, and trust but not necessarily devotion or long-term commitment to the other person, for the romantic relationship may end as soon as the passions that animate it cool.

The deepest ideal of commitment involves dedicating oneself to living a shared life with another person on a permanent basis. A shared life is not simply a life of long-term cooperation on mutually advantageous terms, as might be true of a business partnership. It is founded on values that the persons committed to each other hold together. The central goods realized in such a life are shared in at least two senses. First, their goodness for each partner partially consists in the facts that the other partner also enjoys them, and that each partner knows this fact and knows that the other knows. One committed and loving partner could not rejoice in living with the other if he knew that the other found the relationship to be oppressive. The goods of intimacy are also shared in this first sense. Second, the realization of the good requires an expansive understanding of the self as including another person. The persons to whom the good is good are not selves regarded as isolated individuals, but selves regarded as members of the committed relationship. Commitment to a shared life, such as a marriage, requires redefining one's interests as interests of the *couple* in the marriage. Insofar as one has this commitment, one's interest in the aims of the marriage can neither be defined nor satisfied independently of one's being joined with one's spouse in marriage.[4] This is why marrying just for money is base: it takes advantage of an institutional form of commitment merely for the sake of lower goods definable independently of it.

These ideals inform the ways we value the people with whom we have personal relationships and the ways we value the goods we exchange with them. In this sphere love, affection, trust, and devotion supercede the formal respect of useful persons (acknowledgment of their autonomy) characteristic of the marketplace. The goods exchanged and jointly realized in friendship are valued less through use than through appreciation and cherishing, for they are tokens of shared understandings, affections, and commitments.

If the ways we value the goods proper to friendship differ from the ways we value commodities, then we should expect that the norms that govern the exchange of these goods should also differ; for different modes of valuation are embodied in different norms of exchange, production, and enjoyment. This is what we do find. A fundamental contrast between the sphere of personal relations and that of the market is that the former is properly governed by the spirit of the gift rather than the spirit of commercial exchange. The goods proper to the personal sphere can only be fully realized if they are given as gifts or established through the exchange of gifts. They are goods that cannot be genuinely procured for oneself by paying others to produce them or by appealing to another's merely personal advantage to provide them. The authenticity and worth of these goods depend on the motives that people have in providing them. Among these goods are trust, loyalty, conviviality, sympathy, affection, admiration, companionship, and devotion. None of these goods can be bought (or extracted by threats), although people often deceive themselves in the attempt, mistaking flattery for admiration and subservience for devotion.

The significance of gift exchange differs from that of market exchange in several respects (Hochschild, 1983; Hyde, 1983; Mauss, 1967; Sahlins, 1972; Titmuss, 1971). In the first place, the exchange of gifts affirms and continues the ties that hold the donor and recipient together. This is why refusing a gift is often an insult to a friend, but refusing a trade is merely an unrealized financial gain to a retailer. To reject an appropriate gift is to refuse to acknowledge or sustain a friendship. One point of gift exchange is to realize a shared value in the relationship itself, whereas the point of a market relationship is purely instrumental and realizes distinct goods for each party. Moreover, while both forms of exchange involve reciprocity, the shape and timing of the return of goods differ in the two cases. In market exchange, a delay in reciprocation (unless explicitly arranged in a contract) is cause for legal action. But the exchange of gifts among friends usually incorporates an informal understanding of reciprocity only in the long term. To be anxious to "settle accounts," as when one person insists upon splitting a restaurant tab exactly in half, calculating sums to the penny, or paying a friend for returning a library book, is to reject the logic of friendship. The delay in reciprocation symbolizes the fact that goods are given for the friend's sake, not for the sake of obtaining some good for oneself in return. Moreover, the accounting mentality reflects an unwillingness to be in the debt of another and hence an unwillingness to enter into the longer term commitments that such debts entail. For the debts of friendship—that is, the goods friends owe to one another—are not of a kind that they can be repaid in such a way as to leave nothing between the friends.

Friendly gift exchange is responsive to the personal characteristics of the friends involved and to the particular qualities of their relationship. We seek to give to our friends gifts that have more than merely generic meaning, gifts whose full meaning is conditioned by who gave the gift, to whom it was given, and the character of their friendship. For the gift is a vehicle for the expression of the friends' mutual understanding of how their relationship stands (or how the giver wishes it to be), and not merely a good of impersonal use value to the receiver. This fact is evident not only in cases of such material gifts as engagement rings and Valentine's Day chocolates, but also in the exchange of compliments, affections, and jokes. Max knows that Adam is just the person to appreciate *this* practical joke coming from *him*, but takes care to offer a more serious expression of affection to his girlfriend Marsha, who finds practical jokes rather vulgar. This is why cash is usually such an inappropriate gift between friends. Since it can be used by anyone to acquire any commodity, it expresses nothing of the giver's personality, of any particular thought the giver had for the receiver, or of the receiver's interests.

In the light of this brief account of some fundamental differences between the norms of the market and of personal relations, we can explore some of the ways values are undermined when the norms of the market come to govern the exchange of goods proper to personal relations. Consider the following cases of the importation of market norms in the exchange of personal values: prostitution, the exploitative manipulation of gift relations in commercial transactions, the detailed marriage contract advocated by *Ms.* magazine, and the practice of making loans between friends.

Prostitution is the classic example of the debasement of a gift value through its commodification. But what is base about buying and selling sexual "services" on the market? One cannot understand what makes this practice base without understanding the specifically human good achieved when sexual acts are exchanged as gifts. This good is founded on a mutual recognition of the partners as sexually attracted to each other and as affirming an intimate relationship in their mutual offering of themselves to each other. This is a shared good: one and the same good is realized for both partners in their action, and part of its goodness lies in the mutual understanding that it is shared. The couple rejoices in their *union*, and not simply each in his or her own distinct physical gratification. As a shared good, it cannot be realized except through each partner reciprocating the other's gift *in kind*, offering his or her own sexuality in the same spirit in which the other's sexuality is received—as a genuine offering of the self.

When sexual "services" are sold on the market, the kind of reciprocity required to realize human sexuality as a shared good is broken. The prostitute does not respond to the customer as a sexually attractive person, but merely as someone willing to put down the cash. So it is not the customer as a person that attracts the prostitute, but only his or her wealth. This is simply the counterpart to the impersonality of the market: one need not display any personal characteristics to obtain the goods sold there. And the customer seeks only sexual gratification from the prostitute, not a physical union. Sexuality as a specifically human, shared good cannot be achieved except through gift exchange; market motives cannot provide it.

The failure of reciprocity implied in the sale of sexual services signifies not simply a failure to realize a good, but a degradation of the prostitute, whose sexuality is reduced to the status of a mere service to the customer: sexuality is equated with the lesser good of money.[5] The prostitute's subordination is expressed in the fact that (except in the most blatantly alienated and sterile encounters), he or she must confer on the customer all manner of personal attentions, while the customer need pay attention only to him- or herself, recognizing the prostitute only as an object for satisfaction.

The problems entailed by explicitly exchanging sexual acts for money arise in part because sexual acts, insofar as they are more than means for sheer physical gratification, are valuable as expressions of underlying noncommercial motives and understandings. Since the expressive content of actions cannot be traded on the market, only those goods that are valuable to the receiver apart from their being expressions of the giver's motivations are genuine commodity values. The attempt to sell gift values on the market makes a mockery of those values and subordinates the provider of them.[6]

Other values are undermined when goods offered in the spirit of the gift have been solicited in the spirit of commercial exchange. These arise because the forms of reciprocity appropriate to gift (personal) relationships differ from those appropriate to market relationships. One basic kind of exploitation occurs when one party to an exchange gives goods to the other in accordance with the norms of gift exchange, while the other party returns goods in accordance with the norms of market exchange. Since gift exchange does not involve the demand for an immediate quid pro quo, the party taking a market orientation to the transaction can extract a greater share of goods from the gift giver than one returns.

This kind of exploitation occurs when firms attempt to establish a paternalistic relationship with their employees. By putting them in a dependent position and providing, however meagerly, for their needs, the firm can engender feelings of gratitude and loyalty on the part of its employees. These feelings can then be exploited to extract more labor and obedience from the employees. This has been a common practice of employers of migrant farm workers and sharecroppers. The latter are placed in the position of children to their parents because they have nowhere else to turn for the provision of basic needs. This dependency is reinforced by the fact that wages are paid largely in kind rather than cash. Cash payment would free the worker to purchase his needs from another source and thereby enable him to affirm at least some minimal autonomy from the employer.[7] Paternalistic practices are not confined to backward commercial enterprises. Young women training to be flight attendants are housed by airlines in airport dormitories and encouraged to regard their supervisors as substitute parents to whom they can come to confide any personal problems. They are thus encouraged to develop ties of loyalty and trust with their employers and to work for them in this spirit. But at the same time they are constantly reminded that these ties are not reciprocal: poor performance or disobedience can lead to immediate dismissal, since the tight job market ensures no shortage of job applicants (Hochschild, 1983, pp. 89–101).[8]

Even the impersonal exchanges of civility follow the norms of gift exchange and consequently can be exploited in commercial transactions. One common sales technique is to take advantage of people's desire to be polite, by manipulating them into a position in which it seems that they can back out of a deal only by risking offense or awkwardness. So car salesmen ask reluctant customers questions such as, "Do you doubt the integrity of our dealership?" knowing that most people will go to great lengths to avoid giving offense, and that each "no" they receive to questions like this undermines their ability to explain their reasons against signing the dotted line. The salesman's advantage consists in the fact that he participates in the negotiation strictly in accordance with market norms of pursuing maximum personal advantage, while the customer is manipulated into conceding his bargaining edge because he views some of their verbal exchanges as merely polite ones. Since civility often requires that we hide our frank opinions, we feel uncomfortable in explaining exactly why we don't want to buy. The remark delivered in the spirit of civility ("No, I don't mistrust your dealership") is then seized in the spirit of negotiation and used to the salesman's advantage by being interpreted as a literal expression of the customer's belief.

In these cases of exploitation, one party uses the norms of the market to manipulate the exchange of sentiments and civilities that are properly governed by the norms of gift exchange. When both sides adopt the norms of the market to govern the exchange of gift values, we no longer have a case of exploitation, but other losses still occur. Such is the case with the kind of detailed marriage contract advocated several years ago by *Ms.* magazine.[9] In the interests of avoiding the exploitative tendencies of traditional marriages, in which most of the drudgery involved in maintaining a household and raising children is left for the wife to perform, *Ms.* proposed to place the marriage relationship on an explicit basis of exchange. Henceforth, the duties of husband and wife with respect to the household, children, and sexual interactions were to be laid out in detail in the marriage contract.

While the intentions of *Ms.* in promoting equality in marriage are noble, the attempt to enforce this equality by remaking the marriage on the same terms as a business partnership threatens to undermine the goods of commitment and intimacy proper to marriage. For the realization of these goods depends on each partner carrying out the projects and tasks constitutive of their shared life in a spirit of trust and love rather than of contractual obligation and the piecemeal calculation of individual advantage. Giving and receiving in a spirit of trust is itself one of the goods of marriage. The point of marriage in realizing shared goods is obscured by tending to the terms of the explicit marriage contract, which evaluates the marriage in terms of the distinct advantages accruing to each party. And fixing the terms of exchange in advance undermines the responsiveness of the marriage to the changed needs of the partners, as well as the promise it holds out for deepening their commitment in the light of a more articulate understanding of their shared project, which may require a new division of activities between them. Being open to the possibility of renegotiating the contract in the light of changed wants is not the same thing as committing oneself to love and care for one's spouse "for better, for worse" (Hirsch, 1976, pp. 87–88, 99–101).[10]

These examples show how the norms of the market and of personal relationships are not easily mixed, because adherence to these norms secures quite different kinds of goods. Consider, as a final example of this problem, the basis for discouraging friends from making substantial long-term loans to one another.[11] Loaning money to a friend threatens the friendship in at least two ways. By undermining the equality of friends, it fosters resentment on the part of the debtor. And by tying down his financial resources without prospect for gaining from his friend, it undermines the capacity of the creditor to pursue successfully his advantage on the market and thus fosters resentment on his part. It might be thought that charging interest between friends would restore equality and prevent the creditor from thinking he is losing out by loaning to a friend. But this expedient threatens the friendship even more deeply than a loan without interest. To charge the prevailing interest rate is to permit the norms of strangers interacting merely from self-interest to govern the interactions of friends. Such an act encourages the friends to view their interests as sharply divided and to view themselves as having to be on their guard in protection of their interests when dealing with friends. But friendship is supposed to preserve a sphere of relationships in which one does not have to be on one's guard. Successful participation in both spheres of life thus requires an isolation of their respective concerns.

Political Values and the Market

The preceding section emphasized two qualitative distinctions among goods to which the market is insensitive: between gift values and ordinary exchange values, and between shared goods and divisible goods. I argued that the goods of the personal sphere, which are shared gift values, cannot be adequately realized within the norms of the market. This section will emphasize two further qualitative distinctions among goods that the market does not acknowledge: between ideals and ordinary goods, and between the objects of need and of desire. I shall argue that these distinctions support the application of several norms of democratic political life to the production, distribution, and enjoyment of a variety of goods that could also be provided by the market. As in the case of the economic and personal spheres, the significance of these norms must be understood in the light of the ideals they are supposed to embody. In this section, I focus on two ideals of social democracy: fraternity and democratic freedom.

The ideal of fraternity, while rather vague, seems to involve the following notions. Citizens have fraternal relations with one another when they agree to refrain from making claims to certain goods that come at the expense of those less well off than themselves and when they view the achievement of such relations with their fellow citizens as a part of their own good.[12] People express relations of fraternity with one another in part through providing certain goods in common. Whereas distributing goods through a system of bilateral transactions tends to emphasize either the separateness of persons (in the market) or some special relationship between the two traders (in personal gift relationships), providing goods out of pooled resources obliterates any connection of specific donors with specific recipients. It thereby expresses the idea that the goods are provided by the community as a whole to its members, rather than by some specific individuals to others. Furthermore, where the goods in question are not public but distributed, distribution takes place in accordance with some conception of members' needs. Fraternal relations are need-regarding, not only want-regarding.[13]

Another aspect to the intuitive idea of fraternity connects it to the democratic tradition. This is the idea that citizens are equals engaged in a common cooperative project. In the democratic tradition, this project is collective self-rule. The political freedom of a citizen is the freedom to participate on terms of equality with fellow citizens in deciding the laws and policies that will govern them all. This freedom is meaningless unless citizens have the goods they need (e.g., education) to participate effectively in the project of self-government. Citizens express their fraternity in part by ensuring that these needs are met through community guarantees or outright provision of the goods in question. But the proper interpretation of citizens' needs and, hence, of the ideal of fraternity is itself a subject for democratic deliberation. Citizens cannot interact with one another in the spirit of fraternity without a shared understanding of this ideal forged through participation in democratic institutions. Democratic freedom and fraternity are thus complementary goods.

These ideals of fraternity and democratic freedom are embodied in three norms that conflict with the norms of the market. First, citizens exercise their freedom in a democracy primarily through voice, not exit. Their freedom is the power to take the initiative in shaping the background conditions of their interactions and the content of the goods they provide in common. It is a freedom to participate in democratic activities, not just to leave the country if their government does not satisfy their desires. Second, an uncorrupted democracy distributes goods in accordance with shared principles (including a shared understanding of citizens' needs), not in accordance with unexamined wants. Decisions must be justified in terms acceptable to the public. Third, the goods provided by the public body are provided on a nonexclusive basis—everyone, not just those who pay, has access to them. The different norms of decision-making in the market and in democracy are reflected in the different interpretations of respect we apply to these two spheres. To respect a customer is to respect her privacy by not probing more deeply into her reasons for wanting a commodity than is required to effectively satisfy her want. There is little scope here for challenging her own estimation of what is valuable. But to respect a fellow citizen is to take her reasons for advocating a particular position seriously. It is to consult her judgment about political matters, to respond to it in a public forum, and to accept it if one finds her judgment superior to others'.

Many goods can be secured only through a form of democratic provision that is nonexclusive, principle- and need-regarding, and regulated primarily through voice. To attempt to provide these goods through market mechanisms is to change the kind of good they are for the worse. They contribute to human flourishing in lesser ways when they are provided through the market than when they are provided on a democratic basis. Goods of this kind I shall define as "political goods." This conception of political goods can shed light on two kinds of proposals for subjecting goods to market control. The first is the proposal for "dividing the commons." Many goods, such as streets, parks, and schools, are presently provided on a public, nonexclusive basis and/or subject to public control. Some people argue that freedom (and sometimes also efficiency) would be enhanced if such goods were completely divided into privately owned or controlled parcels that would then be provided on an exclusive basis. The second is the proposal for converting the public provision of goods in kind to the provision of their cash equivalents. I argue that both kinds of proposals fail to recognize the goods realized through democratic provision and also embody a flawed conception of freedom when they are applied to the goods discussed. Let us turn first to the various proposals to "divide the commons."

Since Locke wrote his *Two Treatises of Government,* the argument that both individual freedom and efficiency would be enhanced if publicly provided goods were completely divided into privately controlled parcels has been an enduring one in Western political thought, particularly in libertarian circles. The basic idea behind all of these proposals is that freedom is enhanced when people are granted the power of exit from common control of a good. I argue, however, that in these cases the freedom of exit is no substitute for the loss of voice and of nonexclusive access to the goods in question. Some forms of freedom can be secured only through institutions of voice established over goods to which public access is guaranteed.

Let us begin our investigation of this problem with a relatively uncontroversial case: the value of public streets and parks. Some libertarians have suggested that a system of private, toll-charging roads would be superior to a public system, since these would be paid for through voluntary user fees rather than a coercive tax system, which charges people whether or not they want to use the roads (Rothbard, 1978, Ch. 11). The idea that such a system would enhance individual freedom is rather curious, however. Under a system of public roads, no one need ask anyone else's permission to travel anywhere these roads go. If all roads are privately owned, one must ask the permission of each owner to visit people in areas accessible only by such roads and subject oneself to whatever terms the owner demands for using these roads. Nearly everyone would be subject to arbitrary restraints on their freedom of association by others.[14] Next to this loss, the restriction on my freedom entailed by taxation to maintain public roads is trivial. I would even be reluctant to characterize it as a loss of *freedom* at all—merely a loss of money.

The mistake in the libertarian picture seems to lie in the view that individual freedom is always increased when the common is divided into parcels over which individuals have exclusive control. While this regime would enable each person to be a despot in the territory she owns, she would be a mere subject to others everywhere else. This conception of freedom fails to grasp the point that some freedoms can only be exercised in spaces over which no individual has more control than others. These are the public spaces of free association among equals. I want to make two claims about such goods. First, freedom with respect to these goods requires the right of participation in their enjoyment and control, and not just the right of exit. If the primary spaces of free public association are appropriated by private persons, this amounts to a private appropriation of political power, similar to that found in a comprehensive system of private roads. Second, the goods provided by spaces of free public association are qualitatively different from those provided by exclusive spaces that ostensibly provide the same goods. For these goods extend beyond the privately conceived purposes of each individual using them.[15] Association in public spaces is needed to cultivate relations of civility among citizens of all walks of life. And relations of civility are indispensable for democratic politics.

Consider the goods that are provided by a successful city park. One good lies in its being open without charge to any member of the public. The fact that all members gain access to the park freely and in the same way prevents invidious distinctions from arising among them, enabling all to meet each other on terms of equality—in contrast, say, with an exclusive country club. By providing the park as a common good, citizens thus express fraternal relations with one another. A second good lies in its being a locus for spontaneous interaction and political activity. The users of the park, who may each have separate reasons for being there, together create a lively scene of diverse people and purposes, with many occasions for spontaneous interactions that can build a spirit of trust and civility among the users. Joggers meet on the same trail, one dog takes an interest in another, leading their owners to stop and chat, an old man catches a stray Frisbee and tosses it back to the players, business people eat lunch on the benches to watch the passing show. In virtue of its diverse and open uses, this kind of public space then provides the occasion for political action. Outside of the media, it is only in lively public spaces that people can rapidly and effectively generate concern and support on matters of the public interest among fellow citizens who are strangers to themselves. Here rallies can attract curious bystanders and petitioners gather signatures from those who would feel intruded upon by a door-to-door canvasser.[16]

Sometimes the spaces of public interaction are enclosed under a roof and subjected to private control. This happens whenever a commercial mall leads to the decline of a downtown business district. May the owners of a mall suppress any speech or political activity in it that they find offensive or opposed to their interests? Insofar as they are granted the right to do so, the value of this space deteriorates from one in which people can meet as equal citizens with common interests to one in which they can meet only as private consumers. And there may be no alternative space that can serve the same public functions as the downtown once did. The spirit of a lively public place, and its value as a locus for political action, can be generated only as the unintended byproduct of individuals' other purposes. Public space is good for political action precisely because a wide diversity of people would go there anyway, for their own reasons. Some of the main reasons people use public spaces are to go to work or to shop. When these reasons turn them away from downtown and to the mall, and when their interaction in the mall is then managed by commercial interests, citizens lose this unintended good and cannot recover it through artifice. Their space is depoliticized, and their public life correspondingly impoverished. Under these circumstances, the exercise of a private right to control what people do on one's property becomes in reality an exercise of political power, just as in the case of completely private roads.

So far I have emphasized the ways in which the principle of public access can change the kind of good something is for us by changing the ways in which we can value it. Similar transformations of value occur when we distribute certain goods according to the norms of fraternity rather than those of the market.

In both cases, we not only change the ways we value the goods we enjoy, but we also change the ways we appreciate each other when we adopt the non-market norms. This insight lies at the foundation of Richard Titmuss' famous argument that human blood should be given only as a gift, not sold as a commodity (Titmuss, 1971). By understanding how his argument exemplifies the approach to value defended here, we can see how it illuminates another dispute about welfare policies, namely, whether welfare should be provided in cash or in kind.

Titmuss' fundamental objection to obtaining the blood supply by paying people to provide it is that this policy undermines fraternal relations among people in the community, whereas a purely volunteer system enhances such relations.[17] In a volunteer system, people agree not to extract payment from those needing blood as compensation for donating it. Their actions follow the norms of the gift rather than the market. But these are the norms of the anonymous gift; they create no personal bonds, since no one knows whose blood is transfused into a patient. Blood is regarded as a common resource available to any member of the public. In other words, the provision of blood under the volunteer system follows the norms of fraternity, as I have previously defined this ideal.

As in the case of personal values, the value of blood to both the recipient and the donor is partially dependent on the motives for which it is given, and enhanced when these motives are not commercial. Attempting to increase the blood supply through financial incentives rather than appealing to a sense of civic duty or fraternity promotes the social expectation that people may feel entitled to some merely personal advantage for donating their blood. This attitude makes it seem as if small acts contributing to the health of one's neighbors should be seen merely as inconveniences requiring compensation instead of as enhancing the spirit of the entire community. And this atmosphere of expectations really does make blood donation an onerous task. Patients, forced to pay extravagant amounts for blood, must put pressure on their relatives to donate to keep down costs. The typical circumstances under which people do in fact donate are ones of stress, duress, and punishment. The poor who desperately need money, prisoners who hope to gain parole, and relatives who face the choice of severe financial burden or donation provide most of the supply. But when blood donation is a habit born of a sense of civic duty or benevolence, no such punitive or burdensome circumstances accompany its donation, and the act of giving without pay enhances the donor rather than diminishing her. Virtue *can* be its own reward, but it ceases to be so once people are paid for it, even if some still volunteer. As Peter Singer pointed out, the significance of my volunteer donation is trivialized when other blood is paid for. If blood is also a commodity, then all I have given to the recipient is the cash equivalent of the blood, not the gift of life itself (Singer, 1973, pp. 315–16).

This suggests that there is some good inherent in providing goods in kind rather than in cash. Welfare economics takes the opposed view. According to its analysis, the welfare of the recipient is always increased when she receives her welfare payment in cash rather than in kind. For the cash-equivalent payment offers her more freedom of choice, she could use it to purchase the good for which it was a substitute, but she may wish to purchase preferred bundles of goods that would contribute to her welfare even more. While there is some appeal to this position, it seems that most of us have the intuition that some goods, such as medical care, are still better provided in kind. Is this simply a patronizing position? Why not let the poor decide whether they will spend a cash donation to purchase medical insurance or some other good that they might prefer? Do we not arbitrarily reduce the recipients' welfare by preventing them from exercising this choice?

There is a value, however, in collectively taking a stand on what goods the community regards as so important that it would be a disgrace to let any of its members fall short in them (Kelman, 1986; Thurow, 1977). The ability to take such a stand depends on being sensitive to the distinction between urgent needs and merely intense desires. The scale of urgency is an objective one that the whole community can recognize. It plays a public role in expressing shared principles and fraternal bonds among community members that the policy to simply indulge in individuals' subjective tastes cannot do. Given that we do recognize the distinction between urgent needs and intense desires, we can see that for a community to treat these two as on a par is to trivialize and debase the concerns of those who have the needs and to hold itself hostage to those with extravagant tastes (Scanlon, 1975). To distribute welfare payments on a want-regarding rather than a need-regarding basis would be, for instance, to treat the gourmet's anxiety at her lack of ostrich tongues on a par with the handicapped person's need for a wheelchair.[18]

But what lies at the basis of this distinction between needs and wants? It is our capacity to draw distinctions of worth among goods. In the case of the gourmet and the handicapped person, we understand that gastronomic pleasures are less important to leading a worthwhile life than the power to move about freely without depending on others. For the latter power is needed to lead a life of autonomy and to pursue worthwhile activities such as the development of one's talents. To lack the power to pursue such ends leaves one's life not merely frustrated, as when we lack certain pleasures, but degraded. Moreover, to lack the power to govern one's life in accordance with distinctions of worth between goods is itself debasing.[19] But such distinctions are not the product of private fancy. I cannot draw them in my own life except against a background of shared social understandings that recognizes them. The social practice of distributing goods in accordance with need-regarding rather than want-regarding principles is one means of fixing these social understandings, thereby enabling us to lead not merely pleasurable but worthwhile lives.

A related distinction between ideals and mere wants provides a basis for evaluating the proposal to provide elementary and secondary education by means of a voucher system. This proposal resembles the arguments for "dividing the commons" and for replacing in-kind provision of needs with a cash payment. While it accepts the need for compulsory education, and for providing parents with the means to educate their children, it objects to direct public administration of schools. Instead, the voucher system would provide each parent with a fixed sum of money to be spent on any school of the parents' choice. Schools would be run on a commercial basis, competing for students by offering a variety of educational options to parents. Advocates of the voucher plan argue that it would increase the productive efficiency of schools by introducing competition. And it would enhance the freedom of parents by enabling each parent to obtain the kind of education she wants for her child, rather than having to go along with the majority decision, as is the case when the schools are administered publicly. More of parents' wants could be satisfied under a voucher system than under a system of publicly administered schools (Friedman, 1962, Ch. 6).

As a market-based system, a voucher system would replace institutions of voice with those of exit.[20] Instead of discussing with other parents the proper goals and practices of education in an attempt to arrive at common principles, parents would exercise their power of exit to remove their children from schools that do not suit their tastes. The fundamental problem with this replacement is that it undermines the good of education as a reflection of reasoned ideals. The argument for the voucher system assumes that the relevant wants that an educational system should satisfy are the given, unexamined wants of parents. But the preference for an education of a particular sort is not, like the preference for chocolate over vanilla ice cream, merely a matter of given, primitive tastes for which no reasons can be offered. Such a preference is formulated in the light of particular ideals.

In particular, democratic ideals strongly inform our conception of elementary and secondary education, for one of the main purposes of education at this level is to prepare children for responsible citizenship, exercised in a spirit of fraternity with others of diverse class, racial, and ethnic backgrounds. Reasons can be given for and against different ideals of democratic citizenship, and for and against the claim that a particular educational practice adequately reflects these ideals. An important part of the good of elementary and secondary education is the preservation of its reasoned ties with such ideals. Insofar as people see their preferences for certain kinds of education as backed up by reasons, it is also important for them to have a forum in which these reasons can be evaluated. Since the content of ideals of elementary and secondary education is wrapped up in political ideals of democracy, fraternity, and citizenship, there is a strong argument for determining the shape of education through political institutions, which provide a public forum for the discussion and evaluation of reasoned ideals. Market mechanisms of exit do not respond to reasoned ideals any differently from unreflective wants. When people's choices are removed from the political forum and made in the market, they are reduced to isolated, publicly unarticulated decisions (Sheffrin, 1978).[21]

This argument against the voucher system does not, of course, represent a defense of the status quo, in which the most important decisions about public education are often made by powers far removed from local democratic control. Nor is there any reason to believe that mechanisms of voice need impose a bland uniformity on the educational system. Many public school systems already offer alternative and specialized high school programs, adjusted to the varied needs and interests of the students. The more the mechanisms of voice are opened up to broad, local participation, the greater are the possibilities for parents to realize their preferences as reasoned ideals rather than as merely private tastes.

Conclusion: Some Ethical Limitations of the Market

At the beginning of this article, I proposed to investigate the ethical limitations of the market by means of three questions: Which dimensions of value do the norms and orientations of the market realize, and which do they undermine? Does the market embody an adequate interpretation of its own ideals? In what areas does the market interfere with the realization of other ideals? In the light of our investigation of the differences among economic values and personal and political values, we can sketch some answers to these questions. We have seen that the realization of some values demands that they be open to the public (nonexclusive), or confined to people who have personal ties to one another, or done for reasons other than merely personal advantage, or held to be valuable as a matter of ideals rather than as a mere matter of taste, and so forth. This is to say that the realization of some values demands that certain goods be produced, exchanged, and enjoyed outside of market relations, or in accordance with nonmarket norms.

I have emphasized in particular two classes of goods whose realization must take place within nonmarket norms of exchange: gift values and shared values. Gift values differ from commodity values in that their worth is at least partially constituted by the nonmarket motives for which they are given. They are valued as tokens of love, admiration, respect, honor, and so forth, and consequently lose their value when they are provided for merely self-interested reasons. What is important about these goods as gift values is the fact that they express the giver's acknowledgment and affirmation of a certain relationship to the beneficiary, or of some characteristic she has, which is valued for its own sake.

Shared values differ from commodity values in that their being good for a group of people cannot be fully analyzed in terms of their being independently good for each member of the group, considered in isolation. Part of their being good consists in the fact that they are understood to be held in common—that everyone in the group both acknowledges the thing to be good and participates in its benefits. The value of any noninstrumental relationship is shared in this sense. The realization of shared values needs to take place within social relations that differ from market relations in at least three respects. First, since these values are sustained in part through a common activity of working out how they are valuable for the group, their realization requires a forum for working out these understandings together. Most of these values must be provided by the same people who enjoy them. The people who enjoy the good need to have the opportunity to participate in shaping its character. These characteristics require institutions of voice rather than of exit alone. Second, since part of its value lies in the fact that all members of the relevant group have access to it, some provision must be made for opening access to those members of the group who lack the ability to pay for their share of the costs of providing it. Shared goods are undermined by the market norm of restricting access to those who can afford to pay for it. Finally, since the value of shared goods is realized not in individual, exclusive appropriation and use but in common activities, rights over the physical vehicles of these values cannot be fully distributed in exclusive bundles. This was the basis for my arguments against "dividing the commons."

Gift values and shared values are not the only kinds of goods that are improperly treated as commodities, but our investigation of the problems that arise in attempting to regard them as commodities suggests the general form of arguments that certain goods should not be treated as economic values. By recognizing what this general strategy is, we can both make sense of the heretofore vague objections that some goods should not be treated as commodities and apply it to new cases. When the good in question is some thing or service to be marketed, the argument is as follows: for a certain dimension of value to be realized in a good, or for the good to serve as the vehicle for the realization of our ideals, the production, distribution, and enjoyment of this good must take place within the context of certain social relations. To trade the good on the market, or otherwise to subject its conditions of valuation to market forces and market norms, is to remove it from these social relations or to undermine their integrity. When the good in question is an ideal, the argument is that the social relations that most adequately embody the ideal are undermined when people adopt market norms to regulate their interactions in these relationships. Then we can say that the ideal is not an economic good, where to regard an ideal as an economic good is to regard it as best embodied in market relations.

Arguments of this form do not conclusively show that the goods in question may never be traded on the market. It may be that the distinctive dimensions of value in the goods can be preserved short of prohibiting their sale. Zoning laws represent an attempt to preserve certain public goods while allowing a private market in land. More importantly, the good in question may have more than one dimension of value. Prohibiting or regulating the sale of goods prevents certain economic goods from being realized. If the Grand Canyon is permanently preserved from strip-mining in appreciation of its aesthetic value, its commercial value is unrealized. An argument against marketing a good is stronger if it shows not just that a noneconomic value is lost in marketing it, but that the value is degraded or perverted in marketing the good.[22]

The market has traditionally been defended on two grounds: for its efficiency and for its embodiment of a particular conception of freedom. This argument exposes a serious limitation on the market's claim to efficiency. The market cannot make claims to superior efficiency when it changes the qualities of the goods it provides, since claims to efficiency are valid only when ends are unchanged by alternate means of provision. My account also raises questions about the adequacy of the economic ideal of freedom. The market promises us freedom from the value judgment of others. How much I choose to value a commodity is independent of how much others choose to value it. We have seen, however, that giving a good a place on one's preference ranking is not all there is to valuing a good, unless that good is the object merely of a direct primitive liking. The freedom to value a good as much as one wishes is not the freedom to value it in any *way* one wishes. For the ability of an individual to value a good in some ways requires her participation in a social practice in which others understand its value in the same way. Outside of shared understandings, one can value things only as objects of primitive appeal. And some ways of valuing goods require a shared understanding that the goods are not commodities. The ideal of freedom as consent has also emerged somewhat tarnished. When the outcome of bargaining is influenced by a manipulation of one party's commitment to norms of civility or gratitude, the normative significance of his consent is diminished.

Finally, we may note that the market ideal of freedom is just one among others. Sometimes the realization of one ideal of freedom conflicts with the realization of another. The market ideal interprets freedom as freedom from ties of obligation to others. Committed or involuntary relationships with other people are viewed as entanglements, as constraints on personal autonomy. But we are not free to pursue the goods of deepest significance to human life under these conditions. The personal sphere offers us a different ideal of freedom. Within committed and intimate relationships, we are free to reveal ourselves to others, without having our self-disclosure become the object of another's manipulations. In the market, on the other hand, the successful bargainer must hold his concerns and desires in reserve, lest they be used by the other party to gain a negotiating edge. The sphere of democratic politics offers a different challenge to the market ideal of freedom. The market ideal identifies freedom with the power to exclude others from participation in decisions affecting one's property. But when some realms are completely divided into pieces of private property, nearly everyone is excluded from decision-making power over central areas of their lives. Democratic freedom, on the other hand, is freedom to participate in collective decisions. It is a freedom to be included, rather than to exclude others. When exit is impossible, when decisions concern shared goods, or when freedom can be effectively exercised by all only in public spaces of free and equal association, the freedom of democratic participation supercedes the exclusive freedom of the market.

To argue that the market has limits is to acknowledge that it also has its proper place in human life. There is a wide range of goods that *are* properly regarded as commodities. Among these are the conveniences, luxuries, delights, gadgets, and services found in ordinary stores. The modern market produces and distributes these goods with unsurpassed efficiency and in unsurpassed abundance. It is a good not only to have these goods, but to be able to procure them freely through the anonymous, unencumbered channels the market provides. For harm is done both to personal autonomy and to the integrity of friendship when one's access to consumer goods is dependent on personal connections with political cadres, foreigners, or other well-placed individuals, as is often the case in socialist countries. The difficult task for modern societies is to reap the advantages of the market while keeping its activities confined to the goods proper to it.

Notes

I thank Daniel Hausman, Peter Railton, John Rawls, Thomas Scanlon, and Alan Wertheimer for helpful comments on drafts of this chapter. This is a revised version of a talk I gave at the Conference on Markets and Political Theory at Williams College on April 28, 1989. I thank all those who participated in the discussion of the conference paper.

1. Economic goods are not confined to things or commodities; they can include economic relations, activities, and ideals as well. Things or services are "economic" insofar as their values are best realized through being traded on the market or otherwise treated in accordance with market norms—that is, as commodities. Ideals are "economic" insofar as they are best embodied in practices and relations governed by market norms. Norms are here understood as rules by which the participants in a practice govern and evaluate their behavior, or standards by which they understand the meanings of what they do or value. Often norms are justified as attempts to realize ideals to which we are committed.

The investigation needed to determine the nature of economic goods is a historical and empirical study of the norms and social understandings that govern market practices. What we discover from such investigations of different practices is similar to what Michael Walzer (1983) called the social meanings of goods. I generally endorse Walzer's view that goods can be usefully viewed as occupying different, although often overlapping, spheres of life. However, since social meanings are endlessly nuanced, constantly changing and being reinterpreted, the generalizations I make here about social meanings and norms should not be taken to be unqualified, much less a priori claims. Since modern social practices are deeply pluralistic, I also do not wish to suggest that I have offered an exhaustive account of the values of any particular sphere of life. In every case, the claims I make here should be taken as invitations to further detailed empirical investigation. In taking social meanings as the starting points for ethical argument, I also do not mean to suggest that they are beyond criticism. After all, I criticize later the economic ideal of freedom that informs many of our social practices. A general account of how to criticize social meanings is the task of another paper, however.

2. Friedman (1962) had a particularly clear exposition of the implications of this view.

3. Both aspects of the impersonal freedom of the market are the result of a long process of historical and legal development. My account of the market ethic and its development is indebted to the discussions by Atiyah (1979), Hirschman (1977), Horwitz (1977), Nelson (1969), Polanyi (1944), Simmel (1978), and Weber (1968). In particular, I have been influenced by Polanyi's thesis that societies need to constrain the extent of the market in order to protect themselves.

4. I owe this account of shared goods to Rawls (1971, pp. 523–26) and Taylor (1987).

5. This implied hierarchy of values, according to which one's sexuality is a higher and deeper (more intimate) value than any commodity, is founded on the public meanings embodied in our social practices and not on the possibly idiosyncratic intentions or feelings of individuals who may engage in them. The understanding that a person's sexuality reaches deeper into the self than money, that it is therefore a good that is different in kind from and higher than money, also lies behind our judgment that rape is a deeper violation of the person than robbery. One who would deny that prostitution is degrading would thus be hard pressed for an explanation of why rape is a more serious crime than robbery. To claim simply that rape results in more "disutility" than robbery is not enough—the question is why this is true, and how the claim can be substantiated. Since no one has provided an adequate account of how interpersonal comparisons of subjective utility can be made, it would seem that the basis for the judgment about utilities lies not in such a comparison, but rather in the publicly accessible meanings of the acts themselves: the shared understanding that rape is more degrading than robbery.

6. One could imagine forms of "prostitution" that, while offered on the market, diverge from market norms in ways that could rescue the practice from the criticisms made here. For example, Schwarzenbach (1990) defended a conception of prostitution as a form of sex therapy practiced by professionals who help people liberate themselves from sick, patriarchal forms of sexuality. Such a practice would diverge from the ideal type of market relations presented here in many ways, especially insofar as it is informed by the norms and ideals of a

profession. Professional services, such as legal, medical, and educational services, provide a classic case of "mixed" goods whose production and distribution is determined partly by market norms and partly by nonmarket, professional norms. Notoriously, market norms pose a constant threat to the integrity of professional norms. Yet, market norms may still be needed to ensure the efficient production and allocation of professional services, or to realize certain freedoms for their practitioners or customers.

7. Of course, the mere substitution of cash for in-kind payment does not obviate the exploitative character of such relationships. The firms still take advantage of their employees' duress and lack of decent alternatives; but they would be less likely to be able to evoke the ties of children to parents, from which an extra margin of effort or obedience can be extracted from workers, if their dealings with employees were blatantly self-interested instead of ingratiatingly paternalistic.

8. While gift norms can be used by employers for exploitative purposes, there may be cases where employers themselves come to be guided by them. See Akerlof (1982).

9. "To Love, Honor, and . . . Share: A Marriage Contract for the Seventies," *Ms.* vol. 1, no. 12 (June 1973), pp. 62–64, 102–3.

10. My claim here is not that bargaining can never take place in a worthwhile marriage, but that where the norms of bargaining predominantly govern the relations of the partners, the integrity of their marriage is threatened.

11. It seems obvious to us that friends are not liable for each other's debts. Yet, it was not until the sixteenth century that in England it came to be seen as a foolish act rather than an act of true friendship to guarantee a friend's debts. This change is due to the fact that the present radical separation of the spheres of personal relationships and economic relationships is the product of a long historical development. For some of the details of this history, see Nelson (1969, esp. pp. 142–43). Of course, it is possible that we could rework our practices and understandings of friendship and credit, so that the threats posed to success in each of these practices by combining them would not come about. Ideal-typical analysis does not preclude the reformation or combining of practices in new ways. It simply points out the conflicts and tensions among our present practices, and the conceptions of value they reflect, which would have to be adequately dealt with by any proposal to combine them.

12. Here I am generalizing John Rawls' account of fraternity and of the good of a social union (1971, pp. 105ff, 520–29).

13. On the significance of communal provision, see Sahlins (1972, pp. 188–91).

14. This might violate the norm of impersonality that I previously attributed to the market. However, libertarians do reject the view that impersonality is an appropriate norm to impose on people's use of their private property. Robert Nozick argues that a libertarian would have to accept a proviso on property acquisition that prevents people from trapping others in a small territory. But his proviso doesn't prevent private interference with others' freedom of movement that is less drastic than complete entrapment. For the libertarian

account of freedom doesn't acknowledge that the restrictions mentioned count as interferences in others' freedom at all, since the freedom of movement we are concerned with here is not embodied in some property right. See Nozick (1974, pp. 55, 178–82).

15. Welfare economists differ from libertarians on the issue of dividing common goods that are nonrivals in consumption. It is a theorem of welfare economics that nonrival goods may be more efficiently provided on a nonexclusive (public) basis than on an exclusive one. However, even this view does not recognize the fact that providing a good on an exclusive basis may not merely provide it less efficiently, but change the kind of good it is for the worse. I thank Howard Wial for this point.

16. This account is indebted to Jane Jacobs' (1961) rich description of the goods of public parks and streets.

17. Titmuss has a second argument against selling blood, which relies on the facts that we depend on donors' honesty about their health to keep the blood supply safe and that the prospect of cash reward tempts unhealthy people to donate. In fact, there are many goods for which we are not in a position to verify whether the things offered to us really have the characteristics that make them good, or that are so complex that the costs of supervising the process by which they are provided are prohibitively high. In these cases, we have no choice but to grant a large degree of discretionary power to the providers, on condition that they exercise this power as a trust and not as a private right to exploit for merely personal advantage. This is one powerful basis for opposing the commercialization of hospitals, elementary and secondary schools, and prisons. The profit motive offers a constant incentive for violating this trust, while the complexity of the goods guarantees a wide variety of opportunities for doing so undetected by the public.

18. This is not to claim that providing certain needs on a means-tested basis is better than other alternatives. Arguably, fraternity would be better expressed by making health care a right of all citizens, provided equally on a public basis. Furthermore, the actual meaning of any given form of cash or in-kind provision—whether it expresses respect or contempt for its recipients—depends on the details of its enactment and administration. For example, the petty regulations attending the food stamp program seem more designed to exercise public control over the consumption habits of the poor than to express fraternity with its recipients.

19. Thomas Scanlon expressed this idea in the notion (following Rawls) that we are responsible for our ends (Rawls, 1982, pp. 168–71; Scanlon, 1975, pp. 663–66). One account of distinctions of worth between goods, and its connection with responsibility for one's ends, is provided by Charles Taylor (1985, esp. vol. 1, essays 1, 2, and 4, and vol. 2, essay 9).

20. It would also harness the profit motive to satisfy the demand for education. On the danger of this, see note 17. Some proposals for voucher systems do not envision a world of purely profit-oriented educational providers, but rather a world in which the power of exit is to be used to strengthen institutions of voice, perhaps through the maintenance of a mixture of private and public

schools, with private schools also open to influence by institutions of voice. Here I examine only an "ideal type" of a fully marketized system of educational provision, and leave open the question of how far mixed voucher systems would fall under the same criticisms.

21. Sheffrin (1978) argued that wherever the evolution of preferences in the light of reasons is an important factor, this is a reason for opposing the replacement of mechanisms of voice with those of exit. Where the interests of children are involved, there is an additional reason for ensuring that policies do not rest merely on parental tastes. Voucher systems are more defensible in matters of adult education, where ideals of citizenship do not play as great a role, where the recipients of education choose for themselves, and where providers contain forums for the discussion of educational ideals.

22. The view developed here does not depend on postulating the existence of completely isolable spheres of social practices. Talk of "spheres" is useful, however, because the norms within which we produce and distribute goods typically come in bundles, with distinct bundles defining different spheres. Still, the different norms in the bundles can be separated and combined in different ways, and new norms invented, resulting in hybrid practices, or even in the creation of very new kinds of practices. I would hope that the kind of analysis developed here would be used as an opportunity to think of new kinds of practices that could help us move beyond the sterile dichotomy between market and state that informs so much contemporary political disagreement. The key question to be asked is, "What sets of norms are best for realizing these values?" and the answers need not be confined to the bundles of norms presently in operation.

References

Akerlof, George. 1982. "Labor Contracts as Partial Gift Exchanges." *Quarterly Journal of Economics* 97:543–69.

Atiyah, P. S. 1979. *The Rise and Fall of Freedom of Contract*. Oxford: Clarendon Press.

Fisher, Anthony C. 1981. *Resource and Environmental Economics*. Cambridge: Cambridge University Press.

Friedman, Milton. 1962. *Capitalism and Freedom*. Chicago: University of Chicago Press.

Hirsch, Fred. 1976. *Social Limits to Growth*. Cambridge, MA: Harvard University Press.

Hirschman, Albert O. 1970. *Exit, Voice and Loyalty: Responses to Decline in Firms, Organizations, and States*. Cambridge, MA: Harvard University Press.

———. 1977. *The Passions and the Interests: Political Arguments for Capitalism before Its Triumph*. Princeton: Princeton University Press.

Hochschild, Arlie. 1983. *The Managed Heart: Commercialization of Human Feeling*. Berkeley and Los Angeles: University of California Press.

Horwitz, Morton J. 1977. *The Transformation of American Law: 1780–1860.* Cambridge, MA: Harvard University Press.

Hyde, Lewis. 1983. *The Gift: Imagination and the Erotic Life of Property.* New York: Random House.

Jacobs, Jane. 1961. *The Death and Life of Great American Cities.* New York: Random House.

Kelman, Steven. 1986. "A Case for In-Kind Transfers." *Economics and Philosophy* 2:55–73.

Mauss, Marcel. 1967. *The Gift.* Translated by Ian Cunnison. New York: W. W. Norton.

Nelson, Benjamin. 1969. *The Idea of Usury: From Tribal Brotherhood to Universal Otherhood.* 2nd ed., enlarged. Chicago: University of Chicago Press.

Nozick, Robert. 1974. *Anarchy, State, and Utopia.* New York: Basic Books.

Polanyi, Karl. 1944. *The Great Transformation.* Boston: Beacon Press.

Rawls, John. 1971. *A Theory of Justice.* Cambridge, MA: Harvard University Press.

———. 1982. "Social Unity and Primary Goods." In *Utilitarianism and Beyond,* edited by Amartya Sen and Bernard Williams, pp. 159–85. Cambridge: Cambridge University Press.

Rothbard, Murray. 1978. *For a New Liberty.* New York: Collier (Macmillan). Revised edition of first Collier edition.

Sahlins, Marshall. 1972. *Stone Age Economics.* New York: Aldine.

Scanlon, Thomas. 1975. "Preference and Urgency." *Journal of Philosophy* 72:655–69.

Schwarzenbach, Sibyl, 1990. "Contractarians and Feminists Debate Prostitution." *NYU Review of Law and Social Change.* Forthcoming.

Sheffrin, Steven. 1978. "Habermas, Depoliticization, and Consumer Theory." *Journal of Economic Issues* 7:785–97.

Simmel, Georg. 1978. *The Philosophy of Money.* Translated by Tom Bottomore and David Frisby. Boston: Routledge and Kegan Paul.

Singer, Peter. 1973. "Altruism and Commerce: A Defense of Titmuss against Arrow." *Philosophy and Public Affairs* 2:312–20.

Taylor, Charles. 1985. *Philosophical Papers.* 2 vols. Cambridge: Cambridge University Press.

———. 1987. "The Political Consequences of Communitarianism." Lecture delivered at Harvard University, February 12, 1987.

Thurow, Lester. 1977. "Government Expenditures: Cash or In-Kind Aid?" In *Markets and Morals,* edited by Gerald Dworkin, Gordon Bermant, and Peter Brown, pp. 85–106. New York: Wiley.

Titmuss, Richard M. 1971. *The Gift Relationship: From Human Blood to Social Policy.* New York: Pantheon Books.

Walzer, Michael. 1983. *Spheres of Justice.* New York: Basic Books.

Weber, Max. 1968. *Economy and Society.* 2 vols. Edited by Guenther Roth and Claus Wittich. Berkeley and Los Angeles: University of California Press.

15.

WHAT DO WE OWE THE FUTURE?

Paul Streeten

It is, on the face of it, odd that both growth men and environmentalists, who share a concern for future generations, should be so much at loggerheads. The need to accumulate physical and human capital for greater output and enjoyment later, at the expense of current enjoyment, is at the heart of high growth strategies. Sometimes we hear of the objective of "maximizing growth." This, strictly interpreted, means that we should tighten our belts to the bare minimum consumption for productive survival, accumulate the difference between production and consumption, and then the last generation before Doomsday could indulge in an infinite consumption orgy. While the strategy is nonsensical, what greater concern could there be for the future? But, even more sensible growth strategies aim at higher levels of income and consumption for future generations. On the other hand, conservationists, environmentalists and ecologists wish to preserve a decent natural environment and an adequate supply of raw materials for subsequent generations. They, too, have the welfare of future generations at heart. What then are the issues of disagreement? We might identify five.

Provision for the Future

First, growth men and environmentalists disagree on the form that provision for the future should take. Growth men emphasize reproducible capital and ed-

Resources Policy (March 1986): 4–16.

ucation and training (human capital), anti-growth environmentalists emphasize exhaustible resources—minerals, open space, virgin land, clean air, safe water. They are worried lest rapid growth destroy these and leave future generations worse off. If environmentalists take exhaustibility seriously, the advocacy of zero growth is no remedy. Even zero growth requires depreciation of existing capital and leads eventually to exhaustion, though exponential growth does so sooner. The difference is merely a matter of time. The strategy should lead to the advocacy of not zero growth but zero consumption! But, if the present generation has to be extinguished in order to leave resources over for future generations, there will be no future generations. If, on the other hand, the environmentalists assert that technical substitutes for exhaustible raw materials can be found, so that the issue is a battle between technology and resources, the difference becomes an empirical question about the length of time and the appropriate policies. It is anybody's guess how long it would take for technological innovation to substitute for exhaustible materials. If it were the case that the rate of our technical progress exactly offsets the rate of depletion, pollution and risk creation, intergenerational responsibilities would be met according to both growth men and environmentalists.

Sudden Change for the Worse

A second difference is the degree of probability that the two groups attach to a sudden drastic change for the worse, such as irreversible pollution, or complete exhaustion of an essential resource, or complete dislocation of life that would spell disaster. Growth men tend to attach rather small or zero probabilities to such events and view progress as a more continuous process, while environmentalists attach higher probability to such disasters, if current policies are continued.

Different Time Discount Rates

A third difference may be the rate of time discount that the two groups attach to the welfare of future generations, perhaps together with different estimates of when a disaster might occur. Assume that both groups agreed that it is possible, or even probable, that a disaster will occur in 5 million years. Anti-growth men may have a longer horizon, so that they attach greater negative weights to such a prospect, whereas growth men may discount the very distant future at higher rates. This higher discount rate has to be distinguished from their greater faith in the "technical fix," the human ingenuity of avoiding the disaster, which is a separate point, more fully discussed below.

It may also be that the two schools apply different time discount rates to the not so very distant future. The view that we owe special responsibilities to those near to us would fully take into account the lifetime of our children and their children, but might give decreasing weights to the welfare of subsequent generations. We may reply to this that if we love our children and those they in turn love, the love chain presumably extends into the indefinite future. In fact, however, we attach less weight to an extra dollar accruing to our great-great-great-grandchildren than to our grandchildren. On the other hand, even if we agree that the special relationship of kinship calls for stronger weights to be given to the welfare of those near to us in kinship or space or by some other bonds, it does not call for even lower weights the further they are away in time. Once the special relationship has leveled off, say with our grandchildren, the same weights would apply. And, moreover, we do attach the same weights, irrespective of kinship or other special relationships, to the infliction of some forms of damage for example. We believe that it is wrong to harm intentionally not only our children but any human being anywhere, and at any time.

It could also be that there are some who would want us to apply a negative discount rate to future benefits, so that we should wish to sacrifice more than a dollar now for an extra dollar accruing to a member of a subsequent generation. A value system that attaches great value to the continued existence of the human race might support such negative discount rates.

Costs of Economic Slowdown

A fourth difference is in their estimate of the costs incurred in slowing down economic growth, where such a slowdown is favorable to conserving exhaustible resources and reducing pollution. These costs comprise not only the costs of present forgone consumption, and the consumption forgone in the near future, but also the social and psychological consequences of a slowly growing or stagnating economy. All sorts of adjustments, between occupations, between regions and so on are much easier in a rapidly growing economy, where shrinkage of certain sectors takes the form of redeploying only new entrants, than in a stagnant or slowly growing economy, where dismissal, unemployment and dislocation have to be suffered. Rapid growth makes adjustment not only less difficult and less painful, but whatever adjustments have to be made become easier to bear. More resources are there to maintain the unemployed at a higher level of income, and retrain and relocate them. Anti-growth men, on the other hand, accept these costs and pains of slower growth as an insurance premium that we have to pay in order to avoid the risks of future dislocation or disaster, which they regard as more likely with rapid growth.

Technical Fix

A fifth and final difference lies in the confidence the two schools have in a "technical fix." In the past, technical ingenuity has often substituted for exhaustible natural resources, but what guarantee is there that the future will be like the past? Anti-growth men, who emphasize discontinuities, may quote the story of the man who fell out of the window of the thirtieth floor and, when he reached the fourteenth, said, "so far, so good." In contemporary relations we do not regard it as legitimate to take detrimental actions with the presumption that the potential victims will invent ways of getting out of the scrape. Why should we rely on it in intergenerational relations? Given our ignorance and uncertainty surrounding the future, a sensible moral strategy would be to compare the costs of having relied on a technical fix when it did not turn up, with the costs of having sacrificed options and benefits now for the sake of avoiding such reliance, when in fact it did turn up!

It should also be remembered that growth can be complementary to environmental protection. If we count industrial anti-pollution devices and the technology that produces them and innovations that economize in exhaustible materials, as part of GNP (but for a different approach see the next paragraph), it is possible that a certain type of growth, consisting of many of these inventions, contributes positively to our environmental objectives. Even so, there is probably some trade-off between environmental objectives and economic growth in the short run. Figure 15.1 illustrates temporal paths of GNP growth and of something to be measured by an index of the preservation of the environment and the conservation of resources. We are measuring the log of the GNP and of the environmental index on the vertical axes, in order to show equiproportional increases as equidistant. Until time T the high-growth strategy sacrifices the environment. But forever after T, high growth promotes a purer and safer environment. Which path is chosen depends on the rate of dis-

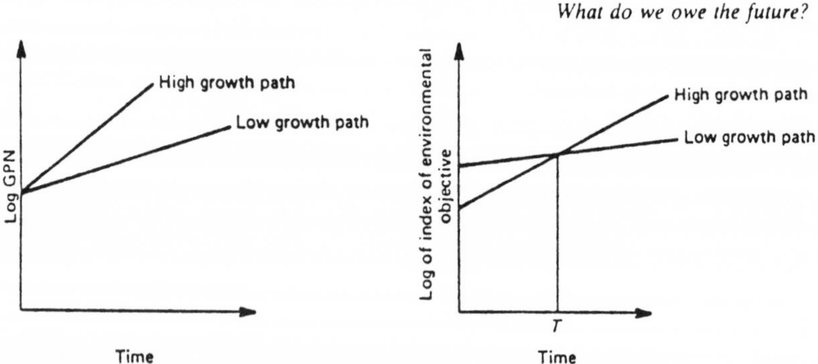

Figure 15.1. Temporal paths of GNP growth and index of environmental objective.

count for environmental objectives, compared with that for GNP. Since the marginal utility of consumption declines with rising income, whereas the relative value of reducing pollution rises with rising income, the rate of discount for environmental objectives is likely to be lower than that for GNP (some have even argued for a zero or negative rate). If this is so, those who lay much store by the environment and by the welfare of future generations ought to advocate a higher, not lower, growth strategy than that dictated by optimizing consumption over time. Only then can devices to protect the environment (a growth industry), the technology that develops anti-pollution techniques, processes and products and innovations that economize in the use of exhaustible materials develop sufficiently rapidly.

Goods and Anti-Bads

Another way of approaching the differences and reconciling them is from the point of view of measurement. Growth men, after all, are concerned with the annual percentage growth of an aggregate of heterogeneous goods and services. Since we do not aggregate these according to their weight or size, but their prices, which are supposed to reflect human valuations, a way to reconcile some of the conflicts is by adjusting the measurement of GNP and its growth. Now it is largely a measure of production and, as the name says, it is gross, not net. We might approach the collection by trying to measure welfare and to measure it net, rather than production measured gross. Some might think that such a revision would bring together growth men and environmentalists. If, for example, it were to be found that what we had been measuring was not goods, but "anti-bads," produced in order to combat the bads produced by the process of growth, we might all agree that economic growth was not all that wonderful. But before discussing these issues, a more fundamental difference might exist. If the divergence between private costs, reflected in market prices, and social costs is so pervasive that it is not the exception (as in the smoke emitted by a factory that raises other people's laundry bills) but the rule, conventional accounting methods might fail. Environmentalists might justifiably ask: can the choice between fresh air and unspoilt land on the one hand, and the motor car with all its implications on the other, be brought under the calculus of the pricing system? The choice between different total lifestyles, it may be said, cannot be subjected to the measuring rod of money.

Let us next assume that we do not have to accept such a radical critique of income measurements, and that shadow pricing can capture all divergencies between private and social costs and benefits. We might still concede that we should not include in our income and welfare measures what have been called "regrettable necessities," or anti-bads. Perhaps growth men and environmentalists might then agree that the growth of properly measured economic welfare is desirable.

Bads derive from three distinct sources: enemies, nature and the economic system itself. Anti-bads made necessary by the activities of our enemies would cover expenditure on the army and the police. Anti-bads made necessary by nature are such things as the provision of shelter, clothing and heating against cold, or of air conditioning against heat. Carried to logical consistency, almost all goods and services are intended to remove some void. We eat because our physiology requires food for survival, and we sleep for the same reason. So food and beds could be regarded as anti-bads against the bads created by our nature. Only the most superfluous frills would, on this approach, be counted as "goods" (it would be an anti-Marxist definition of national income), and even they fulfill some whim, the removal of which could be considered as an anti-bad. But one can drive logical consistency too far. The most relevant bads in the present context are those created by the process of production itself. If production pollutes and we then produce an anti-pollution device, say a scrubber, it is an anti-bad that combats a bad produced in the course of producing other goods.

The anti-bads made necessary by our enemies and by nature are not relevant in the present context, but those made necessary by the production process itself are (as is the appropriate evaluation of exhaustible natural resources) because they affect the fate of future generations. But it does not follow that we must then opt for a lower rate of correctly measured economic growth, that is, growth of income from which anti-bads are subtracted. For although we might opt for fewer goods, if they brought with them more bads and the need for anti-bads, we might also opt for even more goods, compensated by more anti-bads (the solution suggested in figure 15.1). Or we might opt for technical innovation that produces different types of goods, perhaps with fewer of the attractive qualities of goods, but also with fewer complementary bads. What we should avoid doing is just producing more goods that produce bads (such as pollution), without either the anti-bads or the redesign. Some of the differences between growth men and environmentalists can be reduced by a proper redefinition and measurement of net national income as a measure of welfare and its growth.

Future generations are particularly exposed to our creation of bads. As Sidney Holt has argued,[1] they are not only without a voice, without votes in the present, but in addition, they are "downstream" (in time) and therefore vulnerable to any harmful effects we may be inflicting on them, like people who have to live downstream from a polluting factory. They are, therefore, both powerless and vulnerable. It is from this awareness that the claim to appoint a trustee or guardian for the interests of future generations has sprung. What may be needed is a society for the propagation of anti-bads, especially for the protection of future generations.

But deducting anti-bads from a measure of net economic welfare raises more fundamental problems. We have so far concentrated on bads such as pollution that require anti-bads such as scrubbers. The economic system also creates certain desires (or voids), the satisfaction of which calls for scarce resources. Had it not been for this creation, the resources could have been left unused, or used for purposes of satisfying "natural" not "artificially created" desires. Advertisers persuade us that unless we keep ourselves dandruff free, we shall not be rechosen by our loved ones at breakfast. Or they create in us the fear that if we do not use the deodorants or mouthwashes they sell, we shall be shunned by our friends and neighbors. The fear of not being socially acceptable or loved may have been there all the time, but its focus on specific deficiencies that can be removed by buying the advertised product is generated by those producing and selling the product. Is this situation not parallel to the emitter of smoke who imposes the need to install a scrubber? Should we not eliminate from our welfare calculations goods bought only to remove created fears? The situation is like that of a blackmailer or kidnapper or protection racketeer who creates a nuisance for the removal of which he then extracts a payment. Such payments, it might be argued, bring us back to square one, they do not add to our welfare.

Yet, the problem is not so simple. Not only can some of the nastiest feelings of jealousy, competitiveness and fear of ostracism be artificially created, or stimulated, but also some of the highest desires: the desire for beauty, truth and goodness, the wish to buy and enjoy books, paintings and music; these are not "natural" but the result of an often painful process of education. Those of us who are university teachers know. It is not a question of whether the created desires are artificial or natural that should guide us, but whether they are bad or good. We need a value judgment before we can decide whether an item should be included in or excluded from our measure of economic welfare. Not all artificially created "bads" call for "anti-bads" that we should want to exclude from our measure.

The only reason for not including all goods and services responding to the "artificially created" desires of education is that some have to be excluded from net income as replacements of human capital. As older people retire from the labor force, and as skills become obsolete, their replacement calls for educational efforts which are of the same nature as those items of physical capital that replace worn-out plants and equipment.

The main conclusion of this discussion is not that we cannot identify "bads" with voids generated by the society (and not "naturally" given), but that we must exercise value judgments before we can evaluate the net national income as a measure of economic welfare. This leaves an area for possible disagreement between those who put a higher value on resource-using or polluting activities that add to current welfare and those who put a lower value on these things in favor of the welfare of future generations.

The Time Discount Rate

Why should I do anything for the future? The frivolous and facetious question: what has the future done for me? may, as Wilfred Beckerman has pointed out,[2] have an important content worth further exploration. Positive discount rates are powerful instruments for downgrading the future. At a discount rate of 10 percent, a given increase in welfare next year counts for ten times as much as the same increase in twenty years, and at 5 percent, next year's benefit counts for more than a thousand times as much as the same benefit in two hundred years.

Some people regard it as irrational to discount the future at all. Many of the apparent reasons for discounting the future are based on other principles than the passage of time, though some are loosely related to time flow. Events in the future are uncertain, and this would require that we attach probabilities of less than one to them. A special case of the reduced probability of a harmful event in the future is the case where the same event if it occurred now would be very damaging, but we believe that inventiveness will later produce a technology that will enable future generations to overcome the problem. An example would be the disposal of nuclear waste. But the reason for discounting such damaging events is then not that they are in the future, but that their occurrence will be less probable. Although there is a relationship between the future and uncertainty, events do not grow more uncertain the more distant they are in time. Indeed, in some cases it is easier to predict events in the more distant future.

Future generations may be better off than we are now, and the marginal utility of an extra dollar to a richer man is less than to a poorer man. Or his moral desert of getting an extra dollar may be smaller. We should not permit a member of our generation to go hungry in order to add a second car to a member of a future generation. But, again, the reason for discounting his benefit is not future time, but higher income. If someone in the future were to be poorer than we are now, his marginal utility or desert would be greater, and the appropriate "discount rate" would be negative.

Derek Parfit discusses additional apparent reasons for discounting the future, which he rejects.[3] One is the argument from opportunity costs. Earlier benefits can be used to yield greater benefits later. An investment next year can yield much more over the next ten years than had we made the investment after ten years. Delaying the investment therefore imposes opportunity costs. But once again, the reason for putting a premium on nearer events is not time, but their yield. This can be seen when we consider benefits that are not invested but consumed. Parfit uses the example of the enjoyment of a beautiful landscape that results from not building an airport. This enjoyment is the same next year and in ten years' time, and should not be discounted. It is also true that if, for example, we were to compensate for certain genetic deformities, a sum invested now would yield more money for compensation than the same sum invested later. But Parfit argues, correctly, that it is not the distance in time of the later deformity that matters, but the investment and compensation. Were we not to compensate, this would become irrelevant.

Parfit also discusses what he calls the argument from democracy. Since most people care less about the future, the government, reflecting the views of the electorate, should discount it. But unless we believe that what the electorate wants is *ipso facto* right (*vox populi, vox dei*), the question of whether we should or should not care less about the future has to be answered independently of what the majority wants.

Another argument considered by Parfit is the argument from excessive sacrifice. Without a discount rate, any small increase in benefit that extends indefinitely in time could demand any amount of sacrifice in the present, because in time the benefits outweigh the costs. But, once again, the objection to the argument is that no generation can be required to make excessive sacrifices for future generations. Parfit illustrates this by supposing that, at the same costs to us now, we could prevent either a minor catastrophe in the nearer future or a major catastrophe in the further future. "Since preventing the major catastrophe would involve no extra cost, the 'argument from excessive sacrifice' fails to apply."

Finally, Parfit discusses the argument from special relations. We have greater responsibilities to certain people to whom we stand in special relations: our children, parents, students, patients, clients, fellow citizens. And future generations do not stand in any of these relations. But first, it is the distance in the relationship, which may be correlated to distance in space or in time, rather than the distance in time that matters. Second, the discount rate according to special relationships levels off, and does not increase with time. Our obligations to the tenth generation are no less than to the ninth or eighth. Third, the duty to avoid inflicting grave harm applies to all people, now and in the future.

People who argue that we should not discount the future at all would attach the same weight to enjoyment by myself now, in a few years' time and by all future generations. The refusal to do this has been called by A. C. Pigou the lack of telescopic faculty, and by Roy Harrod the conquest of reason by passion. It must be concluded from the previous arguments that there is no case for a positive time discount rate.

Our Responsibilities to Future Generations

What does intergenerational justice demand? A utilitarian approach might suggest that we owe future generations the same level of utility that we are enjoying now. Since we do not know and cannot determine the size of future generations, this may apply to total utility, distributed among their numbers according to a different set of principles. But there are well known difficulties in distributing utility, happiness or welfare equally, and Brian Barry has argued convincingly[4] that it is opportunities, not welfare, that should be distributed equally over generations. For energy this would mean that we should leave future generations the same productive capacity and therefore the same opportunities to produce that we now enjoy. If we deplete some exhaustible resource, we would have to compensate for this by some technological innovation or capital accumulation that makes any given amount of oil or coal yield more energy, or substitutes some other source for the depleted resource. But compensating for depletion presupposes our knowing how much we should have left to future generations without the depletion. Would it be just if we consumed all the capital we inherited from previous generations and only compensated for the depletion of natural resources we caused? Or would it be just if we added to man-made capital as much as the previous generations had added? Or should we leave the same amount of man-made capital that we inherited, plus compensation for the depletion we caused? These are difficult questions and no answer will be attempted here.

Brian Barry discusses the question, "what does adequate compensation in practice mean?"[5] If we develop a technology that enables us to raise the rate of extraction by the same proportion that we have used up the resource, that would be adequate compensation. Or if we invent a technology that gives us as much power as we have used up, effectively maintaining performance, that would also qualify. Such guidelines take us some way, but not all the way, for different forms of energy have different benefits and costs, which it is not easy in practice to bring to a common denominator.

All this presupposes that humanity should survive. Yet, as Wilfred Beckerman and others have shown, the assumption that we should perpetuate mankind is not logically justified. What is the loss of people who were never conceived and born (say, as a result of contraception or abstention or annihilation of the human race)? Who, if anybody, is worse off because these people have not been born, compared with their potential existence?

We have to turn to the basis of our moral obligation to others and specifically to future generations. Different answers have been given. The facetious question raised above suggests that future generations cannot benefit us. But they also cannot harm us. And one tradition in moral philosophy bases moral obligation on the ability to do harm. Hobbes talked about "convenient articles of peace," which prevent us from harming other people in order to avoid being harmed ourselves by them.[6] If this is the social basis of moral law, we would have no obligations towards future generations, for they are not capable of harming us.

Another basis for moral obligations is Locke's theory of entitlement, according to which a man can do whatever he wishes with his own, if he has legitimately acquired it. The main current expositor of his view is Robert Nozick. From it follow no obligations at all to future generations. If we wished to destroy everything we own, or ask our executors to do so after we die, this would be fully consistent with our moral obligations. A third theory is that of Rousseau, who bases moral obligations on our sense of community. But here again, it is hard to see how we can postulate a sense of community with numerous as yet unborn members of future generations.

So neither the approach and tradition of Hobbes, nor that of Locke, nor that of Rousseau help us in formulating moral duties for the welfare, interest or benefit of persons not yet, or never, born. And it is this that we are concerned with when we talk of future generations. Can it be in a person's interest, or, for that matter, against the person's interest, to have been born? Beckerman and Parfit argue that the answer is No.[7] For if we say it is in a person's interest to have been conceived, we say that this person has benefited from receiving life. But to benefit is to be made better off than he would otherwise have been. But if he had not been conceived, he would not "otherwise have been." However happy his life would have been, had he been born, he does not miss this happiness, not having been born. It is therefore meaningless to say that people benefit from having been conceived and born. The argument is taken one step further by Beckerman.[8] He suggests that even happy people should commit suicide. They will not miss their happiness and might miss some unhappiness that they might suffer later on.

Does the same apply to being worse off for having been born? Some time ago there was a lawsuit of an utterly disabled, miserable person against a doctor's inefficient sterilization of that person's mother. Beckerman argues that the situation may not be symmetrical, and that it might be possible to say that a person would be better off not having been born. (There is a tradition in literature going back to Sophocles asserting that "not to be born is best.") But if we accept the argument that we cannot say that a person is better off than if he had never been born (or conceived), we destroy any claims of future generations on our concern.

Is there not a contradiction in maintaining that there is no case for a positive discount rate and that there is no case for assuming the desirability of the existence of future generations? Can we argue simultaneously that the enjoyment of future generations should count the same as our enjoyment, and that their existence is not desirable? I think the contradiction is only apparent. The argument is that if future generations exist, their enjoyment should not be discounted, but there is no case for the perpetuation of the human race.

Parfit suggests an example.[9] Let us assume that we choose a policy with benefits to us that leads to a catastrophe after two centuries. Had we chosen a safe policy and sacrificed these benefits, the catastrophe would have been avoided. But the people who are harmed by the dangerous policy are different people from those who would have existed had we chosen the safe policy. The timing of the meeting of parents, and of the conception is different, and therefore different people are born into the world. According to Parfit, the dangerous policy is not worse for anyone who ever lives.

Various attempts have been made to escape this conclusion. For example, we might "look in the opposite direction."[10] Our duties are not to future generations, but to our ancestors, who labored to make us better off, but not only us: subsequent generations as well. This view fits the views that we are only trustees of the environment which we inherit, and should hand it on in at least as good a condition as the one in which we received it. But the value of the traditions handed on to us by our ancestors has to be independently assessed. Some of the heritage has been bad, and has to be rejected, like slavery or imperialism. So "looking in the opposite direction" for a moral justification may add strength to duties independently regarded as valid, but it does not provide a basis for our responsibilities.

One way out of the repugnant conclusion that there is no basis for our responsibilities to future generations is to say that particular persons not being made worse off by our actions is not the only reason why these actions can be morally condemned. Assume our action produces the result that the population of people, though themselves not worse off, is worse off than an alternative, hypothetical population of the same number, who would have enjoyed greater benefits had we abstained from our action. Derek Parfit and Douglas MacLean have argued that our action may then be regarded as wrong, even although nobody is made worse off by it.[11] Sidney Holt appears to argue along similar lines when he writes that "to the extent that humanity, past, present and future, is perceived as one with the rest of nature—or, at least, with the living world, the biosphere—so discussion of the rights of animals is inseparable from the discussion of the rights of humanity."[12] Others, on the other hand, think that a policy that makes nobody worse off cannot be morally wrong, even if the fate of people who might have lived, but never did, would have been improved by a different policy.

Even if there were no reason in terms of people's interests for accepting responsibility for the fate of future generations, there may be other reasons. Brian Barry ends his article on "Justice between generations" by saying that "if I try to analyse the source of my own strong conviction that we should be wrong to take risks with the continuation of human life, I find that it does not lie in any sense of injury to the interests of people who will not get born but rather in a sense of its cosmic impertinence—that we should be grossly abusing our position by taking it upon ourselves to put a term on human life and possibilities."[13] In spite of the logical difficulty of justifying the continuation of the human race, we shall in the following accept Brian Barry's view and assert instinctively or genetically or on the basis of a new, extended ethics, not based on benefits and harm to the interests of people, the desirability to perpetuate it.

Some Specific Problems

Sometimes the concern for social justice among contemporaries and between generations is presented as a conflict: why be concerned with future generations when we have so many poor and so much inequality among us now? Trade unionists and the unemployed advocate large projects such as hydroelectric dams and call the ecological opponents "gentlemen's kids." The ecologists blame industrialists for greed and causing future ecological disasters.

But there is no such conflict. In principle, having decided upon how much we owe to future generations, the remainder can be distributed in as egalitarian a manner to the present generation as we wish. Any anti-poverty strategy must have a temporal dimension, and it would be as wrong to remove all poverty now by aggravating poverty later, as it would be to starve ourselves in order to provide plenty for the future. Indeed, since it is the present high-income consumers who use up most exhaustible resources, justice requires that compensation be paid both to low-income consumers and to future generations.

A specific obstacle to exercising our responsibility to future generations arises from an institutional lag, or deficiency. Let us suppose that national governments have assumed responsibility for future generations and, as a result, have adopted policies to conserve exhaustible raw materials and avoid excessive pollution. This assumption is not quite unrealistic, for many governments have in fact adopted such policies. Indeed, it could be argued that it is precisely one of the functions of government to take on these responsibilities through public action, because any one individual, however eager he was on achieving the objective, could not give force to his desires in the absence of coordination or even enforcement of other individuals. It is what economists call a public good.

Having achieved the right policies at the national level, the danger arises that the damage will be exported. Resources outside the national boundaries will then be excessively exploited and the air and water beyond the frontiers will be happily polluted. It is likely that these forms of transnational damage would be even greater than if the national government had taken no action. The growing dispersal of acid rain outside national frontiers as a result of high chimney stacks, imposed to avoid national pollution, and the danger of the extinction of whales are examples.

The greater concern shown for future generations inside the national boundaries has led to a situation in which the same concern outside these boundaries is reduced. The reason for this is that we do not have a world government, a global authority, that would enact the appropriate rules. Even if each nation-state were, individually, concerned about the future of the world community, and not only about future generations inside its borders, it would not be able to give effect to this. The result is a prisoner's dilemma in which each nation is made worse off by the impact of the actions of others. There are also difficulties in getting coordinated action on the part of a group of nation-states. For each state will hope to benefit from the actions of others, were these to show global concerns, without itself contributing to the costs and restraints. It is the free rider problem, superimposed upon the prisoner's dilemma. The solution lies in a surrender of national sovereignty to a supranational authority with power to impose laws and regulations that safeguard the interests of future generations of the global community.[14]

What kinds of moral obligations to future generations may arise? If an action now has no consequences affecting future generations, or entirely beneficial ones, no problem arises. But there are two kinds of other actions. First, actions which benefit us may have harmful consequences for future generations and, second, actions which impose a sacrifice on us may have beneficial consequences. In addition to these choices, there may be actions, whether beneficial or harmful to us, that have different impacts on different future generations, beneficial to some, harmful to others.

It should, however, be noted that in many cases actions that impose an apparent sacrifice turn out, on closer inspection, to be profitable, so that the conflict can be avoided. A company called 3M established a program that is called 3P, which stands for "Pollution prevention pays."[15] Once product and process innovation are included in the analysis, it turns out that there are many unexplored and unexploited profit opportunities that manifest themselves in response to the challenge of pollution control. If the costs of these innovations are less than the new profits to be earned, the whole operation turns out to be economical even from the firm's point of view. In this case no conflict between present and future interests arises.

Let us take as the first illustration the exploitation of exhaustible and irreplaceable natural resources, such as the fossil fuels, mineral reserves, ocean fisheries and tropical forests. It is quite possible for the reductions in these nature-given resources to exceed the accumulation of man-made capital. If this is so, we are using up capital that we have inherited and leaving future generations worse off. Even if there is a net addition to the sum of natural and man-made capital, not making full allowances for the exploitation of natural resources in our national income accounts would lead to overstatements of the amount we leave to future generations.

Let us take as another illustration the dangers to future generations that arise from nuclear power. First, there are the technical dangers of accidents in the extreme case of a core melt in a reactor. But there is also great uncertainty about the dangerous effects, some possibly genetic, and over a long period, of milder exposure to radiation.

Second, there is the danger that material may be stolen from a plant and used for the fabrication of nuclear bombs. A proliferation of such bombs, particularly in the hands of terrorists or other extremists who would not hesitate to use them, constitutes a considerable danger.

Third, there is the danger of sabotage at the plant by enemies or opponents of certain policies. Fourth, there is the danger of an attack in war or civil war on the plant and the consequential release of radiation. Fifth, there is the problem of nuclear waste disposal. Such waste has a very long half life and risks continue for hundreds of years, while all the benefits accrue to the present generation.

A very serious, not much discussed sixth risk to future generations arises from the need to protect the plant against terrorists, saboteurs and enemies. The guards that police these stations have to be armed and given a high degree of discretion with regard to the use of their weapons. Armed private armies are a new phenomenon in democracies and constitute a threat to our civil liberties. It may well be that this social and political threat is more serious than the technical risks of breeder reactors.

The crash of an airliner in which forty people are killed makes headline news, but the death of forty motor car accident victims in different places does not. Spatially concentrated death from a nuclear accident or sabotage is judged worse than random or dispersed death. This reinforces the argument that risks of a disaster befalling, simultaneously, groups of people are worse than risks in which the same number of victims are distributed over time.

To this must be added another element: death caused by the actions of others is judged worse than that caused by our own acceptance of risks. We accept the same risks caused by our rock climbing or driving motor cars that we would not accept if they were inflicted on us involuntarily. And risks from nuclear power are among those that are "downstream." Future generations are both powerless and vulnerable.

Notes

This paper was commissioned by Mr. Salvino Busuttil for a UNESCO project on intergenerational responsibilities. I am grateful to UNESCO for allowing me to publish it and to Salvino Busuttil for his encouragement and support.

1. Sidney Holt, "Towards ensuring the rights of future generations: scientific aspects," UNESCO paper, UNESCO, Paris, September 1982, p 4.
2. Wilfred Beckerman, "Human resources: are they worth preserving?" in Paul Streeten and Harry Maier, eds, *Human Resources, Employment and Development,* Vol 2, *Concepts, Measurements and Long-Run Perspective,* International Economic Association, Macmillan, London, 1983.
3. Derek Parfit, "Energy and the further future: the social discount rate," in Douglas MacLean and Peter G. Brown, eds, *Energy and the Future,* Maryland Studies in Public Philosophy, Rowman & Littlefield, NJ, USA, 1983, Chapter 2.
4. Brian Barry, "Intergenerational justice in energy policy," in Douglas MacLean and Peter G. Brown, eds, *Energy and the Future,* Maryland Studies in Public Philosophy, Rowman & Littlefield, NJ, USA, 1983.

5. *Ibid.*

6. Brian Barry, "Justice between generations," in P. M. S. Hacker and J. Raz, eds, *Law, Morality and Society,* essays in honor of H. L. A. Hart, Oxford, 1977.

7. Beckerman, *op cit,* Ref 2. Parfit, *op cit,* Ref 3.

8. Beckerman, *op cit,* Ref 2.

9. Parfit, *op cit,* Ref 3.

10. Douglas MacLean, "A moral requirement of energy policies," in Douglas MacLean and Peter G. Brown, eds, *Energy and the Future,* Maryland Studies in Public Philosophy, Rowman & Littlefield, NJ, USA, 1983, p 187.

11. Parfit, *op cit,* Ref 3. MacLean, *op cit,* Ref 11.

12. Holt, *op cit,* Ref 1, p 2.

13. Barry, *op cit,* Ref 6.

14. See Peter Inglott, "The rights of future generations: some socio-political considerations," UNESCO paper, unpublished.

15. Joseph T. Ling, vice president, environmental engineering and pollution control, "Pollution prevention does pay," 3M Company, USA. *Industry and Environment,* Vol 7, No 2, United Nations Environmental Programme, 17 rue Marguerite, 75017 Paris.

16.

IS WOMEN'S LABOR A COMMODITY?

Elizabeth Anderson

In the past few years the practice of commercial surrogate motherhood has gained notoriety as a method for acquiring children. A commercial surrogate mother is anyone who is paid money to bear a child for other people and terminate her parental rights, so that the others may raise the child as exclusively their own. The growth of commercial surrogacy has raised with new urgency a class of concerns regarding the proper scope of the market. Some critics have objected to commercial surrogacy on the ground that it improperly treats children and women's reproductive capacities as commodities.[1] The prospect of reducing children to consumer durables and women to baby factories surely inspires revulsion. But are there good reasons behind the revulsion? And is this an accurate description of what commercial surrogacy implies? This chapter offers a theory about what things are properly regarded as commodities which supports the claim that commercial surrogacy constitutes an unconscionable commodification of children and of women's reproductive capacities.

What Is a Commodity?

The modern market can be characterized in terms of the legal and social norms by which it governs the production, exchange, and enjoyment of commodities. To say that something is properly regarded as a commodity is to claim that the

Philosophy and Public Affairs 19 (1990): 71–92.

norms of the market are appropriate for regulating its production, exchange, and enjoyment. To the extent that moral principles or ethical ideals preclude the application of market norms to a good, we may say that the good is not a (proper) commodity.

Why should we object to the application of a market norm to the production or distribution of a good? One reason may be that to produce or distribute the good in accordance with the norm is to *fail to value it in an appropriate way*. Consider, for example, a standard Kantian argument against slavery, or the commodification of persons. Slaves are treated in accordance with the market norm that owners may use commodities to satisfy their own interests without regard for the interests of the commodities themselves. To treat a person without regard for her interests is to fail to respect her. But slaves are persons who may not be merely used in this fashion, since as rational beings they possess a dignity which commands respect. In Kantian theory, the problem with slavery is that it treats beings worthy of *respect* as if they were worthy merely of *use*. "Respect" and "use" in this context denote what we may call different *modes of valuation*. We value things and persons in other ways than by respecting and using them. For example, love, admiration, honor, and appreciation constitute distinct modes of valuation. To value a thing or person in a distinctive way involves treating it in accordance with a particular set of norms. For example, courtesy expresses a mode of valuation we may call "civil respect," which differs from Kantian respect in that it calls for obedience to the rules of etiquette rather than to the categorical imperative.

Any ideal of human life includes a conception of how different things and persons should be valued. Let us reserve the term "use" to refer to the mode of valuation proper to commodities, which follows the market norm of treating things solely in accordance with the owner's nonmoral preferences. Then the Kantian argument against commodifying persons can be generalized to apply to many other cases. It can be argued that many objects which are worthy of a higher mode of valuation than use are not properly regarded as mere commodities.[2] Some current arguments against the colorization of classic black-and-white films take this form. Such films have been colorized by their owners in an attempt to enhance their market value by attracting audiences unused to black-and-white cinematography. But some opponents of the practice object that such treatment of the film classics fails to appreciate their aesthetic and historical value. True appreciation of these films would preclude this kind of crass commercial exploitation, which debases their aesthetic qualities in the name of profits. Here the argument rests on the claim that the goods in question are worthy of appreciation, not merely of use.

The ideals which specify how one should value certain things are supported by a conception of human flourishing. Our lives are enriched and elevated by cultivating and exercising the capacity to appreciate art. To fail to do so reflects poorly on ourselves. To fail to value things appropriately is to embody in one's life an inferior conception of human flourishing.[3]

These considerations support a general account of the sorts of things which are appropriately regarded as commodities. Commodities are those things which are properly treated in accordance with the norms of the modern market. We can question the application of market norms to the production, distribution, and enjoyment of a good by appealing to ethical ideals which support arguments that the good should be valued in some other way than use. Arguments of the latter sort claim that to allow certain market norms to govern our treatment of a thing expresses a mode of valuation not worthy of it. If the thing is to be valued appropriately, its production, exchange, and enjoyment must be removed from market norms and embedded in a different set of social relationships.

The Case of Commercial Surrogacy

Let us now consider the practice of commercial surrogate motherhood in the light of this theory of commodities. Surrogate motherhood as a commercial enterprise is based upon contracts involving three parties: the intended father, the broker, and the surrogate mother. The intended father agrees to pay a lawyer to find a suitable surrogate mother and make the requisite medical and legal arrangements for the conception and birth of the child, and for the transfer of legal custody to himself.[4] The surrogate mother agrees to become impregnated with the intended father's sperm, to carry the resulting child to term, and to relinquish her parental rights to it, transferring custody to the father in return for a fee and medical expenses. Both she and her husband (if she has one) agree not to form a parent-child bond with her child and to do everything necessary to effect the transfer of the child to the intended father. At current market prices, the lawyer arranging the contract can expect to gross $15,000 from the contract, while the surrogate mother can expect a $10,000 fee.[5]

The practice of commercial surrogacy has been defended on four main grounds. First, given the shortage of children available for adoption and the difficulty of qualifying as adoptive parents, it may represent the only hope for some people to be able to raise a family. Commercial surrogacy should be accepted as an effective means for realizing this highly significant good. Second, two fundamental human rights support commercial surrogacy: the right to procreate and freedom of contract. Fully informed autonomous adults should have the right to make whatever arrangements they wish for the use of their bodies and the reproduction of children, so long as the children themselves are not harmed. Third, the labor of the surrogate mother is said to be a labor of love. Her altruistic acts should be permitted and encouraged.[6] Finally, it is argued that commercial surrogacy is no different in its ethical implications from many already accepted practices which separate genetic, gestational, and social parenting, such as artificial insemination by donor, adoption, wet-nursing, and day care. Consistency demands that society accept this new practice as well.[7]

In opposition to these claims, I shall argue that commercial surrogacy does raise new ethical issues, since it represents an invasion of the market into a new sphere of conduct, that of specifically women's labor—that is, the labor of carrying children to term in pregnancy. When women's labor is treated as a commodity, the women who perform it are degraded. Furthermore, commercial surrogacy degrades children by reducing their status to that of commodities. Let us consider each of the goods of concern in surrogate motherhood—the child, and women's reproductive labor—to see how the commercialization of parenthood affects people's regard for them.

Children as Commodities

The most fundamental calling of parents to their children is to love them. Children are to be loved and cherished by their parents, not to be used or manipulated by them for merely personal advantage. Parental love can be understood as a passionate, unconditional commitment to nurture one's child, providing it with the care, affection, and guidance it needs to develop its capacities to maturity. This understanding of the way parents should value their children informs our interpretation of parental rights over their children. Parents' rights over their children are trusts, which they must always exercise for the sake of the child. This is not to deny that parents have their own aspirations in raising children. But the child's interests beyond subsistence are not definable independently of the flourishing of the family, which is the object of specifically parental aspirations. The proper exercise of parental rights includes those acts which promote their shared life as a family, which realize the shared interests of the parents and the child.

The norms of parental love carry implications for the ways other people should treat the relationship between parents and their children. If children are to be loved by their parents, then others should not attempt to compromise the integrity of parental love or work to suppress the emotions supporting the bond between parents and their children. If the rights to children should be understood as trusts, then if those rights are lost or relinquished, the duty of those in charge of transferring custody to others is to consult the best interests of the child.

Commercial surrogacy substitutes market norms for some of the norms of parental love. Most importantly, it requires us to understand parental rights no longer as trusts but as things more like property rights—that is, rights of use and disposal over the things owned. For in this practice the natural mother deliberately conceives a child with the intention of giving it up for material advantage. Her renunciation of parental responsibilities is not done for the child's sake, nor for the sake of fulfilling an interest she shares with the child, but typically for her own sake (and possibly, if "altruism" is a motive, for the intended parents' sakes). She and the couple who pay her to give up her parental rights over her child thus treat her rights as a kind of property right. They thereby treat the child itself as a kind of commodity, which may be properly bought and sold.

Commercial surrogacy insinuates the norms of commerce into the parental relationship in other ways. Whereas parental love is not supposed to be conditioned upon the child having particular characteristics, consumer demand is properly responsive to the characteristics of commodities. So the surrogate industry provides opportunities to adoptive couples to specify the height, IQ, race, and other attributes of the surrogate mother, in the expectation that these traits will be passed on to the child.[8] Since no industry assigns agents to look after the "interests" of its commodities, no one represents the child's interests in the surrogate industry. The surrogate agency promotes the adoptive parents' interests and not the child's interests where matters of custody are concerned. Finally, as the agent of the adoptive parents, the broker has the task of policing the surrogate (natural) mother's relationship to her child, using persuasion, money, and the threat of a lawsuit to weaken and destroy whatever parental love she may develop for her child.[9]

All of these substitutions of market norms for parental norms represent ways of treating children as commodities which are degrading to them. Degradation occurs when something is treated in accordance with a lower mode of valuation than is proper to it. We value things not just "more" or "less," but in qualitatively higher and lower ways. To love or respect someone is to value her in a higher way than one would if one merely used her. Children are properly loved by their parents and respected by others. Since children are valued as mere use-objects by the mother and the surrogate agency when they are sold to others, and by the adoptive parents when they seek to conform the child's genetic makeup to their own wishes, commercial surrogacy degrades children insofar as it treats them as commodities.[10]

One might argue that since the child is most likely to enter a loving home, no harm comes to it from permitting the natural mother to treat it as property. So the purchase and sale of infants is unobjectionable, at least from the point of view of children's interests.[11] But the sale of an infant has an expressive significance which this argument fails to recognize. By engaging in the transfer of children by sale, all of the parties to the surrogate contract express a set of attitudes toward children which undermine the norms of parental love. They all agree in treating the ties between a natural mother and her children as properly loosened by a monetary incentive. Would it be any wonder if a child born of a surrogacy agreement feared resale by parents who have such an attitude? And a child who knew how anxious her parents were that she have the "right" genetic makeup might fear that her parent's love was contingent upon her expression of these characteristics.[12]

The unsold children of surrogate mothers are also harmed by commercial surrogacy. The children of some surrogate mothers have reported their fears that they may be sold like their half-brother or half-sister, and express a sense of loss at being deprived of a sibling.[13] Furthermore, the widespread acceptance of commercial surrogacy would psychologically threaten all children. For it would change the way children are valued by people (parents and surrogate brokers)—from being loved by their parents and respected by others, to being sometimes used as objects of commercial profit-making.[14]

Proponents of commercial surrogacy have denied that the surrogate industry engages in the sale of children. For it is impossible to sell to someone what is already his own, and the child is already the father's own natural offspring. The payment to the surrogate mother is not for her child, but for her services in carrying it to term.[15] The claim that the parties to the surrogate contract treat children as commodities, however, is based on the way they treat the *mother's* rights over her child. It is irrelevant that the natural father also has some rights over the child; what he pays for is exclusive rights to it. He would not pay her for the "service" of carrying the child to term if she refused to relinquish her parental rights to it. That the mother regards only her labor and not her child as requiring compensation is also irrelevant. No one would argue that the baker does not treat his bread as property just because he sees the income from its sale as compensation for his labor and expenses and not for the bread itself, which he doesn't care to keep.[16]

Defenders of commercial surrogacy have also claimed that it does not differ substantially from other already accepted parental practices. In the institutions of adoption and artificial insemination by donor (AID), it is claimed, we already grant parents the right to dispose of their children.[17] But these practices differ in significant respects from commercial surrogacy. The purpose of adoption is to provide a means for placing children in families when their parents cannot or will not discharge their parental responsibilities. It is not a sphere for the existence of a supposed parental right to dispose of one's children for profit. Even AID does not sanction the sale of fully formed human beings. The semen donor sells only a product of his body, not his child, and does not initiate the act of conception.

Two developments might seem to undermine the claim that commercial surrogacy constitutes a degrading commerce in children. The first is technological: the prospect of transplanting a human embryo into the womb of a genetically unrelated woman. If commercial surrogacy used women only as gestational mothers and not as genetic mothers, and if it was thought that only genetic and not gestational parents could properly claim that a child was "theirs," then the child born of a surrogate mother would not be hers to sell in the first place. The second is a legal development: the establishment of the proposed "consent-intent" definition of parenthood.[18] This would declare the legal parents of a child to be whoever consented to a procedure which leads to its birth, with the intent of assuming parental responsibilities for it. This rule would define away the problem of commerce in children by depriving the surrogate mother of any legal claim to her child at all, even if it was hers both genetically and gestationally.[19]

There are good reasons, however, not to undermine the place of genetic and gestational ties in these ways. Consider first the place of genetic ties. By upholding a system of involuntary (genetic) ties of obligation among people, even when the adults among them prefer to divide their rights and obligations in other ways, we help to secure children's interests in having an assured place in the world, which is more firm than the wills of their parents. Unlike the consent-intent rule, the principle of respecting genetic ties does not make the obligation to care for those whom one has created (intentionally or not) contingent upon an arbitrary desire to do so. It thus provides children with a set of pre-existing social sanctions which give them a more secure place in the world. The genetic principle also places children in a far wider network of associations and obligations than the consent-intent rule sanctions. It supports the roles of grandparents and other relatives in the nurturing of children, and provides children with a possible focus of stability and an additional source of claims to care if their parents cannot sustain a well-functioning household.

In the next section I will defend the claims of gestational ties to children. To deny these claims, as commercial surrogacy does, is to deny the significance of reproductive labor to the mother who undergoes it and thereby to dehumanize and degrade the mother herself. Commercial surrogacy would be a corrupt practice even if it did not involve commerce in children.

Women's Labor as a Commodity

Commercial surrogacy attempts to transform what is specifically women's labor—the work of bringing forth children into the world—into a commodity. It does so by replacing the parental norms which usually govern the practice of gestating children with the economic norms which govern ordinary production processes. The application of commercial norms to women's labor reduces the surrogate mothers from persons worthy of respect and consideration to objects of mere use.

Respect and consideration are two distinct modes of valuation whose norms are violated by the practices of the surrogate industry. To respect a person is to treat her in accordance with principles she rationally accepts—principles consistent with the protection of her autonomy and her rational interests. To treat a person with consideration is to respond with sensitivity to her and to her emotional relations with others, refraining from manipulating or denigrating these for one's own purposes. Given the understanding of respect as a dispassionate, impersonal regard for people's interests, a different ethical concept—consideration—is needed to capture the engaged and sensitive regard we should have for people's emotional relationships. The failure of consideration on the part of the other parties to the surrogacy contract explains the judgment that the contract is not simply disrespectful of the surrogate mother, but callous as well.[20]

The application of economic norms to the sphere of women's labor violates women's claims to respect and consideration in three ways. First, by requiring the surrogate mother to repress whatever parental love she feels for the child, these norms convert women's labor into a form of alienated labor. Second, by manipulating and denying legitimacy to the surrogate mother's evolving perspective on her own pregnancy, the norms of the market degrade her. Third, by taking advantage of the surrogate mother's noncommercial motivations without offering anything but what the norms of commerce demand in return, these norms leave her open to exploitation. The fact that these problems arise in the attempt to commercialize the labor of bearing children shows that women's labor is not properly regarded as a commodity.

The key to understanding these problems is the normal role of the emotions in noncommercialized pregnancies. Pregnancy is not simply a biological process but also a social practice. Many social expectations and considerations surround women's gestational labor, marking it off as an occasion for the parents to prepare themselves to welcome a new life into their family. For example, obstetricians use ultrasound not simply for diagnostic purposes but also to encourage maternal bonding with the fetus.[21] We can all recognize that it is good, although by no means inevitable, for loving bonds to be established between the mother and her child during this period.

In contrast with these practices, the surrogate industry follows the putting-out system of manufacturing. It provides some of the raw materials of production (the father's sperm) to the surrogate mother, who then engages in production of the child. Although her labor is subject to periodic supervision by her doctors and by the surrogate agency, the agency does not have physical control over the product of her labor as firms using the factory system do. Hence, as in all putting-out systems, the surrogate industry faces the problem of extracting the final product from the mother. This problem is exacerbated by the fact that the social norms surrounding pregnancy are designed to encourage parental love for the child. The surrogate industry addresses this problem by requiring the mother to engage in a form of emotional labor.[22] In the surrogate contract, she agrees not to form or to attempt to form a parent-child relationship with her offspring.[23] Her labor is alienated, because she must divert it from the end which the social practices of pregnancy rightly promote—an emotional bond with her child. The surrogate contract thus replaces a norm of parenthood, that during pregnancy one create a loving attachment to one's child, with a norm of commercial production, that the producer shall not form any special emotional ties to her product.

The demand to deliberately alienate oneself from one's love for one's own child is a demand which can reasonably and decently be made of no one. Unless we were to remake pregnancy into a form of drudgery which is only performed for a wage, there is every reason to expect that many women who do sign a surrogate contract will, despite this fact, form a loving attachment to the child they bear. For this is what the social practices surrounding pregnancy encourage. Treating women's labor as just another kind of commercial production process violates the precious emotional ties which the mother may rightly and properly establish with her "product," the child, and thereby violates her claims to consideration.[24]

Commercial surrogacy is also a degrading practice. The surrogate mother, like all persons, has an independent evaluative perspective on her activities and relationships. The realization of her dignity demands that the other parties to the contract acknowledge rather than evade the claims which her independent perspective makes upon them. But the surrogate industry has an interest in suppressing, manipulating, and trivializing her perspective, for there is an ever-present danger that she will see her involvement in her pregnancy from the perspective of a parent rather than from the perspective of a contract laborer.

How does this suppression and trivialization take place? The commercial promoters of surrogacy commonly describe the surrogate mothers as inanimate objects: mere "hatcheries," "plumbing," or "rented property"—things without emotions which could make claims on others.[25] They also refuse to acknowledge any responsibility for the consequences of the mother's emotional labor. Should she suffer psychologically from being forced to give up her child, the father is not liable to pay for therapy after her pregnancy, although he is liable for all other medical expenses following her pregnancy.[26]

The treatment and interpretation of surrogate mothers' grief raises the deepest problems of degradation. Most surrogate mothers experience grief upon giving up their children—in 10 percent of cases, seriously enough to require therapy.[27] Their grief is not compensated by the $10,000 fee they receive. Grief is not an intelligible response to a successful deal, but rather reflects the subject's judgment that she has suffered a grave and personal loss. Since not all cases of grief resolve themselves into cases of regret, it may be that some surrogate mothers do not regard their grief, in retrospect, as reflecting an authentic judgment on their part. But in the circumstances of emotional manipulation which pervade the surrogate industry, it is difficult to determine which interpretation of her grief more truly reflects the perspective of the surrogate mother. By insinuating a trivializing interpretation of her emotional responses to the prospect of losing her child, the surrogate agency may be able to manipulate her into accepting her fate without too much fuss, and may even succeed in substituting its interpretation of her emotions for her own. Since she has already signed a contract to perform emotional labor—to express or repress emotions which are dictated by the interests of the surrogate industry—this might not be a difficult task.[28] A considerate treatment of the mothers' grief, on the other hand, would take the evaluative basis of their grief seriously.

Some defenders of commercial surrogacy demand that the provision for terminating the surrogate mother's parental rights in her child be legally enforceable, so that peace of mind for the adoptive parents can be secured.[29] But the surrogate industry makes no corresponding provision for securing the peace of mind of the surrogate. She is expected to assume the risk of a transformation of her ethical and emotional perspective on herself and her child with the same impersonal detachment with which a futures trader assumes the risk of a fluctuation in the price of pork bellies. By applying the market norms of enforcing contracts to the surrogate mother's case, commercial surrogacy treats a moral transformation as if it were merely an economic change.[30]

The manipulation of the surrogate mother's emotions which is inherent in the surrogate parenting contract also leaves women open to grave forms of exploitation. A kind of exploitation occurs when one party to a transaction is oriented toward the exchange of "gift" values, while the other party operates in accordance with the norms of the market exchange of commodities. Gift values, which include love, gratitude, and appreciation of others, cannot be bought or obtained through piecemeal calculations of individual advantage. Their exchange requires a repudiation of a self-interested attitude, a willingness to give gifts to others without demanding some specific equivalent good in return each time one gives. The surrogate mother often operates according to the norms of gift relationships. The surrogate agency, on the other hand, follows market norms. Its job is to get the best deal for its clients and itself, while leaving the surrogate mother to look after her own interests as best as she can. This situation puts the surrogate agencies in a position to manipulate the surrogate mothers' emotions to gain favorable terms for themselves. For example, agencies screen prospective surrogate mothers for submissiveness, and emphasize to them the importance of the motives of generosity and love. When applicants question some of the terms of the contract, the broker sometimes intimidates them by questioning their character and morality: if they were really generous and loving they would not be so solicitous about their own interests.[31]

Some evidence supports the claim that most surrogate mothers are motivated by emotional needs and vulnerabilities which lead them to view their labor as a form of gift and not a purely commercial exchange. Only 1 percent of applicants to surrogate agencies would become surrogate mothers for money alone; the others have emotional as well as financial reasons for applying. One psychiatrist believes that most, if not all, of the 35 percent of applicants who had had a previous abortion or given up a child for adoption wanted to become surrogate mothers in order to resolve their guilty feelings or deal with their unresolved loss by going through a process of losing a child again.[32] Women who feel that giving up another child is an effective way to punish themselves for past abortions, or a form of therapy for their emotional problems, are not likely to resist manipulation by surrogate brokers.

Many surrogate mothers see pregnancy as a way to feel "adequate," "appreciated," or "special." In other words, these women feel inadequate, unappreciated, or unadmired when they are not pregnant.[33] Lacking the power to achieve some worthwhile status in their own right, they must subordinate themselves to others' definitions of their proper place (as baby factories) in order to get from them the appreciation they need to attain a sense of self-worth. But the sense of self-worth one can attain under such circumstances is precarious and ultimately self-defeating. For example, those who seek gratitude on the part of the adoptive parents and some opportunity to share the joys of seeing their children grow discover all too often that the adoptive parents want nothing to do with them.[34] For while the surrogate mother sees in the arrangement some basis for establishing the personal ties she needs to sustain her emotionally, the adoptive couple sees it as an impersonal commercial contract, one of whose main advantages to them is that all ties between them and the surrogate are ended once the terms of the contract are fulfilled.[35] To them, her presence is a threat to marital unity and a competing object for the child's affections.

These considerations should lead us to question the model of altruism which is held up to women by the surrogacy industry. It is a strange form of altruism which demands such radical self-effacement, alienation from those whom one benefits, and the subordination of one's body, health, and emotional life to the independently defined interests of others.[36] Why should this model of "altruism" be held up to *women*? True altruism does not involve such subordination, but rather the autonomous and self-confident exercise of skill, talent, and judgment. (Consider the dedicated doctor.) The kind of altruism we see admired in surrogate mothers involves a lack of self-confidence, a feeling that one can be truly worthy only through self-effacement. This model of altruism, far from affirming the freedom and dignity of women, seems all too conveniently designed to keep their sense of self-worth hostage to the interests of a more privileged class.[37]

The primary distortions which arise from treating women's labor as a commodity—the surrogate mother's alienation from loved ones, her degradation, and her exploitation—stem from a common source. This is the failure to acknowledge and treat appropriately the surrogate mother's emotional engagement with her labor. Her labor is alienated, because she must suppress her emotional ties with her own child, and may be manipulated into reinterpreting these ties in a trivializing way. She is degraded, because her independent ethical perspective is denied, or demoted to the status of a cash sum. She is exploited, because her emotional needs and vulnerabilities are not treated as characteristics which call for consideration, but as factors which may be manipulated to encourage her to make a grave self-sacrifice to the broker's and adoptive couple's advantage. These considerations provide strong grounds for sustaining the claims of women's labor to its "product," the child. The attempt to redefine parenthood so as to strip women of parental claims to the children they bear does violence to their emotional engagement with the project of bringing children into the world.

Commercial Surrogacy, Freedom, and the Law

In the light of these ethical objections to commercial surrogacy, what position should the law take on the practice? At the very least, surrogate contracts should not be enforceable. Surrogate mothers should not be forced to relinquish their children if they have formed emotional bonds with them. Any other treatment of women's ties to the children they bear is degrading.

But I think these arguments support the stronger conclusion that commercial surrogate contracts should be illegal, and that surrogate agencies who arrange such contracts should be subject to criminal penalties.[38] Commercial surrogacy constitutes a degrading and harmful traffic in children, violates the dignity of women, and subjects both children and women to a serious risk of exploitation. But are these problems inherent in the practice of commercial surrogacy? Defenders of the practice have suggested three reforms intended to eliminate these problems: (1) give the surrogate mother the option of keeping her child after birth; (2) impose stringent regulations on private surrogate agencies; (3) replace private surrogate agencies with a state-run monopoly on surrogate arrangements. Let us consider each of these options in turn.

Some defenders of commercial surrogacy suggest that the problem of respecting the surrogate mother's potential attachment to her child can be solved by granting the surrogate mother the option to reserve her parental rights after birth.[39] But such an option would not significantly change the conditions of the surrogate mother's labor. Indeed, such a provision would pressure the agency to demean the mother's self-regard more than ever. Since it could not rely on the law to enforce the adoptive parents' wishes regardless of the surrogate's feelings, it would have to make sure that she assumed the perspective which it and its clients have of her: as "rented plumbing."

Could such dangers be avoided by careful regulation of the surrogate industry? Some have suggested that exploitation of women could be avoided by such measures as properly screening surrogates, setting low fixed fees (to avoid tempting women in financial duress), and requiring independent counsel for the surrogate mother.[40] But no one knows how to predict who will suffer grave psychological damage from surrogacy, and the main forms of duress encountered in the industry are emotional rather than financial. Furthermore, there is little hope that regulation would check the exploitation of surrogate mothers. The most significant encounters between the mothers and the surrogate agencies take place behind closed doors. It is impossible to regulate the multifarious ways in which brokers can subtly manipulate the emotions of the vulnerable to their own advantage. Advocates of commercial surrogacy claim that their failure rate is extremely low, since only five out of the first five hundred cases were legally contested by surrogate mothers. But we do not know how many surrogate mothers were browbeaten into relinquishing their children, feel violated by their treatment, or would feel violated had their perspectives not been manipulated by the other parties to the contract. The dangers of exploiting women through commercial surrogacy are too great to ignore, and too deep to effectively regulate.

Could a state-run monopoly on surrogate arrangements eliminate the risk of degrading and exploiting surrogate mothers?[41] A nonprofit state agency would arguably have no incentive to exploit surrogates, and it would screen the adoptive parents for the sake of the best interests of the child. Nevertheless, as long as the surrogate mother is paid money to bear a child and terminate her parental rights, the commercial norms leading to her degradation still apply. For these norms are constitutive of our understanding of what the surrogate contract is for. Once such an arrangement becomes socially legitimized, these norms will govern the understandings of participants in the practice and of society at large, or at least compete powerfully with the rival parental norms. And what judgment do these norms make of a mother who, out of love for her child, decides that she cannot relinquish it? They blame her for commercial irresponsibility and flighty emotions. Her transformation of moral and emotional perspective, which she experiences as real but painful growth, looks like a capricious and selfish exercise of will from the standpoint of the market, which does not distinguish the deep commitments of love from arbitrary matters of taste.[42]

The fundamental problem with commercial surrogacy is that commercial norms are inherently manipulative when they are applied to the sphere of parental love. Manipulation occurs whenever norms are deployed to psychologically coerce others into a position where they cannot defend their own interests or articulate their own perspective without being charged with irresponsibility or immorality for doing so. A surrogate contract is inherently manipulative, since the very form of the contract invokes commercial norms which, whether upheld by the law or by social custom only, imply that the mother should feel guilty and irresponsible for loving her own child.

But hasn't the surrogate mother decided in advance that she is not interested in viewing her relationship to her child in this way? Regardless of her initial state of mind, once she enters the contract, she is not free to develop an autonomous perspective on her relationship with her child. She is contractually bound to manipulate her emotions to agree with the interests of the adoptive parents. Few things reach deeper into the self than a parent's evolving relationship with her own child. To lay claim to the course of this relationship in virtue of a cash payment constitutes a severe violation of the mother's personhood and a denial of the mother's autonomy.

Two final objections stand in the way of criminalizing commercial surrogacy. Prohibiting the practice might be thought to infringe two rights: the right of procreation, and the right to freedom of contract. Judge Harvey Sorkow, in upholding the legality and enforceability of commercial surrogate parenting contracts, based much of his argument on an interpretation of the freedom to procreate. He argued that the protection of the right to procreate requires the protection of noncoital means of procreation, including commercial surrogacy. The interests upheld by the creation of the family are the same, regardless of the means used to bring the family into existence.[43]

Sorkow asserts a blanket right to procreate, without carefully examining the specific human interests protected by such a right. The interest protected by the right to procreate is that of being able to create and sustain a family life with some integrity. But the enforcement of surrogate contracts against the will of the mother destroys one family just as surely as it creates another. And the same interest which generates the right to procreate also generates an obligation to uphold the integrity of family life which constrains the exercise of this right.[44] To recognize the legality of commercial surrogate contracts would undermine the integrity of families by giving public sanction to a practice which expresses contempt for the moral and emotional ties which bind a mother to her children, legitimates the view that these ties are merely the product of arbitrary will, properly loosened by the offering of a monetary incentive, and fails to respect the claims of genetic and gestational ties to children which provide children with a more secure place in the world than commerce can supply.

The freedom of contract provides weaker grounds for supporting commercial surrogacy. This freedom is already constrained, notably in preventing the purchase and sale of human beings. Yet one might object that prohibiting surrogate contracts could undermine the status of women by implying that they do not have the competence to enter into and rationally discharge the obligations of commercial contracts. Insofar as the justification for prohibiting commercial surrogacy depends upon giving special regard to women's emotional ties to their children, it might be thought to suggest that women as a group are too emotional to subject themselves to the dispassionate discipline of the market. Then prohibiting surrogate contracts would be seen as an offensive, paternalistic interference with the autonomy of the surrogate mothers.

We have seen, however, that the content of the surrogate contract itself compromises the autonomy of surrogate mothers. It uses the norms of commerce in a manipulative way and commands the surrogate mothers to conform their emotions to the interests of the other parties to the contract. The surrogate industry fails to acknowledge the surrogate mothers as possessing an independent perspective worthy of consideration. And it takes advantage of motivations—such as self-effacing "altruism"—which women have formed under social conditions inconsistent with genuine autonomy. Hence the surrogate industry itself, far from expanding the realm of autonomy for women, actually undermines the external and internal conditions required for fully autonomous choice by women.

If commercial surrogate contracts were prohibited, this would be no cause for infertile couples to lose hope for raising a family. The option of adoption is still available, and every attempt should be made to open up opportunities for adoption to couples who do not meet standard requirements—for example, because of age. While there is a shortage of healthy white infants available for adoption, there is no shortage of children of other races, mixed-race children, and older and handicapped children who desperately need to be adopted. Leaders of the surrogate industry have proclaimed that commercial surrogacy may replace adoption as the method of choice for infertile couples who wish to raise families. But we should be wary of the racist and eugenic motivations which make some people rally to the surrogate industry at the expense of children who already exist and need homes.

The case of commercial surrogacy raises deep questions about the proper scope of the market in modern industrial societies. I have argued that there are principled grounds for rejecting the substitution of market norms for parental norms to govern the ways women bring children into the world. Such substitutions express ways of valuing mothers and children which reflect an inferior conception of human flourishing. When market norms are applied to the ways we allocate and understand parental rights and responsibilities, children are reduced from subjects of love to objects of use. When market norms are applied to the ways we treat and understand women's reproductive labor, women are reduced from subjects of respect and consideration to objects of use. If we are to retain the capacity to value children and women in ways consistent with a rich conception of human flourishing, we must resist the encroachment of the market upon the sphere of reproductive labor. Women's labor is *not* a commodity.

Notes

The author thanks David Anderson, Steven Darwall, Ezekiel Emanuel, Daniel Hausman, Don Herzog, Robert Nozick, Richard Pildes, John Rawls, Michael Sandel, Thomas Scanlon, and Howard Wial for helpful comments and criticisms.

1. See, for example, Gena Corea, *The Mother Machine* (New York: Harper and Row, 1985), pp. 216, 219; Angela Holder, "Surrogate Mother-

hood: Babies for Fun and Profit," *Case and Comment* 90 (1985): 3–11; and Margaret Jane Radin, "Market Inalienability," *Harvard Law Review* 100 (June 1987): 1849–1937.

2. The notion of valuing something more highly than another can be understood as follows. Some preferences are neither obligatory nor admirable. To value a thing as a mere use-object is to treat it solely in accordance with such nonethical preferences. To value a thing or person more highly than as a mere use-object is to recognize it as having some special intrinsic worth, in virtue of which we form preferences about how to treat the thing which we regard as obligatory or admirable. The person who truly appreciates art does not conceive of art merely as a thing which she can use as she pleases, but as something which commands appreciation. It would be contemptible to willfully destroy the aesthetic qualities of a work of art simply to satisfy some of one's nonethical preferences, and it is a mark of a cultivated and hence admirable person that she has preferences for appreciating art. This account of higher and lower modes of valuation is indebted to Charles Taylor's account of higher and lower values. See Charles Taylor, "The Diversity of Goods," in *Utilitarianism and Beyond,* ed. Amartya Sen and Bernard Williams (Cambridge: Cambridge University Press, 1982), pp. 129–44.

3. This kind of argument shows why treating something as a commodity may be deplorable. Of course, more has to be said to justify prohibiting the commodification of a thing. I shall argue below that the considerations against the commodification of children and of women's labor are strong enough to justify prohibiting the practice of commercial surrogacy.

4. State laws against selling babies prevent the intended father's wife (if he has one) from being a party to the contract.

5. See Katie Marie Brophy, "A Surrogate Mother Contract to Bear a Child," *Journal of Family Law* 20 (1981–82): 263–91, and Noel Keane, "The Surrogate Parenting Contract," *Adelphia Law Journal* 2 (1983): 45–53, for examples and explanations of surrogate parenting contracts.

6. Mary Warnock, *A Question of Life* (Oxford: Blackwell, 1985), p. 45. This book reprints the Warnock Report on Human Fertilization and Embryology, which was commissioned by the British government for the purpose of recommending legislation concerning surrogacy and other issues. Although the Warnock Report mentions the promotion of altruism as one defense of surrogacy, it strongly condemns the practice overall.

7. John Robertson, "Surrogate Mothers: Not So Novel after All," *Hastings Center Report,* October 1983, pp. 28–34; John Harris, *The Value of Life* (Boston: Routledge and Kegan Paul, 1985).

8. See "No Other Hope for Having a Child," *Time,* 19 January 1987, pp. 50–51. Radin argues that women's traits are also commodified in this practice. See "Market Inalienability," pp. 1932–35.

9. Here I discuss the surrogate industry as it actually exists today. I will consider possible modifications of commercial surrogacy in the final section.

10. Robert Nozick has objected that my claims about parental love appear to

be culture-bound. Do not parents in the Third World, who rely on children to provide for the family subsistence, regard their children as economic goods? In promoting the livelihood of their families, however, such children need not be treated in accordance with market norms—that is, as commodities. In particular, such children usually remain a part of their families, and hence can still be loved by their parents. But insofar as children are treated according to the norms of modern capitalist markets, this treatment is deplorable wherever it takes place.

11. See Elizabeth Landes and Richard Posner, "The Economics of the Baby Shortage," *Journal of Legal Studies* 7 (1978): 323–48, and Richard Posner, "The Regulation of the Market in Adoptions," *Boston University Law Review* 67 (1987): 59–72.

12. Of course, where children are concerned, it is irrelevant whether these fears are reasonable. One of the greatest fears of children is separation from their parents. Adopted children are already known to suffer from separation anxiety more acutely than children who remain with their natural mothers, for they feel that their original mothers did not love them. In adoption, the fact that the child would be even worse off if the mother did not give it up justifies her severing of ties and can help to rationalize this event to the child. But in the case of commercial surrogacy, the severing of ties is done not for the child's sake, but for the parents' sakes. In the adoption case there are explanations for the mother's action which may quell the child's doubts about being loved which are unavailable in the case of surrogacy.

13. Kay Longcope, "Surrogacy: Two Professionals on Each Side of Issue Give Their Arguments for Prohibition and Regulation," *Boston Globe,* 23 March 1987, pp. 18–19; Iver Peterson, "Baby M Case: Surrogate Mothers Vent Feelings," *New York Times,* 2 March 1987, pp. B1, B4.

14. Herbert Krimmel, "The Case against Surrogate Parenting," *Hastings Center Report,* October 1983, pp. 35–37.

15. Judge Sorkow made this argument in ruling on the famous case of Baby M. See *In Re Baby M,* 217 N.J. Super 313. Reprinted in *Family Law Reporter* 13 (1987): 2001–30. Chief Justice Wilentz of the New Jersey Supreme Court overruled Sorkow's judgment. See *In the Matter of Baby M,* 109 N.J. 396, 537 A.2d 1227 (1988).

16. Sallyann Payton has observed that the law does not permit the sale of parental rights, only their relinquishment or forced termination by the state, and these acts are subject to court review for the sake of the child's best interests. But this legal technicality does not change the moral implications of the analogy with baby-selling. The mother is still paid to do what she can to relinquish her parental rights and to transfer custody of the child to the father. Whether or not the courts occasionally prevent this from happening, the actions of the parties express a commercial orientation to children which is degrading and harmful to them. The New Jersey Supreme Court ruled that surrogacy contracts are void precisely because they assign custody without regard to the child's best interests. See *In the Matter of Baby M,* p. 1246.

17. Robertson, "Surrogate Mothers: Not So Novel after All," p. 32; Harris, *The Value of Life*, pp. 144–45.

18. See Philip Parker, "Surrogate Motherhood: The Interaction of Litigation, Legislation and Psychiatry," *International Journal of Law and Psychiatry* 5 (1982): 341–54.

19. The consent-intent rule would not, however, change the fact that commercial surrogacy replaces parental norms with market norms. For the rule itself embodies the market norm which acknowledges only voluntary, contractual relations among people as having moral force. Whereas familial love invites children into a network of unwilled relationships broader than those they have with their parents, the willed contract creates an exclusive relationship between the parents and the child only.

20. I thank Steven Darwall and David Anderson for clarifying my thoughts on this point.

21. I am indebted to Dr. Ezekiel Emanuel for this point.

22. One engages in emotional labor when one is paid to express or repress certain emotions. On the concept of emotional labor and its consequences for workers, see Arlie Hochschild, *The Managed Heart* (Berkeley and Los Angeles: University of California Press, 1983).

23. Noel Keane and Dennis Breo, *The Surrogate Mother* (New York: Everest House, 1981), p. 291; Brophy, "A Surrogate Mother Contract," p. 267. The surrogate's husband is also required to agree to this clause of the contract.

24. One might ask why this argument does not extend to all cases in which one might form an emotional attachment to an object one has contracted to sell. If I sign a contract with you to sell my car to you, can I back out if I decide I am too emotionally attached to it? My argument is based upon the distinctive characteristics of parental love—a mode of valuation which should not be confused with less profound modes of valuation which generate sentimental attachments to things. The degree to which other modes of valuation generate claims to consideration which tell against market norms remains an open question.

25. Corea, *The Mother Machine*, p. 222.

26. Keane and Breo, *The Surrogate Mother*, p. 292.

27. Kay Longcope, "Standing Up for Mary Beth," *Boston Globe*, 5 March 1987, p. 83; Daniel Goleman, "Motivations of Surrogate Mothers," *New York Times*, 20 January 1987, p. C1; Robertson, "Surrogate Mothers: Not So Novel after All," pp. 30, 34 n. 8. Neither the surrogate mothers themselves nor psychiatrists have been able to predict which women will experience such grief.

28. See Hochschild, *The Managed Heart*, for an important empirical study of the dynamics of commercialized emotional labor.

29. Keane and Breo, *The Surrogate Mother*, pp. 236–37.

30. For one account of how a surrogate mother who came to regret her decision viewed her own moral transformation, see Elizabeth Kane, *Birth Mother: The Story of America's First Legal Surrogate Mother* (San Diego:

Harcourt Brace Jovanovich, 1988). I argue below that the implications of commodifying women's labor are not significantly changed even if the contract is unenforceable.

31. Susan Ince, "Inside the Surrogate Industry," in *Test-Tube Women,* ed. Rita Arditti, Ranate Duelli Klein, and Shelley Minden (Boston: Pandora Press, 1984), p. 110.

32. Philip Parker, "Motivation of Surrogate Mothers: Initial Findings," *American Journal of Psychiatry* 140 (1983): 117–18.

33. The surrogate broker Noel Keane is remarkably open about reporting the desperate emotional insecurities which shape the lives of so many surrogate mothers, while displaying little sensitivity to the implications of his taking advantage of these motivations to make his business a financial success. See especially Keane and Breo, *The Surrogate Mother,* pp. 247ff.

34. See, for example, the story of the surrogate mother Nancy Barrass in Anne Fleming, "Our Fascination with Baby M," *New York Times Magazine,* 29 March 1987, p. 38.

35. For evidence of these disparate perspectives, see Peterson, "Baby M Case: Surrogate Mothers Vent Feelings," p. B4.

36. The surrogate mother is required to obey all doctor's orders made in the interests of the child's health. (See Brophy, "A Surrogate Mother Contract"; Keane, "The Surrogate Parenting Contract"; and Ince, "Inside the Surrogate Industry.") These orders could include forcing her to give up her job, travel plans, and recreational activities. The doctor could confine her to bed, and order her to submit to surgery and take drugs. One can hardly exercise an autonomous choice over one's health if one could be held in breach of contract and liable for $35,000 damages for making a decision contrary to the wishes of one's doctor.

37. See Corea, *The Mother Machine,* pp. 227–33, and Christine Overall, *Ethics and Human Reproduction* (Boston: Allen and Unwin, 1987), pp. 122–28. Both emphasize the social conditions which undermine the claim that women choose to be surrogate mothers under conditions of autonomy.

38. Both of these conclusions follow the Warnock commission's recommendations. See Warnock, *A Question of Life,* pp. 43–44, 46–47. Since the surrogate mother is a victim of commercial surrogacy arrangements, she should not be prosecuted for entering into them. And my arguments are directed only against surrogacy as a commercial enterprise.

39. Barbara Cohen, "Surrogate Mothers: Whose Baby Is It?" *American Journal of Law and Medicine* 10 (1984): 282; Peter Singer and Deane Wells, *Making Babies* (New York: Scribner, 1985), pp. 106–7, 111.

40. Harris, *The Value of Life,* pp. 143–44, 156.

41. Singer and Wells support this recommendation in *Making Babies,* pp. 110–11. See also the dissenting opinion of the Warnock commission, *A Question of Life,* pp. 87–89.

42. See Fleming, "Our Fascination with Baby M," for a sensitive discussion of Americans' conflicting attitudes toward surrogate mothers who find they cannot give up their children.

43. *In Re Baby M,* p. 2022. See also Robertson, "Surrogate Mothers: Not So Novel after All," p. 32.

44. The Catholic Church makes this principle the fundamental basis for its own criticism of surrogate motherhood. See Congregation for the Doctrine of the Faith, "Instruction on Respect for Human Life in Its Origin and on the Dignity of Procreation: Replies to Certain Questions of the Day," reproduced in *New York Times,* 11 March 1987, pp. A14–A17.

17.

METAPHORS OF DISCRIMINATION: A COMPARISON OF GUNNAR MYRDAL AND GARY BECKER

Steven Shulman

Introduction

The critique of positivism is old news. Marxian and institutionalist economists have long believed that economics is an interpretive, value laden and historically conditioned discipline, and have argued against the simplistic empiricism and rationalism characteristic of the neoclassical majority (e.g., Dobb, 1973, ch. 1). In recent years, however, the writings of Donald McCloskey (especially 1985) have brought this critique into much wider currency. This may be due to his orthodox credentials, his stature as an economic historian, the grace and wit of his writing style, or the sheer quantity of his publications. No matter; his point is well taken. Economics is another form of communication, an ongoing conversation conducted in terms of metaphorical allusions, established conventions, appeals to authority and other rhetorical devices. If economics is not physics, perhaps it is a form of literature, albeit one which would elicit little praise for the typical quality of its prose.[1]

McCloskey's description of economics as rhetoric is seductive, but it is not without its dangers. The communicative nature of economics leaves open the

Review of Social Economy 50, no. 4 (Winter 1992): 432–52.

question of what it is that economists communicate about. Though all economists engage in rhetoric, the differences in their questions and answers are nonetheless real. Sassower (1988, p. 554) suggests that McCloskey glosses over these differences by ignoring non-neoclassical paradigms. In a similar vein, Waller and Robertson (1990) accuse McCloskey of being anti-rhetorical in the sense that he is so tied to the premises of neoclassicism that he cannot acknowledge the validity of alternative perspectives. Dyer goes so far as to chide McCloskey for his "intolerance for theoretical variety" (1988, p. 163). Sebberson agrees that McCloskey's belief that rhetoric will not affect the substance of economics demonstrates his blindness to the relative character of his own point of view, and Sebberson wonders, "What happens if there is more at stake than just winning a given argument? What happens if the truth of the matter has to be discerned so that the best course of action may be followed" (1990, p. 1021)?

This chapter explores the relation between argumentative rhetoric and analytical substance in the economics of discrimination. I shall try to follow the advice of Robert Solow to "analyze the connection between particular lines of economic analysis and particular rhetorical conventions," though I would have put the word "connection" in the plural (1988, p. 35). A metaphor not only expresses an idea by combining disparate images; it also relates that idea to a larger system of social beliefs. Metaphors, in other words, convey an ideology as well as an analysis. For example, one popular model of racial inequality in the 1960s was based on a concept called "internal colonialism." The metaphor of colonialism explained inequality as a consequence of unequal exchange between the center—the white metropolis—and the periphery—the black ghetto. But it also provided a condemnation of inequality insofar as colonialism is an undemocratic exercise of domination and exploitation. In this way, metaphors establish a criteria for judgment as well as analysis. They reflect beliefs as well as ideas. The metaphor chosen will have moral as well as theoretical and empirical interest. Metaphors matter not just because they are metaphors, but because of the choice to employ one rather than another. McCloskey just has trouble taking the second step.[2]

To illustrate this point, I will compare two classic texts on discrimination: Gunnar Myrdal's *An American Dilemma* (1972; first edition 1944) and Gary Becker's *The Economics of Discrimination* (1971; first edition 1957). These are undoubtedly the two most influential books ever written by economists on the subject of race, but two more different books could hardly be imagined. Myrdal headed one of the largest and most complex social research projects of his time (Southern, 1987, ch. 2); his findings span two volumes and over a thousand pages of text with nearly five hundred additional pages of appendices, notes, bibliography and index. He was world famous and could count on the resources of the Carnegie Corporation, not the least of which were a vast amount of research assistance and contacts with some of the most influential people of the day. In contrast, Becker's volume is less than two hundred pages and represents the product of a single mind, albeit with the help of a fellowship and the comments of a dozen highly respected economists. It was originally written as a Ph.D. dissertation before the author's reputation was established. Yet, despite these apparent inequities in scope, support, and prestige, Becker's book has become so dominant within the profession that articles on the economics of inequality and discrimination now routinely take it to be the standard reference in the field while entirely ignoring Myrdal (e.g., O'Neill, 1987).

Clearly, the ascendency of Becker over Myrdal reflects the relative fortunes of neoclassicism and institutionalism, but I will argue that more is at stake than methodology. Myrdal and Becker propose different interpretations of racial ideologies. Myrdal stressed their historical and psychological uniqueness while Becker focused on their commonalities with the other beliefs of economic actors. By interpreting racial ideologies in terms of their particularity, Myrdal elevated them to the ultimate moral crisis of capitalism. In contrast, Becker's interpretation of racial ideologies in terms of their generality meant that they were reduced to one among many arguments in a utility function. This contrast can be appreciated by comparing the metaphors each used to conceptualize discrimination, metaphors which remain relevant—despite their age—to our understanding of racial inequality in the post–Civil Rights era.

Discrimination as a Vicious Circle: Gunnar Myrdal

Racial inequality is a distinctive area of study as a result of the particular history of black people in the United States. With the exception of native Americans, no other group has suffered as much at the hands of the white majority. Blacks were the only people to arrive here involuntarily; they were the only people to be enslaved; they were the only people to be subject to the elaborate apartheid of Jim Crow; they were the only people who were terrorized by lynching and other forms of mass violence; they were the only people who aroused passionate white fears of miscegenation; they were segregated and oppressed unlike any other people; and they were the only people whose resistance movement was able to crack the facade of white supremacy. Inequality between blacks and whites is not akin to inequality in general, nor is discrimination against blacks equivalent to other types of discrimination.

Any analysis of racial inequality is immediately forced to confront its distinctive character, but at the same time it must connect it to the general forces which are perceived to define and shape American society. These forces can be conceived of in various ways. Myrdal's method was to posit racism as a "dilemma" insofar as it contradicted the American credo of democracy. The belief in the equality of rights contradicts itself in the inequality of the races—

or at least in the treatment of the races. Thus, the connection between the particularity of the black condition and the generality of American society was seen by Myrdal to be fundamentally ideological in the sense that the connection consisted of a clash between belief systems.

This clash meant that the "race problem" was at root a moral problem, one which forced white people to compromise in order to maintain the coexistence of mutually exclusive beliefs. But Myrdal thought this compromise was unstable. He optimistically believed that the larger belief system about equality would overwhelm the particularistic belief system about race. However, it is important to recognize that he was not an idealist: he connected white beliefs about blacks to the actual condition of blacks and thought that improvements in that condition would change beliefs and thus add further momentum to the change in actual conditions. By the same token, discrimination also could become a self-fulfilling prophecy insofar as it depressed the standard of living of blacks and thereby reinforced white prejudice. He advocated vigorous social planning exactly because he did not believe that the ideological contradiction would resolve itself.

The mutually reinforcing connection between discrimination and its consequences was used by Myrdal to explain black poverty (1944, p. 208). He identified "three bundles of interdependent causative factors"—general economic conditions, black standards and manners of living, and discrimination—and argued that changes in any one would generate corresponding changes in the other two. Each, of course, consisted of many subfactors so that "No single factor . . . is the 'final cause' in a theoretical sense." He ridiculed such reductionism as "theoretically unclear," "contradicted by easily ascertainable facts and factual relations" and scientifically "narrow" (Myrdal, 1972, p. 1069). The circumstances of blacks were then explicable by what he called the "vicious circle of cumulative causation." This vicious circle meant that discrimination was self-perpetuating by virtue of its interaction with its consequences. Discrimination influenced the patterns of economic development and black life conditions, which in turn influenced white beliefs, which in turn influenced discrimination: "Discrimination breeds discrimination" (Myrdal, 1972, p. 381). Myrdal therefore believed that "little is explained when we say that 'discrimination is due to prejudice'" (1972, p. 52). Prejudice is just as well due to discrimination.

Round circles are geometric; vicious circles are metaphoric. Why this choice of metaphor? It clearly expresses Myrdal's concerns with the dynamics of feedback. Feedback between multiple and interconnected factors was the basis of Myrdal's principle of cumulation, which he believed "has given us, for the first time, something which approaches a real theory of economic dynamics" (1972, p. 1065).[3] A vicious circle connotes positive feedback effects in which problems fuel themselves *via* the consequent adjustments in their context. White beliefs were the mechanism which created the vicious circle in

Myrdal's explanation for racial subordination. They accounted for the positive feedback between the various components of black poverty: "Poverty itself breeds the conditions which perpetuate poverty" (1972, p. 208).

Myrdal's statement sounds like an early version of the culture of poverty, but he lays the explanatory emphasis on whites rather than blacks. He was emphatic that "little if anything could be scientifically explained in terms of the peculiarities of the Negroes themselves"—it was a "white man's problem" (1972, p. lxxiii). Whites had all the power; they were willing and able to limit the opportunities and resources available to blacks; to the extent that black behaviors differed from the norm, it was because of the exercise of white prerogatives. White actions were the primary cause of the "race problem," and those actions were predicated upon certain beliefs. The vicious circle worked by connecting the factors behind racial subordination in terms of white beliefs: changes in one factor would alter white attitudes and thereby impact on other factors when those altered white attitudes led to altered white behaviors. White beliefs thus had to be of the type which would serve to connect and reinforce the "facets of the Negro problem."

Myrdal described white beliefs in terms of the "anti-amalgamation doctrine." Unlike other minorities who were urged to assimilate, blacks were believed to be inevitably set apart. Even whites who decried racism in the society at large would never accept a black person as an equal within their own family, and they encouraged blacks "to keep to themselves and develop a race pride of their own" (Myrdal, 1972, p. 54). Amalgamation was opposed because it would detract from racial purity. According to Myrdal, the "white man's rank order of discrimination" had the ban against intermarriage first while economic discrimination was sixth (1972, pp. 60–61).[4] This did not mean that racism was purely a psychological phenomenon: Myrdal acknowledged that economic motives could be important, and when they were, the psychological need for racial purity would not be the dominant factor. Nonetheless, Myrdal saw prejudice primarily in psychological terms, and surprisingly he found this to be a source of optimism. On the one hand, the rank order of discrimination for blacks was the opposite of that for whites. Blacks were most concerned about ending job discrimination and least concerned about intermarriage. What they most wanted was what whites were most likely to accept. On the other hand, the irrational and psychological nature of racism made it susceptible to attack. Whites were prone to rationalize their prejudice by blaming black poverty on black behaviors (the vicious circle) but they could also see the contrast between their beliefs about blacks and their beliefs about America. They were neither stupid nor blind, and Myrdal thought their prejudice would survive only as long as their ignorance.

In order for white beliefs to generate a vicious circle, they must be able to respond to actual changes in the circumstances of blacks. White people cannot be immutably prejudiced; instead their prejudice must confront their rationality and their inner drives to act ethically. Myrdal was certainly an optimist with respect to his view of human nature: "Behind all outward dissimilarities, behind their contradictory valuations, rationalizations, vested interests, group allegiances and animosities, behind fears and defense constructions, behind the role they play in life and the mask they wear, people are all much alike on a fundamental level. And they are all good people. They want to be rational and just. They all plead to their conscience that they meant well even when things went wrong" (Myrdal, 1972, p. 1023). The racial beliefs of whites were the critical variable in Myrdal's explanation for the subordinate status of blacks, but his attitude about whites was far from cynical. He believed that racial prejudice would become more and more contradictory as its scientific basis was undermined (1972, p. 1003), as it became more ethically implausible in the aftermath of Nazism (p. 1008) and as it confronted the formal organizations in which "people invest their highest ideals" (p. 1023). The vicious circle was dynamically unstable; racism was not an inevitability.

What does this metaphor do? In the first place a vicious circle is vicious: it expresses moral condemnation, which Myrdal self-consciously emphasized in order to drive home the point about the "American dilemma." But it is also a circle, an image which denies both beginning and end and thereby suggests the ongoing and interconnected nature of the problem. The vicious circle is both vicious and a circle because of white attitudes and actions: it points a finger as it explains why the problem of racial subordination is self-perpetuating. It also tells us something hopeful about the white beliefs which drive the vicious circle: they are not fixed or permanent; they will change as circumstances change; they coexist uneasily with the human instinct for rationality and morally defensible behavior. A vicious circle can become a virtuous circle. The principle of cumulative causation can work in both directions. Even though circles can endlessly repeat themselves, in the end it is a metaphor of the change which Myrdal foresaw.[5]

Discrimination as a Commodity: Gary Becker

An American Dilemma was immediately perceived to be a classic, and for two decades after its publication it was the leading work in the field. Its boldness of expression and almost overwhelming comprehensiveness made it a definitive text, but it was dropped into a vacuum as research funding fell in the conservative political climate of the 1940s and 1950s. Few of Myrdal's suggestions were actually acted upon. Eventually, of course, it became representative of the mainstream in the aftermath of the Brown decision and the civil rights movement, but then its star paradoxically fell in the academic world as Myrdal went elsewhere and times seemed to pass the book by. As Jackson notes, Myrdal's book "underwent a process of ossification and by the mid-

1960s would seem irrelevant to many intellectuals" (1990, p. 273). At the same time, Gary Becker's *The Economics of Discrimination* became established as the leading work in the field, one which broke new ground methodologically and which replaced Myrdal's institutionalist orientation with an aggressive neoclassicism.

Becker's innovation was simple but powerful. He labeled discrimination as a "taste" held by employers, employees, and consumers. If whites have a taste for discrimination, they will be willing to pay to maintain their distance from blacks. Becker was then able to define a "discrimination coefficient" (d) which represented the monetary value of this taste: wage costs to employers are w for whites but w(1+d) for equally productive blacks; wage incomes are w for whites working with other whites but w(1-d) for whites working with blacks; and the price paid by white consumers is p if it is produced or served by whites but p(1+d) if it is produced or served by blacks. The theory of discrimination thus becomes analogous to the theory of compensating wage differentials. Just as workers must be compensated for working in undesireable physical circumstances, they must also be compensated for working in undesirable, as they see it, social circumstances. The degree of discrimination can then be measured by the extent of compensation.

Cain summarizes the advantages to this formulation: "Discrimination has the appealing property of continuity, rather than being merely present or absent. It is potentially measurable, and the monetary units have an intuitive meaning to experts and laypersons alike. . . . There are explicit behavioral and even policy implications" (1986, p. 710). Furthermore, it provides a means of understanding how markets respond to discriminatory preferences. Discrimination is conceived to have a price or, in other words, to be a commodity, and as such it becomes amenable to the traditional tools of supply and demand.

Where Myrdal concentrated on the consequences of discrimination with respect to black living standards and white beliefs, Becker's concern was the reaction of markets. If discrimination raises wage costs, it will lower profits. This can have two possible effects. On the one hand, it provides an incentive for segregation. Discriminatory employers will hire only whites to avoid the disutility of associating with blacks or to avoid paying prejudiced white workers a wage premium. Nondiscriminatory employers will hire only blacks to take advantage of their lower wages, though this incentive is temporary since black wages will be bid up over time. Discrimination thus creates segregation rather than wage differences. On the other hand, the combination of nondiscriminatory employers with nondiscriminatory white workers will mean lower costs and higher profits. Eventually, these firms should drive discriminators out of the market. As O'Neill notes, "Competitive markets can . . . accommodate discriminatory behavior for a time, but through the profit motive they also provide a mechanism that works to diminish [its] extent" (1987, p. 171).

It is important to note that this conclusion is not inherent in the metaphor of discrimination as a commodity. Discrimination can be costly to the individual firm, but any conclusion about market-wide outcomes will depend upon the application of restrictive assumptions such as full-employment. Slack labor markets will mean that white wages will not have to be raised nor search time lengthened for employers to reject qualified black applicants. Other assumptions—for example, about the cost structure of production, factor substitutability, the relative size of the black population, and the number of nondiscriminatory firms—are also presumed by the conclusion that competition will automatically erode discrimination. Becker himself, in contrast to both his proponents and opponents, refused to conclude that discrimination could not be sustained in competitive markets. In an article for the *International Encyclopedia of the Social Sciences* published 11 years after his book, Becker wrote that "A few of the more extreme nineteenth-century advocates of a competitive market economy believed that eventually its extension and development would eliminate most discrimination. . . . Unfortunately, this has not yet taken place; discrimination exists, and at times even flourishes, in competitive economies, the position of Negroes in the United States being a clear example" (quoted in Cain, 1986, p. 715).

The popularity of Becker's model thus does not rest upon its predictions. These could be anything depending upon the assumptions within which the metaphor of discrimination as a commodity is embedded.[6] Nor can its influence be traced to its presumption that whites "pay" to achieve physical distance from blacks. The implication that intraoccupational wage differentials have historically been the most basic symptom of discrimination is simply false (Higgs, 1989). While Becker's book has generated empirical debates about matters such as the relative degree of discrimination in monopolies, it has received no clear-cut factual support (Cain, 1986, sec. 4).[7] Its influence lies almost entirely in the realm of theory. The comparison with Myrdal is striking: a cursory glance through the *Social Sciences Citation Index* over the last two decades shows that *An American Dilemma* is much more likely to be cited in sociology, political science, and law journals while *The Economics of Discrimination* is still widely cited by economists. Yet Myrdal provided an enormous mass of factual material in an effort to describe the circumstances of African-Americans and to support his thesis of a moral dilemma; the preference for Becker among economists rests almost entirely on his theoretical contribution.

The simplest reason for this preference is methodological: it reflects the sway of neoclassical thought. Myrdal was an institutionalist; his empirical work was descriptive, his theoretical work lacked formal structure, and he wrote self-consciously about values in a manner now commonly considered to be "unscientific." Becker found this approach to be so devoid of interest that he referred to Myrdal only once in passing. Instead of focusing on the concrete behavior of institutions and social groups, Becker concentrated his attention on the decision making process of hypothetically rational individuals. In the process he founded a framework for the analysis of social problems which has become so widely applied that the term "economic imperialism" has been coined to characterize the invasion of neoclassical methodology into the traditional domains of sociology (Swedberg, 1990). Indeed, Becker today holds a joint appointment in economics and sociology at the University of Chicago. The profession would appear to have simply left Myrdal behind.

But the question of content is equally important. Consider the metaphor of discrimination as a commodity. Becker understood that this metaphor was not only applicable to the problem of discrimination against blacks, but could be applied to discrimination against "Jews, women, or persons with 'unpleasant' personalities"; furthermore, it could "stimulate the quantitative analysis of non-pecuniary motivation in other areas" aside from discrimination (1971, p. 11). In its generalizability lay its strength. It provided a perspective on discrimination in general, not just against blacks, and a means of quantifying the analysis of many other social behaviors previously considered to be off-limits to economists. In this respect it is similar to the theory of compensating wage differentials. The nonwage aspects of a job—its danger, its status, its unpleasantness, its convenience, etc.—can be analyzed as trade-offs against the wage, but only by being made equivalent, as utilities, to the monetary reward from work. Discrimination becomes just another compensating wage differential: two white workers of equal human capital receive equal total returns even though the one who must work with blacks receives a higher wage.

The metaphor of the commodity means that discrimination loses its specific qualities by being equated with other commodities. Commodities are similar in that they are values in exchange and different in that they are values in use. By calling discrimination a commodity, we abstract from its distinguishing features in use—history, customs, institutions, practices, etc.—in favor of the characteristic it has in common with other commodities (i.e., its ability to be exchanged in specific proportions). It is a metaphor with wide applicability precisely because it abstracts from specific in favor of the general. In this manner, the decision to have children, to commit crimes, to discriminate, or to do virtually anything else can be modeled by defining an argument in a utility function and grinding through the usual cost-benefit machinations.[8]

By placing race discrimination on par with all other utility maximizing decisions, the commodity metaphor denies that discrimination means something in particular. Becker begins his book by stating that the preference for looking at a glamorous actress is equivalent to the preference for living next to whites rather than blacks, or at least that "calling just one of these actions 'discrimination' requires making subtle and rather secondary distinctions" (1971, p. 13). In a like vein, Becker's mentor, Milton Friedman, comments that "It is hard to see that discrimination can have any meaning other than a 'taste' of others that one does not share. We do not regard it as 'discrimination' . . . if an individual is willing to pay a higher price to listen to one singer than to another, although we do if he is willing to pay a higher price to have services rendered to him by a person of one color than by a person of another" (1962, p. 110). Discrimination against blacks is collapsed into discrimination in general, which in turn is collapsed into all nonpecuniary motivations, which in the end are equivalent to the usual maximizing decisions that explicitly involve money.

Becker's model has frequently been criticized for its reduction of discrimination to prejudice, its assumption that discriminatory preferences are exogenous and constant, and its focus on voluntary exchange rather than domination and power (e.g., Reich, 1981, pp. 83–85). These are equivalent to the criticisms which are typically heard of the neoclassical theory of demand: purchases depend upon preferences, with a weak wave toward budget constraints, which are assumed to be given and to reflect consumer sovereignty rather than corporate hegemony. When discrimination is a commodity, the theory of discrimination is nothing more than a subset of the theory of demand. It adopts its strengths and its weaknesses. The metaphor is more than a rhetorical flourish: it contains a content, and it is on that content that it is ultimately evaluated.

The Relevance of Metaphors

The "content" of metaphors refers to their explanatory power or, in other words, to their contribution to the telling of a believable story. Economic stories become believable by virture of their relevance to concrete circumstances. Yet relevance is notoriously uninteresting to orthodox theorists who tend to be more entranced with aesthetics (e.g., consistency or simplicity) than empirics. One would have hoped that the emphasis on rhetoric, as opposed to science, would have restored relevance to its rightful place in the pantheon of intellectual respectability. Unfortunately, the analysis of economic metaphors has remained stuck at a literary level, with little attention paid to their content.[9] This has made the whole enterprise appear (I hate to say it) irrelevant (e.g., Heilbroner, 1988; Solow, 1988).[10]

Yet economic metaphors can and should be assessed in terms of their explanatory power. To illustrate, I will show how Myrdal's and Becker's metaphors of discrimination can be combined into a story about black unemployment. The black unemployment rate has shown no tendency to converge with the white unemployment rate; if anything, the 2-to-1 gap has widened since the late 1970s (Shulman, 1991). Yet the wage gap among employed blacks and whites has narrowed among men and virtually collapsed among women (Freeman, 1989). These two trends are difficult to reconcile. If supply side factors (i.e., human capital) account for the decline in the wage gap, they should also have resulted in a decline in the unemployment gap. If demand side factors (e.g., a drop in discrimination) account for a decline in the wage gap, they too should have resulted in a decline in the unemployment gap. Since 1964 we have witnessed the passage of antidiscrimination and affirmative action laws as well as a narrowing of the gap between black and white educational attainment; it therefore seems likely that the wage trend is due to both supply and demand factors. The failure of the racial gap in unemployment to fall is thus a puzzle from both sides of the labor market.

Of all the models of racial inequality and discrimination, the only one which can reconcile the trends in wages and unemployment is the "race relations model" (Shulman, 1991). This model acknowledges Becker's argument that discrimination can raise the costs of production, but it also notes that ceasing discrimination can be costly as well. The costs of ceasing discrimination can arise from disrupting established patterns of association and authority, reducing team efficiency, increasing intra-class and inter-class conflict, raising the costs of on-the-job training, adding risk by hiring workers whose backgrounds are known with less certainty, and overthrowing tried-and-true methods of recruitment, screening, allocation, pay and promotion. The firm's propensity to discriminate is then determined by the balance between the costs of continuing discrimination and the costs of ceasing discrimination. This makes discrimination a matter of history and circumstance rather than theoretical necessity. In particular, it provides a means of relating the intensity and type of discrimination to macroeconomic fluctuations and changes in the institutional context for business decision making.

The race relations model reconciles the trends in wages and unemployment by predicting a shift in the composition of discrimination. Social, legal, educational and economic developments in the post-War period reduced the likelihood of wage discrimination among blacks with jobs (and improved their occupational mobility), but at the same time they raised the likelihood of employment discrimination among blacks without jobs. Of the many factors at play, the key one was the secular rise in aggregate unemployment. Persistent labor market slackness reduced the costs of discrimination while increasing the costs of ceasing discrimination. Employment discrimination is more difficult to monitor than wage discrimination and is more important to white workers in a period when jobs are scarce. Employers had more to gain (from improved relations with their white workers in a period of heightened class conflict) and less to lose (from the risk of discovery and penalty) from employment discrimination. The increase in black educational attainment and the expansion of the federal apparatus designed to monitor discrimination thus worked to improve the circumstances of employed blacks, but at the same time the scarcity of jobs and the decreasing ability of employers to keep black wages artificially low reduced the employment prospects of unemployed and underemployed blacks. As a result, the wage gap narrowed while the unemployment gap stagnated or grew.

The metaphors of discrimination as a vicious circle and as a commodity are both foundation stones in this story. Discrimination as a vicious circle is key to understanding the costs of ceasing discrimination while discrimination as a commodity is key to understanding the costs of continuing discrimination. Ceasing discrimination can be costly due to the social relations of race: white workers trust and communicate with each other more readily than with their black counterparts, and white workers are concerned about maintaining their influence over informal job distribution networks and reducing job competition in a period when the demand for labor, especially highly skilled labor, is weak. Because of the history of exclusion and segregation, whites identify their interests racially, and employers are able to raise productivity by bonding with them on this basis. This history then becomes self-perpetuating as whites use race as an in-group signifier. Blacks continue to be victimized by racial bonding among whites because the history of racial solidarity reduces the ability of whites to communicate or trust blacks or to see their common interests. Discrimination thus breeds discrimination, i.e., there is a vicious circle. At the same time, competitive pressures may force firms to rationalize their human resource utilization, especially in a period when many blacks are acquiring more experience and education. Discriminatory firms also face the risks of penalties if they are convicted of discrimination, not the least of which is bad publicity. Discrimination as a commodity means that discrimination has a "price"; or in other words, it can be costly. The race relations model acknowledges this possibility, especially when labor markets are tight and antidiscrimination agencies are adequately staffed and motivated.

Firms thus face potential costs from both continuing and ceasing discrimination; their actual behavior will be determined by the balance between the two, itself a function of the specific circumstances (e.g., local labor market conditions, industrial structure, the degree of governmental activism, etc.) in which the firms operate. The race relations model thus allows for changes in the intensity and composition of discrimination as circumstances change, a distinct advantage over other models of discrimination which tend to be historically invariant. Yet this model is itself a combination of pieces from other models, albeit put together in a manner which consciously connects them to external conditions. These "pieces" did not drop out of the sky. They emerged as thinkers such as Becker and Myrdal expressed themselves through relevant metaphors. Discrimination as a commodity is a relevant metaphor because it gives rise to the concept that continuing discrimination can be costly; discrimination as a vicious circle is a relevant metaphor because it gives rise to the concept that ceasing discrimination can be costly. These two concepts form the foundation of a model which is capable of reconciling the divergent trends in wages and unemployment. It is their content—not just the simple fact that they are metaphors—which makes them interesting and important.

Conclusions

Becker and Myrdal are similar in that both saw racism to be a contradiction for capitalism. For Becker discrimination was antithetical to rational business practices while for Myrdal the belief system which justified and perpetuated racial inequality came into conflict with the American self-image as a democracy. An economic anachronism for one, a moral dilemma for the other, an unstable pattern of behavior for both. Curiously, it was Myrdal who expressed the most optimism concerning the future of American race relations. He believed that conflicts created by discrimination with the beliefs of ordinary Americans and the workings of public and private institutions would eventually make discrimination unsustainable. He had complete confidence in the ability of government planners to create policies which would improve black circumstances and reduce white prejudice. Becker, in contrast, was more cautious with regard to his predictions. As noted in the previous section, he did not believe that competitive forces would necessarily be a powerful deterrent to discrimination, and his analysis of trends in racial inequality from the turn of the century until 1950 led him to conclude that "almost all the increase in the absolute occupational position of Negroes was caused by forces increasing the position of whites as well . . . [so that] it seems probable that a large secular decrease in discrimination did not occur" (1971, p. 141). Although Becker did not discuss the role of government with much concrete detail, he certainly would have adopted a dim view of policy activism as an alternative to market mechanisms. Becker thus cannot be accused of over-optimism about the future of discrimination. Though Myrdal foresaw that the beliefs in democracy and individual rights would eventually triumph as popular ideologies, he failed to grasp the tenacity of racial stereotypes and their ability to reconcile continuing inequality with the conviction that equal opportunity has been achieved. Despite his empiricism, Myrdal comes off as the idealist; despite his theoreticism, Becker comes off as the realist.

Both Becker and Myrdal conceived of discrimination metaphorically. This recognition in and of itself does not reveal much about the similarities and differences of their conceptions. The actual content of the metaphor is more important. This content is in part analytical and in part ideological. With regard to the former, Myrdal's vicious circle connotes positive feedback effects so that discrimination becomes self-perpetuating in the absence of deliberate policies to eradicate it. Discrimination is thus perceived to be systemic. In contrast, Becker's commodity metaphor captures the opportunity cost associated with discrimination as a resource absorbing activity. Discrimination is thus perceived to be an individualized process of decision making, one which coexists uneasily with the rationality of competition. Each metaphor thereby expresses a dynamic process connecting capitalism to racism, and each, therefore, expresses a vision about ending racism. Myrdal's vicious circle means that capitalism will not automatically end racism even if its ideology of individual rights makes it a moral dilemma; hence, the solution lies in deliberate government policies. For Becker, discrimination is a costly commodity with a limited demand while racial inequality is in part due to factors aside from discrimination; government policy is inherently less efficient than market mechanisms.[11] Capitalism is thus the only solution.

Each of their metaphors also expresses a particular ideology, or a particular set of racial beliefs. For Myrdal, the anti-amalgamation doctrine means that the racial beliefs of whites are a unique psychosexual phenomenon created by specific historical circumstances. The beliefs of whites about blacks are different from other belief systems; white discrimination against blacks is therefore also unique. Myrdal's "American dilemma" derives its power from the fact that it is unprecedented and unparalleled. It is the special character of racism which elevates it to the level of a moral conflict facing the country at large. For Becker, racial prejudice is just one more argument in a utility function. It has no special features and character; the power of his analysis is entirely based on its generality. Because prejudice is just another taste, it cannot create a moral dilemma. Myrdal's lengthy discussion of "values premises" simply has no place in this conception of economics. As Cain puts it, "Economics does not distinguish among the ethical merits of different tastes; between, say preferences for physical attractiveness or for race. As economists we have nothing to say about the justness of laws that prohibit an employer from refusing to hire someone on the basis of color but that permit that hiring on the basis of physical attractiveness. As citizens, of course, we may have strong opinions about such matters" (1986, p. 775).

Of course, the refusal to "distinguish among the ethical merits of different tastes" presumes that those ethical merits are irrelevant to the workings of the economy, a presumption which would only be true if they were irrelevant to human behavior. This leads us to a slightly different concept of ideology which also plays a role in the metaphors of discrimination. Ideology can be understood as a belief system which rationalizes the existing social order by interpreting it to be "natural," "just," or "inevitable" (Heilbroner, 1988). Ideology in this sense is not about racial beliefs *per se*, but rather about their relation to the belief systems of the society at large.

For Myrdal, this ideology is democracy. Democratic rights are for him a teleological force which will inevitably subsume the more parochial forces such as racism. Democracy is the future; racism is the past. The ideology of individual rights rationalizes our society in terms of its inherent justness. Rather than seeing the racial beliefs as primary—after all, they have rationalized genocide, slavery, Jim Crow, segregation, colonialism, and imperialism, all of which could be held to be the historically fundamental driving forces of our society—he sees the democratic tradition to be primary. For this reason, many on the left have interpreted *An American Dilemma* as an exercise in apologetics (Southern, 1987, ch. 4).

For Becker, on the other hand, the ideology which rationalizes society at large is that of self-interest. Voluntary exchange explains diverse behaviors in terms of utility maximization; society is rationalized with respect to its efficiency. Racial discrimination is just one among many types of social interaction. Economists have no right to comment on its desirability, only on its effects, which are presumed to be independent of its ethical character. Racial beliefs are expensive and therefore scarce. Society is driven by the desire to improve standards of living. Racism is the past; growth is the future. The tradition of work, investment and achievement is primary. Again America is seen to be driven by future-oriented qualities which will leave racism behind.

The interpretation of each metaphor taken separately or isolated within its original framework is different than when they are combined. Taken together in the race relations model, the metaphors of Becker and Myrdal are equally relevant in telling a believable story about contempory trends in racial inequality. Metaphors are not rigidly attached to particular paradigms; their power lies in their ability to acquire new significance as they are redeployed in new models and systems of thought. Their use lies partly in their ability to be applied in new frameworks and thereby to acquire new meanings. The metaphors of Becker and Myrdal are not incompatible or mutually exclusive; they can be combined to new effect in our attempts to understand such puzzling phenomenon as the trend in the black/white unemployment gap. Their relevance gives them ongoing life. It is a far more interesting quality than the overly-acclaimed rigor (mortis) of particular paradigms.

Metaphors of discrimination thus express a vision of how discrimination interacts with the economic system and with the belief system of the society at large. They are a statement about racial ideologies and their relation to the images which rationalize the existing social order. They matter as metaphors, not just as forms of expression, but also in terms of their specific content. Metaphors are worth analyzing not just as figures of speech, but as expressions of debatable ideas with concrete consequences. We care about them because we care about our world and how to best behave in it.

Notes

J. R. Stanfield made helpful comments on an earlier draft of this chapter.

1. McCloskey's short book on the writing of economics (1987) should be required reading for all graduate students of the dismal science.

2. McCloskey's discussion of significance tests shows that he is aware that the choice of metaphor matters and that rhetoric can be "poor" or badly used (1985, ch. 9). These are relative terms; but relative to what? If rhetoric is poor, style is being judged relative to substance. It is not an end in and of itself.

3. Toward this end he also contrasted different conceptions of equilibrium by inventing metaphors of a pencil in different positions—upright on its end, rolling on a plane surface, etc. (see Myrdal, 1944, p. 1065).

4. Myrdal's rank ordering for whites continued to hold two decades after his book was first published. A 1964 poll in metropolitan Houston showed 67 percent of the respondents opposed a federal law barring segregation in restaurants and hotels, yet 73 percent favored legislation protecting the rights of blacks to vote and 62 percent favored equal employment opportunity laws (Morley, 1992, pp. 19–20).

5. Myrdal later insisted that he was a realist and not an optimist, but it is clear that he had great faith in the underlying goodwill of the American people and in their institutions (1973, pp. 300–301). It would be easy to praise him for foreseeing the civil rights movement and the moral power which drove it and gave it its impact. It would also be easy to criticize him in light of the mean-spirited experience of the 1980s.

6. This is true about all economic models. For example, new classical and neo-Keynesian models both presume rational expectations yet yield different predictions due to their auxiliary assumptions about market clearing. This has led Herbert Simon (1987) to remark that the "action" is all in the assumptions. Despite the positivist pretenses of the profession, economic theories are rarely if ever rejected on the basis of falsified predictions.

7. Nor has any other model. Cain concludes that "theories of discrimination have been useful for providing definitions and for suggesting measurements of discrimination but not for providing convincing evidence of the phenomenon nor of its patterns" (1986, p. 781). What makes Becker's model stand out, however, is its widespread acceptance among economists despite its weak empirical basis.

8. Becker (quoted in Swedburg, 1990, p. 40) does acknowledge that there are social phenomenon such as war which have so far been impervious to rational choice models, though it is unclear if he means that they cannot be modeled or if they just have not so far been modeled.

9. McCloskey elsewhere denounces such an emphasis on substance over speech by asking, "Is one accomplished in the substance of skiing, stripped of mere style, if one rolls down the hill or falls every ten feet" (1988, p. 286)? This is a play on the word "accomplished." In fact, a beginner falling down the slopes in Colorado is accomplishing more skiing than an expert who is unhappily stranded on the plains of Iowa. If substance is not style-less, neither is style substance-less.

10. Relevance may be irrelevant if one agrees with Ruccio that economic "knowledges" are textual and thereby "fictions" (1990, p. 503). But if economics is nothing more than a conversation about itself, why should we care about it? Resnick and Wolff assure us that "social theories matter enormously," though not "in terms of the futile and fetishistic game of asking which one is closer to some absolute truth." Rather, they "matter in the different ways they affect our lives" (1988, p. 61). Instead of Truth, we are left with Consequences, though how we are to "know" what those consequences (pre-

dictions?) are, or why choosing on the basis of consequences is any different than choosing on the basis of truth, remain unasked questions.

11. "An analysis of income and occupational differentials between men and women should be very useful not only because much discrimination has occurred against women but also because it has long been recognized that 'productivity' differences between men and women explain a significant part of these differentials. Discussions of other minorities usually reveal an unwillingness to admit that important differences in 'productivity' and 'taste' exist between them and the majority. I believe that these differences *are* important, although the discussion in this monograph is probably also biased toward underestimating them" (Becker, 1971, pp. 161–2, emphasis in original). This passage presages Becker's turn toward human capital theory and displays the same confusion which would later emerge in the efforts to use human capital theory to explain racial inequality: even if blacks and whites do differ in terms of tastes and productivities (a proposition which is notoriously difficult to empirically establish), those differences may be due to discrimination and hence cannot substitute for it as an explanation of inequality. For example, does the lower educational attainment of blacks mean that racial inequality is due to productivity differences or to discrimination in the provision of education?

References

Becker, Gary. *The Economics of Discrimination,* Chicago: University of Chicago Press, 1971.

Cain, Glen. "The Economic Analysis of Labor Market Discrimination: A Survey," Chapter 13 of *The Handbook of Labor Economics, Volume I,* O. Ashenfelter and R. Layard eds. NY: Elsevier Science Publishers, 1986.

Dobb, Maurice. *Theories of Value and Distribution since Adam Smith: Ideology and Economic Theory*. NY: Cambridge University Press, 1973.

Dyer, Alan. "Economic Theory as an Art Form." *Journal of Economic Issues* 22, no. 1 (March 1988).

Freeman, Richard. "Black Economic Progress: Erosion of the Post-1965 Gains in the 1980s?" In Steven Shulman and William Darity Jr., eds., *The Question of Discrimination: Racial Inequality in the U.S. Labor Market*. Middletown, CT: Wesleyan University Press, 1989.

Friedman, Milton. *Capitalism and Freedom*. Chicago: University of Chicago Press, 1962.

Heilbroner, Robert. "Rhetoric and Ideology." In A. Klamer, D. McCloskey and R. Solow, eds., *The Consequences of Economic Rhetoric*. NY: Cambridge University Press, 1988.

Higgs, Robert. "Black Progress and the Persistence of Racial Economic Inequalities, 1865–1940." In *The Question of Discrimination: Racial Inequality in the U.S. Labor Market*. Middletown, CT: Wesleyan University Press, 1989.

Jackson, Walter. *Gunnar Myrdal and America's Conscience: Social Engi-*

neering and Racial Liberalism, 1938–1987. Chapel Hill: University of North Carolina Press, 1990.

McCloskey, Donald. *The Rhetoric of Economics*. Madison: University of Wisconsin Press, 1985.

———. *The Writing of Economics*. NY: Macmillan, 1987.

———. "The Consequences of Rhetoric." In *The Consequences of Economic Rhetoric*. NY: Cambridge University Press, 1988.

Morley, Jefferson. "Bush and the Blacks: An Unknown Story." *New York Review of Books* 39, nos. 1–2 (16 Jan. 1992).

Myrdal, Gunnar. *An American Dilemma: The Negro Problem and Modern Democracy*. NY: Pantheon Books, 1972.

Myrdal, Gunnar. *Against the Stream: Critical Essays on Economics*. NY: Pantheon Books, 1973.

Reich, Michael. *Racial Inequality: A Political-Economic Analysis*. Princeton, NJ: Princeton University Press, 1981.

Resnick, Stephen and Richard Wolff. "Marxian Theory and the Rhetoric of Economics." In *The Consequences of Economic Rhetoric*. NY: Cambridge University Press, 1988.

Ruccio, David. "Postmodernism and Economics." *Journal of Post Keynesian Economics* 13, no. 4 (Summer 1991).

Sassower, Raphael. "Economics: Rhetoric or Mathematics?" *Philosophy of the Social Sciences* 18 (1988).

Sebberson, David. "The Rhetoric of Inquiry or the Sophistry of the Status Quo? Exploring the Common Ground between Critical Rhetoric and Institutional Economics." *Journal of Economic Issues* 24, no. 4 (December 1990).

Shulman, Steven. "Why Is the Black Unemployment Rate Always Twice as High as the White Unemployment Rate?" In R. Cornwall and P. Wunnava, eds., *New Approaches to Economic and Social Analyses of Discrimination*. NY: Praeger, 1991.

Simon, Herbert. "Rationality in Psychology and Economics." In *Rational Choice: The Contrast between Economics and Psychology,* R. Hogarth and M. Reder, eds. Chicago: University of Chicago Press, 1987.

Solow, Robert M. "Comments from Inside Economics." In *The Consequences of Economic Rhetoric*. NY: Cambridge University Press, 1988.

Southern, David. *Gunnar Myrdal and Black-White Relations: The Use and Abuse of an American Dilemma, 1944–1969*. Baton Rouge: Louisiana State University Press, 1987.

Swedburg, Richard. *Economics and Sociology: Redefining Their Boundaries*. Princeton, NJ: Princeton University Press, 1990.

Waller, William and Linda Robertson. "Why Johnny (Ph.D., Economics) Can't Read: A Rhetorical Analysis of Thorstein Veblen and a Response to Donald McCloskey's *Rhetoric of Economics*." *Journal of Economic Issues* 24, no. 4 (December 1990).

18.

TOWARD DEVELOPMENT ETHICS

David A. Crocker

1. Introduction

Policy makers and project managers involved in international "development" often confront ethical questions in their work. Similarly, it is increasingly common to recognize that theories and models of "Third World" "development" and "underdevelopment" have ethical or valuational as well as scientific components.[1] Finally, some have called for and a few have practiced "development ethics."

By development ethics I mean the normative or ethical assessment of the ends and means of Third World and global development.[2] The questions of this ethical inquiry include the following: What should take place in Third World development? What ends should poor countries pursue? What should be their fundamental economic, cultural, and political goals? Should we continue using the concept of development instead of, for example, "progress," "transformation," "liberation," or "revolution"?[3] If we continue to speak of development, how should we define it? Should the concept be ethically positive, negative, or neutral? Should development be descriptive, prescriptive or both? How should the benefits and burdens of development be distributed? What ethical and other value issues emerge in development policies and practices and how should they be resolved? What moral responsibilities, if any, do

World Development 19, no. 5 (1991): 457–83.

rich countries, regions, and classes have toward impoverished countries, regions, and classes? What international structures are called for by international or global justice? What can "developed" areas learn from "developing" areas with respect to their own "authentic" development? Who ought to decide these questions? Social "insiders," "outsiders" or both?[4] Technical experts, government officials, the market, social scientists, philosophers, the people? Which people? How or by what procedures or methods, should these "should questions" be answered? By internal or external ethical criticism and inquiry?[5] What are the implications of political realism, moral skepticism, and moral relativism for the possibility and practice of development ethics?

My objectives in this essay are twofold. First, I describe recent interest in the ethical aspects of Third World and international social change, and in the forging of development ethics. Second, I explain why different groups have such concerns, and I argue that their concerns are justified. What is needed are explicit development ethics. In a companion article, I have systematically sketched the nature of such an ethic of development, emphasizing that it should be part of what I call "the theory-practice" of development.[6] Although my model in these two essays is not ethically neutral, neither proposes a specific development ethic. My hope is that readers will be persuaded of the need for and importance of a general style of ethical reflection in the theory and practice of international development.

Informing my work is a certain conception of the nature and role of philosophy and applied ethics. I have been influenced particularly by Rorty's "pragmatism"; the critical social theory of two members of the Yugoslav Praxis Group, Marković and Stojanović; Jaggar's idea of a "feminist framework"; the feminist concept of the unity of theory and practice; and Fals-Borda's notion of "investigation-action."[7]

2. The Emergence of Development Ethics

Denis Goulet has been called—correctly—the pioneer of a "new discipline, the ethics of development."[8] Since the early 1960s, Goulet has argued that "'development' needs to be redefined, demystified, and thrust into the arena of moral debate."[9] Reflecting academic training in philosophy, political science, and social planning as well as "grassroots" or project experience in numerous countries, Goulet seeks answers to "the ethical and value questions posed by development theory, planning, and practice."[10] One of the most important lessons to be learned from Goulet's work over the past three decades is that well-intentioned "development" can have a terrible human cost:

> The essential task of development ethics is to render development decisions and actions humane. Stated differently, it is to assure that the

> painful changes launched under the banners of development and progress not result in antidevelopment which destroys cultures and individuals and exacts undue sacrifices in suffering and societal well-being—all in the name of profit, some absolutized ideology, or a supposed efficiency imperative. Development ethics as a discipline is the conceptual cement which binds together multiple diagnoses of problems with their policy implications, this through an explicit phenomenological study of values which lays bare the value costs of various courses of action.[11]

Independently, sociologist Peter Berger prefaced his influential *Pyramids of Sacrifice: Political Ethics and Social Change* (1974) with the following:

> This book deals with two topics which are intertwined throughout. One is Third World Development. The other is political ethics applied to social change. It seems to me that these two topics belong together. No humanly acceptable discussion of the anguishing problems of the world's poverty can avoid ethical considerations. And no political ethics worthy of the name can avoid the centrally important case of the Third World.[12]

Development ethics has also been taken up by the Third World. In 1979–80 a group of over 100 Asian scholars, policy makers, and development professionals participated in seminars and joint research that culminated in the book *Ethical Dilemmas of Development in Asia,* edited by members of the Marga Institute, the Sri Lanka Center for Development Studies.[13] The anthology includes what editor Godfrey Gunatilleke calls a "normative framework . . . to help us define and analyze the nature of the dilemmas inherent in the processes of development."[14] This framework, says Gunatilleke, is informed not only by recent innovations in development theory but also by "ethical ideals from cultural and religious traditions of Asian societies."[15] Many of the essayists apply the framework (or refinements thereof) to particular Asian societies such as India, the Philippines, South Korea, Singapore, and Sri Lanka.

Latin American philosophers and social theorists have also rallied around the banner of development ethics. In 1974, the Third National Conference of Philosophy in Costa Rica addressed the theme of "Philosophy and Development." Roberto Murillo presented a paper in which he argued for the necessity of "a developed notion of development."[16] While no one used the concept of "development ethics," some participants took up ethical issues and others discussed the role of philosophy in relation to development. For example, Claudio Gutiérrez treated the need for and risks of philosophy in Costa Rican development:

> A marriage of action and reflection, of work and philosophy, seems to be . . . the precondition of development worthy of the name. . . . That philosophy might be a positive factor in a nation's development assumes and

> requires that the philosopher correctly understand his mission and not be a vehicle of obscurantist influences in social life and that he not be an instrument of paralyzing and fatalistic class ideologies or of projects that sublimate the collective desires of humanity. On the contrary, the philosopher should be a witness to reality, truth, and reason, not understood accommodatingly but with respect to their true value.[17]

In 1980, the Argentine philosopher Mario Bunge published *Ciencia y Desarrollo* (Science and Development).[18] In this important book Bunge criticizes one-sided concepts of development and proposes "authentic and sustained development," which he calls "the integral conception of development."[19] In Bunge's normative vision, integral development ought to be simultaneously biological, economic, political, and cultural.

More recently, Bunge's influence can be seen in the work of two Costa Rican philosophers who are working in the field of development ethics: E. Roy Ramírez and Luis Camacho. According to Ramírez, it is important to forge a new concept of development "in order not to confuse it with modernization" and "because it is preferable to decide things for ourselves than to have others decide them for us."[20] For Ramírez, "the great ethical impact" of Bunge's approach is its

> constant vigilance not to let forms of oppression pass for liberty, commercial pseudo-culture and the consumption of fantasies for superior culture, diverse manifestations of plunder for progress. Superstition should not pass for rationality, economic inequalities for justice or fear for peace.[21]

Ramírez also offers an ethical critique of and alternative to what he calls "technological determinism," the belief that technology—whether imported or produced nationally—is both necessary and sufficient for development:

> In the same way that development cannot be restricted to economic growth, so development cannot be reduced merely to a technological matter. It involves a culture's identity, self-confidence, important degrees of independence, the search for its own answers, the satisfaction of basic needs, an openness to the future, social and mental changes that transform members of a society capable of sustaining, at its own pace and by its own means, more human forms of life.[22]

In the light of these ethical principles, Ramírez goes on to propose ethical criteria for deciding whether a technology is appropriate for a poor country:

> What is not appropriate technology? A technology excessively contaminating, expensive, and difficult to repair, one that deepens dependency, consumes much fuel, and is capital intensive. On the other hand, what is

> appropriate technology? It is technology that is friendly to the user and the environment, that is, appropriate in not damaging the human and non-human environment, one with low consumption of energy and fuel, one which doesn't require the payment of large sums for patents and prerequisites, one that helps resolve some of our problems and that, by not submerging the country in greater dependence, stimulates independence and confidence in ourselves as a people.[23]

Camacho also contributes to an ethics of science and technology (especially) in developing countries, evaluates different notions of crisis and development, and proposes a new and expanded concept of human rights which "does justice to the problem of the relations between advanced countries and Third World countries, including the treatment of the problem of individual development within socio-economic development."[24]

Interest in development ethics has also surfaced in Oceania. The 17th Waigani Seminar held at the University of Papua New Guinea in September 1986 was devoted to the topic "The Ethics of Development." One theme pursued during the seminar was that the "crisis" of Pacific development, including the disruption of traditional societies, calls for renewed ethical reflection if not a new ethic. Reflecting on the seminar, John D'Arcy May argues for a grounding of development ethics in both liberation theology and the "consensus of the suffering":

> In Papua New Guinea, the "lucky colony" which at times seems to behave like the spoiled brat of the developing world, the voice of the poor is just beginning to be heard. In searching for foundations on which to develop ethics, we should look beyond the quibbles of the philosophers to the "consensus of the suffering" among the slum dwellers and squatter settlers whose "base communities" are perhaps the most important seedbed of development ethics in our day.[25]

Three recent anthologies, with essays by authors of various countries, supply additional evidence of the increase in international interest in the evaluative dimension of development: *The Political Economy of Development and Underdevelopment,*[26] edited by the economist Charles K. Wilber; *Dialectics of Third World Development,* edited by geographers Ingolf Vogeler and Anthony De Souza;[27] and *Poverty, Amidst Plenty: World Political Economy and Distributive Justice,* edited by political scientist Edward Weisband.[28] In these three collections, social scientists either presuppose some value perspective on development or explicitly take up ethical issues in Third World and global development. What we see in these anthologies is a salutary movement within the social scientific community from narrowly empirical development studies to normative development analysis and development ethics.

Wilber indicates that his anthology "emphasize[s] the *political economy* rather than the narrowly *economic* approach and issues" and that the contributions "are radical in the sense that they are willing to question and evaluate the most basic institutions and values of society."[29] Wilber joins Kenneth P. Jameson in arguing that each development paradigm, whether "radical" or not, presupposes some conception of progress, good development, or other basic goals.[30]

Vogeler and De Souza assemble essays that exhibit "conservative," "liberal," and "radical" development perspectives:

> These three paradigms are based on different presuppositions about human nature, normative values, and social authority; and employ different concepts to describe the nature and causes of underdevelopment.[31]

The Weisband volume, a combination of readings and the editor's analyses, seeks to promote an empirical-normative discipline that Weisband calls "world political economy":

> World political economy examines the relationships between poverty and justice within, between, and across societies. It allows us to ask how political and economic factors perpetuate injustice and, in turn, how injustice sustains poverty. World political economy as a field of investigation focuses on the questions of how poverty arises, how it is sustained, and under what circumstances expansions in poverty levels reflect injustice.[32]

One value of Weisband's anthology is that it shows how "the political economy of development" must be situated in the context of the political economy of international relations and institutions. Moreover, to his credit Weisband sees that the very definition of "world political economy" includes a moral element, for this study "combines the analytical question of how poverty can persist in a world of plenty with the moral or normative question of when and why this is unjust."[33] To talk about "injustice" requires the use of moral concepts and the making of moral judgments. Hence, Weisband says that "this book applies moral norms—specifically distributive justice—to the social, economic, and political events associated with poverty amidst plenty."[34]

We complete our survey of the emergence of development ethics by noting some "analytically" trained Anglo-American philosophers who have taken up the field.[35] Onora O'Neill, a British social philosopher, explains the purpose of her recent book, *Faces of Hunger: An Essay on Poverty, Justice, and Development:*

> This book will not try to resolve debates about *how* hunger and destitution can best be ended. Some of the deepest disagreements about world hunger and poverty are not about methods, but about *whether* and *why* those with power to make fundamental changes ought to do so. Beyond

> the bland and superficial agreement that hunger and destitution should be ended, sceptical and self-seeking views are common. Poverty is indeed seen as a problem—for the poor. The rich and powerful often see no reason why they should help end distant poverty. This books asks *whether* and *why* development should be pursued, not only by the poor and vulnerable, but by the rich and powerful.[36]

In her book and in an important earlier article, O'Neill develops a Kantian, duty-based ethic that stresses the moral obligation of the rich and powerful to meet the basic needs of the world's poor. Her goal is to articulate and apply a secular ethic that avoids the "restricted outlook" of either a religious ethic, such as liberation theology, or the parochial value assumptions of many "development studies" professionals: "Since hunger and poverty are global problems, . . . their relief standardly requires communication between those whose categories and outlooks diverge. Retreat into the cosiness of shared tradition and rhetoric cannot resolve global predicaments."[37] Although she wants to transcend narrow outlooks, O'Neill also advocates a development ethic that is not so abstract that it would be blind to urgent needs or irrelevant to particular change agents in particular situations.

In two unpublished papers, Jerome M. Segal explicitly calls for development ethics, evaluates the moral assumptions of standard development paradigms, articulates a nicely nuanced version of a "basic human needs" perspective, and explores what development ethics can learn from the history of the idea of progress.[38]

British philosopher Nigel Dower argues that moral philosophy has much to offer in (a) clarifying the general concept of development as "a process of change which ought to take place,"[39] (b) evaluating particular development conceptions or paradigms, (c) advocating alternative visions, and (d) encouraging morally informed action. Dower defends and applies to problems of global poverty and the relations between rich and poor countries an ethic that includes a comprehensive conception of the "good life," an expanded notion of the right to life, and an employment of Rawls's contractarian theory of justice.[40]

At the forefront of a very recent movement that seeks to combine international development ethics and environmental ethics is J. Ron Engel. Rather than conceiving of social change as an inevitable trade-off between people and pandas or ponds, Engel challenges theorists and practitioners to forge an ethics of "ecodevelopment" or "sustainable development." To this end, Engel recently chaired the Ethics Working Group that drafted a new ethics chapter, "Building a World Conservation Ethic," for the second edition of the World Conservation Strategy of the International Union for the Conservation of Nature.[41] In addition, he has edited a cross-cultural and multidisciplinary volume entitled *Ethics of Environment and Development: Global Challenge, International Response*.[42]

Finally, in "The Hope for Just, Participatory Ecodevelopment in Costa Rica," Crocker evaluates competing development models and argues for an alternative vision.[43] In a series of other papers he treats less substantive and more methodological or "meta" questions about development ethics.[44]

The International Development Ethics Association (IDEA) had its origins in 1984 as the Development Ethics Working Group when Crocker and Yugoslav philosopher Mihailo Marković organized a seminar on "Ethics and Third World Development" as part of the VIII World Conference on Future Studies. In June 1987, the Development Ethics Working Group changed its name to IDEA and sponsored the First International Conference on Ethics and Development, at the University of Costa Rica. IDEA's second conference took place in Mérida, Mexico, July 3–9, 1989. One hundred philosophers, development theorists, and development practitioners from 15 countries treated the theme "Economic Crisis, Ethics, and Development Alternatives."[45]

It must be emphasized that these authors are not saying the same thing. For example, there is a difference between (a) the recognition that development theories, policies or practices have evaluative assumptions and (b) the articulation and defense of ethical principles and their application to development. Further, these thinkers sometimes have different conceptions of the nature, tasks, and methods of development ethics. Differences also exist among the ethical principles that are advocated. Nevertheless, this diverse group of academics and development professionals is united by the common recognition that pressing ethical questions exist and need to be answered, in what I shall call the "theory-practice" of development.

3. The Need for Development Ethics

Five considerations explain and justify the recent emergence of international development ethics.

(a) Moral questions in development practice

Development planners and project personnel often confront moral issues and difficult choices. This is true for professionals, whether members of local, national, or international organizations, and their "clients." A moral issue emerges when one must decide which possible action is ethically better. A moral dilemma occurs when one must decide, when considering the available action or policy options, between either two (or more) ethical principles or different ways of balancing these principles.

Another sort of ethical question occurs when the agent's moral obligation conflicts with personal or group self-interest. Then the question is not, "What is morally right?" but "Should I do what is right or should I do what is prudent?" Sometimes this second sort of dilemma is avoided; sometimes—but not always—ethics and prudence require the same thing. Let us consider some hypothetical and actual examples.[46]

(i) An Indian engineer invents a rice transplanter, and his state government of Orissa subsidizes production of the transplanters and distributes them to selected farmers. But each transplanter puts twenty agricultural laborers, mostly poor women, out of work. Is that morally right? What, if anything, does morality require after the fact of invention, distribution, and declining employment? What should have been done before the fact if these job consequences were (or should have been) foreseen? Who ought to have done what? Who should answer these questions?[47]

(ii) The United States Agency for International Development (USAID) funds an agricultural economist to set up small-farmer credit unions in Somoza's Nicaragua. If she comes to believe that her achievements and even her presence help legitimate an unjust regime, what should she do?[48] Should she honor her contract and continue her project, resign and go home, or aid the Sandinistas? What if her pulling out would mean the collapse of a necessary part of genuine rural development? What if her refusal to continue would destabilize Somoza and help the Sandinistas come to power? What if she believes that her credit unions are important for farmers regardless of the government in power and that an eventual Sandinista government would benefit from her institutional innovations? What if she knows what we now know about Nicaragua's revolutionary government? (What *do* we know, and how should we evaluate it?)

(iii) A national planner has to choose between two policies. The first policy would establish a national park in an area noted for its exotic but endangered flora and fauna. The land has also been home for generations to scores of small-scale slash-and-burn farmers. The second policy would permit the farmers to stay on their land and sell their trees to sawmills. Moreover, this second policy would contribute to the economic growth of the region and save these farm families from severe poverty. Which policy would be morally better? Would the answer be different if fears were justified about deforestation's role in global warming? If the crop were coca leaves rather than trees? Is there some third policy that would provide environmental protection without uprooting or undermining the economic livelihood of the human population? Now suppose that the planner cannot get the best policy adopted unless he resorts to bribery and deception of other officials. What should the planner do? Is it wrong for a representative of a foreign government or international agency to try to influence the planner's decision by attaching strings to assistance?[49] (What if those conditions are population controls or economic privatization? What if they are debt-equity or debt-for-nature "swaps?") Is it wrong for foreigners to assist policy they think unjust or unsound?

(iv) In Costa Rica more than 1,000 workers suffer from sterility due to bodily absorption of the chemical DBCP contained in the pesticides fumazone and nemagon. In spite of the fact that the World Health Organization and U.S. government scientists established that the substance is "extremely toxic," U.S. manufacturers kept exporting the product to other nations even though these same producers stopped production and alerted U.S. consumers to the dangers of continued use. In the period 1972–78, transnational corporations in Costa Rica used the substance without adequate safeguards. The Costa Rican government knew of the problem but prohibited neither the importation nor the use of the pesticides.[50] We need not waste time asking whether these policies and acts are morally wrong. But a development ethic should pose at least the following questions: Why are these policies morally objectionable?[51] Who is morally culpable, to what degree, and why? How should the workers be compensated and who should pay? Most generally, what are the moral responsibilities of transnational corporations and their host governments?

(v) In October 1986, Costa Rican President Oscar Arias suspended the executive president, Dr. Roger Churnside, and the directors of the Board of Port Administration and Economic Development of the Atlantic Slope (JAPDEVA). Arias's decree stated that JAPDEVA had not achieved "integral development" of the underdeveloped region of Costa Rica's Atlantic Coast. According to the ousted Churnside, these development goals had included the decentralization of "public sector decisions in order to respond to the realities and aspirations of the region and its specific communities" and "the importance of small businesses and communal organizations as instruments to promote employment and economic democracy."[52] Churnside contended that Costa Rica's "new development paths" necessitated that JAPDEVA have representatives from the Atlantic region's unions, cooperatives, and communal development associations. Earlier, Churnside had ruffled feathers by publicly arguing that some of JAPDEVA's directors were caught in "contradictions between their public functions and their duties in private business." One director answered that JAPDEVA had no serious problems and that the issue was simply one of "a difference in criteria."[53]

This episode raises several general questions for development ethicists: How should conflicts of interest and (possible) corruption be treated? Who should decide on regional development goals and strategy? The central government, regional governmental bodies, popular organizations, representatives of private business? Is it possible and morally desirable to have a "moral and rational dialogue" about development criteria when there are serious ideological clashes among groups with significantly unequal amounts of economic and political power?

(vi) Perhaps the most fundamental ethical question in development practice concerns the cultural identity of groups, populations, and societies on the path toward development. Throughout the world we find groups that are culturally different from the surrounding society and that now must decide if or how they ought to combine economic growth and modernization with their traditional identity. As Paula Palmer argues, "the needs of 'development' compete with the traditions and ethnic-cultural concepts of the 'good life.'"[54]

One option, called "absurd sentimentalism"[55] by Alphaeus Buchanan, would be to reject modern life and return to the past. This answer is absurd because changes are already on the way and the past cannot be recaptured. Another option would be to embrace the new and erase or suppress the old. But this choice would endanger community and personal identity rooted in cultural tradition. The blacks that live in Talamanca, Costa Rica seek a third alternative. According to Palmer,

> The Afro-Caribbean people of the coast do not want to return to the isolation of a past that provided fertile soil for culture but not for the economy. Neither do they want to follow blindly the classical model of development that eradicates Talamanca's unique cultural character. The Talamancans are searching for a creative alternative, in accord with their communal values, and insist that they should be the ones to establish what model to follow.[56]
>
> The people want to enjoy fully the rights of Costa Rican citizenship, the means of communication, the public services, and the economic development of their communities. At the same time they want to conserve the unique characteristics of their Afro-Caribbean heritage: their English and *creole* languages, their West Indian identity, their cooking, music, communal life, religious and ethnic customs; in short, their way of life. They want to progress but not at the cost of their cultural identity.[57]

Urgent questions persist even within this third perspective. For example, what sort of balance between the past and present should be chosen? Should the meaning of "development" or traditional identity (or both) be modified? In what way? Who should decide? How should the autonomy of the culturally unique groups be related to national development? When do the violations of minority rights become obstacles to genuine development in the wider society?[58] These issues take on an explosive character in contemporary Guatemala, India, and Sri Lanka. Taking these questions beyond national borders, development ethics similarly probes the relations between national identity, on the one hand, and regional and continental development, on the other. What balance should be sought between, for example, Costa Rican or Nicaraguan identity and improved Central (and Latin) American economic and political arrangements?

(vii) Richer countries provide foreign aid to poorer countries, and such aid is accompanied by an ongoing moral debate concerning whether such aid is morally impermissible, permissible, or obligatory. This debate turns on the factual question of the actual impact and use of such aid in Third World countries. But it is equally important to assess foreign aid morally in relation to whether it promotes good or authentic development. For this evaluation, we need a concept of "good development." As Roger C. Riddell has argued, the

> range of attack on foreign aid suggests that the view that governments have a moral obligation to provide foreign aid is, in fact, a highly complex claim. This is not only because the proposition contains three distinct elements—moral obligation, governments, and foreign aid—but also because foreign aid is not an end in itself. Development assistance, as it is technically known, is provided for the purpose of achieving secondary objectives. At its most general level, it is provided to promote or to assist the achievement of development, a term itself open to a variety of interpretations.[59]

This sample of moral issues and dilemmas reflects present realities and current debates. Decision makers often are keenly aware of the moral ambiguities that surround their work. Many express, sometimes only privately, their doubts and struggles to do what is right. Some have worked out for themselves or their enterprises moral codes, such as the Sullivan principles concerning investment in South Africa, to guide hard choices.[60] But many are convinced that a good deal more is needed if urgent problems are to be confronted in a morally responsible way. Rather than restricting moral judgments to one's private closet or to an inflexible professional code, many are coming to recognize the positive role to be played by ethical reflection that is explicit, contextually sensitive, public, and engaged. Such reflection would provide guidance for resolving such dilemmas. It would identify relevant features of the situation and supply help as to how these factors should be weighed.

Of course, not everyone involved recognizes the need for development ethics. Such dogmas as moral skepticism, political realism, some versions of moral relativism, value neutrality in the social sciences, and the utilitarian assumptions of economics are obstacles here. Moreover, some analysts worry that a self-conscious ethics may make things worse by overstressing good intentions and neglecting the bad consequences of well-intended actions. A related danger is that development ethics will preach utopian values that make no contact with the value content of realizable policy options. Development ethics might easily become a method of self-deception. It could make people—especially the privileged of the North and the West—feel good about doing bad things. Ethics, as an instrument of dominant societies and classes, can be used to celebrate rather than condemn unjust practices. Critiques, both Marxist and non-Marxist, of "moralism" and "a global ethic" are motivated by this concern.[61] Finally, development project personnel often worry that development ethics will be either naively utopian, too abstract to be useful, or so concrete as to make project people have to jump through yet another set of burdensome hoops.

My view is that these obstacles and dangers can be avoided by the right type of ethical reflection. Development personnel will become clearer and more unwavering in their recognition of the need for development ethics when they understand and practice the approach I will recommend. Goulet perceptively addresses some of these worries when he argues that "the best way to characterize how development ethics must operate is to say that it must become a 'means of the means'":[62]

> Ethicists do not discharge themselves of their duty merely by posing morally acceptable values as goals or ends of economic or political action. Nor does it suffice for them to evaluate the economic and political instrumentalities employed to pursue those ends in the light of some extrinsic moral rule. Rather, ethicists must analyze and lay bare the value content of these instrumentalities from within their proper dynamism. For example, they must ask whether a policy of export promotion favors economic equity or not, whether it consolidates fragile local culture or not, and so on. A kind of "peeling away" of the value content—positive and negative—latently present in the means chosen by technicians of decision-making must take place. Any moral judgment must relate to the technical data pertinent to the problem under study in realistic terms. Moreover, such a judgment must utilize those data in ways which professional experts can recognize as faithful to the demands of their discipline. This is the sense in which ethics must serve as a "means of the means," that is, as a moral beacon illuminating the value questions buried inside instrumental means appealed to by decision-makers and problem solvers or all kinds. . . . The greatest danger faced in this enterprise is that development ethicists will fall into the role played by plantation preachers in the days of slavery, namely, giving good conscience to the rich while providing spiritual, other-worldly solace to the victims of unjust structures.[63]

(b) Changes in theories of development and underdevelopment

Theory as well as practice shows the need for development ethics. In the post-WWII period, economists tried to describe and causally explain development and underdevelopment. W. W. Rostow's *The Stages of Economic Growth: A Non-Communist Manifesto*[64] is the best and most influential example of development theory in the 1950s and 1960s. Aidan Foster-Carter helpfully identifies some basic assumptions then shared by orthodox development theory.[65] I paraphrase Foster-Carter's analysis:

(i) Development does not involve irreconcilable interests—either between developed and undeveloped countries or among social groups in the latter. In the long run, at least, there are no losers.

(ii) No connection exists between development and underdevelopment. Development in some places is never causally linked to underdevelopment in others.
(iii) What is modern is good, and what is traditional is bad.
(iv) Development means becoming modern like the West.

Like fish oblivious to the water in which they swim, mainline theorists tended to be unaware of these basic beliefs, especially the normative ones. Only with the subsequent rise of a rival paradigm did these commitments become visible and subject to debate. A new perspective, dependency theory, negated each of the above assumptions. Exemplifying Foster-Carter's categories, F. H. Cardoso and Enzo Faletto, and Andre Gunder Frank proposed that:

(i) There are winners and losers in development because there are irreconcilable interests between developed and undeveloped countries and among groups within the latter (and former).
(ii) A structural link exists between development and underdevelopment. The countries of the "center" have developed precisely by causing the "peripheral" countries to become underdeveloped. Some indigenous groups have made themselves rich by impoverishing other groups. There has been, in Frank's now famous phrase, a "development of underdevelopment."
(iii) What is modern is not (necessarily) good and what is traditional is not (necessarily) bad.
(iv) (Real) development does not mean (or ought not mean) Western-style modernization.[66]

Development theory is currently in a state of contention. Whatever map is provided of the landscape, academics recognize that there is a plurality of general perspectives and a variety of versions within each paradigm.[67] Contrary to Kuhn's theory of scientific change, no theory has gained hegemony; alternative paradigms exist side by side.[68] Moreover, part of this variety consists of differences in value assumptions. Theories of development and underdevelopment are value-laden, and each theory has some conception of desirable ends for developing countries. As early as 1967, for example, Peter J. Henriot remarked that "the entire field of development has been in considerable disarray" and that we must speak of "defining the *problems* of development," "proposing *strategies* faced in development," and "specifying the *values* guiding development."[69]

Steidlmeier, a theological ethicist, explicitly discusses what he calls "social ethics of development."[70] He correctly sees that any development theory, model or policy presupposes *inter alia* a normative answer to the question

"What is the ultimate purpose of development?"[71] Steidlmeier clarifies ethical principles, based on what he calls "an ecumenical tradition of Christian humanism."[72] Then, in the light of these principles, he argues that any development perspective (i) should presuppose that societal members have the freedom and opportunity to participate in their society's development dialogue and (ii) does and should make proposals concerning the nature of good growth, fair distribution, citizen responsibility, and just incentives and sanctions. Steidlmeier goes on to advocate (but not argue) for an ethically based development vision:

> When it gets down to the concrete, then, I advocate a certain qualitative orientation in development policy based on the following priorities: the liberty of the oppressed over the freedom of the more powerful, the social opportunity of the marginalized over their exclusion by certain elites, the needs of the poor over the mere wants of the wealthy, the duty to contribute to the common good according to ability rather than be apathetic or merely seek narrow self-interest, and the reinforcement of patterns of social justice through social incentives and sanctions rather than surrendering the determination of due process to mere group egoism or vindictiveness. Each of these goals is a value statement in the sense that it indicates priorities regarding what should happen. I am well aware that others may disagree. Nonetheless, the positions that any society takes with respect to any of these questions will directly determine the overall orientation of development as well as the policy instruments and strategies involved.[73]

Steidlmeier proceeds to employ his value orientation to evaluate the ends, means, and agents of several leading development policies or models, *viz.*, growth plus trickle-down, revolution, redistribution with growth, basic needs, self-reliance and popular participation, and integrated rural development in a social market economy.[74]

The Wilber anthology gives us a selection from the voluminous writings of the most important practitioner of development ethics emerging from within economics in general and development economics in particular, namely, Amartya Sen. Acclaimed for his ground-breaking work in welfare economics and social choice theory as well as in development economics, Sen—without using the term—has increasingly taken up many of the questions of development ethics.

Sen argues that "traditional development economics has not been particularly unsuccessful in identifying factors that led to *growth* in developing countries,"[75] namely, capital accumulation and investment, industrialization, mobilization of underemployed labor, and state activism in the economy. For Sen, however, traditional development economics has mistakenly identified economic growth as the end of economic development. At best, economic growth is only a means—and often not a very efficient means—for the goals of development. The concept of development is, for Sen and philosopher Martha Nussbaum, "value-relative": "without some idea of ends that are themselves external to the development process and in terms of which the process may be assessed, we cannot begin to say what changes are to count as 'development.'"[76] It is not enough to describe and explain a society's values nor to treat its values merely as instruments (or obstacles) to development. In addition, cultural insiders as well as outsiders need "some sort of evaluation *of* those practices and values: which ones are, in fact, the most valuable":[77]

> Values cannot be treated, as they often are in the literature on economic development, as purely instrumental objects in promoting development. Indeed, the very idea of "development"—whether seen from within a culture or in the stylized impersonal context of development economics—is inevitably based on a particular class of values, in terms of which progress is judged and development is measured.[78]

Sen and Nussbaum distinguish two forms of ethical inquiry about development. The externalist or Platonic model is one in which "rational criticism is detached and external." From a transcendent, ahistorical standpoint, the ethicist looks down and "recommends certain values as best for the development and flourishing of a people" and excludes "any influence from the beliefs of those people as to what lives are best to live, or from wishes as to the sort of lives they want to live."[79] Sen and Nussbaum criticize this Platonic model and advocate an Aristotelian approach that blends cultural immersion and internalist assessment.

> Aristotle holds that any good account of development . . . will be genuinely rooted in the experience of the people and genuinely practical, and yet be evaluative in such a way as to help leaders structure things for the best, enabling people to live as good and flourishing a life as possible . . . we do not inquire in a vacuum. Our conditions and ways of life, and the hopes, pleasures, pains, and evaluations that are a part of these, cannot be left out of the inquiry without making it pointless and incoherent. . . . Ethical truth is in and of human life; it can be seen only from the point of view of immersion.[80]

Practicing this second model for development ethics, Sen conceives development as "a process of expanding the capabilities of people":[81]

> Ultimately the process of economic development has to be concerned with what people can or cannot do, e.g., whether they can live long, escape avoidable morbidity, be well nourished, be able to read and write and communicate, take part in literary and scientific pursuits, and so forth. It is to do, in Marx's words, with "replacing the domination of cir-

> cumstances and chance over individuals by the domination of individuals over chance and circumstances."[82]

In defending this conception of development, Sen explicitly formulates and argues for a distinctive ethical vision. This ethical outlook, stressing "positive freedom" and "goal rights," is offered as a superior alternative to the "welfarism" and "sum ranking" of much welfare economics as well as the nonconsequentialist deontology of much Anglo-American ethics and moral philosophy.[83] In Sen's ethical theory we find a pluralism that seeks (i) to do equal justice to the "well being" and "agency" aspect of human beings and (ii) to combine cross-cultural moral "minimums" or absolutes with appropriate sensitivity to cultural relativity and differences.[84] It is also important to note that Sen offers his "capabilities approach" as building on but deepening and improving the "basic needs" development strategy, a development perspective that emerged in the 1970s in which moral arguments were wedded to theoretical explanation and practical recommendations.[85]

What we find in Sen's ongoing work is a subtle and well-argued vision of humane development, ethically based criteria for development success and failure, and careful attention to issues in methodology and meta-ethics. Sen is our best contemporary example of the move from (development) economics to (development) ethics in which both economics and (philosophical) ethics are undergoing a long overdue transformation. An important task of the emerging field of development ethics will be to grasp and assess Sen's proposals.

What is true of general theories is also true of treatments of the development models or styles in particular countries and regions. Consider, for example, the explicit norms in the following critique of Costa Rican economic and social change:

> In spite of undeniable social, economic and political advances, the country's reigning development model has enormous limitations with respect to achieving a more autonomous and self-sufficient development that satisfies the basic needs of all Costa Ricans, that generates an adequate distribution of income and absorption of manpower that keeps being "incorporated" every year, and, most importantly, that maintains and improves the country's present democratic system.[86]

Let us pause to consider an objection. It is often said that the concept of development simply refers to economic growth, industrialization, or modernization. These objective changes need not be subjectively evaluated at all or, if they are assessed, they can be either approved or disapproved. One can describe a country as developed and then leave open whether its state of being economically developed is good, bad, or indifferent. So, the argument goes, there is nothing inherently valuational about development theories and, consequently, an ethics of development has no place in development studies.

It is true that development is often used in a relatively value-neutral way. Sometimes, for example, we ask if it is better to be or not to be (economically) developed. Or we ask, as Palmer did above, whether development can be compatible with a group's cultural identity. In this sense, development does more or less neutrally signify economic growth, industrialization, or (more vaguely) modernization. Moreover, it is possible, although sometimes difficult, to refrain from evaluating such economic and social conditions. As Segal remarks, the question "What is development?" is sometimes merely the request for a description of economic growth and an identification of its key causes.

But this relatively neutral use of "development" must not be confused with the concept's normative meaning. For Segal, the central usage of "development" is related to the maturation of a living thing and, as such, is inherently valuational. A living thing develops not simply when it changes, let alone when it merely gets bigger. Rather, it "develops itself" when its changes stem more or less from within itself and it realizes its inner goals, inherent potential, or "fullness of being."[87] To use "development" in this normative sense is to *approve* of the inner goals and their realization. With respect to theories of development and underdevelopment, then, an important question becomes, "Which goals ought a country (or other unit) try to achieve?":

> "Development" is the most widely used concept for thinking about the great changes that are occurring throughout the world. Moreover, it is a concept for which there are no good substitutes. The call for development exerts a special power in that it is a call for change in order that Third World people should more fully come into being. At the same time, just what we mean or should mean by "greater fullness of being" is not at all clear.[88]

Various theories of development have different answers to this question. They agree that the general concept of development implies desirable change, but they differ as to what that change should be. Identifying development with economic growth is, for both Sen and Segal, only one answer and not a very good one at that.

Dower makes a similar point. For Dower the concept of "development" has both a more general normative sense, which most everyone can accept, and more specific meanings, "conceptions" of development, in which what is advocated as development is expected to be controversial.[89] To the question "What is development?" in the first sense, Dower answers that development is a process of social change that can be influenced by human action and ought to take place.[90] To answer the question in the second, more specific sense, Dower contends one has to answer the additional question "What ought to happen?"[91] To answer this "ought question" explicitly is one of the tasks of development ethics.

The objection with which we began this digression now can be answered. Just because "development" is sometimes used in a value neutral way to designate such things as economic growth or modernization does not mean that we do not need development ethics. Indeed, such ethical reflection is important precisely because there are also two widely employed and important normatives senses of development. Development in the general normative sense means "beneficial alterations," social changes that humans can and should influence. Development in the more determinant normative sense is that particular kind of social change advocated as, in Dower's apt phrase, "the object of moral commitment."[92] We need moral reflection on a society's basic goals because such things as economic growth and modernization may be morally problematic and in need of replacement, modification, or supplementation with more adequate concepts of "fullness of being." We need critical and explicit reflection on the ends as well as the means of development, on the *what* as well as the *how*. Given that the non-normative sense of development can be easily confused with the normative sense, it is often best to speak of "authentic" or "good" development as the theoretical and practical goal of development ethics.

With this understanding of the ambiguity of development, let us draw out the implications for my principal argument. It is a step forward to realize the importance of clarifying the normative assumptions of development theories. But we need something more. As Sen recognizes and practices, development theorists need to engage in explicit "moral dialogue" in which values and ethical principles are articulated, defended, and applied. We need prescription as well as description, interpretation, explanation, and prediction. We need good goals as well as causal linkages. But if valuational dimensions are part of all development theory, they must not function as unexamined commitments. If we want to improve these beliefs, in our own as well as other societies, we ought to elucidate and defend them in ways appropriate to any basic beliefs—through critical dialogue.[93] A development ethic, then, would go well beyond many current development theories. But such an ethic alone would not be sufficient; it would be executed in conjunction with the various empirical investigations of development.

One objection to such a development ethic is that it would prescribe an impossible dream that projects sublimated desires and stimulates unrealizable hopes. The result would be frustration and paralysis when the dream encounters reality. Consequently, it is sometimes argued, we must eschew a development ethic because it will do more harm than good.

This argument must be taken seriously. But the proper response is not to reject all ethics in this field but only moral reflection that is isolated from the sciences, politics, and practice of development. In this context, I want to stress that an explicit development ethic ought to be in close relation with empirical development theories. There are, in general, two ways to understand this linkage.

The first way is to modify both ethics and the sciences of development so that they in some sense work together but retain some autonomy or separateness. The sciences describe and explain what is, was, and can be. To discern what *ought* to be is the task of ethics. Science and ethics, however, are not isolated from each other. Social scientists must realize that their very choices of descriptive and explanatory categories often reflect moral judgments, and the better the moral judgments, the more helpful are the descriptions and explanations.[94] If, for example, poverty is defined as the relation of the least well-off to the best-off and the gap between the two is erased, poverty magically disappears even though all fail to satisfy their basic needs. More generally, certain kinds of factual information are included and certain kinds excluded depending on one's ethical and other paradigmatic commitments.[95] On the other hand, ethicists must remember that to know what ought to be, we must first know what can be. For, as Kant said, "ought" implies "can." Hence, development ethicists must reject a utopian ethic in favor of an ethic that clarifies, justifies, and applies realizable ideals and identifies efficient as well as morally permissible means.[96] Just as development theorists need to be conscious of and evaluate their implicit values, so ethicists of development need to do their work in relation to the best available empirical theory and factual information. But there is still a disciplinary division of labor, and multidisciplinary cooperation is needed. Examples would be Sen and Nussbaum's collaboration and IDEA's multidisciplinary focus.

A second model for the relation of development ethics and science would be to advocate a new field of normative development science (or studies) which fuses or dialectically combines in one "discipline" the ethics and philosophy of development with the various sciences (economics, sociology, political science) of development. For example, Sen talks of "normative economics" and "normative economic analysis" within development economics, and Weisband advocates a conception of "world political economy" that includes both empirical and normative elements.[97] Practitioners of this enterprise would do both empirical and normative research. The Costa Rican philosopher Manuel Formoso illustrates this second model when he argues that moral critique and ethical inquiry into better alternatives is part of the social scientist's responsibilities.

> It is enough for the investigator of nature to know the being of nature in order to dominate it and utilize its forces. But knowledge of social reality is not enough, above all when this reality is ethically unacceptable. There will be no dignity in the work of social scientists if they stop in the face of the simple fact that in the Third World millions of children die of hunger every year.

> Social scientists are obliged to move from the knowledge of social reality to a formulation of duty. They are obliged to elaborate alternative proposals for change, for transformation, in order that the social order can be ethically acceptable.[98]

One task of development ethics is to see if there is a "difference that makes a difference" between these approaches. My judgment at this point is that it does not greatly matter which way we choose to integrate our normative and non-normative research on development. Given the nature of current academic training and disciplinary separation, the first model is probably more realistic. But with more comprehensive education we may approximate the second model. What clearly is important is that the science and ethics of development—whether or not each investigator engages in both—be done in relation to each other and in the context of development as a "theory-practice." We now turn to the practical origin, context, and impact of both the ethics and science of development.

(c) The "theory-practice" of development

A more fundamental case can be made for development ethics when we understand the field of "development" by means of what I call a "theory-practice." With this concept we can link up both normative and empirical development theory with development policy, politics, and practice.

An interesting recent turn in the history and philosophy of science is the recognition that our image of science should transcend the traditional distinction of theory vs. practice as well as that of pure science vs. applied science vs. technology.[99]

According to the first dichotomy, real science consists of a body of propositions—conceptual systems, confirmed theories, and scientific laws. Of secondary importance is the transitory activity that generates these allegedly timeless truths. In the second set of distinctions the significance of science as a human activity is recognized, but *pure* science is viewed as having priority precisely because it is more general than applied science and is untainted by practical interests. As an example of this second approach, Bunge considers pure or fundamental science to be an activity motivated solely by the search for truth about the natural and social world.[100] The product of pure science is general scientific knowledge that is valuable in and of itself. Applied or practical science, for Bunge, is motivated by the purpose of changing the world in order to satisfy human needs. Its product, resulting from deduction from general truths, is more particular causal knowledge designed to solve particular social problems. For Bunge, the technician then employs applied science to "design artifacts and plan courses of action that have some practical value for some social group."[101] Finally, human agents construct the artifacts (technologies) and put the plans into action (practice).

Applying these distinctions to the field of development, Bunge identifies (i) pure (value-neutral) and general theories of development and underdevelopment, (ii) general theories deductively applied to particular social contexts in order to understand and thereby eliminate particular examples of underdevelopment, (iii) the technical design of practical strategies to bring about development and reduce underdevelopment, and (iv) the practical implementation of development plans and the construction of progressive institutions.

I do not want to deny that Bunge's fourfold demarcation has some merit and utility. A distinction is sometimes possible and desirable between a relatively pure and a relatively applied science, between scientific theory and (technological or political) practice *informed* by it. (Relatively) pure scientists certainly need to be free from control by political, religious, and scientific authorities. (Relatively) applied scientists, technicians, and practitioners can be aided by general empirical theory, although they rarely deductively apply such theory and often revise it on the basis of their grasp of concrete particulars.[102] Technological innovations often follow theoretical breakthroughs.

But we need to soften Bunge's distinctions and see them as dialectically related "moments" of a continuum and as aspects of a more comprehensive reality: a "theory-practice." Bunge does help us advance beyond the earlier, "propositional" image of science in order to see science as a human activity. Instead of understanding science, pure or applied, as merely—or most importantly—a conceptual product published in books, Bunge conceives science as different sorts of human activity motivated by various interests and integrated with other kinds of activity. We also need, however, to modify Bunge's view of the relations between pure and applied (scientific) theory. Pure science is motivated not only, as Bunge would have it, by an interest in general knowledge but also by practical concerns. Human beings seek general truths about their natural and social environments in order to be able to cope with them better. Moreover, science's long-run social utility precisely requires that science be motivated by truth and characterized by freedom of investigation. We cope best when we see clearly.

Practical context often motivates and shapes even abstract and general scientific theory. Theory normally informs practice: it tells us what is and why, what is (likely) to be and why, and how to arrive at the better future from the actual present. Relatively pure theory is possible. Relatively "pure" practice is possible. But it is typical and, more importantly, often desirable to have a "practice-theory" or a "theory-practice" in which more or less abstract thought, site-specific experience, and practical conduct are dialectically related.

What we find when we turn to the actual world is a profusion of "theory-practices." As a working definition, let us conceive a theory-practice as, among other things, a complex, cooperative human activity, with both theoretical (normative and non-normative) and practical aspects, that achieves certain goods by striving to fulfill norms definitive of that activity.[103] One category of "theory-practices" would be fields such as medicine, sports, agriculture, and education.[104] A good soccer coach, for instance, will emphasize the normative goal of soccer excellence and the norm of fair play but also will apply scientific knowledge from such fields as nutrition and physiology. On the other hand, such a coach can make contributions to the normative and non-normative theories of soccer excellence, sportsmanship, strategy and tactics, training, and the prevention and cure of injuries.

Another category of "theory-practices" would be social and political movements such as environmentalism and feminism, for each is a fusion of science, ethics, politics, and practice. Feminism is important in another way, for it is one important source for the idea of a "theory-practice" that I am proposing. Nancy Hartsock, drawing on some ideas of Antonio Gramsci, explains what she means by feminist theory:

> Our [feminist] theory gives us a description of the problems we face, provides an analysis of the forces which maintain social life, defines the problems we should concentrate on, and acts as a set of criteria for evaluating the strategies we develop . . . theory itself can be a force for change. . . . For feminists, the unity of theory and practice refers to the use of theory to make coherent the problems and principles expressed in our practical activity. Feminists argue that the role of theory is to take seriously the idea that all of us are theorists. The role of theory, then, is to articulate for us what we know from our practical activity, to bring out and make conscious the philosophy embedded in our lives.[105]

In her book *Feminist Politics and Human Nature,* Alison Jaggar employs this general concept of theory to examine different "feminist frameworks," diverse treatments of the nature, cause, and cure of women's oppression. One constructs theories to understand as well as end the oppression. Knowledge is necessary (but insufficient) for the cure (as well as vice versa). Diagnosis and prognosis lead to prescriptions for cure. Cure involves both a vision of a desirable goal and strategic recommendations for achieving it. Feminist (normative and non-normative) theory guides and is revised by feminist practice. Science (both pure and applied), ethics (both abstract and applied), technology, and politics are not isolated nor merely yoked together. They do and should mingle in cooperative activity in various and subtle ways.[106]

What I have done is to take this notion of the dialectical continuum of feminist theory and practice and generalized it as the concept of "theory-practice" in order to illumine other fields and movements. Among these is what is called the field of Third World and international development. People involved in development need not be just theorists or exclusively activists or practitioners. What we sometimes find and urgently need are people who are both—albeit in a variety of proportions and with various measures of success. What these theorist-practitioners can do is to bring about (authentic) development, however defined, as a cure for underdevelopment. To do so requires an identification of those factors that cause underdevelopment and that block and produce development. Such causal explanation is the scientific side of development theory-practice. But reflection should also be *ethical* reflection. We should ask "In what direction *should* (poor) societies develop themselves?" and "Who should decide?" Finally, the answers to both empirical and normative theoretical questions may not only guide but also be informed by practical experience and efforts to make changes—especially the experience and action of poor people.[107]

If our focus is on development as a "theory-practice," we must also reflect ethically on practical development strategy and tactics. As Goulet argues, we need an ethics of means as well as an ethics of goals and limits. We should evaluate which means are morally permissible, impermissible, and obligatory as well as which means are effective and which goals are worthwhile. We need to inquire empirically with respect to what concrete social and economic conditions are needed if appropriate moral principles and development visions are to be realized in people's lives and institutions. We need to reflect ethically if the end justifies the means. When and why? Given the means at our disposal, which ends should we adopt? Why? How much weight should we give to the values of (economic) efficiency and growth, especially when they conflict with other values?

An ethics in the context of development theory-practice explicitly poses and answers these questions both on a general level and in relation to particular societies and specific problems. We need to be as good at concrete moral judgment (*phronesis*) as we are at doing scientific and ethical theory and producing technical innovations.

Just as feminism is one source of the idea of a theory-practice, so recent steps toward the "feminization" of international development give promise of a new and ethically justified approach in development theory-practice. Far from accepting their exploitation, neglect, or token recognition in development, women—especially Third World women—have initiated a new consideration of their actual and ideal social roles and a new approach to Third World and global change. For example, Gita Sen and Caren Grown, members of Development Alternatives with Women for a New Era (DAWN), write:

> The group . . . affirmed that it is the experiences lived by poor women throughout the Third World in their struggles to ensure the basic survival needs of their families that provide the clearest lens for an understanding of the development processes. And it is *their* aspirations and struggles for a future free of the multiple oppression of gender, class, race, and nation that can form the basis for the new visions and strategies that the world now needs.[108]

(d) The end of value neutrality

The dogma of the ethical neutrality of science and technology is a major reason that development theorists-practitioners have been uncomfortable with and have even repudiated ethics. The dogma, as an uncritical belief, says that science is (ideally) objective. What objectivity means here is that the scientist should provide (disinterested) information about facts and laws and not permit an intrusion of his or her subjective values. Description, interpretation, explanation, and prediction are scientific activities that should be free of all values, especially ethical values.[109] Similarly, the dogma affirms that technology is ethically neutral. Humans can *use* technology for good or ill, but in itself it is valuationally neutral.

This dogma has impeded and continually threatens to rupture the fruitful dialectical relation that I have sketched between the theory and practice of development. There is pressure to put the pure and applied development sciences on the "objective" side and ethics or values on the "subjective" side of the great divide. Even Charles Wilber shows a residue of this neutrality when he confesses his ethical "commitments" in contrast to his "objective" compilation of options in development theory:

> While I hope that the work presented here is objective, there is no artificial stance of neutrality. I am committed to certain values that undoubtedly influence the choice of questions asked and the range of variables considered for selection. In general, my system of values posits material progress (at least up to some minimum level), equality, cooperation, democratic control of economic as well as political institutions, and individual freedom as positive goods. It should be noted that there may be contradictions among these criteria, and thus society is faced with choices. With these values in mind the reader can judge the degree of objectivity attained.[110]

What is interesting about this passage is that objectivity is sharply disconnected from values and that values are matters of personal commitment and social choice. Wilber clarifies but refrains, at least in his preface, from trying to justify or apply his own values to the ends and means of development. But that is precisely one trouble with the dogma of value neutrality. It makes people in the development field uncomfortable about employing ethical reflection as *part* of their theory and/or practice. Over a drink after work, moral debate can become heated. But on the job, development scientists and professionals often see ethical decisions as something that someone else—for instance, "society" or ethicists—ought to make. The scientist as scientist and the professional as professional, so the argument goes, have no ethical responsibility.

To a certain extent this attitude is justified. First, although our "hopes and fears" may motivate development inquiry, Berger correctly cautions us not to permit them to distort our grasp of what is, was, and might be.[111] But instead of implying neutrality, this prohibition shows us that science itself presupposes some ethical principles; for example, those of honesty and the search for truth.[112] Likewise, technology, as a product of human activity, is not neutral. The use of time and resources to produce a technology instead of employing them for other purposes is a matter for ethical choice. Ethical judgment ought to inform the production of technologies because we should evaluate the probable consequences—both good and bad—of a proposed technology and compare them with alternative innovations and the status quo. Nuclear policy, genetic engineering, pesticides, and Nestlé baby formulas all have ethical implications.

Second, I would agree with Wilber that citizens have the *right* to participate in decisions affecting national development. Moreover, development professionals need to respect and learn from traditional practices as well as popular knowledge and aspirations.[113] Going further, Goulet and others compellingly argue "the need for new forms of non-elite participation in the transition to equitable development strategies."[114] But none of this means that there is no need for ethical reflection by development theorists and practitioners. They are more than their society's hired hands. They also have a moral responsibility as human beings, as fellow citizens, and as professionals to engage in ethical reflection about development. I would argue that one result of this reflection would be a reasoned defense of the right to and importance of popular participation in macro as well as micro arenas of decision making.[115]

Now is not the time to argue further against the dogma of scientific and technological neutrality. That has been done elsewhere.[116] We have seen that values and ethics enter into development theory-practice at many points. It is increasingly recognized that this state of affairs is valuable as well as unavoidable. Now that the obstacle of value neutrality is being removed, development scientists and practitioners have the opportunity as well as *moral responsibility* to attend carefully to the normative aspect, be it theoretical or practical, of their field.

(e) From philosophy to development ethics

So far I have explained and justified the need for development ethics by reference to development practice, theory, and "theory-practice." The call for such an ethics also can be linked to certain recent changes in and continuing deficiencies of Anglo-American philosophy. For the present we must leave open similar questions with respect to the philosophy practiced in other countries.[117]

Recently, much Anglo-American philosophy has taken a decidedly "practical" turn. Following John Dewey's dictum and example, many Anglo-American "postanalytic" philosophers have switched their attention away from the traditional problems of philosophy and toward the problems of human beings (and, one should add, nonhuman beings). Toulmin puts it well:

> Taking "philosophy" in this *practical* sense, as a contribution to the reflective resolution of quandaries that face us in enterprises with high stakes—even life and death— . . . it is time for philosophers to come out of their self-imposed isolation and reenter the collective world of practical life and shared human problems.[118]

Renouncing the exclusively neutral analyses of moral discourse popular in the 1950s and 1960s, not satisfied with constructing abstract ethical systems as was done in the 1970s, and eschewing the "technicality" of much "analytic" philosophy, increasing numbers of Anglo-American moral philosophers are applying ethical reflection to concrete human practices, problems, and policies.[119] The results—variously called "applied philosophy," "practical philosophy," "applied ethics," "practical ethics," and "philosophy and public policy"—have proliferated in courses, articles, journals,[120] books, conferences, and institutes.[121] Philosophers testify before the U.S. Congress and are members of hospital ethics committees and "think-tanks."[122] Philosophical subdisciplines such as medical ethics, environmental philosophy and ethics, legal ethics, economic philosophy, and nuclear ethics are being energetically pursued.

My claim is that philosophical attention to the ethical issues in development theory and practice would benefit both development ethics and Anglo-American philosophy. Development ethics would gain from the role philosophers can play in criticizing myths, identifying ethical issues, clarifying fundamental assumptions, and constructing, advocating, justifying, and applying ethical principles. It is not the case that philosophers are the moral experts or have unique expertise in ethical reflection. We need to abandon the Platonic model of the philosopher-king and the Kantian model of the transcendental adjudicator of basic and jurisdictional disputes. Rather, philosophers should exemplify the Aristotelian-Deweyan model defended by Nussbaum, Sen, Rorty and others. They should be participants and critics in a society-wide moral dialogue and facilitators of ethical practice.[123] It is important, especially in a democratic society, that the ability to engage in moral reflection be widely shared.

Anglo-American philosophy would also benefit. If philosophers take up international development ethics, it would reduce ethnocentrism in other areas of Anglo-American applied ethics. For example, we must rethink environmental ethics if the preservation of tropical rain forests turns out to be in irreconcilable conflict with an acceptable level of infant mortality in Brazil or Costa Rica.[124] We need to question U.S. food aid and trade policies when U.S. food exports to Third World countries contribute to a reduction in local food production, migration of small farmers to overcrowded cities, and an unfavorable balance of payments.[125] We need to wonder about improving our treatment of U.S. pets when they eat more and better than many Third World people.[126] We ought to challenge the employment of costly and exotic North American medical techniques when many Third World people lack minimal health care. We should question our traditional notions of (domestic) economic justice when North American workers make many times more in wages (with much less physical risk) than do Third World workers who do exactly the same jobs, sometimes for the same transnational corporation. The Anglo-American feminist demand for "*the* woman's voice" in public affairs, when that voice is First World (white, middle class, academic), needs to be corrected by the demand for many Third World (colored, poor, illiterate) women's voices.[127] We should not confine ourselves to "ethics in (and for) one country"; for, if we do, our ethics can easily become an ideological camouflage for group egoism and a new form of imperialism.

Anglo-American moral philosophers and other ethicists have begun to tackle *some* of the moral questions that emerge in international affairs and, in particular, in the relations between developed and developing countries.[128] In the early 1970s, philosopher Peter Singer and biologist Garrett Hardin sparked a lively debate on the ethics of famine relief and development transfers from rich to poor countries.[129] Michael Walzer's attempt to revive and improve the traditional just-war theory has stimulated a vigorous discussion about the ethics of military and nonmilitary intervention that crosses national boundaries.[130] The Institute for Philosophy and Public Policy has scrutinized the ethical issues involved in U.S. food, foreign, and immigration policies, especially as the latter applies to Mexican undocumented workers.[131] Charles Beitz has developed a "cosmopolitan ethic" that extends Rawls's methods and conception of distributive justice to the global arena.[132] The Carnegie Council on Ethics and International Relations sponsors conferences and the Working Group on International Ethics, and publishes a newsletter, an annual journal, *Ethics and International Affairs,* and a series of books on the ethics of foreign policy and international relations.[133] Although the council's focus is interdisciplinary, several philosophers and theological ethicists have been involved.

Yet this salutary "internationalization" of Anglo-American philosophy and applied ethics is not enough. For at least four reasons, we also need an ethics of Third World and international development. First, an ethics of foreign policy and international relations requires an understanding of the Third World. For example, an ethics of famine relief and development assistance demands an intimate acquaintance with the impact of aid as well as with history, problems, development styles, values, and prospects of particular poor societies.[134] Because development ethics, as part of development "theory-practice," would treat these non-normative issues, the ethicist would be informed about the concrete context of moral choice. Indeed, development ethics would help Anglo-American philosophers to fulfill their *own* moral obligations to understand what is going on in the country that is a possible object of aid:

> An evaluation of how developing countries manage their transition is itself an exacting moral task . . . there must be a profound understanding of the historical processes in these societies, a capacity to see the ethical issue in relation to these processes, and a sensitivity to the inner struggle of a society in the midst of an unprecedented transition.[135]

Second, the ethics of foreign aid must be dialectically linked to development ethics. What kind of aid, if any, rich countries should give to poor countries depends on answers to questions such as "In what direction should a poor country develop itself?" and "Who should decide?" Short-term aid ought to promote authentic, long-range development. Hence to decide on the case for aid requires a conception of "good" development.[136]

Third, Anglo-American ethics would benefit from involvement in international development ethics because it would expand the Northern and Western moral discussion to one that includes the South and the East. A truly global moral dialogue would be promoted. Defects in Northern and Western moral visions would have a better chance of being identified and corrected when Anglo-American thinkers and practitioners enter into a moral give-and-take with ethicists from other moral traditions.[137] For example, many people in rich countries are trying to redefine the good life so that material affluence is kept in its proper place. Development ethics executed in dialogue with Third World theorist-practitioners would include consideration of the appropriate role of material well-being. Moreover, the pronounced teleological character of much development ethics—with its stress on national goals and human flourishing—should contribute to the recent search for an ethic with a strong consequentialist but nonutilitarian component.[138]

Fourth and finally, development ethics would provide Anglo-American and other philosophers and ethicists with additional resources to help forge an international social morality and a public transnational ethics.[139] Given increasing world interdependence, we need not only international law but also a nonethnocentric "ethical consensus" on some basic matters in order to regulate and guide the interactions of nation states, international agencies—such as the World Bank, the International Monetary Fund, and refugee organizations—and transnational corporations. The global society stands to gain from the global moral dialogue to which development ethics, practiced in and for various cultures, would contribute.

In summary, these four considerations have stimulated the Anglo-American philosophical interest in international development and justify the emergence of international development ethics that was charted in this essay's introduction.

4. Agenda and Conclusion

Much remains to be done in the further evolution of development ethics. We need to clarify further its nature and function in relation to other aspects of "development theory-practice." In particular, we need to consider how the normative and empirical elements in "development theory-practice" should be related. Should our efforts be multidisciplinary or should we be forging a new empirical-normative discipline? We need to understand more fully how development ethics should be related to other fields of ethics, for example, environmental ethics and international ethics. We need to elucidate and comparatively evaluate various ethical visions for development. We need to consider further the challenges of ethical relativism and political realism and the charge that development ethics is but a new form of U.S. or Northern cultural imperialism. We need to perform ethical reflection on the development goals, strategies, and institutions of particular societies and regions. We need to forge ethically based but operational criteria for what counts as development success and failure. We need detailed ethical evaluations of the goals and performances of national and international development agencies. We need more work on the empirical conditions necessary if persons, communities, and institutions are to comply with the principles that development ethics prescribes.

But some things should be clear as we draw together the threads of this essay and work toward development ethics in the context of "development theory-practice."

It is best, at least in our present age of disciplinary and practical divisions, that this "theory-practice" includes the work of many hands so that various components can make their contribution. The ongoing dialogue should include many voices. It ought to be at least multidisciplinary and perhaps a new integrated field to ensure the presence of the various theoretical elements—not only economics but also sociology, political science, history, ecology, agronomy, law, and philosophy. It ought to transcend the distinction between the pure and applied sciences and therefore include such fields as agricultural economics, education, social work, and engineering. The moral dialogue ought to include theological ethics, so as not to neglect the resources of the religious communities, as well as secular ethics, in order to forge an improved global and public moral consensus.

Development ethics ought to go beyond theoreticians and include development policy makers, politicians, activists, and journalists. It ought to involve rural as well as urban participants if urban bias is to be corrected without neglecting crucial rural/urban linkages. The dialogue must involve both women and men in order to diminish sexism. Members of minority groups must participate to reduce racism, classism, and an academic bias against traditional practices and popular wisdom. The participants should come from the South as well as the North to avoid ethnocentric imperialism and counterimperialism. We need participants from the East as well as the West so that the issues of development and peace can be intimately linked. The dialogue must involve citizens as well as governmental experts and private consultants if citizens are to have a real opportunity to exercise their right to effective participation.

Development ethics, then, requires a global dialogue. Perhaps what is most important for this dialogue is that it occur in a context in which the big, strong, and rich do not coerce the small, weak, and poor. Our notion of authentic international development itself should include this ideal of unrestricted and unforced moral dialogue.[140]

If these persons and groups are integrated in moral dialogue, we will be moving toward the right kind of development ethics and, hopefully, toward authentic development and a better world.

Notes

An antecedent of this essay was presented in the symposium "Ethical Issues in International Development," a part of the VIII World Conference on Future Studies, San José, Costa Rica, December 1984. The present essay, a translation and greatly expanded version of Crocker (1987), is closely related to Crocker (1988, 1990b). I am grateful to the following colleagues at the University of Costa Rica and Colorado State University for valuable comments on earlier versions: Rafael Angel Herra, Jorge Rovira Mas, Bernard E. Rollin, and Holmes Rolston III. A decade of students in my graduate seminar, "Ethics and International Development," have contributed in many ways to my thinking on this topic. Four of them—Alison Bailey, Cynthia Botteron, Chris Johnston, and Charles Kolic—made helpful suggestions about this paper. Finally, the anonymity of three referees for *World Development* does not preclude me from expressing appreciation for their insightful and constructive criticisms of an earlier draft. Remaining problems, of course, are my own responsibility.

1. In this first paragraph I employ quotation marks to indicate that the meaning and evaluation of the following concepts are contested: "development," "underdevelopment," and "Third World."

2. Although I usually use "normative" and "ethical" as synonyms, it should be noted that I mean to say neither that all values are moral values nor that all normative reflection is moral reflection. For example, aesthetic values are different from ethical values, and normative assessment of development policies and projects should include aesthetic questions such as the aesthetic value of an endangered rain forest or a traditional ritual.

3. See Goulet (1971b); Mansilla (1989).

4. Crocker (1991).

5. See Nussbaum and Sen (1989).

6. Crocker (1988, 1990b).

7. See especially, Crocker (1983); Rorty (1979, 1982, 1989); Marković (1983, 1990); Stojanović (1988); Jaggar (1983); and Fals-Borda (1982).

8. Goulet (1977), p. 319. L. J. Lebret, with whom Goulet studied in France in the 1950s, also deserves credit as a founder of the discipline. In dialogue with Goulet, Lebret remarked: "It seems to us that when we treat the achievement of human progress we cannot leave out these [ethical] considerations and that the ethics of development would deserve an entire book by itself" (Lebret, 1966, p. 35). All translations from Spanish are my own.

9. Goulet (1971), p. xix.

10. Goulet (1977), p. 5.

11. Goulet (1988), p. 162. See also Goulet and Wilber (1988), pp. 459–467.

12. Berger (1974), p. vii. Goulet reviews Berger's book in Goulet (1975). Berger, now a free market conservative, returns to these themes and defends a capitalist development model in Berger (1984). Hinkelammert (1984) makes important objections to Berger.

13. Gunatilleke, Tiruchelvam, and Coomaraswamy (1983).

14. Gunatilleke (1983), p. 1.

15. Gunatilleke (1983), p. 1. Mehta (1978) sets forth what he believes to be a distinctively Indian development model with its own "normatively-defined goals." See also Kothari (1989).

16. Murillo (1974).

17. Gutiérrez (1974), p. 171.

18. Bunge (1980).

19. Bunge (1980), p. 23.

20. Ramírez (1986), p. 23. Wiarda (1988, p. 65) makes the more general point that Third World criticisms of Western development models: "Western modernization and development theory is . . . seen as still another imperialist Cold War strategy aimed at tying Third World nations into a Western and liberal (that is, United States) development pattern, of keeping them within our sphere of influence, of denying them the possibilities of alternative development patterns. . . . Since that time [the early 1970s] . . . development has been increasingly tarred with the imperialist brush and discredited throughout the Third World, and hence a whole new generation of young Third World leaders and intellectuals no longer accepts Western developmentalist concepts and perspectives and is searching for possible alternatives."

21. Ramírez (1986), p. 25.

22. Ramírez (1988b), p. 48

23. Ramírez (1988b), p. 49.

24. Camacho (1985a), p. 26. Also see Camacho (1982, 1985b, 1986a, 1986b, 1988).

25. May (1987), p. 244. See also Goulet (1987b).

26. Wilber (1988). The Wilber anthology has gone through four editions, each one of which has had a somewhat different focus. In the preface to the third edition (1984, p. v), Wilber indicates that the first edition (1973) reflected a disillusionment with the 1960s' optimism that world poverty could be conquered with economic growth. In contrast, the second edition (1979) "explored the principles" of a new optimism founded in the paradigm of development as

"growth with equity" or a strategy of targeting "basic human needs." The third edition (1984) exhibited the more cautious debate among contending paradigms, all recognizing complex obstacles to the reduction of world poverty, for example, resource shortages, protectionism, militarism, the arms race, and the international economic order. Finally, Wilber (1988, p. v) remarks "this fourth edition updates the continuing debate among contending schools of thought, highlights the international debt crisis along with the attendant stabilization and readjustment programs, and charts the resurgence of free market economics with its attack upon 'development' economics."

27. Vogeler and De Souza (1980).

28. Weisband (1989). Another anthology should also be mentioned. Seligson (1984) has collected essays that focus on the gaps between rich and poor nations and between the rich and poor within poor countries. Although these essays largely address the *empirical* questions of the causes of the gaps and whether they are narrowing or widening, moral assumptions and judgments are implicit.

29. Wilber (1988), p. v.

30. Wilber and Jameson (1975), pp. 5–7.

31. Vogeler and De Souza (1980), p. 7.

32. Weisband (1989), p. 10.

33. Weisband (1989), p. 13.

34. Weisband (1989), p. 11.

35. Williams (1985, p. viii) offers a helpful if self-serving definition of "analytic philosophy": "What distinguishes analytical philosophy from other contemporary philosophy (though not from much philosophy of other times) is a certain way of going on, which involves argument, distinctions, and, so far as it remembers to try to achieve it and succeeds, moderately plain speech. As an alternative to plain speech, it distinguishes sharply between obscurity and technicality. It always rejects the first, but the second it sometimes finds a necessity. This feature peculiarly enrages some of its enemies. Wanting philosophy to be at once profound and accessible, they resent technicality but are comforted by obscurity." According to Rajchman and West, a characteristic of "post-analytic philosophy," one I would argue that fits those Anglo-American philosophers taking up development ethics, is a "move to other fields." This move has been "less a collaboration between specialized fields than a questioning of basic assumptions in those fields and an attempt to create new ones" (Rajchman and West, 1985, p. xiii). International development ethics is precisely a "new field" that also requires substantial changes in disciplines such as philosophy, ethics, economics and political science. For the need for changes in both ethics and economics, see Sen (1987).

36. O'Neill (1986), p. xi.

37. O'Neill (1986), pp. xii–xiii.

38. Segal (1986, 1987).

39. Dower (1985), p. 3.

40. See Dower (1983). Desmond Gaspar and Geoffrey Hunt are two other

British philosophers who treat ethical or methodological assumptions in development theory. See Gaspar (1986) and Hunt (1986).

41. In February, 1988 the Ethics Working Group presented the draft chapter to the IUCN's 17th General Assembly in San José, Costa Rica.

42. See Engel (1988, 1990).

43. Crocker (1989, 1990a). These essays come from a book manuscript entitled *The Costa Rican Path: An Analysis and Ethical Evaluation.*

44. Crocker (1979, 1983, 1987, 1988, 1990b, 1991).

45. The following declaration was signed by a majority of the participants in the Second International Conference on Ethics and Development:

Merida Declaration

We, the undersigned participants in the Second International Conference on Ethics and Development, make the following declaration upon finishing our deliberations. In the face of the profound inadequacies of modernization development strategies, We propose:

1. To intensify the search for and study of an alternative for social transformation, supported by at least the following ethical principles:

(a) The absolute respect for the dignity of the human person, regardless of gender, ethnic group, social class, religion, age or nationality.

(b) The necessity of peace based on a practice of justice that gives to the great majorities access to goods and eliminates the conditions of their misery.

(c) The affirmation of freedom, understood as self-determination, self-management, and participation of peoples in local, national, and international decision processes.

(d) The recognition of a new relation of human beings with nature, facilitating responsible use, respectful of biological cycles and the equilibrium of ecosystems—especially those of tropical forests—and in solidarity with future generations.

(e) The stimulus to construct a rationality suited to exploited peoples, one that accords with their cultural traditions, their thought, their interests, and their needs and that involves a new valuing of self-esteem based on their being subjects rather than objects of development.

2. To strengthen IDEA's efforts to maintain an international, intercultural, and interdisciplinary dialogue that brings together intellectuals, grassroots organizations, and decision-making groups with the purpose of constructing an ethic applicable to different "development" alternatives.

46. Shue (1980, p. 41) discusses the strengths and weaknesses in ethical argument of both hypothetical and actual examples.

47. The U.S. President Theodore Roosevelt was watching a steam shovel (a new technology at the beginning of the twentieth century) when someone commented on the number of workers it was putting out of work: "Think of how many laborers we could hire to do that with shovels!" Roosevelt replied,

"Think of how many we could hire to do it with tablespoons!" I owe this example to my colleague Professor Holmes Rolston.

48. Nagel (1983) considers the moral issues regarding his presence as a lecturer in South Africa.

49. For a "no strings attached" view, see O'Neill's application of a version of Kantian ethics to famine relief in O'Neill (1986). For a justification of some strings in some aid situations, see Singer (1977), pp. 34–36.

50. "Lecciones de una tragedia" (1986). The reluctance of this conservative Costa Rican newspaper to report on the wrongdoings of U.S. business (Reagan administration) is only surpassed by its eagerness to discredit the current social democratic government of Costa Rica. Ramírez has been particularly concerned to call attention to this sort of "substance abuse." See Ramírez (1986).

51. Shue (1984) brilliantly treats this issue. For a moral argument, based on "fiduciary morality," for more restrictive forms of export control, see Paine (1989).

52. Churnside (1986), p. 16A.

53. "Gobierno intervino JAPDEVA," (1986), pp. 1A, 4A.

54. Palmer (1986), p. 19. An earlier, less political, English version is Palmer (1977). For an important study that evaluates Palmer's work and other grassroots development projects, see Dorfman (1984). See also Dorfman (1988). In these two studies commissioned by the Interamerican Foundation, Dorfman, a noted Chilean novelist, examines the relation between development, in the sense of economic survival, and cultural identity.

55. Palmer (1986), p. 373.

56. Palmer (1986), p. 383.

57. Palmer (1986), p. 14.

58. See also Goulet (1981, 1987a); Stavenhagen (1990).

59. Riddell (1987), p. 12. Foreign assistance, of course, is also given for a variety of nondevelopmental objectives such as donor "security" considerations and economic advantages. Development ethics assesses the intentions as well as the consequences of aid transfers to developing countries.

60. See Elbinger (1979), p. 36. Sullivan finally repudiated his principles because he believed that their promulgation and (partial) compliance tended to stabilize the unjust and repressive South African government.

61. See, for example, Nielsen and Patten (1981); Herra (1988).

62. Goulet (1988), p. 156.

63. Goulet (1988), pp. 157–158.

64. Rostow (1960).

65. Foster-Carter (1976). See also Sunkel and Paz (1986).

66. Cardoso and Faletto (1969), and Frank (1966, 1967). See also the related "structuralism" of Prebisch and the Comisión Económica para America Latina (CEPAL) in Prebisch (1981).

67. The orthodox or capitalist paradigm also exhibits important variants that Wilber and Jameson distinguish as *laissez-faire,* planning, and growth-with-equity. See Wilber and Jameson (1975). Examples of the *laissez-faire* model are Bauer (1981) and Harrison (1985). Culbertson (1971) illustrates the

"planning" perspective in which governments are urged to intervene to "sell" modernization and regulate and sometimes replace the market to achieve economic growth. The "growth-with-equity" perspective has many proponents and variations: for example, Adelman and Morris (1973). To the orthodox paradigm's stress of economic growth is wedded—as means or end (or both)—the reduction of relative and absolute poverty of the bottom half of the population. Likewise, variation exists within the leftist or "political economy" development paradigm. In addition to dependency theory and structuralism, one finds Marxist or radical alternatives such as the "mode of production school." See Chilcote (1982) and Ruccio and Simon (1988).

68. Foster-Carter (1976). See also Kuhn (1970).

69. Henriot (1979), p. 5.

70. Steidlmeier (1987), p. 204. Steidlmeier's book is excerpted in Weisband (1989), pp. 89–109.

71. Steidlmeier (1987), p. 202.

72. Steidlmeier (1987), pp. 176, 178–181.

73. Steidlmeier (1987), p. 204.

74. Steidlmeier (1987), pp. 207–235.

75. Sen (1984), p. 504; emphasis mine. Sen's essay is reprinted in Wilber (1988), pp. 37–58.

76. Nussbaum and Sen (1989), p. 299.

77. Nussbaum and Sen (1989), p. 307.

78. Nussbaum and Sen (1989), p. 299.

79. Nussbaum and Sen (1989), p. 309.

80. Nussbaum and Sen (1989), pp. 308, 311.

81. Sen (1984), p. 497.

82. Sen (1984), p. 497.

83. See Sen (1981, 1982a, 1982b, 1983, 1984, 1985, 1987a, 1987b, 1988, 1989a, 1989b); Sen and Williams (1982).

84. Nussbaum and Sen (1989), pp. 317–321.

85. Sen (1984), pp. 513–515. See Streeten (1981).

86. Fallas (1981), p. 115. For normative analysis of development policy in Costa Rica, see Crocker (1989, 1990a); in Mexico, see Goulet (1983) and Goulet and Kim (1989); in India, see Mehta (1978); Sen (1982b); Kothari (1989b); and Nussbaum and Sen (1989); in Latin America, see Mansilla (1989).

87. Segal (1986), p. 2.

88. Segal (1986), p. 3. Nussbaum and Sen (1989), p. 307: "The very concept of 'development' as it is most often used in the discourse that surrounds it has an evaluative dimension. A change that is not thought to be in some way beneficial would not usually be described as part of 'development.' But then in order to know which changes count as development, that is, as beneficial alterations, we need to have not only a description of the practices and the values of a culture but also some sort of evaluation *of* those practices and values: which ones are, in fact, the most valuable."

89. Dower (1988), pp. 5–6.

90. Dower (1988), p. 9.
91. Dower (1988), p. 8.
92. Dower (1988), p. 8.
93. See Crocker (1983), pp. 23–32, 145–188, and 189–224.
94. See, for example, Sen's discussion of (a) various definitions and indices of poverty and (b) the relations of description to both prediction and evaluation in Sen (1982a) essays 17 and 19, (1984) essay 14, (1989).
95. See Sen (1985), pp. 169–184.
96. For a more complete treatment of this issue, see Crocker (1983), pp. 179–188.
97. Sen (1984), p. 25; Weisband (1989), pp. 7–13.
98. Formoso (1986), p. 5.
99. See, for example, Brown (1979) and Kuhn (1970).
100. Bunge (1980a), pp. 27–38.
101. Bunge (1980a), p. 36.
102. In contrast, Toulmin (1988) emphasizes scientific knowledge of particulars as more important than and the basis for scientific generalities.
103. My conception is derived from that of MacIntyre who defines a practice as "any coherent and complex form of socially established cooperative activity through which goods internal to that form of activity are realized in the course of trying to achieve those standards of excellence which are appropriate to, and partially definitive of, that form of activity, with the result that human powers to achieve excellence, and human conceptions of the ends and goods involved, are systematically extended" (MacIntyre, 1984, p. 18). My view of a theory-practice narrows MacIntyre's definition to include both theory and conduct as elements but broadens it so as not to *require* the extension of excellent human powers.
104. For a suggestive exploration of how the field of education includes various theoretical and practical dimensions, see Frankena (1965), pp. 1–10.
105. Hartsock (1986), pp. 8–9, 13.
106. See Jaggar (1983), pp. 15–21, 353–389.
107. See Fals-Borda (1982); Edwards (1989).
108. Sen and Grown (1987), pp. 9–10. See also Sen (1984), essays 15 and 16.
109. In welfare and development economics the problem is not the dogma of value neutrality so much as a dogmatically held utilitarian ethical theory. One of Sen's achievements is the normative analysis and critique of both utilitarian (a) conceptions of well-being such as utility, for example, happiness, desire-satisfaction, or choice; and (b) use of "sum ranking," defined as "the goodness of any set of individual utilities must be judged entirely by their sum total" (Sen, 1984, p. 278).
110. Wilber (1988), p. viii.
111. Berger (1974), p. 24.
112. Bunge (1980b), pp. 11–20; (1980a), pp. 122–124.
113. See Fals-Borda (1982); Edwards (1989).
114. Goulet (1989c), p. 165. See also Goulet (1989b).

115. Goulet (1989b, 1989c).

116. For example, see the works mentioned in note 7 as well as Ramírez (1980a, 1987).

117. In a future essay I shall explore the convergence between development ethics and the Latin American philosophical movement called "philosophy of liberation." For a profile of this philosophical tendency, see Cerutti-Guldberg (1988–89).

118. Toulmin (1988), p. 352.

119. In the early 1970s, the two most important works in the Anglo-American (re)turn to normative ethics in general and economic justice in particular were undoubtedly Rawls (1971) and Nozick (1974). But both of these books remained excessively abstract and failed to apply ethics to concrete policies and practices. For an account of "applied ethics" as well as an argument that we need to concentrate our attention on elaborating "different moralities for different contexts" rather than striving for a "comprehensive morality," see Held (1985). See also DeMarco and Fox (1986).

120. See, for example, *Agriculture and Human Values, Economics and Philosophy, Environmental Ethics, Ethics and Animals, Journal of Business Ethics, Journal of Medical Ethics, Journal of Philosophy of Sport, Journal of Applied Philosophy, Philosophy and Public Affairs, QQ-Report from the Institute for Philosophy and Public Policy, Social Philosophy and Policy,* and *Social Theory and Practice.*

121. Philosophers are prominent in the following institutions: Institute for Philosophy and Public Policy (University of Maryland), Center for the Study of Values (University of Delaware), Center for Values and Social Policy (University of Colorado), Social Philosophy and Policy Center (Bowling Green State University), and The Hastings Center.

122. See *QQ-Report from the Institute for Philosophy and Public Policy* (1987).

123. See Nussbaum and Sen (1989); Rorty (1979, 1982, 1989).

124. See Engel and Engel (1990).

125. Much philosophical (and nonphilosophical) discussion of the ethics of foreign aid has been vitiated by a failure to consider the actual impact of various kinds of aid, especially with respect to aid's contribution to various definitions of development. For an excellent contribution to remedying this defect, see Riddell (1987).

126. Rollin (1988) has made a good start on this topic.

127. See Lugones and Spelman (1986).

128. The most important single work remains, in my opinion, Shue (1980). See also Shue (1988). A helpful recent anthology with essays treating international justice, foreign intervention, and world government is Luper-Foy (1988).

129. See Aiken and La Follette (1977); Brown and Shue (1977).

130. Walzer (1977); see Beitz, Cohen, Scanlon, and Simmons (1985). Much recent work on nuclear and security policy examines the global relevance of traditional or revised just-war theory. In addition, see Sterba (1985) and Bailey (1989).

131. Brown and Shue (1977); Brown and MacLean (1979); Brown and Shue (1981); Brown and Shue (1983).

132. Beitz (1979a, 1979b). See also Hoffman (1981); Hare and Joynt (1982); Nardin (1983); *Philosophy in Context* (1985). For debate on the ethical significance of national boundaries and nationality, see "Symposium on duties beyond borders" (1988).

133. For example, Thompson (1985).

134. Analytic philosophy's penchant for "conceptual" analysis has often resulted in a cavalier disregard if not disdain for the facts. Once the distinction between analytic and synthetic truth is rejected or "relativized" to practices, the philosopher becomes responsible for the factual premises of his or her arguments. With respect to facts of foreign aid, see Riddell (1987).

135. Gunatilleke (1983), p. 8.

136. See Field and Wallerstein (1977); Minear (1988–89). Riddell is aware of how foreign aid arguments depend not only on factual questions of the actual impact of aid on development but also on development models: "The total moral case for governments to provide development aid would seem to be dependent upon a blend of three interrelated factors: narrow ethical beliefs (the basis for action), theories of development (constructs of how the world works) and an assessment of the performance of aid in practice" (Riddell, 1987, p. 16). Riddell does an excellent job with the third factor, an adequate job with the second, and basically ignores *ethical* evaluation of development theories and models.

137. In Crocker (1991), I consider the opportunities and risks involved in practicing development ethics in and for another culture.

138. Sen's ethical writings, especially (1982, 1984, 1985, 1987, 1988, 1989b) are the most impressive example. See also Dower (1983, 1988) and Crocker (1983, 1989, 1990a). For a suggestive exploration of nonutilitarian consequentialism, see Miller (1981).

139. See Crocker (1979, 1991); Pogge (1988). For an interesting analysis of both Third World critiques of Western Development models and "indigenous Third World development models," see Wiarda (1988).

140. For an explication and defense of dialogue as both a means to and part of the content of a good society, see Crocker (1983), especially chapter 6. For the way in which consensus and dialogue can be (mis)used by elites as instruments of domination, see Fischel (1987).

References

Adelman, Irma, and C. T. Morris, *Economic Growth and Social Equity in Developing Countries* (Stanford, CA: Stanford University Press, 1973).

Aiken, William, and Hugh La Follete (Eds.), *World Hunger and Moral Obligation* (Englewood Cliffs, NJ: Prentice-Hall, 1977).

Bailey, Alison, *Posterity and Strategic Policy: A Moral Assessment of Nuclear Policy Options* (Lanham, MD: University Press of America, 1989).

Bauer, P. T., *Equality, the Third World and Economic Delusion* (London: Weidenfeld, 1981).

Beitz, Charles, "Democracy and developing societies," in Peter G. Brown and Henry Shue (Eds.). *Boundaries: National Autonomy and Its Limits* (Totowa, NJ: Rowman and Littlefield, 1981).

Beitz, Charles R., *Political Theory and International Relations* (Princeton, NJ: Princeton University Press, 1979).

Beitz, Charles, "Global egalitarianism: Can we make out a case?" *Dissent,* Vol. 26, No. 1 (1979).

Berger, Peter, "Underdevelopment revisited," *Commentary,* Vol. 78, No. 1 (1984).

Berger, Peter, *Pyramids of Sacrifice* (New York: Basic Books, 1974).

Brown, Harold I., *Perception, Theory and Commitment: The New Philosophy of Science* (Chicago and London: University of Chicago Press, 1979).

Brown, Peter G., and Douglas MacLean (Eds.), *Human Rights and U.S. Foreign Policy* (Lexington, MA: Lexington Books, 1979).

Brown, Peter G., and Henry Shue (Eds.), *The Border That Joins: Mexican Migrants and U.S. Responsibility* (Totowa, NJ: Rowman & Littlefield, 1983).

Brown, Peter G., and Henry Shue (Eds.), *Boundaries: National Autonomy and Its Limits* (Totowa, NJ: Rowman & Littlefield, 1981).

Brown, Peter G., and Henry Shue (Eds.), *Food Policy: The Responsibility of the United States in the Life and Death Choices* (New York: The Free Press, 1977).

Bunge, Mario, *Ciencia y Desarrollo* (Buenos Aires: Ediciones Siglo Veinte, 1980).

Bunge, Mario, "La ciencia ¿es éticamente neutral?" in E. Roy Ramírez and Mario Alfaro (Eds.), *Etica, Ciencia y Tecnología* (Cartago, Costa Rica: Editorial Tecnológica de Costa Rica, 1980).

Camacho, Luis A., "Uso y abuso de las nociones de "crisis" y "modelo" en ciencias sociales en Costa Rica," *Revista de Filosofia de la Universidad de Costa Rica,* Vol. 26, No. 63–64 (1988).

Camacho, Luis, "Desarrollo y tecnología," in *Ciclo de Conferencias sobre Ciencia y Tecnología* (San José, Costa Rica: CONICIT, August–October 1986).

Camacho, Luis, "La ciencia pura en el subdesarrollo," *Desarrollo,* No. 3–4 (1986).

Camacho, Luis, "Cuando se habla de ciencia, tecnología y desarrollo ¿de qué se está hablando?" *Tecnología en Marcha,* Vol. 7, No. 9 (1985).

Camacho, Luis, "Ciencia, tecnología y desarrollo desde el punto de vista de los derechos humanos," in E. Roy Ramírez (Ed.), *Ciencia, Responsabilidad y Valores* (Cartago: Editorial Tecnológica de Costa Rica, 1985).

Camacho, Luis, "Desarrollo y cultura: enfoques y desenfoques," *Revista de Filosofía de la Universidad de Costa Rica,* Vol. 22, No. 55–56 (1982).

Cardoso, F. H., and Enzo Faletto, *Dependencia y Desarrollo en America Latina* (Mexico: Siglo XXI Editores, 1969).

Cerutti-Guldberg, Horacio, "Actual situation and perspectives of Latin American philosophy for liberation," *Philosophical Forum,* Vol. 20, No. 1–2 (1988–89).

Chilcote, Roger H. (Ed.), *Dependency and Marxism: Toward a Resolution of the Debate* (Boulder, CO: Westview Press, 1982).

Churnside, Roger, "JAPDEVA y los nuevos rumbos," *La Nación* (October 22, 1986).

Crocker, David A., "Insiders and outsiders in international development ethics," *Ethics and International Affairs,* Vol. 5 (1991).

Crocker, David A., "The hope for just, participatory ecodevelopment in Costa Rica," in J. Ronald Engel and Joan Gibb Engel (Eds.), *Ethics of Environment and Development: Global Challenge, International Response* (London: Belhaven Press; Tucson, AZ: University of Arizona Press, 1990a), pp. 150–163.

Crocker, David A., "Development ethics and development theory-practice," Mimeo (Fort Collins, CO: Colorado State University, 1990b).

Crocker, David A., "Cuatro modelos del desarrollo costarricense: análisis y evaluación ética," *Revista de Filosofía de la Universidad de Costa Rica,* Vol. 27, No. 66 (1989).

Crocker, David A., "La naturaleza y la práctica de una ética del desarrollo," *Revista de Filosofía de la Universidad de Costa Rica,* Vol. 26, No. 63–64 (1988).

Crocker, David A., "Hacia una ética del desarrollo," *Revista de Filosofía de la Universidad de Costa Rica,* Vol. 25, No. 62 (1987).

Crocker, David A., *Praxis and Democratic Socalism: The Critical Social Theory of Marković and Stojanović* (Atlantic Highlands, NJ: Humanities Press; Sussex: Harvester Press, 1983).

Crocker, David A., "Moral relativism and international affairs," *Technos,* Vol. 8 (1979).

Culbertson, John M., *Economic Development: An Ecological Approach* (New York: Alfred A. Knopf, 1971).

DeMarco, Joseph P., and Richard M. Fox (Eds.), *New Directions in Ethics: The Challenge of Applied Ethics* (New York and London: Routledge and Kegan Paul, 1986).

Dorfman, Ariel, "Into another jungle: The final journey of the Matacos?" *Grassroots Development: Journal of the Inter-American Foundation,* Vol. 12, No. 2 (1988).

Dorfman, Ariel, "Bread and burnt rice: Culture and economic survival in Latin America," *Grassroots Development: Journal of the Inter-American Foundation,* Vol. 8, No. 2 (1984).

Dower, Nigel, "What is development? A philosopher's answer," *Centre for Development Studies,* Occasional Paper No. 3 (Glasgow: Centre for Development Studies, 1988).

Dower, Nigel, *World Poverty: Challenge and Response* (York, UK: Ebor Press, 1983).

Edwards, Michael, "The irrelevance of development studies," *Third World Quarterly,* Vol. 11, No. 1 (1989).

Engel, J. Ron, "Ecology and social justice: The search for a public environmental ethic," in Warren R. Copeland and Roger D. Hatch (Eds.), *Issues of Justice—Social Resources and Religious Meanings* (Macon, GA: Mercer University Press, 1988).

Engel, J. Ron, and Joan Gibb Engel (Eds.), *Ethics of Environment and Development: Global Challenge, International Response* (London: Belhaven Press; Tucson, AZ: University of Arizona Press, 1990).

Fallas, Hellio, *Crisis Económica en Costa Rica* (San José; Editorial Nueva Decada, 1981).

Fals-Borda, Orlando, "Teoría de la investigación-acción," *Praxis Centroamericana,* Vol. 91 (1982).

Field, John Osgood, and Mitchel B. Wallerstein, "Beyond humanitarianism: A developmental perspective on American food aid," in Peter G. Brown and Henry Shue (Eds.), *Food Policy: The Responsibility of the United States in the Life and Death Choices* (New York: The Free Press, 1977).

Fischel, Astrid, *Consenso y Represión: Una Interpretación Socio-politica de la Educación Costarricense* (San José, Costa Rica: Editorial Costa Rica, 1987).

Foster-Carter, Aidan, "From Rostow to Gunder Frank: Conflicting paradigms in the analysis of underdevelopment," *World Development,* Vol. 4, No. 3 (1976).

Frank, Andre Gunder, *Capitalism and Underdevelopment in Latin America: Historical Studies of Chile and Brazil* (New York and London: Monthly Review Press, 1967).

Frank, Andre Gunder, "The development of underdevelopment," *Monthly Review,* Vol. 18, No. 4 (1966).

Frankena, William, *Philosophy of Education* (New York: Macmillan Company, 1965).

Gaspar, Desmond, "Distribution and development ethics: A tour," in R. Apthorpe and A. Krahl (Eds.), *Development Studies: Critique and Renewal* (Leiden: E. J. Brill, 1986).

"Gobierno intervenio JAPDEVA," *La Nación* (October 23, 1986).

Goulet, Denis, "Development ethics and ecological wisdom," in J. Ron Engel and Joan Gibb Engel (Eds.), *Ethics of Environment and Development: Global Challenge, International Response* (London: Belhaven Press; Tucson, AZ: University of Arizona Press, 1990).

Goulet, Denis, *Incentives for Development: The Key to Equity* (New York: New Horizons Press, 1989).

Goulet, Denis, "Participation in development: New avenues," *World Development,* Vol. 17, No. 2 (1989).

Goulet, Denis, "Tasks and methods in development ethics," *Cross Currents,* Vol. 38, No. 2 (1988).

Goulet, Denis, "Cultural and traditional values in development," in Susan Stratigos and Philip J. Hughes (Eds.), *The Ethics of Development in the 21st Century* (Port Moresby: University of Papua New Guinea, 1987).

Goulet, Denis, "Ethics in development theory and practice," *Catalyst: Social Pastoral Magazine for Melanesia,* Vol. 17, No. 4 (1987).

Goulet, Denis, "Three rationalities in development decision-making," *World Development,* Vol. 14, No. 2 (1986).

Goulet, Denis, *Mexico: Development Strategies for the Future* (Notre Dame, IN: University of Notre Dame Press, 1983).

Goulet, Denis, "Obstacles to world development: An ethical reflection," *World Development,* Vol. 11, No. 7 (1983).

Goulet, Denis, "In defense of cultural rights: Technology, tradition and conflicting models of rationality," *Human Rights Quarterly,* Vol. 3, No. 4 (1981).

Goulet, Denis, "Development experts: The one-eyed giants," *World Development,* Vol. 8, No. 7/8 (1980).

Goulet, Denis, *The Uncertain Promise: Value Conflicts in Technology Transfer* (New York: IDOC/North America, 1977).

Goulet, Denis, "The high price of social change—on Peter Berger's *Pyramids of Sacrifice,*" *Christianity and Crisis,* Vol. 35, No. 16 (1975).

Goulet, Denis, *The Cruel Choice: A New Concept in the Theory of Development* (New York: Atheneum, 1971a).

Goulet, Denis, "Development' . . . or liberation?" *International Development Review,* Vol. 13, No. 3 (1971b).

Goulet, Denis, and Kwan S. Kim, *Estrategias de Desarrollo para el Futuro de México* (Guadalajara: ITESCO, 1989).

Goulet, Denis, and Charles K. Wilber, "The human dilemma of development," in Charles K. Wilber (Ed.), *The Political Economy of Development and Underdevelopment,* 4th edition (New York: Random House, 1988).

Gunatilleke, Godfrey, "The ethics of order and change," in Godfrey Gunatilleke, Neelen Tiruchelvam, and Radhika Coomaraswamy (Eds.), *Ethical Dilemmas of Development in Asia* (Lexington, MA: Lexington Books, 1983).

Gunatilleke, Godfrey, Neelen Tiruchelvam, and Radhika Coomaraswamy (Eds.), *Ethical Dilemmas of Development in Asia* (Lexington, MA: Lexington Books, 1983).

Gutiérrez, Claudio, "Papel del filósofo en una nación en desarrollo," *Revista de Filosofía de la Universidad de Costa Rica,* Vol. 12, No. 35 (1974).

Hare, J. E., and Carey B. Joynt, *Ethics and International Affairs* (New York: St. Martin's Press, 1982).

Harrison, Lawrence, *Underdevelopment Is a State of Mind* (Lanham, MD: Madison Books, 1985).

Hartsock, Nancy, "Feminist theory and the development of revolutionary strategy," in Marilyn Pearsall (Ed.), *Women and Values: Readings in Recent Feminist Philosophy* (Belmont, CA: Wadsworth Publishing Company, 1986).

Held, Virginia, *Rights and Goods: Justifying Social Action* (New York: Free Press, 1985).

Henriot, Peter J., "Development alternatives, problems, strategies, and values," in Charles K. Wilber (Ed.), *The Political Economy of Development and Underdevelopment,* 2nd edition (New York: Random House, 1979).

Herra, Rafael Angel, "Kritik der globalphilosophie," in Franz M. Wimmer (Ed.), *Vier Fragen zur Philosophie in Afrika, Asien und Lateinamerika* (Wien: Passagen Verlag, 1988).

Hinkelammert, Franz, *Critica a la Razón Utópica* (San José: Departamento Ecuménico de Investigaciones, 1984).
Hoffman, Stanley, *Duties Beyond Borders: On the Limits and Possibilities of Ethical International Politics* (Syracuse: Syracuse University Press, 1981).
Hunt, Geoffrey, "Two methodological paradigms in development economics," *Philosophical Forum,* Vol. 17, No. 1 (1986).
Jaggar, Alison, *Feminist Politics and Human Nature* (Totowa, NJ: Rowman & Allanheld; Sussex: Harvester Press, 1983).
Kothari, Rajni, "Environment, technology, and ethics," in J. Ron Engel and Joan Gibb Engel (Eds.), *Ethics of Environment and Development: Global Challenge, International Response* (London: Belhaven Press; Tucson, AZ: University of Arizona Press, 1990).
Kothari, Rajni, *Politics and the People: In Search of a Humane India* (New York: New Horizons Press, 1989).
Kothari, Rajni, *Rethinking Development: In Search of Humane Alternatives* (New York: New Horizons Press, 1989).
Kuhn, Thomas S., *The Structure of Scientific Revolutions,* 2nd edition (Chicago: University of Chicago Press, 1970).
Lebret, Luis-Joseph, *Dinámica Concreta del Desarrollo* (Barcelona: Editorial Herder, 1966).
"Lecciones de una tragedia," *La Nación* (September 23, 1986).
Lugones, Maria C., and Elizabeth V. Spelman, "Have we got a theory for you! Feminist theory, cultural imperialism, and the demand for 'The woman's voice,'" in Marilyn Pearsall (Ed.), *Women and Values: Readings in Recent Feminist Philosophy* (Belmont, CA: Wadsworth Publishing Company, 1986).
Luper-Foy, Steven (Ed.), *Problems of International Justice* (Boulder, CO: Westview Press, 1988).
MacIntyre, Alasdair, *After Virtue,* 2nd edition (Notre Dame, IN: University of Notre Dame Press, 1984).
Mansilla, H. C. F., *Desarrollo y Progreso como Ideologías de Modernización Tecnocrática* (La Paz: Hisbol, 1989).
Marković, Mihailo, "The development vision of socialist humanism," in J. Ron Engel and Joan Gibb Engel (Eds.), *Ethics of Environment and Development: Global Challenge, International Response* (London: Belhaven Press; Tucson, AZ: University of Arizona Press, 1990).
Marković, Mihailo, *Democratic Socialism: Theory and Practice* (Sussex: Harvester Press, 1983).
May, John D'Arcy, "Toward a development of ethics," *Catalyst: Social Pastoral Magazine for Melanesia,* Vol. 17, No. 3 (1987).
Mehta, Raj Vrajenda, *Beyond Marxism: Towards an Alternative Perspective* (New Delhi: Manohar Publications, 1978).
Miller, Richard W., "Marx and Aristotle," in Kai Nielsen and Steven C. Patten (Eds.), *Marx and Morality* (Guelph, Ont.: Canadian Association for Publishing in Philosophy, 1981).
Minear, Larry, "The forgotten human agenda," *Foreign Policy,* No. 73 (1988–89).

Murillo, Roberto, "Noción desarrollada del desarrollo," *Revista de Filosofía de la Universidad de Costa Rica,* Vol. 12, No. 35 (1974).

Nagel, Thomas, "A month in the country," *New Republic* (March 14, 1983).

Nardin, Terry, *Law, Morality and the Relations of States* (Princeton: Princeton University Press, 1983).

Nielsen, Kai, and Steven C. Patten (Eds.), *Marx and Morality* (Guelph, Ont.: Canadian Association for Publishing in Philosophy, 1981).

Nozick, Robert, *Anarchy, State, and Utopia* (New York: Basic Books, 1974).

Nussbaum, Martha C., and Amartya Sen, "Internal criticism and Indian rationalist traditions," in Michael Krausz (Ed.), *Relativism, Intrepretation and Confrontation* (Notre Dame, IN: University of Notre Dame Press, 1989).

O'Neill, Onora, *Faces of Hunger: An Essay on Poverty, Justice, and Development* (London: Allen & Unwin, 1986).

O'Neill, Onora, "The moral perplexities of famine and world hunger," in Tom Regan (Ed.), *Matters of Life and Death: New Introductory Essays in Moral Philosophy,* 2nd edition (New York: Random House, 1986).

Paine, Lynn Sharp, "Responsibilities of exporters of hazardous products: Pesticides, a case in point," Paper presented to the Second International Conference on Ethics and Development (Merida, Mexico: Autonomous University of Yucatán, July 3–9, 1989).

Palmer, Paula, *"Wá apin Man": La Historia de la Costa Talamanqueña de Costa Rica, Según sus Protagonistas* (San José: Instituto del Libro, 1986).

Palmer, Paula, *"What Happen": A Folk-History of Costa Rica's Talamanca Coast* (San José, Costa Rica: Ecodesarrollos, 1977).

Pogge, Thomas, "Moral progress," in Steven Luper-Foy (Ed.), *Problems of International Justice* (Boulder, CO: Westview Press, 1988).

Prebisch, Raul, *Capitalismo Periférico* (Mexico City: Fondo de Cultura Económica, 1981).

"The public turn in philosophy," *QQ-Report from the Institute for Philosophy and Public Policy,* Vol. 7, No. 1 (1987).

Rajchman, John, and Cornel West (Eds.), *Post-Analytic Philosophy* (New York: Columbia University Press, 1985).

Ramírez, E. Roy, "El 'argumento' tecnológico, la tecnología perniciosa, y la ética," in Mario Alfaro, Guillermo Coronado, E. Roy Ramírez, and Alvaro Zamora (Eds.), *Dedalo y su Estirpe: La revolución industrial* (Cartago: 1988).

Ramírez, E. Roy, "Etica y tecnología," *Revista Communicación,* Vol. 3, No. 2 (1988).

Ramírez, E. Roy, *La responsabilidad ética en ciencia y tecnología* (Cartago: Editorial Tecnológica de Costa Rica, 1987).

Ramírez, E. Roy, "Desarrollo y ética," *Revista Comunicación,* Vol. 2, No. 2 (1986).

Ramírez, E. Roy, "Entre ética y ciencia," in E. Roy Ramírez (Ed.), *Ciencia, responsibilidad y valores* (Cartago, Costa Rica: Editorial Tecnológica de Costa Rica, 1980).

Ramírez, E. Roy, "Responsibilidad y neutralidad," in E. Roy Ramírez (Ed.),

Ciencia, responsibilidad y valores (Cartago, Costa Rica: Editorial Tecnológica de Costa Rica, 1980).

Rawls, John, *A Theory of Justice* (Cambridge, MA: Belknap Press of Harvard University Press, 1971).

Riddell, Roger C., *Foreign Aid Reconsidered* (Baltimore: Johns Hopkins University Press, 1987).

Rollin, Bernard, "Environmental ethics and international justice," in Steven Luper-Foy (Ed.), *Problems of International Justice* (Boulder, CO: Westview Press, 1988).

Rostow, W. W., *The Stages of Economic Growth: A Non-Communist Manifesto* (New York: Cambridge University Press, 1960).

Rorty, Richard, *Contingency, Irony, and Solidarity* (Cambridge: Cambridge University Press, 1989).

Rorty, Richard, *Consequences of Pragmatism* (Minneapolis: University of Minnesota Press, 1982).

Rorty, Richard, *Philosophy and the Mirror of Nature* (Princeton, NJ: Princeton University Press, 1979).

Ruccio, David F., and Lawrence H. Simon, "Radical theories of development: Frank, the modes of production school, and Amin," in Charles K. Wilber, (Ed.), *The Political Economy of Development and Underdevelopment,* 4th edition (New York: Random House, 1988).

Segal, Jerome M., "What can the history of the idea of progress tell us about what development should be?" Paper presented to the First International Conference on Ethics and Development (San José: University of Costa Rica, June 7–14, 1987).

Segal, Jerome M., "What is development?" Working Paper DN-1 (College Park, MD: Institute for Philosophy and Public Policy, October 1986).

Seligson, Mitchell A. (Ed.), *The Gap between Rich and Poor: Contending Perspectives on the Political Economy of Development* (Boulder, CO: Westview Press, 1984).

Sen, Amartya, "Economic methodology: Heterogeneity and relevance," *Social Research,* Vol. 56, No. 2 (1989).

Sen, Amartya, "Food and freedom," *World Development,* Vol. 17, No. 6 (1989).

Sen, Amartya, "Freedom as choice: Concept and content," *European Economic Review,* Vol. 32 (1988).

Sen, Amartya, *On Ethics and Economics* (Oxford: Basil Blackwell, 1987).

Sen, Amartya, "Well-being, agency and freedom: The Dewey Lectures 1984," *Journal of Philosophy,* Vol. 82, No. 4 (1985).

Sen, Amartya, *Resources, Values and Development* (Oxford: Blackwell; Cambridge, MA: Harvard University Press, 1984).

Sen, Amartya, "Evaluator relativity and consequential evaluation," *Philosophy and Public Affairs,* Vol. 12, No. 2 (1983).

Sen, Amartya, *Choice, Welfare and Measurement* (Oxford: Blackwell; Cambridge, MA: MIT Press, 1982).

Sen, Amartya, "How Is India Doing?" *New York Review of Books,* Vol. 21 (December 1982).

Sen, Amartya, "Rights and agency," *Philosophy and Public Affairs,* Vol. 11, No. 1 (1982).

Sen, Amartya, *Poverty and Famines: An Essay on Entitlement and Deprivation* (Oxford: Clarendon Press, 1981).

Sen, Gita, and Caren Grown, *Development, Crises, and Alternative Visions: Third World Women's Perspectives* (New York: Monthly Review Press, 1987).

Sen, Amartya, with K. Hart, R. Kanbur, J. Muellbauer, B. Williams and G. Hawthorn, *The Standard of Living* (Cambridge: Cambridge University Press, 1987).

Sen, Amartya, and Bernard Williams (Eds.), *Utilitarianism and Beyond* (Cambridge: Cambridge University Press, 1982).

Shue, Henry, "Mediating duties," *Ethics,* Vol. 98, No. 4 (1988).

Shue, Henry, "Transnational transgressions," in Tom Regan (Ed.), *Just Business: New Introductory Essays in Business Ethics* (New York: Random House, 1984).

Shue, Henry, *Basic Rights: Subsistence, Affluence, and U.S. Foreign Policy* (Princeton: Princeton University Press, 1980).

Singer, Peter, "Famine, affluence, and morality," in William Aiken and Hugh La Follette (Eds.), *World Hunger and Moral Obligation* (Englewood Cliffs, NJ: Prentice-Hall, 1977).

Stavenhagen, Rodolfo, "Culturas indígenas y desarrollo auténtico," *Revista de la Universidad Autónoma de Yucatán,* special edition (February 1990), pp. 25–32.

Steidlmeier, Paul, *The Paradox of Poverty: A Reappraisal of Economic Development Policy* (Cambridge, MA: Ballinger, 1987).

Sterba, James (Ed.), *The Ethics of War and Nuclear Deterrence* (Belmont, CA: Wadsworth, 1985).

Stojanović, Svetozar, *Perestroika: From Marxism and Bolshevism to Gorbachev* (Buffalo, NY: Prometheus Books, 1988).

Sunkel, Osvaldo, and Pedro Paz, *El Subdesarrollo Latinoamericano y la Teoría del Desarrollo,* 20th edition (Mexico: Siglo Veintiuo Editores, 1986).

"Symposium on duties beyond borders," *Ethics,* Vol. 98, No. 4 (1988).

Thompson, Kenneth W., *Ethics and International Relations* (New Brunswick, NJ: Transaction Press, 1985).

Toulmin, Stephen, "The recovery of practical philosophy," *American Scholar,* Vol. 57, No. 3 (1988).

Vogeler, Ingolf, and Anthony De Souza (Eds.), *Dialectic of Third World Development* (Montclair: Allanheld, Osmun, 1980).

Walzer, Michael, *Just and Unjust Wars: A Moral Argument with Historical Illustrations* (New York: Basic Books, 1977).

Weisband, Edward (Ed.), *Poverty Amidst Plenty: World Political Economy and Distributive Justice* (Boulder, CO: Westview Press, 1989).

Wiarda, Howard, "Toward a nonethnocentric theory of development: Alternative conceptions from the Third World," in Charles K. Wilber (Ed.), *The Political Economy of Development and Underdevelopment,* 4th edition (New York: Random House, 1988).

Wilber, Charles K. (Ed.), *The Political Economy of Development and Underdevelopment,* 4th edition (New York: Random House, 1988).

Wilber, Charles K. (Ed.), *The Political Economy of Development and Underdevelopment,* 3rd edition (New York: Random House, 1984).

Wilber, Charles K., and Kenneth P. Jameson, "Paradigms of economic development and beyond," in Kenneth P. Jameson and Charles K. Wilber (Eds.), *Directions in Economic Development* (Notre Dame, IN: University of Notre Dame Press, 1975).

Williams, Bernard, *Ethics and the Limits of Philosophy* (Cambridge: Harvard University Press, 1985).

PART V

ECONOMIC POLICIES AND ETHICS

Rational actor theory is more than an empirical theory of behavior. This is perhaps most clearly evident when economists use the concept of Pareto optimality as a tool for gauging the relative efficiency of alternative economic arrangements and, therefore, the desirability of policies. Since the definition of welfare in this case is preference satisfaction, the utility function becomes a normative benchmark. Another example is perhaps more crude in its use of the preference-satisfaction standard but equally important—cost-benefit analysis (CBA). In this controversial practice, the merit of projects or policies is determined by adding up their costs and benefits. The benefits are usually measured in terms of the willingness of the affected parties to pay for them, with willingness to pay the normatively relevant piece of data because it reflects preferences. Thus, when applying either the Pareto criterion or CBA, economists rely on the notion that welfare amounts to the satisfaction of observed individual preferences. In this section, two chapters pursue the issue, one that assesses the role of preference satisfaction generally and another that focuses specifically on CBA.

Tyler Cowen is critical of the use of preference-satisfaction as a yardstick for policy choice, arguing not that it gives the wrong policy recommendations, but that in some cases it fails to issue in any coherent recommendations at all. His argument is analogous to a problem raised by economist Tibor Scitovsky. Incomes depend in some cases on which policy is chosen and, in turn, partly determine the measured benefit of any particular policy. Thus, the valuation of benefits, which is the basis for policy choice, itself depends on the policy chosen; the economist's logic is circular.

Cowen's argument is based on this paradox. He claims that preferences, and not just income, shift in response to policy. Thus, there is a second potential source of circularity in the use of preferences to guide policy. An example from chapter 19 will serve to illustrate this point. Suppose that liberal education instills in students liberal values and a tendency to favor government support for liberal education; at the same time, those educated in a more authoritarian system tend to support authoritarian educational policies. In this situation, the preference sovereignty standard fails to provide any consistent advice to the policy maker. Which policy satisfies preferences best depends upon which policy is implemented in the first place. Thus, "preference sovereignty" as a criterion for policy selection is not only incorrect; it is incoherent, Cowen argues.

These problems are compounded, Cowen says, when considering the problem of how to count the welfare of future generations. The shape (and existence!) of future individuals' preferences are determined in part by the policies adopted today, so again one is faced with the question of which preferences to count.

A related problem arises when we deal with the problem of imperfectly informed preferences. It has been empirically documented that in the real world, preferences are affected by all kinds of irrational influences. How, then, can one justify relying on those preferences to guide policy? This problem leads to efforts by some theorists to save the preference-sovereignty criterion by using preferences that are "cleansed" of malign influences such as imperfect information. Cowen rejects this approach, pointing out that it only introduces new problems. For example, people often value things or not—such as a surprise birthday present—because of the very uncertainty surrounding them. In such situations, the "cleansing" process may not just cleanse but also distort preferences. Thus, the supporter of preference sovereignty has a dilemma. Either he or she must accept "bad" preferences or tolerate an alien version of preferences, which may lack the moral appeal of more authentic, but ill-informed, ones. The preference sovereignty standard thus fails even when modified to take account of imperfect information.

In chapter 20, Donald Hubin examines the justification of one application of preference sovereignty—CBA. First, it is necessary to describe some details of the practice of CBA. Costs are perhaps more straightforward to estimate than benefits. Benefits can be measured by what is known as *compensating variations*—the amount that must be subtracted from a person's income to restore his or her utility to its pre-project levels. Economists have used a variety of ingenious strategies to measure compensating variations, usually by consulting market prices. The value of a good that is not traded on the market can sometimes be inferred, for example, when the value of life is estimated by observing wage premiums for unsafe jobs. In order to compare costs and benefits over a period of time, an appropriate rate of discount is determined and present values are computed. Some controversy surrounds the choice of an appropriate discount factor, and this can strongly influence the results. The bottom line of the CBA is a comparison of costs and benefits, which indicates whether the project should be chosen.

Should analyses of this type be used to make policy? One way of answering this question is to tie CBA to utilitarian moral theory and assess the latter. Hubin eschews this approach, saying that CBA does not stand or fall with any one moral philosophy; rather, he endorses a limited role for CBA on other grounds. He begins by arguing that there is not necessarily a straightforward connection between good moral theory and good practice. A practice such as CBA may be justified even if it is not a direct implementation of the correct moral theory. This can happen if we have what Hubin calls a *self-effacing* moral theory, that is, one that does not call for its own implementation. Directly justifying CBA with a moral theory is impossible at any rate, Hubin says, because the moral theories that might be said to provide the basis for CBA are all implausible.

But, then, how can CBA be justified? To begin his justification, Hubin argues that the kind of information provided by a CBA is relevant for decision making from the point of view of several different moral perspectives. For example, CBA reflects people's preferences, which are important to utilitarianism. Similar arguments can be made for deontological and contract-based theories. So, Hubin argues, even if CBA itself is not the exact embodiment of a correct moral theory, it would provide information relevant to the moral decisions of a deontologist or utilitarian.

Two arguments lead from this claim to the justification of CBA: a probabilistic argument and a political one. The probabilistic one is that since CBA information is useful under many plausible moral theories, chances are it may be useful under the correct one. The political argument is that because of its wide moral appeal, CBA is likely to gain the assent of a broad spectrum of citizens. Despite this justification of CBA, Hubin argues that there are limits to its applicability, in part because it weights preferences by willingness to pay, which reflects the influence of the morally arbitrary (and possibly unjust) current distribution of income. Thus Hubin argues for the use of CBA, but neither makes use of the most obvious justification for it, nor endorses an absolutist position in favor of all CBA.

The selections by Hubin and Cowen serve the function of reminding the reader that preferences serve an explicitly normative and action-guiding role, and not merely an empirical one. They also demonstrate that this role is no less subject to debate than the empirical one.

19.

THE SCOPE AND LIMITS OF PREFERENCE SOVEREIGNTY

Tyler Cowen

1. Preference Sovereignty and Idealized Welfare Standards

Economists use tastes as a source of information about personal welfare and judge the effects of policies upon preference satisfaction; neoclassical welfare economics is the analytical embodiment of this preference sovereignty norm. For an initial distribution of wealth, the welfare-maximizing outcome is the one that exhausts all possible gains from trade. Gains from trade are defined relative to fixed ordinal preferences. This analytical apparatus consists of both the Pareto principle, which implies that externality-free voluntary trades increase welfare, and applied cost-benefit analysis, which attempts to weight costs and benefits when evaluating policies that are not Pareto improvements.[1]

The economic approach to policy analysis stands in stark contrast to the methods espoused and practiced by philosophers, sociologists, politicians, and others. While most economists find the ethical standing of preference obvious, philosophers and other social scientists (for example, Sagoff, 1986) generally find revealed choices uncompelling as a standard of welfare, much less as an overall theory of the good. These writers question both whether preference sovereignty offers an adequate theory of welfare and whether policy should aim at increasing welfare.

Some critics grant that we should use preference information as one mea-

Economics and Philosophy 9, no. 2 (1993): 253–69.

sure of welfare, but argue also that preference information is not the only standard of welfare and that welfare is not the only value that matters. These views suggest that we should supplement preference sovereignty with other ethical considerations. I do not consider these criticisms, which are widely (although not universally) accepted. Most economists agree with Robbins's (1932/1984) judgment that policy prescriptions require explicit value judgments in addition to economic analysis.[2]

Other critics argue that preference sovereignty has inadequate building blocks and does not even offer a coherent theory of welfare (reasons for this claim, and references, are presented below). In this view, the rankings given by preference sovereignty standards do not give us inputs for use in making judgments of welfare. I focus upon this more fundamental criticism. Incoherence of the preference sovereignty norm implies the radical conclusion that welfare economics does not have a positive marginal product in judging welfare or making social decisions.

Sections 2, 3, and 4 of this chapter are devoted to specific examples of this more radical criticism. Section 2 considers the issue of endogenous preferences; section 3 covers issues of population choice and future generations; and section 4 examines the status of imperfectly informed preferences in policy evaluation. In each case, I argue that even applications of the Pareto principle involve versions of the Scitovsky double-switching problem, usually associated only with applied cost-benefit analysis. The chapter closes with some concluding remarks on the implications of the analysis.

2. Endogenous Preferences and Scitovsky Double-Switching

Endogenous preferences create problems for welfare economics when preferences (or metapreferences) are determined by the policies being chosen or evaluated. When valuing education, for instance, should we use the *ex ante* or *ex post* preferences? If subsidies to liberal and authoritarian educations give rise to different demand curves, a circularity problem arises because policy rankings depend upon which preferences we use to judge welfare.[3]

This issue can be interpreted in familiar terms, as the preference circularity dilemma is analogous to the Scitovsky (1941) double-switching problem in traditional cost-benefit analysis. The Scitovsky problem arises when *ex ante* and *ex post* distributions of income result in different policy evaluations. Policy options can no longer be ranked unambiguously, because rankings depend upon the distribution of wealth, which in turn depends upon policy.[4]

In both the Scitovsky problem and the preference circularity problem, the policy instituted shifts market demand curves; this shift itself changes the evaluation of policy. The only difference is whether these demand curves shift because of changes in the distribution of wealth, or because of changes in tastes. The logical structure of the two problems is the same.

To illuminate this link, consider the nature of the Scitovsky problem in more detail. The Scitovsky problem points out a paradox with standards (such as the Kaldor-Hicks principle) that use *ex post* results to evaluate policy changes. Consider, for instance, the claim made by the Kaldor-Hicks principle: World-state A is welfare-superior to B if, when the status quo is B, the total of compensating variations in moving from B to A is positive.[5]

The Scitovsky paradox shows that accepting this claim could require us to claim both that A is welfare-superior to B and that B is welfare-superior to A. The compensating variations involved with moving to world-state B may sanction B, and the compensating variations involved with moving to world-state A may sanction A. Each policy may create income effects that shift demand curves and thus the evaluation of each policy. Subsidizing a liberal education, for instance, may redistribute income toward individuals who prefer a more liberal educational system. Similarly, subsidizing an authoritarian education may redistribute income toward individuals who prefer a more authoritarian educational system.

In the case of endogenous preferences, inconsistent policy rankings may result from the same logic. We need only postulate standards of welfare defined in *ex post* terms; these standards may include a Kaldor-Hicks rule or even the Pareto principle requiring unanimity *ex post*. World-states A and B, rather than having different distributions of wealth, now have different preferences. But different preferences affect compensating variations just as different distributions of wealth do. If we institute world-state A, the compensating variations resulting from those preferences may rank world-state A as welfare-superior to B. Similarly, if we institute world-state B, the summed compensating variations may rank world-state B welfare-superior A. In the education example, we can imagine that subsidies to a liberal education create individuals who value liberality highly, and subsidies to the authoritarian education create individuals who value strictness and discipline. We might even imagine that each policy change, *ex post,* is approved of unanimously.

As the above example shows, Scitovsky-like problems do not require the specific Kaldor-Hicks aggregation rule, but can result more generally from aggregation rules that make the final measure of welfare dependent upon the policy that is chosen. Given that market demands shift (through either movements along demand schedules, caused by income effects, or through change of preferences), the social welfare function needs only to be based upon *ex post* preferences and wealth levels, even if the rule is one of *ex post* unanimity.

The link between the Scitovsky problem and the endogenous preferences problem becomes even closer if we consider the argument of Stigler and Becker (1977) that "taste changes" can be redefined as changes in constraints, such as human capital endowments. Developing one's taste for liberality through a liberal education, for instance, can be considered either a taste change or an investment in human capital, and thus a change in constraints. Rather than saying that an individual now places a greater value upon a liberal education, we can say that the individual's human capital endowments increase the shadow value of a liberal education to him or her. Similarly, other taste changes can be redefined in terms of our increasing ability to enjoy intermediate goods, given a constant set of underlying tastes for final goods but a changing "utility production function."

If we accept this principle, taste changes are no different in principle than changes in endowments. Whether a given change in compensating variations results from "endowment changes" or "taste changes" becomes a matter of how the theorist classifies terms.[6]

The preference circularity problem is more general than the traditional Scitovsky problem in one sense: the preference circularity problem can arise with only one individual (although two sets of preferences must be involved). The traditional Scitovsky problem requires changes in the distribution of wealth among different individuals to shift compensating variations. In contrast, the preference circularity problem allows compensating variations to shift through changing the tastes of a single individual. Even in this case, however, we can think of the changing tastes as shifting an entire wealth endowment from *ex ante* preferences to *ex post* preferences, as if the two different preference sets were different individuals with a changing distribution of wealth. Rather than saying that one preference set "ceases to exist" we can also say that this preference set receives a zero endowment (and thus does not affect policy evaluation).

Related to Scitovsky problems and circularity problems is the "sour grapes" phenomenon (Elster, 1982). One example of the sour grapes phenomenon arises when for any status quo, all individuals wish to switch to the alternative. Consider, for instance, a world where an authoritarian educational system produces rebellious preferences and the desire for a more liberal education. Conversely, educations that encourage introspection and self-criticism may produce preferences that partially or wholly condemn the institutions that created such preferences. The sour grapes problem is the mirror image of the Scitovsky problem. Rather than world-states A and B creating compensating variations that favor themselves in terms of welfare, they lead to compensating variations that favor the other world-state.[7]

Implications

Economists have not solved the Scitovsky problem in the context of traditional income effects, despite numerous attempts. Little (1957), for instance, combines the Kaldor-Hicks potential compensation principle with judgments about wealth distributions; we might approve of policies that increase total wealth and have favorable effects on the distribution of wealth. Such standards are open to criticism on the grounds of arbitrariness and potential intransitivity (Chipman and Moore, 1978, pp. 576–77). But even if these standards can be applied in the case of traditional wealth effects, they cannot be used to evaluate changing preferences. We can judge the distribution of monetary wealth as more or less equal, but how do we judge the distributional implications of changing preferences?

Preference sovereignty can provide coherent rankings if and only if we can choose a baseline level of preferences (or wealth level) for comparing policies. One obvious choice is to use equivalent variations, and define these equivalent variations from a unique, well-defined set of *ex ante* relative prices, preferences, and levels of wealth. Status quo preferences then evaluate the desirability of different policies, taking into account that these policies also may change preferences.

Using the equivalent variation based upon status quo preferences, however, encounters time consistency problems. Use of *ex ante,* status quo preferences provides a consistent solution only if we are making a once-and-for-all policy evaluation. When we make policy evaluations over time, *ex ante* preferences change and so do equivalent variations, thus changing our policy decisions. A status quo that changes over time is no longer unique and does not rule out time inconsistency and circularity problems. We are now confronted with an intertemporal version of the Scitovsky problem, as policies can switch back and forth over time as tastes change. Isolating a unique status quo is not possible in a changing world when policies are made each period.[8]

3. The Welfare of Future Generations

Assessing the welfare of future generations involves issues closely related to the problem of endogenous preferences. When considering the welfare of future generations, we must consider preferences that do not yet exist, or whose existence is contingent upon our actions. Again, we are faced with the possible lack of a unique status quo point for measuring welfare.

For the purposes of discussion, I assume that we attach some weight to the welfare of future generations. Refusing to count future preferences involves myopic decision-making. We may choose, and later regret, options with horrific future consequences. Or we may choose certain options and later incur costs reversing them, after the "once-future" preferences come into being (see Cowen, 1990).

Counting the welfare of future individuals, however, produces conundrums of circularity. We are again faced with a Scitovsky-like problem, even when applying the Pareto principle. The number of potential future preference sets is very large, and the preferences that actually materialize are contingent upon choices that we make today. Assume that the Germans must decide whether to save the Black Forest by adopting costly controls on automobile emissions. Once the Black Forest is gone, preferences for it will greatly weaken or disappear; future generations will have difficulty conceiving what they are missing. If the Black Forest remains, however, future Germans will grow up to value this resource greatly. Just as with the education example, we are faced with a potential circularity problem. Two directly opposed policies (save the forest, let the forest die) might both command unanimous assent from the respective future preferences that each creates.

The problems that arise with future generations go even deeper than the problems with endogenous preferences examined above. Consider the biological fact that even small changes in the timing of conception will involve different sperm/egg fertilizations and thus produce offspring with different identities. Most policies change our lives enough to influence the timing of conceptions, either by influencing us directly or through interactions with others. Even individuals far removed from the policy in question will be affected if they must wait at one additional traffic light because another individual drove a different route home that evening. These individuals will now conceive the children they have at different times. For this reason, different policies give rise to identifiably distinct sets of future generations (Parfit, 1984).

With this in mind, consider the example of nuclear waste policy. Assume that by burying nuclear wastes in the ground today, we save some small cost, but we also ensure that some individuals in future generations will be born with serious genetic defects. These lives will be very deprived, but still be worth living to some slight degree. If the nuclear wastes are not buried, however, identifiably different individuals with no genetic defects will be born.[9]

If we bury the nuclear waste, everyone who lives in this scenario will approve of the policy. Current generations will benefit, because they do not have to dispose of the waste by more costly means. The children born with genetic defects will approve also. If the nuclear wastes were not buried, these children would never have been born. Other children would have been born in their place. Despite their defects, the handicapped children still prefer to live than to have been replaced by different children (that is, never to have been born at all).

Unless we count the preferences of those contingent individuals who never come to be, the Pareto principle yields counterintuitive results. The policy of burying the nuclear waste receives unanimous approval. Unanimity, however, is not an intuitively appealing concept when the identities of those who vote are themselves the subject of policy choice.

Again, we can portray the problem in terms of wealth effects and a Scitovsky-like circularity problem. When choosing policies that result in the birth of some individuals and the nonbirth of others, we are affecting the distribution of wealth among these individuals. Life itself is the endowment being distributed. If a policy distributes the endowment of life, the receiving individual is likely to approve of that policy, regardless of its other consequences. Potential individuals who fail to receive endowments of life have no incomes (or voices) through which they can register their protest. Parfit's work can be read as suggesting that Scitovsky problems are unavoidable when we deal with policies that change the identities of future generations.

Endogenous Preferences and Contingent Persons

The problems of endogenous preferences and contingent future generations possess strong common elements. Past and future preferences may belong either to past or future generations, or to current individuals whose tastes have changed or will be changing. For most individuals, the primary source of preference endogeneity is the family. Our genetic background and family experience shape us in many ways; population ethics simply focuses upon one form of "shaping"—the polar issue of whether or not we are born at all.

Since neoclassical economic theory treats the utility function as a complete description of an individual, preference sovereignty norms have the option of treating past and future preferences as different individuals and aggregating accordingly. Different preferences can be treated the same, regardless of whether they belong to the "same" individual. Past preferences that are no longer held are treated as dead individuals. Even if we accept this parallel without qualification, however, difficult conundrums remain when evaluating policies that affect future and contingent generations.[10]

Evaluating policies when the identities or preferences of future generations are contingent is even more difficult than evaluating policies when preferences are endogenous. In the case of future generations, we do not have a well-defined status quo or *ex ante* even at a single point in time. Future generations do not yet exist, and a status quo cannot be defined on their behalf. Without a well-defined status quo, the potential scope for circularity problems increases greatly.

For this reason, we might choose to bypass the Pareto principle and move to applied cost-benefit analysis by comparing sums of future wealth when evaluating policy options. This approach would avoid the unappetizing conclusions considered above, since the burial of nuclear waste does decrease total wealth. Without an underlying Pareto principle, however, cost-benefit analysis is left without microfoundations. We might defend wealth maximization as a proxy for other aspects of welfare, but this underlying concept of welfare remains ill defined. Furthermore, comparisons of national income are themselves subject to intransitivity, as demonstrated by Samuelson (1950).[11]

4. Imperfect Information

Imperfectly informed preferences are another critical issue for the preference sovereignty theory of welfare. Recent work on biases in cognitive decision-making indicates that individuals make ill-informed or "irrational" choices on a systematic basis (Kahneman, Slovic, and Tversky, 1982). Measured effects include misestimation of small probability events (Kunreuther, Ginsberg, Miller, Sagi, Slovic, Borkan, and Katz, 1978), an overestimation of the importance of nominal losses, illusions created by framing effects (Kahneman and Tversky, 1979), a tendency to overestimate one's probability of success, and noticing patterns in data that are not present, to name but a few examples. In some cases, observed or reported preferences cannot be represented by any well-defined ordering at all (Grether and Plott, 1979). In asking how welfare economics should account for imperfectly informed preferences, we once again raise the question of finding an appropriate status quo.[12]

Consider the evaluation of consumer protection legislation, specifically, the prohibition of asbestos insulation. An individual may prefer asbestos insulation if he or she does not understand the accompanying risk of cancer. Yet, the advocate of preference sovereignty is presumably unwilling to recommend asbestos insulation for this individual. Utilitarian arguments that paternalism is generally self-defeating and inefficient are beside the point; asbestos insulation is still not the morally best outcome for the uninformed.[13]

We might attempt to correct for imperfect information by considering what an individual would want if he or she were fully informed. I refer to this as the "cleansed-preference" standard. Poorly informed preferences are discarded in favor of a thought experiment that generates hypothetical preferences. What would an individual want if he or she were fully informed about the world and in a clear state of mind? The cleansed-preference standard does not require that an individual's preferences actually be changed, only that we use these counterfactual questions to generate information for policy evaluations.[14]

Although the cleansed-preference standard appears to address the case of asbestos, use of cleansed preferences is not a generally satisfactory solution. The preferences of perfectly informed individuals are not always relevant for imperfectly informed choice. By considering perfectly informed preferences, we are hypothetically changing an individual's human capital endowment. What an individual would want with a different human capital endowment cannot necessarily be extrapolated usefully into information about what improves the welfare of an individual now.

The problems with using cleansed preferences can be illustrated by example. With perfect information and cleansed preferences, I would prefer red wine to Coca-Cola, but this hypothetical taste has little bearing on my welfare in a world where my preferences are not cleansed. For this reason, we cannot use perfect information demand curves to evaluate, say, a tax on Coca-Cola or a ban on Coca-Cola advertising.[15]

The cleansed-preference standard fails to measure welfare accurately because so much of the value in our lives arises from imperfect information. I prefer certain goods precisely because I do not have perfect information about these goods. Surprise, for instance, is a component of our enjoyment of many goods, including personal relationships; art, jobs, and food are just a few examples of goods that we value because they offer surprise and discovery. I would find a choice of job or spouse less attractive and exciting if I knew the outcome of my decision in advance. We enjoy our ability to learn from our decisions, and the sense of suspense and anticipation we experience in the meantime. The temporal creation and resolution of uncertainty produces many of our most important joys (Cowen, 1991b).

The cleansed-preference standard also misjudges the value of goods and services that are complementary to surprise and discovery goods. A large and comfortable house may not appear to be a discovery good, but is a complement to a discovery good, namely a spouse. Upon examination, most of the well-being in our lives is closely linked to discovery and surprise; that is, imperfect information. A perfectly informed life would be a curse, rather than a blessing. We would know the date of our death, how each meal would taste, what we would get for Christmas, the solutions to whodunits, and which jokes would be funny. Imperfect information also possesses value as a protection against discomfort. Most of us do not wish, for instance, to know what other individuals think about us at each moment.

Imperfectly informed preferences serve other valuable functions as well, such as protecting the vividness of our experiences from the evils and suffering that occur in the world. How many of us would wish to be fully and continually aware of the enormous amount of suffering in the world? Small pleasures of life, such as country drives or ice cream cones, would be overwhelmed by this awareness, and we would have a difficult time enjoying life. In other cases (perhaps cocaine?), perfect or even adequate information can only be obtained at the cost of addiction. Other problems result when having too good a memory binds us to our past. Mnemonists, for instance (that is, individuals with a near-perfect memory), usually have difficulty adjusting to life and cannot think abstractly because they are unable to ignore the strong images and pictures that they retain in their memories.[16]

The cleansed-preference standard masks uncertainty not only as a protective device but also as a source of discomfort. By evaluating the effects of a policy under the assumption of perfect information, we are ignoring the costs of anxiety. The costs of building a new nuclear power plant, for instance, include not just the possibility of radiation death, but also the anxiety experienced by potential victims before the uncertainty about their health is resolved. Much of the misery we experience comes not from bad events that actually happen, but from our fears about what might happen. We are all familiar with the comfort of knowing the worst.[17]

Saving Cleansed Preferences?

We might try to save the cleansed-preference standard by modifying the initial cleansed-preferences thought experiment. If we compare the asbestos and red wine examples presented above, relevant differences are evident. Even if I desire asbestos insulation, I presumably have a higher-order preference that my demand be overridden if I am mistaken about the effects of asbestos (for the time being, I treat this higher-order preference as actual, not cleansed). In the case of Coca-Cola and red wine, I have no higher-order preference that my "mistakes" be overridden by cleansed preferences.[18]

Respecting cleansed preferences only when higher-order preferences so dictate, however, simply pushes the problem back another step. Higher-order preferences for giving priority to cleansed tastes are themselves imperfectly informed. I may think I do not want my Coca-Cola preference overridden in a welfare evaluation, but in fact I would prefer the wine if I were to taste it. My higher-order preferences may be just as imperfectly informed as lower-order preferences, and these higher-order preferences do not offer a reliable guide as to when the cleansed preference should enter the welfare calculation.

The fallibility of higher-order preferences can be illustrated by examples from experimental economics. Individuals who choose inconsistently in the Allais paradox and violate the independence axiom, for instance, do not always change their choice when their inconsistency is explained to them. These individuals may be exhibiting inconsistent higher-order preferences by sticking with their originally inconsistent lower-order preferences. Some psychologists even offer evidence that introspection reduces the quality of preferences and decisions (Wilson and Schooler, 1991).[19]

We can imagine a further refinement of the cleansed-preference standard designed to avoid the problem of imperfect higher-order preferences. I can be given perfect information as a counterfactual thought experiment, and then asked when I want my cleansed preferences to override my actual preferences in welfare evaluations. My perfectly informed self can then make a judgment about how much cleansing would maximize the welfare of my imperfectly informed self; that is, we can use the cleansed higher-order preferences of the perfectly informed self.[20]

Once again, this approach requires a judgment of my welfare external to my actual preferences. A self with radically different brain endowments and capacities (even if based upon my genetic patterns) cannot judge my welfare without going outside of my preferences. In effect, the ideally informed self is a different individual altogether; from my point of view a perfectly informed self is another dictator. Because imperfect information is so pervasive, a perfectly informed self is perhaps even more different from my current preferences than a traditional political dictator would be.

With different modifications of the cleansed-preference standard, we end up abandoning or at least subordinating preference sovereignty by defining welfare in terms external to individual preferences. Rather than going through the machinations of the cleansed-preference theory as an amendment of preference sovereignty, Occam's razor would dictate using this underlying theory of welfare to evaluate policies and preferences directly.[21]

We might try to avoid problems with the cleansed-preference standard by modifying full-information thought experiments to avoid these problems. For instance, we may try to set up experiments that give us just enough knowledge to know how much we will enjoy an outcome, but not enough specific knowledge to ruin the joy of discovery. But attempted modifications of the cleansed-preference standard, no matter how many difficulties they take account of, encounter similar basic problems. The level of information provided to preferences in these modified thought experiments is arbitrary and requires justification in terms of a theory of the good external to preferences. Furthermore, the level of information we are trying to create by our thought experiments may not even be possible. Even the simple knowledge that "a choice has an outcome that I will like" can diminish the joy of being pleasantly surprised. For instance, I prefer going to see good movies with low expectations; that is, with poor information.

Postulating hypothetical levels of information as bases for determining preference valuations is arbitrary. The shadow prices generated by hypothetically increasing an individual's information set to a certain level do not possess greater moral relevance than the shadow prices that could be generated at any other level of information. Furthermore, additional shadow prices can be derived by hypothetically varying goods or inputs other than an individual's information. The hypothetical shadow prices at full or near-full information have no more validity than other hypothetical shadow prices. Fully informed preferences do not offer an Archimedean point for value theory in a world of imperfect information.

Implications

Adjusting for imperfect information through thought experiments distorts policy evaluations. All versions of the cleansed-preference standard change informational constraints, alter human capital endowments, and shift demand curves. The preferences derived from such demand curves are not directly relevant to the well-being of individuals who do not have these human capital endowments.

Interpreting imperfect information in terms of endowment effects returns us to the traditional dilemma of welfare economics. We should not judge welfare for a world with one set of endowments (ill-informed preferences) with demand curves taken from another set of endowments (perfectly informed preferences). By changing the information set, the cleansed-preference standard adds yet another wealth effect to issues of policy evaluation. If the welfare of alternative policies is evaluated in terms of a hypothetical status quo and thus a different level of wealth, chosen policy may be unsuitable for actual preferences.

If the cleansed-preference standard cannot deal adequately with imperfect information, we are faced with a troublesome decision. If we allow preference sovereignty to be overridden when information is imperfect, our conception of preference sovereignty is supported ultimately by some welfare standard external to preferences. Respecting preferences would then be a pragmatic means of attaining our underlying theory of welfare, but preferences would not be a fundamental source or definition of welfare. Conversely, if we never allow preference sovereignty to be overridden when information is imperfect, we may be required to endorse consequences that even ardent defenders of preference sovereignty would probably find uncomfortable. Since recent work on cognitive decision-making indicates that poorly informed or inconsistent preferences are common, the magnitude of this problem is likely considerable.

5. Concluding Remarks

Upon examination, the problems of endogenous preferences, future generations, and imperfect information are variants of the traditional problems of endowment effects and Scitovsky double-switching. In these cases, we do not have a plausible status quo benchmark available for use. Welfare economics remains logically consistent if we restrict its application to situations when endowment effects are small. Nonetheless, the condition of small endowment effects is extremely restrictive, and rules out evaluating many policies that affect preferences, future generations, and imperfectly informed individuals. These limitations of welfare economics apply not only to cost-benefit analysis but also to situations where the Pareto principle can be invoked.

Recognition of the link between preferences and endowment effects also points out disturbing conclusions about the relationship between government policy and individual preferences. Government cannot be neutral across different preferences any more than it can be neutral across the distribution of wealth. Indeed, the two issues are directly analogous. With respect to both wealth and preferences, government policy implies either an endorsement of the outcomes that already obtain or a positive desire to shape society in a particular direction. Preferred policies, including laissez-faire, must ultimately be judged not only on traditional efficiency grounds, but also as a program for favoring one set of preferences over another. While we cannot eliminate the arbitrariness in policy evaluation, we should at least be more explicit about the subjective nature of the underlying values we choose to promote.

Notes

I wish to thank Timothy Brennan, James Buchanan, Jack High, Joseph Kalt, Greg Kavka, Daniel Klein, Randy Kroszner, Julius Margolis, Susanne Paine, Thomas Schelling, Alex Tabarrok, Larry Temkin, the editors, and two anonymous referees for useful comments and discussions.

1. Gibbard (1986, p. 168) defines the preference satisfaction standard of welfare: "[G]iven two possible histories of the universe, x and y, a person j is better off in x than in y if and only if j prefers x to y. . . ." Normative standards can be based upon preference sovereignty without accepting the entire structure of modern welfare economics; Cowen (1991a) considers such standards. Penz (1986, p. 13) surveys various definitions of consumer sovereignty.

2. Sen's (1979, 1982) critique of the "poverty of welfarism" is one example of this criticism. Sen does not argue that preferences do not matter, simply that preferences and utility considerations are not all that matters. Few economists have committed themselves to the view that policymakers should consider only the information contained in utility functions; Ng (1981) is one exception.

3. The circularity problem with endogenous preferences is spelled out most clearly in Penz (1986). Approaches to welfare theory with endogenous preferences include utility map comparisons (Harsanyi, 1953–54), Rawlsian thought experiments (Weisbrod, 1977), and a distinction between conditional and unconditional preferences (Pollak, 1978). Dixit and Norman (1978) consider *ex ante* and *ex post* comparisons. Brandt (1979) attempts to compare different preferences in terms of their ability to produce happiness. von Weizsacker (1971) analyzes endogenous preferences when myopia is present.

I consider time consistency problems below. I do not, however, treat time inconsistent preferences (for example, Elster, 1979; Schelling, 1984) as a separate problem. Inconsistent preferences may arise from several different sources. If time inconsistency arises because preferences change, the discussion in this section applies. Alternatively, if time inconsistency arises because of imperfectly informed preferences, the discussion offered in section 4 applies. Time inconsistency may also arise because a single body has two distinct utility functions (Schelling, 1984). The welfare economics of time inconsistency then becomes a problem of aggregation, similar to aggregation across different individuals. On this issue, see Kavka (1991).

4. See Scitovsky (1941) and Samuelson (1950). Hause (1975) and Chipman and Moore (1978) offer a modern treatment of the Scitovsky problem.

5. The compensating variation is the dollar amount required to restore an individual to his *ex ante* utility level given his *ex post* situation; compensating variation is thus positive for policies that affect an individual adversely and negative for policies that benefit an individual. Equivalent variation starts from

the status quo and is the potential dollar value of a change (for example, how much an individual would be willing to pay for an improvement from his *ex ante* level of wealth). Being defined over a unique *ex ante* level of wealth, use of equivalent variations does not encounter Scitovsky problems of the traditional sort; more on this below.

6. Cowen (1989a) argues that the Stigler and Becker model cannot handle certain kinds of taste changes, such as those involving intrapersonal conflict or weakness of will. These features are not at stake in the problem under consideration.

7. A sour grapes problem may arise through income effects as well, by moving along a demand curve, without resort to endogenous preferences. Imagine that for Southerners, authoritarian education is preferred at high levels of income and liberal education is preferred at low levels of income. For Northerners, the contrary is true. The South is rich and the North is poor so everyone prefers a move to authoritarian education. The subsidy to authoritarian education, however, redistributes income from the South to the North. Now, authoritarian education is in place, but, with the new levels of income, both regions prefer liberal education. In either case the social welfare functions suggest we implement whichever kind of education is not present.

8. Using *ex ante* preferences is also vulnerable to the charge of conservative bias and favoring the status quo; see, for instance, Veblen (1936/1964). I find this criticism less compelling because individuals may have metapreferences that their preferences change over time. The use of *ex ante* preferences places no restrictions on the possible strength of this desire and does not unduly restrict change and novelty.

9. The nuclear waste conundrum comes from Derek Parfit (1984, chap. 16). Parfit, however, does not consider the implications for welfare economics or the link to the theory of endogenous preferences. See Broome (1985) and Cowen (1989b, 1990) on other parts of Parfit's work, including the Repugnant Conclusion.

10. The idea of treating different preferences as different individuals comes from Allais (1947) and Malinvaud (1972). Past preferences that are no longer held are analogous to individuals who have died and are not counted. (Why we should not count the preferences of the dead is puzzling, however, unless we invoke a mental state theory of welfare, contrary to the ordinalist foundations of economic theory.) Assuming that the interests of future generations should be counted, Cowen and Parfit (1992) consider the proper choice of discount rate for future preferences.

11. I do not consider whether cost-benefit analysis has satisfactory microfoundations, even if the Pareto principle were available. Posner (1981) defends a wealth maximization standard; Dworkin (1980) criticizes wealth maximization.

12. Earl (1990) surveys how psychology influences economic decision-making. Two older critiques of preference sovereignty, Veblen (1936/1964) and Knight (1936) concur in this attitude as well. For the purposes of this dis-

cussion, I treat errors of calculation as similar in effect to imperfect information. In both cases an "incorrect" choice will be made.

13. Sen (1973), Gibbard (1986, 1990), Griffin (1986), and Braybrooke (1987) treat the potential conflict between preference and welfare. Also, see Glover (1977, p. 63), who considers the following statement: "My husband wants me to be faithful to him while he is in prison, but he will never know about this." Is the husband worse off if his wife has the affair? Haslett (1990) analyzes problems of this sort.

14. Versions of the cleansed-preference standard are advocated by Musgrave (1959), Head (1969, p. 215), Rawls (1971), Brandt (1979), Hammond (1983), Railton (1986), Broome (1989, p. 11), Marshall (1989), Ng (1989), and Haslett (1990, p. 83). On the concept of meta-preferences more generally, see Jeffrey (1974), Elster (1979), and McPherson (1982). Criticisms of the cleansed preference standard, or related ideas, are found in Velleman (1988); Smith, Lewis, and Johnston (1989); and Gibbard (1990), which are considered further below.

15. Brandt (1979, p. 161) admits briefly that we cannot always ignore what he calls "neurotic" or "irrational" desires, but does not consider the points raised below. The criticism of Velleman (1988) argues that there is no single, correct way of presenting information to an individual that counts as informing him or her correctly. Gibbard (1990, pp. 18–22) argues that full information preferences can be misleading but focuses upon cases of instrumental rationality rather than evaluation of final ends. An individual lost in the forest, for instance, should not be advised to seek the shortest route out. If this individual has imperfect information, he or she should follow rules of thumb for finding a suitable path out of the forest. Smith, Lewis, and Johnston (1989, pp. 124, 126) consider cases where not all values can be contemplated or considered at once (for example, struggle and tranquility), and thus cannot be represented in terms of perfect information.

16. Gibbard (1986) also argues that imperfect information insulates from experiencing too much suffering. See also Smith, Lewis, and Johnston (1989, p. 126), who argue that vivid awareness of the entire cosmos might extinguish our desires altogether. On addiction, see Smith, Lewis, and Johnston (p. 117n), citing Michael Tooley. On mnemonism, see Luria (1968).

17. Weil (1990) surveys theories of utility maximization that treat the resolution of uncertainty as an economic good or bad different from the value of outcomes.

18. In the case of Coca-Cola and red wine, not only might I reject cleansed preferences as a counterfactual thought experiment, but I might also reject the actual cleansing of my preferences, even if it could be performed costlessly. Better informed preferences are not always preferable, as ignorance is sometimes bliss. Those who have developed a taste for good wines might have a harder time meeting their budget constraint, for instance.

19. Marshall (1989, pp. 16–17) notes: "[R]isk-taking behavior remains stubbornly divergent from what it 'should' be. Subjects in the laboratory persist in violating the strong assumptions. Consumers at large persist in ignoring hazards, in spite of extensive campaigns of education, warning, and threat."

20. Railton (1986, pp. 173–74) suggests this procedure.

21. Along these lines, defenders of the cleansed-preference standard tend to assume that their favored ethical views are less controversial than they really are. Railton (1986, p. 179), for instance, notes: "Surely our well- or ill-being are among the things that matter to us most, and most reliably, even on reflection." Here Railton is invoking external values under the guise of informed choice. While I am sympathetic to the invocation of well-being as an ultimate normative standard, this question has proved controversial, to say the least, throughout the history of philosophy.

References

Allais, Maurice. 1947. *Economie et Intérêt*. Paris: Imprimerie Nationale.

Brandt, Richard. 1979. *A Theory of the Good and the Right*. New York: Oxford University Press.

Braybrooke, David. 1987. *Meeting Needs*. Princeton: Princeton University Press.

Broome, John. 1985. "The Welfare Economics of the Future: A Review of *Reasons and Persons* by Derek Parfit." *Social Choice and Welfare* 2:221–34.

———. 1989. "Should Social Preferences Be Consistent?" *Economics and Philosophy* 5:7–17.

Chipman, John S., and James C. Moore. 1978. "The New Welfare Economics 1938–1974." *International Economic Review* 19:547–84.

Cowen, Tyler. 1989a. "Are All Tastes Constant and Identical?: A Critique of Stigler and Becker." *Journal of Economic Behavior and Organization*. January:127–35.

———. 1989b. "Normative Population Theory." *Social Choice and Welfare* 6:33–43.

———. 1990. "Distribution in Fixed and Variable Number Problems." *Social Choice and Welfare* 7:47–56.

———. 1991a. "What a Non-Paretian Welfare Economics Would Have to Look Like." In *Hermeneutics and Economics,* edited by Donald C. Lavoie, pp. 285–98. London: Routledge.

———. 1991b. "Self-Liberation versus Self-Constraint." *Ethics* 101:360–73.

Cowen, Tyler, and Derek Parfit. 1992. "Against the Social Discount Rate." In *Philosophy, Politics, and Society,* 6th series, edited by P. Laslett and J. Fishkin, pp. 144–61. New Haven: Yale University Press.

Dixit, Avinash, and Victor Norman. 1978. "Advertising and Welfare." *Bell Journal of Economics* 9(1):1–18.

Dworkin, Ronald M. 1980. "Is Wealth a Value?" *Journal of Legal Studies* 9:191–226.

Earl, Peter E. 1990. "Economics and Psychology: A Survey." *Economic Journal* 100:718–55.

Elster, Jon. 1979. *Ulysses and the Sirens*. New York: Cambridge University Press.

———. 1982. "Sour Grapes—Utilitarianism and the Genesis of Wants." In *Utilitarianism and Beyond,* edited by A. Sen and B. Williams, pp. 219–38. New York: Cambridge University Press.

Gibbard, Allan. 1986. "Interpersonal Comparisons: Preference, Good, and the Intrinsic Reward of a Life." In *Foundations of Social Choice Theory,* edited by J. Elster and A. Hylland, pp. 165–94. Cambridge: Cambridge University Press.

———. 1990. *Wise Choices, Apt Feelings: A Theory of Normative Judgment.* Cambridge, MA: Harvard University Press.

Glover, Jonathan. 1977. *Causing Death and Saving Lives.* Harmondsworth: Penguin Books.

Grether, David M., and Charles R. Plott. 1979. "Economic Theory of Choice and the Preference Reversal Phenomenon." *American Economic Review* 69:623–38.

Griffin, Robert. 1986. *Well-Being.* New York: Oxford University Press.

Hammond, Peter. 1983. "Ex-Post Optimality as a Dynamically Consistent Objective for Collective Choice under Uncertainty." In *Social Choice and Welfare,* edited by P. Pattanaik and M. Salles, pp. 175–205. Amsterdam: North-Holland.

Harsanyi, John. 1953–54. "Welfare Economics of Variable Tastes." *Review of Economic Studies* 21:204–13.

Haslett, D. W. 1990. "What Is Utility?" *Economics and Philosophy* 6:65–94.

Hause, John C. 1975. "The Theory of Welfare Cost Measurement." *Journal of Political Economy* 83:1145–82.

Head, John. 1969. "Merit Goods Revisited." *Finanzarchiv* 28:214–25.

Jeffrey, Richard. 1974. "Preference among Preferences." *Journal of Philosophy* 71:377–91.

Kahneman, Daniel, and Amos Tversky. 1979. "Prospect Theory: An Analysis of Decision under Risk." *Econometrica* 47:263–91.

Kahneman, Daniel, Paul Slovic, and Amos Tversky. 1982. *Judgment under Uncertainty: Heuristics and Biases.* Cambridge: Cambridge University Press.

Kavka, Gregory S. 1991. "Is Individual Choice Less Problematic Than Collective Choice?" *Economics and Philosophy* 7:143–65.

Knight, Frank H. 1936. *The Ethics of Competition.* New York: Harper and Brothers.

Kunreuther, Howard, Ralph Ginsberg, L. Miller, Phillip Sagi, Paul Slovic, B. Borkan, and N. Katz. 1978. *Disaster Insurance Protection: Public Policy Lessons.* New York: John Wiley and Sons.

Little, I. M. D. 1957. *A Critique of Welfare Economics.* London: Oxford University Press.

Luria, A. R. 1968. *The Mind of a Mnemonist.* New York: Basic Books.

Malinvaud, Edmond. 1972. *Lectures on Microeconomic Theory.* Amsterdam: North-Holland.

Marshall, John M. 1989. "Welfare Analysis without Expected Utility." Department of Economics, University of California, Santa Barbara, Working Paper #23-89.

McPherson, Michael. 1982. "Mill's Moral Theory and the Problem of Preference Change." *Ethics* 92:252–73.

Musgrave, Richard. 1959. *Theory of Public Finance*. New York: McGraw-Hill.

Ng, Y.-K. 1981. "Welfarism: A Defence against Sen's Attack." *Economic Journal* 91:527–30.

———. 1989. "Individual Irrationality and Social Welfare." *Social Choice and Welfare* 6:87–101.

Parfit, Derek. 1984. *Reasons and Persons*. New York: Oxford University Press.

Penz, G. Peter. 1986. *Consumer Sovereignty and Human Interests*. Cambridge: Cambridge University Press.

Pollak, Robert. 1978. "Endogenous Tastes in Demand and Welfare Analysis." *American Economic Review* 68:374–79.

Posner, Richard. 1981. "The Ethical and Political Basis of Wealth Maximization." In *The Economics of Justice,* by Richard Posner, pp. 88–115. Cambridge, MA: Harvard University Press.

Railton, Peter. 1986. "Moral Realism." *The Philosophical Review* 2:163–207.

Rawls, John. 1971. *A Theory of Justice*. Cambridge: Harvard University Press.

Robbins, Lionel. 1984 (first ed. 1932). *An Essay on the Nature and Significance of Economic Science*. New York: New York University Press.

Sagoff, Mark. 1986. "Values and Preferences." *Ethics* 96:301–16.

Samuelson, Paul. 1950. "The Evaluation of Real National Income." *Oxford Economic Papers* 1:1–29.

Schelling, Thomas. 1984. *Choice and Consequence*. Cambridge, MA: Harvard University Press.

Scitovsky, Tibor. 1941. "A Note on Welfare Propositions in Economics." *Review of Economic Studies* 9:77–88.

Sen, Amartya. 1973. "Behaviour and the Concept of Preference." *Economica* 40:241–59.

———. 1979. "Personal Utilities and Public Judgements: Or What's Wrong with Welfare Economics." *Economic Journal* 89:537–58.

———. 1982. *Choice, Welfare and Measurement*. Cambridge, MA: MIT Press.

Smith, Michael, David Lewis, and Mark Johnston. 1989. "Dispositional Theories of Value." *Proceedings of the Aristotelian Society,* Supplementary Vol. LXIII:113–37.

Stigler, George J., and Gary S. Becker. 1977. "De Gustibus Non Est Disputandum." *American Economic Review* 67(2):76–90.

Veblen, Thorstein. 1964 (first ed. 1936). *What Veblen Taught*. New York: Augustus M. Kelley.

Velleman, J. David. 1988. "Brandt's Definition of 'Good.'" *The Philosophic Review* 98(3):353–71.

Weil, Philippe. 1990. "Nonexpected Utility in Macroeconomics." *Quarterly Journal of Economics* 105:29–42.

Weisbrod, Burton. 1977. "Comparing Utility Functions in Efficiency Terms, or What Kinds of Utility Functions Do We Want?" *American Economic Review* 77:291–95.

von Weizsacker, C. C. 1971. "Notes on Endogenous Changes in Tastes." *Journal of Economic Theory* 3:345–72.

Wilson, Timothy D., and Jonathan W. Schooler. 1991. "Thinking Too Much: Introspection Can Reduce the Quality of Preferences and Decisions." *Journal of Personality and Social Psychology* 60:181–92.

20.

THE MORAL JUSTIFICATION OF BENEFIT/COST ANALYSIS

Donald C. Hubin

Benefit/cost analysis is a technique for evaluating programs, procedures, and actions; it is not a moral theory. There is significant controversy over the moral justification of benefit/cost analysis. When a procedure for evaluating social policy is challenged on moral grounds, defenders frequently seek a justification by construing the procedure as the practical embodiment of a correct moral theory. This has the apparent advantage of avoiding difficult empirical questions concerning such matters as the consequences of using the procedure. So, for example, defenders of benefit/cost analysis (BCA) are frequently tempted to argue that this procedure *just is* the calculation of moral rightness—perhaps that what it *means* for an action to be morally right is just for it to have the best benefit-to-cost ratio given the accounts of "benefit" and "cost" that BCA employs.[1] They suggest, in defense of BCA, that they have found the moral calculus—Bentham's "unabashed arithmetic of morals." To defend BCA in this manner is to commit oneself to one member of a family of moral theories (let us call them *benefit/cost moral theories* or *B/C moral theories*) and, also, to the view that if a procedure is (so to speak) the direct implementation of a correct moral theory, then it is a justified procedure. Neither of these commitments is desirable, and so the temptation to justify BCA by direct appeal to a B/C moral theory should be resisted; it constitutes an unwarranted shortcut to moral foundations—in this case, an unsound foundation. Critics of

Economics and Philosophy 10, no. 2 (1994): 169–94.

BCA are quick to point out the flaws of B/C moral theories, and to conclude that these undermine the justification of BCA. But the failure to justify BCA by a direct appeal to B/C moral theory does not show that the technique is unjustified. There is hope for BCA, even if it does not lie with B/C moral theory.

In defense of these claims, I begin (in section 1) with a slightly fuller account of the strategy of moral justification to be criticized and a brief sketch of what B/C moral theory would look like. There are several different versions it might take, but certain features will be common to all variants. In virtue of these common features, I dismiss all variants of B/C moral theory without detailed consideration. I argue in section 2 that even if some version of B/C moral theory were correct, it is unlikely that unrestricted use of B/C would be morally justified—that is, it is unlikely that B/C moral theory would endorse unrestricted employment of BCA. BCA appears to be doubly damned. However, in section 3 I sketch two arguments for the justification of a restricted use of BCA. Both arguments depend on the assertion that BCA yields information that it is reasonable to suppose is of moral importance. Different moral theories will interpret the information in different ways and accord it different roles, but most moral theories current in our society, and indeed most plausible moral theories, will take a higher benefit-to-cost ratio to be correlated, *ceteris paribus,* with moral preferability.

1. Benefit/Cost Moral Theories

The short-cut defense of BCA holds that BCA is the direct implementation of the correct moral theory. But the notion of "directly implementing" requires some clarification. It is difficult to define this term in a way that is neutral between axiological and deontological theories. Perhaps a pair of examples will illustrate the concept of *direct implementation.* Imagine, first, a moral theory according to which actions are right if and only if they maximize some value, v. The procedure that directly implements this theory is that of determining the set of alternative actions that maximize v and then performing one member of that set. In contrast, such a theory might be *indirectly* implemented by attempting to produce a merely satisfactory, rather than a maximum, quantity of v, by attempting to maximize some other value, or by attempting to conform to certain constraints. It is possible for v to be more effectively produced by indirect than by direct means.[2] Second, consider a theory that holds that actions are right just in case they don't violate any member of a set of rules. Such a theory would be directly implemented by the procedure of determining the set of actions that satisfy the rules in question and performing one of those actions. An *indirect* implementation might have us attempt to conform to some other sets of rules or to maximize some value. It is possible that an indirect implementation of a set of rules would be more effective in producing conformance with the rules than would a direct implementation. (I shall use "directly grounds" as the converse of "directly implements," so that a moral theory directly grounds a procedure that directly implements it.)

A theory that does not endorse its direct implementation will be called *self-effacing,*[3] while one that does recommend its direct implementation will be called *self-promoting*. Defenders of the short-cut strategy, then, assume that some variant of B/C moral theory is both correct and self-promoting. Before attacking each of these assumptions, we will briefly consider two forms of B/C moral theory.

At the heart of any moral theory that could directly ground BCA will be the concept of a Potential Pareto Improvement (PPI) as measured by individuals' willingness to pay (or accept compensation) for proposed changes. We should begin our examination of the moral theories that can be said to directly ground BCA with a discussion of the concept and moral significance of a Potential Pareto Improvement.

One state, s_1, represents a PPI over another, s_2, just in case (roughly) there exists *in principle* some way to redistribute the benefits in s_1 so as to achieve a third state, s_3, which is Pareto superior to s_2. (The in-principle method of redistributing need not take account of transfer costs.) For present purposes, *Pareto superiority* is defined as follows: A state, s_1, is Pareto superior to another, s_2, if and only if no one is worse off in s_2 than in s_1 and at least one person is better off in s_2 than in s_1. There is nothing in the concept of a PPI itself that implies anything about the specific interpretation of "better off" and "worse off," but B/C moral theories interpret these in terms of the individual's willingness to pay for a proposed change (WTP) and willingness to accept compensation for a proposed change (WTA).

Perhaps the most obvious candidate for a moral theory that directly grounds BCA would be one that prescribes those actions that produce the best consequences where the goodness of the consequences is proportional to the ratio of benefits to costs, with these being measured by the willingness to pay for a proposed change and the willingness to accept compensation for a proposed change of contemporary individual agents. Let us call this the *consequentialist version of B/C moral theory.*

We could view BCA as being the implementation of a nonconsequentialist moral theory, too. For example, consider the following rights-based theory that is not wholly consequentialistic (indeed, is not wholly axiological). Let us call it *deontological B/C moral theory*. This theory holds that people have *ab initio* a presumptive right to their current endowments. The theory does not offer a basis for these rights; rather, it employs these rights to impose restrictions on actions. Unlike most popular rights-based theories, this theory is quite permissive with respect to rights violations. These presumptive rights are to be violated, according to the theory, when and only when doing so brings about a Potential Pareto Improvement (with this measured according to the WTP/WTA standard).[4] Projects, of course, change endowments, and the new endowments define the rights that must be employed in evaluating future changes.

Though these two moral theories are structured quite differently, they both have as a cornerstone the notion of a PPI and they both determine PPIs by reference to WTP/WTA information. Therein lies their undoing. Any moral theory committed to the PPI criterion (measured by WTP/WTA) is unacceptable for a variety of independent reasons. While I argue later that BCA is not undermined by the refutation of B/C moral theory, many of the criticisms of BCA are, in fact, criticisms of B/C moral theory. And, construed as such, they are effective.[5] I make no attempt here to justify this claim nor even to be exhaustive in listing the criticisms I believe *are* effective against B/C moral theory. But here are a few:

1. Because of its commitment to the PPI criterion and the WTP/WTA test, B/C moral theory accords a morally unjustified status to the current state of affairs. The desirability of a state of affairs is always measured against the *status quo* and the magnitude of improvements is measured by WTP/WTA, which is, notoriously, sensitive to current endowments.
2. Because of its commitments to the PPI criterion, B/C moral theory fails to accord the appropriate role to considerations of distributive justice.
3. Because of its commitment to the WTP/WTA test, B/C moral theory fails to accord the proper moral status to future generations and to those individuals (both human and nonhuman) lacking in the cognitive capacities necessary to display a WTP/WTA.
4. Because of its commitment to the WTP/WTA test, B/C moral theory exhibits a naïve form of subjectivism, endorsing whatever errors and ignorance are incorporated in an individual's WTP/WTA.

These are not flaws in the finish of B/C moral theory; they are cracks—perhaps chasms—in the core. If the justification of BCA depends on the acceptability of B/C moral theory, it is doomed.

2. Theory and Practice: From B/C Moral Theories to Benefit/Cost Analysis

The attempt to justify BCA on the grounds that it is the direct implementation of the correct moral theory—that it *is* the moral calculus—depends on two claims: first, that some variant of B/C moral theory is the correct moral theory; and, second, that if a practice is the direct implementation of a moral theory, then that moral theory endorses the practice. The first is false. But suppose it weren't; suppose that some form of B/C moral theory were an adequate moral theory. Would this alone serve to justify the practice of BCA?

No. That is to say, the correctness of some version of B/C moral theory does not guarantee that the practice of BCA is morally justified; B/C moral theories may be self-effacing—they may not recommend engaging in a practice of BCA (indeed, they may recommend *against* doing so).

This is not a peculiarity of B/C moral theories—nor is it even unique to *moral* theories. Any consequentialistic normative theory (be it one of morality, rationality, prudence, or whatever) that does not define the goodness of an outcome (at least in part) by whether the theory is directly implemented is open to this possibility.[6] (Self-effacement can occur with nonconsequentialist theories as well. A moral theory that tells us, as much as possible, to conform our behavior to some set of rules might, depending on empirical considerations, recommend that we not *try* to conform to those rules.)

Jeremy Bentham seemed unaware of the possibility that utilitarianism is self-effacing when he wrote, "[t]he principle of utility is capable of being consistently pursued; and *it is but tautology* to say, that the more consistently it is pursued, the better it must ever be for humankind" (1948, p. 13; emphasis added).[7] But John Stuart Mill's discussion of the importance of secondary moral rules as a solution to the problem of calculating utility shows a subtle awareness of the possibility that utilitarianism is self-effacing (Mill, 1968, p. 265).

Some have taken self-effacement to be an indictment of a moral theory. The thinking appears to go as follows: the *raison d'être* of a normative theory is to guide action. If a normative theory fails *by its own lights* to be an adequate action guide—that is, if it is self-effacing—it cannot be an acceptable normative theory. It is analogous to a descriptive theory entailing its own falsity; such a theory cannot be true and hence cannot be acceptable.

If this is correct, then there is yet another serious problem with the shortcut defense of BCA, for there is reason to suspect that B/C moral theory *is* self-effacing. Indeed, it is surely *partly* self-effacing, since there are undoubtedly situations in which the attempt to determine which action maximizes the B/C ratio is more costly than the difference between the best and the worst alternative. In such a situation, B/C moral theory is wisely self-effacing. But B/C moral theory may be self-effacing for more profound reasons—reasons having nothing to do with the costs of calculation. As a result, B/C moral theory may be self-effacing even when the results of BCA are obtained cost-free. Consider social decisions that concern issues about which people have strong moral convictions. These may well be cases in which there are likely to be costs attached to the reliance on BCA information in public decision-making. The costs in question might involve the perception instilled in citizens that the government is without principle and views its citizens as consumers to be satisfied rather than as rational agents with political and moral arguments to be given and weighed. People may well be willing to pay to live in a society in which certain issues (the punishment of criminals, the legal status of abortion, the laws securing freedom of religion and association, for example) are not decided by doing benefit/cost analysis.[8] If so, then B/C moral theories may be self-effacing as a result of these sorts of costs.

While B/C moral theories are certainly self-effacing in some actual cases, the fact is that no one really knows when B/C moral theories would recommend their direct implementation—that is, the use of benefit/cost analysis on individual occasions to determine social policy. B/C moral theories tell us that an action, program, project, policy, or practice is morally permissible if, and only if, the ratio of WTP to WTA is higher for that action, etc., than for any available alternative. The justification of the practice of using BCA to evaluate, rank, and choose between various social projects, then, would require demonstration that the ratio of WTP to WTA is higher for this practice than for any available alternative. A BCA establishing this has yet to be done.[9]

One attempting to defend the use of BCA by appeal to some form of B/C moral theory is confronted, then, not only with the problem of defending that form of B/C moral theory—an impossible task in itself—but of showing that the doing of BCA passes the BCA test. This latter thesis is empirical and undefended.[10] There are reasons to suspect that B/C moral theory would *not* endorse unqualified use of BCA; we should not begin with the assumption that it would.

Suppose it did not; indeed, suppose that B/C moral theory entails that we ought never to do a benefit/cost analysis, nor even to base any of our policies on such an analysis if the results were given to us cost-free. Would this provide yet another reason to reject B/C moral theory? Is the fact that a theory is completely self-effacing a reason to reject it?

No. Suppose a normative theory, *T,* tells us that we ought to maximize some value, *V*. Suppose, further, that circumstances were such that, *I,* the direct implementation of *T* (that is, the direct pursuit of *V* by trying to measure the degree to which alternatives promote *V* and performing those actions that are believed to maximize *V*) did not maximize *V*. If *T* were an otherwise adequate theory, it would hardly be an objection to it that it didn't recommend *I*. After all, *I* does not maximize the value that *T* tells us to maximize; it would be inconsistent for *T* to tell us to make an exception here. *T* tells us to maximize *V*; it tells us to follow *I* only contingently, if at all (Hubin and Perkins, 1986; see also Parfit, 1984, chap. 1).

As Mill notes (1968, p. 265), people are not inclined to reject self-effacing principles in areas of practical concern outside of ethics (and, one should now add, rationality and public policy). It is no flaw in the principle of maximizing profit that this is sometimes best achieved by forgetting about profit altogether and focusing on such other considerations as customer service, product quality, and corporate integrity. Telling a novice bowler to forget about the pins and try to throw the ball through the lane markers at a certain point hardly commits one to the view that the ultimate standard of bowling is not the number of pins knocked down.

It is sometimes alleged that the moral principles of a just society must be public. That is to say, a principle cannot be a principle of justice if it would be wrong for that principle to be publicly known.[11] While I am not sympathetic to this requirement, its validity need not detain us here. It is irrelevant. In the sense in which I have been using the term, a self-effacing theory need not advocate deception or concealment. A theory is self-effacing if it does not recommend its direct implementation. This is fully consistent with a publicity requirement. A self-effacing utilitarian theory could endorse its public recognition consistent with recommending that public policy be limited by certain side-constraints "entitled to govern absolutely [such things as] the dealings of society with the individual in the way of compulsion and control" (Mill, 1968, p. 129).

There is no reason for taking the potential (or even actual) self-effacement of B/C moral theories to be a further criticism of those theories. The correctness of B/C moral theories is logically independent of the correctness of actually *using* B/C moral theory by directly implementing it. This fact, and the difficult empirical questions involved in bridging the logical gap, render bleak the prospects for the direct approach to the justification of BCA by appeal to a B/C moral theory. Such an approach has two hurdles to clear. Clearing the first seems completely impossible; clearing the second only slightly less so. Some may take this to result in dim prospects for any justification of BCA. But such a conclusion would be hasty and unwarranted. In fact, the recognition that the correctness of a moral theory doesn't ensure the correctness of its direct implementation opens up an entirely new approach for the justification of a practice, for it suggests that even if B/C moral theories are inadequate, the practice of BCA may still be justified.[12]

An analogy may illuminate. Many accept the moral justification of allowing certain sorts of social decisions to be decided by a majority vote. How could this be defended? Surely the most naïve way would be to argue for what we might call *democratic moral theory*—the theory that the right action just *is* that action approved of by the majority—and that the democratic procedure is, therefore, the moral calculus. Democratic moral theory is clearly unacceptable. But this is a matter of no concern for the democrat; he has never felt that his commitment to democratic institutions committed him to democratic moral theory. Rather, the democrat sets about justifying democracy by appeal to other, more plausible moral theories. The proponent of BCA should do likewise.

3. The Justification of BCA

The attempt to justify the funding of and reliance on BCA by claiming it to be the direct implementation of the correct moral theory is not promising. But, were this the only way to justify a decision-making procedure, democracy itself would be in trouble. Democratic decision-making may be morally justified for a range of issues confronting the public, despite the failure of its corresponding moral theory. Similarly, there is a range of public issues for which it is plausible to suggest that the funding of benefit/cost analyses and the reliance on the results of those analyses to guide (or possibly even to determine) public policy are warranted. The failure of B/C moral theories no more undermines the use of BCA than does the failure of democratic moral theory undermine the use of democratic mechanisms.[13]

Various approaches to the justification of BCA are available. Justifications will differ both with respect to the range of application and the role in deliberation they assign to BCA. Some will hold that it is appropriate for all social decisions (or, conceivably, for all decisions of *any* sort). More modest versions will restrict the range of applicability, holding that the technique has, for example, no place in the individual acts of sentencing criminals or the establishment of the basic freedoms that make liberal democracy possible. Justifications will also vary in the role given to BCAs. The most ambitious view would hold that, where BCA is applicable, it determines the correct decision. That is, society should implement those projects with the highest benefit-to-cost ratio until its budget is expended or the costs exceed the benefits regardless of other considerations. Less ambitious approaches would hold that BCA plays some "less than definitive" role in decision-making, even where its use is appropriate. (And, of course, one might wish to assign a differential role to BCA depending on the issue to which it is being applied.)

There are two distinct but compatible kinds of reasons one might have for assigning a less than determining role to BCA (or to any decision process, for that matter). First, one might hold that the unaugmented procedure is less likely to come to the correct decision than is the procedure when supplemented in specified ways. Call this an *outcome-oriented reason.* One might believe, for instance, that when social decisions involve infringement on important rights or risks to life, BCA must be augmented in order to arrive at (or maximize the likelihood of arriving at) the correct answer.[14] In addition to reasons of this sort, there are also *process-oriented reasons* for limiting the role of benefit/cost analysis. These reasons can, perhaps, best be understood negatively, as non-outcome-oriented reasons. An example will illustrate a common variety of process-oriented reasons. Parents typically allow children some say so in matters that affect them and, if the consequences of error are not too great, sometimes even a determining role. This is frequently *not* because the decision made is likely to be better given the child's role in making it. It is because of other benefits of the child's playing that role in the process. Similarly, one might hold that while certain decisions are likely to be better if made strictly in accordance with B/C criteria, allowing democratic procedures to determine the outcome, while almost certain to cause deviations from the best decisions, is justified because of the value (intrinsic or instrumental) of participatory democracy.[15]

Whatever range and role one seeks to justify for BCA, the best way to give a full moral justification of a procedure would be to begin with the correct moral theory and show that the procedure in question is endorsed by it. But, since there is significant disagreement about what is the correct moral theory, no noncontroversial starting place presents itself. One could, of course, simply assume some moral theory to be correct and then show that it endorses the procedure. This might be of broad intellectual interest but would be of practical interest only to those who accepted the moral theory assumed to be correct. Absent antecedent agreement on moral theory, the ideal approach would be to *demonstrate* the unique adequacy of a particular moral theory thereby forcing rational assent to it; then, one could set about showing that this theory endorsed the procedure. Such an ambitious approach is beyond my present scope (not to mention ability). Another alternative, more closely related to the one pursued here, is this: Show that BCA is endorsed by *every* viable moral theory—an ambitious project in its own way, to be sure—too ambitious to undertake here. The strategy pursued here is a poor second-cousin of this bold strategy.

I want to sketch two different approaches to the justification of a practical decision procedure. These approaches promise less than those just outlined and, so, are more likely to fulfill their promise. One might be labeled a probabilistic moral argument for the funding of and reliance upon benefit/cost analyses. It is founded on the observation that the information contained in a competently conducted benefit/cost analysis will be deemed morally significant and useful by most plausible moral theories. That is to say, it is likely that, whatever the correct moral theory turns out to be, it will take a higher BCA ranking to be *prima facie* evidence that there is a *pro tanto* reason to prefer a project. Moreover, it is likely to recommend use of the information contained in the benefit/cost analysis in making a social decision. This fact provides some moral reason for conducting and employing benefit/cost analyses, and perhaps for supporting institutions that employ a strict B/C rule for certain types of decisions.

Another line of argumentation, which runs parallel to the above in certain respects, is suggested by a long-standing strategy implicit in the liberal justification of the state.[16] This strategy does not seek agreement on ultimate values; it explicitly eschews, for example, appeal to the nature of the good life as a basis for justifying the institutions it aims to justify. Rather, it attempts to justify an institution (the state, for example) as a necessary means to the attainment of whatever the individual citizens aim at. In this respect, the justification is not philosophical but political; it is quite frankly an *ad hominem* argument, appealing to the ends and values of the audience to which it is addressed.[17]

On the liberal view, people with radically different moral ideals and conceptions of the good life can, nevertheless, agree on common political institutions because these institutions are necessary to the achievement of whatever ideals these people might have.[18] This is the founding faith of pluralistic society. The relative stability of many liberal pluralistic societies is some evidence that it is not misplaced faith. Following this insight, I suggest that the use of BCA is warranted by the moral views that enjoy currency in our society. That is to say, according to the (often partly inchoate) moral views held in our society, the information incorporated in a competent benefit/cost analysis is morally relevant. To the extent that citizens want to make choices about public policy that are, by their own lights, morally responsible, there is a reason for them to attend to the results of benefit/cost analyses.

In making this argument, I do not assume the B/C moral theory is a widely held moral theory. Few, presumably, would hold that the information contained in a benefit/cost analysis is all that is morally relevant or that the procedure attaches all the appropriate weights to the individual costs and benefits measured. The conclusions of a benefit/cost analysis will be judged by most to be readily defeasible; *what* may serve as a defeater will vary from one moral view to another, but the fact of defeasibility remains. Still, a recommendation founded appropriately on morally relevant information is useful even if defeasible.[19] Some may hold that, by itself, a favorable B/C ratio provides *no* reason (not even a defeasible—that is, *pro tanto*—one) to pursue a project (Copp, 1987, p. 80). Even if this were true, to the extent that BCA provides us with a measure (even an imperfect one) of the degree to which people expect that their intrinsic preferences will be satisfied by various programs or projects, it provides us with *information* that is morally relevant.[20] This is what I mean by the claim that the fact that a project has a high B/C ratio is *prima facie* evidence of a *pro tanto* moral reason to undertake it. In a particular case, the evidence itself may be defeated, undermining the claim that there is any reason, even a *pro tanto* one, to undertake the project. Even if the reason does exist, though, it may be overridden by other moral considerations.

The Role and Range of Benefit/Cost Analysis

I shall limit discussion of the justification of BCA to those positions holding that such a procedure has restricted applicability and, even within this range of issues, is not to play the role of determining decision. This is a modest, but still contested, position. The objections leveled against B/C moral theory suggest that enforcing such a doubly limited role for BCA is prudent.

While the possibility that the correct moral theory is self-effacing entails that the correct moral theory *could* endorse the unrestricted and determinative use of BCA, this seems unlikely in light of the nature and severity of problems with B/C moral theory, which suggest limitations of the procedure of BCA.

It is relatively easy to generate a list of plausible reasons for rejecting a strict and unrestricted adherence to BCA in deciding matters of public policy. I make no attempt to be encyclopedic; rather, I present several considerations that seem salient.

1. *Benefit/cost analysis itself does not allow any role for side-constraints on government action.* Those who accept a deontological moral theory will obviously have reason to be concerned with this omission. (It is, of course, *possible* that one has the best chance of complying with the side-constraints morality imposes, if there are any, by following decision procedures that do not incorporate side-constraints. But this seems a *bare* possibility—not worth taking seriously for practical purposes unless some evidence of its truth is forthcoming.) It is important to see that the absence of side-constraints on government action—indeed the absence of any provisions for handling such constraints—will be of concern not only to deontologists but to many consequentialists as well. The most brilliant defense of individual liberty in the English language, John Stuart Mill's *On Liberty,* grounds moral side-constraints on government action solely on considerations of utility. Mill offers a variety of utilitarian arguments in favor of liberty. The most interesting from our point of view is also the one on which Mill rests the most weight:

> [T]he strongest of all the arguments against the interference of the public with purely personal conduct is that when it does interfere, the odds are that it interferes wrongly and in the wrong place. (1968, p. 198)

Mill gives here, and in the subsequent passages, an argument that the *direct* implementation of a utilitarian theory is dangerous—that it is better to accept rigid side-constraints on government action as a *strategy* for maximizing utility. He would not endorse a procedure lacking such side-constraints as one that should determine government policy.[21]

An argument of similar structure may well show the desirability from a consequentialist point of view of imposing side-constraints on government action. Presumably, constitutional limitations like the Bill of Rights (which are intended to serve this purpose) are attractive to consequentialists as well as to deontologists.

2. *The subjective expectation of preference satisfaction is the only value directly measured by BCA.* While it is plausible to assume that this is an indicator of states of affairs that are morally important, it is quite implausible to assume that it is a perfect indicator of all that is morally relevant. People's estimates of intrinsic preference satisfaction may be distorted by ignorance or er-

ror, and individual good (and *a fortiori* overall moral good) plausibly consists in more than intrinsic preference satisfaction. Furthermore, to the extent that BCA equates people's estimates of their intrinsic preference satisfaction with WTP/WTA and measures this behaviorally, behavioral irrationalities will sometimes deprive the numbers of even their usual significance.

3. *The reliance of BCA on the WTP/WTA criterion skews its analysis in favor of those with greater initial endowments (see Copp, 1987).* Equal WTP does not entail equal expected intrinsic preference satisfaction, equal happiness, or equality of any other quantity reasonably held to be of intrinsic moral value.

4. *BCA shows its utilitarian roots by being indifferent to matters of distribution.* Individual costs and benefits are summed; the recommendation is based on the aggregate net benefit. This is a damning objection—even if it is not seen as such by all.[22]

These considerations, and more that could be stated, suggest that there are quite likely to be result-oriented objections to BCA. Were it possible to define a sphere of social issues with regard to which BCA incorporated all that was morally relevant and weighed it in the proper way in coming to a recommendation, there would be no result-oriented objections to allowing BCA to be determinative within that sphere. I am not optimistic about the possibility of doing this in any helpful way.[23] And, in any event, this would not defuse process-oriented objections, which I take seriously. There is an important moral difference between democratic institutions and bureaucratic or dictatorial ones even if they reach the same decisions.[24]

For both result- and process-oriented reasons, it is appropriate to limit the role of BCA to that of informational input into a broader decision-making framework. The exact nature of this broader practice is a problem in applied political philosophy that is far beyond the present scope. Presumably, though, it will involve administrative, democratic, and judicial elements.

Taking the role of BCA to be the weak, but important, one of informational input into a broader decision mechanism may seem to make the procedure so noncontroversial that there is no need to restrict its application. But this is not so. Information is not cost-free; there are costs involved in gathering information and, sometimes, in using it. With respect to some judgments, BCA may be so unlikely to give us new, morally relevant information that it is not worth the expenditure required to do it. More interestingly, there may be areas in which the information contained in a BCA even if attained cost-free should not be considered. These might be cases in which the use of benefit/cost information tends to lead people to the wrong conclusion.[25]

The question of what areas of social decision-making should not be informed by BCA (because of either sort of costs discussed above) will not be answered precisely or conclusively here. It seems plausible, though, to suppose that BCA will have little to tell us about the determination of fundamental moral principles upon which governmental policy is based: the rights of individuals, the goals of government, and so on. It would be inappropriate, also, to decide issues of individual criminal guilt and sentencing by BCA (though issues of what actions to criminalize and what sorts of sentences to impose generally may benefit by being informed by BCA). In contrast, the allocation of scarce resources seems to be a problem about which BCA is likely to provide useful morally relevant information.[26]

If BCA is to be used to provide informational input into a broader social decision mechanism, it is important to consider what information is included in such an analysis and how this information is aggregated and analyzed. What BCA purports to offer us is a measure of collective intrinsic preference satisfaction. It begins with individual WTP/WTA information. This is, I believe, an indication of intrinsic preference satisfaction. It is not a perfect indication by any means. People can be wrong about their intrinsic preferences; they can, because of ignorance or error, have a willingness to pay for a change that does not reflect their intrinsic preferences; and they can behave in ways that do not reflect their true willingness to pay. These problems do not undermine the claim that individual WTP/WTA is an indication of intrinsic preference satisfaction. This is important because, as I shall argue soon, plausible moral theories will take such information to be, *prima facie,* of moral relevance.

It is, of course, one thing to believe that individual WTP/WTA is an indicator of individual intrinsic preference satisfaction and quite another to think that when this information has been aggregated as it is in BCA it gives us any morally relevant information. Perhaps the BCA procedure turns signal into noise; it would not be the first procedure to do so. There is no doubt that the aggregation of individual WTP/WTA information introduces additional problems because of the sensitivity of an individual's willingness to pay (and willingness to accept compensation) for changes to that individual's current endowment. Recognizing the respect in which BCA might be thought to skew that morally relevant information conveyed by individual WTP/WTA is not sufficient to show that the BCA process "turns signal into noise." Skewed indicators may still be useful indicators, provided we understand the ways in which they are skewed.[27]

There are, though, grounds for worrying that the results of BCA are genuinely without informative content. Consider the following analogy:

> Suppose everyone is given a ballot and a crayon. Each person is asked to indicate his preference among alternative projects by coloring the square next to the most preferred alternative the darkest, the square next to the least preferred the lightest, and so on. The relative darkness of the colors on the ballot give us an individual's ranking of the alternatives. Now suppose that a color wheel is made up for each alternative, with each person's colored square for the alternative being put on the wheel. We spin the

> wheels, and rank the alternatives in order of the darkness of the spinning wheels. Call this method, *color analysis*. Is there any reason to think that color analysis gives us *prima facie* evidence of a *pro tanto* reason to choose the project with the darkest looking color wheel? Remember, each person has a different-colored crayon and there is no standard for how dark one should color the square beside the thing one prefers most.[28]

This challenge raises issues to which I certainly can't respond adequately here. For example, the problem of interpersonal comparisons of utility (hinted at in the analogy) is not likely to be resolved quickly. It is worth noting, though, that the analogy need not be accepted in its entirety. First, it does not appear that BCA involves anything analogous to aggregating the darkness of "different-colored crayons."[29] BCA measures individual intrinsic preference satisfaction in terms of an individual's WTP/WTA, which employs a common measure, typically money. It seems the analogy should be one in which all are given the same color crayon. Someone denying the possibility of interpersonal comparisons of utility might well object to BCA precisely because it gives to each the same color crayon to represent things that are incommensurable.

In addition, it is true that there is nothing in color analysis that indicates how darkly to color each of one's choices. (This seems a virtue of the theory since any attempt to do so would impose an—arbitrary, I think—interval scale on individuals. For some, the difference in the preferability of the first and last place alternative may be great, while for others it may be negligible.) But it is also true that each person's crayon is of finite length, and the more darkly one colors a square, the more of one's crayon is consumed. Individuals have to budget their crayons accordingly. Of course, individuals begin with crayons of different lengths, and this has to be taken into account after one has spun the wheels and completed one's color analysis. But, this does not seem to be the sort of problem that deprives color analysis of conveying morally relevant information. The issue may not divide along the "length-of-crayon" dimension. Even where it does, we may find that the options preferred by those with the longer crayons do not fare well in color analysis. Since such analysis, as a technique for determining intrinsic preference satisfaction, favors those with longer crayons, to the extent that we deem the satisfaction of intrinsic preferences morally valuable, we have reason *a fortiori* to oppose that alternative. Finally, unlike color analysis, BCA, if based on market behavior rather than interviews, looks at behavior that agents engage in for reasons independent of the analysis; that is, the behavior is not engaged in for the purpose of providing information for BCA. This tends to lessen the risk of "strategically" motivated behavior—behavior that intentionally misrepresents preferences in order to better satisfy them.

Clearly, much more needs to be said in defense of the aggregation procedure involved in BCA. I think, though, that it is quite plausible to assert that BCA gives us a view of overall intrinsic preference satisfaction. It must be remembered that few will think that overall intrinsic preference satisfaction is all that is morally relevant. Furthermore, the view of overall intrinsic preference satisfaction BCA affords is flawed and distorted, but still contains useful information.

A Multitude of Justifications

After discussing some of the more straightforward approaches to the justification of BCA, I will develop the previously outlined defense of the funding and use of benefit/cost analyses for certain types of social projects. It is inspired by the liberal insight alluded to earlier. This political justification will run parallel to a somewhat unconventional probabilistic moral argument that has the more conventional *aim* of giving a moral justification of a practice.

THE UTILITARIAN DEFENSE OF BENEFIT/COST ANALYSIS

In attempting to justify BCA, one might naturally look to a utilitarian theory. BCA is not the direct implementation of any standard version of utilitarianism;[30] rather, it directly implements some version of B/C moral theory. But, as I have argued, a theory may well justify employing some practical decision mechanism other than its direct implementation. It could be, then, that BCA would find a utilitarian defense acceptable, despite not being the direct practical implementation of utilitarianism.

The defense might go like this. Institutions are justified by their beneficial consequences. While utilitarian theories differ concerning their standard of value, plausible theories will hold that individual well-being is at least partly constituted by the degree to which individual intrinsic desires are satisfied. For a number of reasons, it is reasonable to suppose that, in general, individuals are likely to be the best judges of what will satisfy their intrinsic desires. (The fact that people sometimes fail spectacularly does not refute this.) It is also reasonable to suppose that, in general, people's willingness to pay for some change reflects their *ex ante* evaluation of the degree to which the change will satisfy their intrinsic desires. Thus, we may plausibly take individual willingness to pay to be a *defeasible* indicator of the relative *intra*-personal benefit of changes. That is, if an individual is willing to pay more for one change than another, it is reasonable to suppose (in the absence of contrary or undermining evidence) that the former satisfies her intrinsic desires more than the latter.

Summing the WTP (and WTA) across individuals involves, of course, a large additional step—especially because WTP is influenced by ability to pay. A poor man, willing to pay half his annual salary for an operation to save the life of his child, desires his end more, I would suppose, than a wealthy man who is willing to spend the same *amount* of money to jet overseas to watch the

Wimbledon finals desires his. To use BCA as a final arbiter for all public decisions would be objectionable to a utilitarian for this reason if for no other.[31] One could seek to rectify this in a number of ways. For example, one could introduce a weighting factor to adjust for differential incomes. Or, one could attempt to measure WTP hypothetically upon equal incomes, though this magnifies the practical problems of measurement. An alternative approach would be to restrict either the range of applicability or the role of BCA. While some public projects may divide people along lines of wealth, many do not. The use of BCA could be restricted to issues unlikely to show such division. Alternatively, if BCA is not taken to be the final arbiter, division along lines of wealth could be noted and taken into account in the broader procedure in which BCA plays a part. I have explicitly provided for this last approach by restricting our discussion to the justification of BCA within a limited range and with a limited role.

A society may choose *on utilitarian grounds* to do benefit/cost analyses and to take the recommendations very seriously—even to follow a B/C rule—for many kinds of projects. Surely, a BCA constitutes something much less than a full utilitarian appraisal of all of society's actions and expenditures. Its aims are more modest than that. It seeks to guide action piecemeal—making adjustments at the margin—in a way that can be expected, at least if conjoined with policies based on more traditional utilitarian evaluations of the basic structure of society, to lead to desirable outcomes in the long run. As a utilitarian can defend the market, so she can defend BCA as a rectification for market imperfections. And, of course, as she can justify limiting the scope or effect of the unfettered marketplace, so she can justify diverging from the action recommended by BCA. But limiting the scope or effect of the market hardly constitutes a rejection of the market. And diverging from the recommendations of BCA hardly constitutes a rejection of BCA.

Hypothetical Agreement

One of the most influential approaches to the justification of procedures and institutions is based on the notion of hypothetical agreement (which I will understand broadly to include both hypothetical contract and hypothetical consent). Sometimes combined with a utilitarian standard (for example, Harsanyi, 1977) but more frequently used to ground an explicitly nonutilitarian alternative, this approach seeks to show that institutions, procedures, or practices are justified because they would have been agreed to by certain relevant parties in some nonactual situation. The roots of this approach are traceable at least to the political philosophy of Thomas Hobbes. (See Hobbes, 1969.)

Although it is sometimes missed, it is absolutely crucial to note that the considerable force of this approach comes not from the notion of agreement (contract or consent) so much as from the hypothesis under which the agreement would take place. Hypothetical agreement is not a kind of agreement, it is a kind of hypothesis. Because it is only hypothetical, the agreement does not, in itself, have actual moral force. Its moral force rests entirely on the nature of the situation in which people would make the agreement. Thus, employment of the PPI criterion cannot be justified on the grounds that actual Pareto improvements are agreeable to all and, thus, *potential* Pareto improvements are *hypothetically* agreeable because they are hypothetically Pareto improvements. That is, the fact that the losers *would* agree to the project if the winners compensated them at their WTA (and that the winners *could* do so) does not, by itself, show anything of moral significance. Such a naïve approach is a caricature of hypothetical agreement.[32]

But a more traditional and plausible defense of BCA along hypothetical consent lines can be offered. To a large extent, it mirrors that sketched for the utilitarian defense. Plausible hypothetical agreement theories make justification turn (at least partly) on the degree to which institutions function to satisfy individual intrinsic desires. They ask us to imagine people in an initial bargaining situation that is (claimed to be) ideal for making decisions about institutions and procedures and to determine what such people would agree to. There can be no general answer to the question of what people would agree to from the initial bargaining situation in a contractarian theory because there is no generally accepted characterization of that situation. However, the idealizing assumptions typically involve improved knowledge of the consequences of actions, idealized reasoning abilities, and (frequently) ignorance of one's own station in life.

It is eminently arguable that people thus situated would approve of the use of BCA as a part of a broader process of public decision-making because of the degree to which the results of BCA can indicate desirable changes. Such people would, many contractarians argue, be especially worried about how the worst-off will fare,[33] but even if this is a pressing concern it is certainly not the only concern such contractors would have. While I do not argue, indeed I deny, that they would accept a B/C moral theory as a conception of justice, this does not show that they would not accept the use of BCA as a means of generating relevant and important information for decisions about public policy for a variety of different issues, or even as a decisive rule for certain social institutions having a limited scope.

Concern for the distribution of individual goods is characteristic of hypothetical agreement theories. As we have seen, BCA does not share this concern. But the conception of the bargaining solution accepted by a hypothetical contractarian need not be indifferent to distributive considerations for the theory to endorse institutions that rely on a B/C rule, much less to endorse ones that rely on B/C information. If such institutions are significantly more efficient in satisfying people's intrinsic preferences, and a theory takes such preference satisfaction to be part of the good of an individual, then there may be compelling reasons for agreeing to such institutions regardless of one's conception of the rational bargaining solution. Unless contractors are omniscient, they do not agree to the future course of the universe in all detail. They accept institutions that they expect will work to the long-run advantage of the worst-off, or that they expect will maximize their benefit given the similar demands of other rational agents. These institutions may well be guided by (indeed be controlled by) a rule that the contractors, themselves, do not employ in choosing institutions. But even if contractors would reject BCA as a final arbiter, they would almost certainly take the information contained in a BCA to be morally relevant information.

RIGHTS-BASED DEONTOLOGICAL THEORY

Some of the most persistent and principled objections to the use of BCA appear to be based on deontological moral theories—in particular, rights-based versions of these theories. It might seem, then, that there is little likelihood of BCA being justified on familiar versions of such theories. Such a conclusion would be hasty. Provided that the role played by BCA were one of informational input into a broader social decision process, there is good reason to suppose that plausible rights-based deontological theories would endorse the use of BCA. This is because plausible deontological theories must hold that the function of government is not merely to refrain from violating people's rights. Were this the only moral consideration relevant to government, it would be better if there were no government: What doesn't exist cannot violate rights. Presumably, at the very least, the rights-based deontologist will hold that government has a moral obligation to protect people against rights violations. If this is all that is admitted, the rights-based theorist is advocating a minimal, "night-watchman" state (Nozick, 1974, pp. 26–27).

Even the slim goal of protecting citizens against rights violations seems enough to establish the point that BCA may be endorsed by the rights-based deontologist. This is because, consistent with not violating rights, she will have reason for promoting the most efficient means of protecting rights. And, to the extent that BCA indicates efficient means, the rights-based deontologist should be interested in the information it offers. This, however, might be seen as reducing BCA to what Sagoff calls "cost-effectiveness analysis" (1988, p. 38 and pp. 195–224). While Sagoff is not particularly clear in drawing this distinction, it appears to be the following: cost-effectiveness evaluation does not take individual preference to be relevant in determining the goals of public policy. Rather, these goals are to be set entirely by political procedures. The role of the policy analyst is merely to compare the efficiencies of means to the politically determined goals. BCA, on the other hand, aspires to either set or inform the process of setting the social goals. Defenders of the night-watchman conception of the state might hold that the legitimate goals of the state are given, not by some political procedure, but by the correct moral theory. The role of BCA must be confined to determining cost-effective ways to attain these goals.

I will not attempt to clarify this distinction further,[34] nor to determine whether the night-watchman conception of the state necessarily demotes BCA to a less significant role than its proponents would like. The night-watchman conception of the state seems to me neither plausible enough, nor popular enough, to warrant such sustained discussion. More plausible rights-based theories hold that, *provided it is consistent with respect for rights,* governments have a moral reason to promote the ends of distributive justice, economic efficiency, and environmental protection. If these goals are admitted, the argument for the relevance of BCA information proceeds as it did in the consideration of the utilitarian and contractarian theories above. This may well warrant its having an official role in the determination of and administration of governmental policies.

Clearly, a rights-based deontologist will hold that there are constraints (possibly overrideable) on the projects that government may permissibly carry out. How a project affects people's rights will typically, if not always, trump B/C considerations. A person holding such a position will not be tempted by the view that BCA provides us with conclusive moral guidance. But it doesn't follow that the information in a benefit/cost analysis is morally irrelevant from this point of view. Frequently, proposed projects do not violate rights, or there are modifications to them that can avoid doing so. Furthermore, the potential benefits as measured by BCA may be sufficient to warrant overriding the rights in question (assuming the theorist allows that these rights are overrideable).

I have sketched the barest outlines of justifications for the use of BCA on a variety of fundamentally different moral theories. While the theories considered do not begin to exhaust the possibilities, they suggest the breadth of the appeal of B/C information. I think that this can reasonably be generalized. That is to say, I believe that one can reasonably conclude that B/C information will be deemed morally relevant and useful information from a wide variety of moral views. In particular, I conclude, first, that a wide variety of moral theories *currently accepted* will hold such information to be morally relevant and useful. Secondly, I believe that most *plausible* moral theories will come to this conclusion. On the first premise, I found a political argument for the use of benefit/cost analysis; on the second, a probabilistic moral argument.

The Political Argument

The determination of a procedure for the setting of social policy is a political matter. It is a mistake to think that political issues are always to be decided by appealing to basic principles. Often, perhaps usually, it is better to seek agreement on means, on procedures, and on middle- and low-level goals than to "begin at the beginning"—attempting to forge agreement on foundational principles and/or ultimate goals.

The fact that the information contained in a B/C report is morally relevant information from a broad variety of moral theories that represent the theoretical elaborations of the moral views actually current in our society means that most people should be interested in this information. That is to say, the vast majority of people in our society (I speculate) hold moral theories according to which this information is morally relevant. In the absence of a reason to suppose that gathering and employing the information in reaching a decision is too costly (either for outcome- or process-oriented reasons), most people should support the doing of BCAs and the use of information contained therein to arrive at a social decision.

This is compatible, of course, with most people believing that the recommendations of BCA are defeasible on any of a number of grounds. Those who believe this—most likely the vast majority—will view the possibility of BCA recommendations being accepted without further evaluation, or being given undue weight in the process of social deliberation, as a potential outcome-oriented reason for refraining from the doing of benefit/cost analyses. These concerns are alleviated significantly by the explicit recognition that BCA is *not* the moral calculus, that arguments based on B/C considerations are *not* the only impartial, morally relevant considerations that bear on an issue, and that there is a place for other considerations to have an appropriate role.

THE PROBABILISTIC MORAL ARGUMENT

The fact that the information contained in a properly done benefit/cost analysis is deemed morally relevant by the moral theories current in a society doesn't seem to provide any reason, in itself, to think that the information *is* morally relevant. These moral theories could be so seriously flawed that there would be no reason to think that the information they take to be morally relevant really is. But if we look to the argument made above rather than merely to its conclusion, we will see the basis for an argument that does address the moral significance of the BCA information—at least in a probabilistic way.

I have argued that according to several approaches to moral theory the information contained in a benefit/cost analysis is morally relevant. Without settling the issue of the precise nature of the correct moral theory, I claim not only that these theories are representative of those current in our society but that they are representative of the range of plausible moral theories.[35] This means that it is reasonable to expect that whatever moral theory turns out to be correct, it is likely to assign positive moral value to the satisfaction of intrinsic preferences. Therefore, it is likely to take information (even less than perfect information) about the degree to which such preferences are satisfied to be morally relevant information. And, so, it would take BCA reports to be valuable informational input into social decision procedure. This means that BCA information is likely, in general, to be morally relevant information. If it is reasonable to expect that the costs of doing such an analysis would be recouped by following a better policy as a result of the analysis, then there is reason to support the doing of and reliance upon a benefit/cost analysis.

Conclusion

To justify the use of BCA, it would be desirable first to establish the unique correctness of a specific moral theory and then to demonstrate that the use of BCA is endorsed by this theory—both daunting tasks. I set my sights much lower; I sketched two arguments, new in the literature, for a weaker result: there are good grounds for believing that institutions that employ B/C information, and perhaps follow a B/C rule, for public policy decisions on a variety of issues are endorsed by a wide range of moral theories that are both currently accepted and plausible. If so, this provides both a reason for believing that such institutions are, in fact, morally justified *and* a political argument for supporting such institutions.

Notes

This work was partly supported by the National Science Foundation (Award No. 8710153). I am very grateful for the help of Alan Randall, my co-principal investigator, and of his research assistant, Mike Farmer, who did much to bridge the disciplinary gap between philosophy and economics. I am also indebted to Dan Farrell, Diana Raffman, Daniel Hausman, and especially David Copp for assistance in clarifying and presenting my thoughts.

1. If they reject descriptive analyses of moral terms, the claim might be that the judgment that one ought to maximize the ratio of benefits to costs (given the account of "benefits" and "costs" employed by BCA) is a fundamental moral judgment—what R. M. Hare calls a "decision of principle" (1969, pp. 56–78).

2. This fact has been noticed by many at least since John Stuart Mill's discussion of it in chapter 2 of *Utilitarianism* (1968, pp. 264–66). For several recent discussions of this and related matters, see Parfit (1984, chap. 1), Elster (1983, chap. 2), and Hubin and Perkins (1986).

3. I use this term rather than "self-defeating" or "self-subverting." The former is used in Derek Parfit's (1984) discussion of these matters, the latter by myself in earlier work (Hubin and Perkins, 1986). The reason for my preference is that I am specifically speaking of a property of the moral theory in question (not, for example, a property of our attempts to realize the goals set by the moral theory), and the two alternatives might suggest to some that the-

ories that do not endorse their own direct implementation are somehow self-*refuting*. As will become clear, I mean to suggest nothing of the sort.

4. The full deontological B/C moral theory would have to incorporate the comparative aspect of BCA. This could be done by inclusion of a consequentialistic element (requiring that, when the presumptive rights are violable, they are to be violated in the way that maximizes the ratio of benefits to costs). Alternatively, and less plausibly, it could be held that individuals have a right to the most cost-effective violation of their presumptive rights.

5. There are notably bad criticisms of the PPI criterion and the WTP/WTA test, as well. This philosophical "piling on" has produced arguments designed to show that any theory that directly grounds BCA must treat things that are intrinsically valuable as merely instrumentally valuable. (Daniel Schwartzman discusses and endorses such an argument [1982, p. 73]. He attributes the argument to Steven Kelman's "Economic Incentives and Environmental Policy: Politics, Ideology, and Philosophy," a then unpublished paper, pp. 103, 106–7.) In fact, though, B/C moral theories are, in themselves, absolutely agnostic on the question of what things are of intrinsic value—or perhaps it would be better to say that, on this issue, B/C moral theories are completely deferential to individuals' preferences. If we value something intrinsically, then B/C moral theory will take it to be of intrinsic value. B/C moral theory doesn't offer a substantive theory of intrinsic value; it offers a procedure for determining what has intrinsic value.

6. For a further discussion of this specific claim, see Hubin and Perkins (1986). See also Gibbard (1986b, especially pp. 102ff. and 108–9).

7. What *is* "but tautology" is that, if the utilitarian standard is correct, then the more it is *complied with* the better it is morally. What Bentham fails to appreciate is that *pursuit* of a standard may not be in compliance with it. (Surprisingly, he also fails to appreciate here that even *compliance* with the utilitarian standard may not be best for *humankind,* since, for Bentham, the utilitarian standard counts the welfare of all sentient creatures equally.) For an interesting recent discussion of related issues, see Elster (1983, Part II). See also Hubin (1986).

8. See, for example, Rawls (1955) for the now classic statement of the argument that a direct implementation of utilitarian principles is not likely to pass the utilitarian test of moral permissibility. Rawls is wrong to think that this constitutes an objection to act utilitarianism. If his thesis about the disutility of a direct implementation of act utilitarianism is correct, it shows only that act utilitarianism is self-effacing in the sense used here. A similar point could be made with even greater plausibility about B/C moral theories.

9. The specter of regress lurks here. To know whether the practice of BCA is justified on a B/C moral theory, we would have to have done a benefit/cost analysis. And how could we know whether *this* project was justified? Apparently, only by having done another benefit/cost analysis. And so on. We are not here concerned with *how we could know* whether the practice of BCA is justified, however, but with whether it *is* justified. And, if some form of B/C moral theory is correct, then it is justified if, and only if, the ratio of WTP to WTA is greater than any alternative. And this fact is, I assume, independent of its discovery.

10. While not offering an opinion on this matter precisely, Herman Leonard and Richard Zeckhauser (1986), in their defense of BCA, suggest that the prospects for the use of BCA techniques to pass the BCA test are dim: "Cost-benefit analysis, particularly applied to public decisions involving risks to life and health, has not been notably popular" (p. 31). They suggest that the unpopularity of BCA is based on ignorance and misinformation. Alas, even if this suggestion were correct, the WTP/WTA standard fails to distinguish preferences based on ignorance and misinformation from those based on knowledge. So, whatever the source of the unpopularity of BCA, it may well be true that the use of BCA would not pass a BCA test.

11. One of the best-known exponents of this position is Rawls (1971, p. 133).

12. Diana Raffman pointed out to me that the reasoning here is rather complex. Roughly, it goes as follows: A correct moral theory need not endorse its direct implementation; but plausible moral theories will endorse *some* practical decision procedure. Every decision procedure is the direct practical implementation of *some* moral theory; therefore, the correct moral theory may endorse a decision procedure that is the direct practical implementation of some other (incorrect) moral theory. It is possible, then, that BCA, the direct implementation of an inadequate moral theory, is nevertheless endorsed by an adequate moral theory.

13. Closer to home, many who would reject what might be called a "market morality"—that is, that what is morally right is whatever the free market produces—would still endorse the use of a free market. (Witness the rise in popularity of the theory of market socialism.) The attempt to justify a practice or institution on the grounds that it is the direct implementation of the correct theory is simplistic. The idea that this is the only way to justify a practice or institution is nonsense. BCA should no more be held to this standard than should market or democratic mechanisms.

14. This is an oversimplification. One may reasonably accept a procedure that is less likely than an alternative to arrive at the correct answer if it guarantees avoidance of disaster. This can provide yet a different basis for an outcome-oriented objection to a procedure: one might hold that the procedure in question should not be definitive, even if it is the most reliable procedure available, on the grounds that, when it fails, it fails spectacularly.

15. The consequentialist will see the problem here as being one of an unsuitably narrow understanding of "outcome." If the procedure has intrinsic value, then the proper description of the outcome must be an inclusive one—including the fact that what might ordinarily be considered the outcome in a narrower sense is *produced by this procedure*. If the procedure has instrumental value apart from the correctness of the decision, then the correct account of the outcome must include not only the decision but the fact that it was produced by a procedure that has this additional benefit. An entertaining and instructive parable about excessively narrow understandings of outcomes is given by Ernest J. Weinrib:

> Assume that Jones loves playing golf and plays eighteen holes every Sunday morning. One particular Sunday Jones realizes that he cannot spare

the time to play his usual game. Instead he goes out into his back yard, digs a hole, and drops the ball into it eighteen times. (1980, p. 321); quoted in Byrne (1983, p. 574)

16. "Liberal" here refers to the tradition of liberal individualism as exemplified by such thinkers as Thomas Hobbes (1969), John Locke (1960), John Rawls (1971), Robert Nozick (1974) and David Gauthier (1986).

17. It does not, of course, seek to show that a proposition is true because of its relation to beliefs held by the audience (as certain forms of a circumstantial *ad hominem* fallacy would). Rather, it aims at showing that a procedure or an institution is *desirable* for individuals with certain specified aims. It seeks consensus, not truth.

18. The power of this argument can be exaggerated. It is unlikely, for example, that we can find *any* institutions that are necessary means to *whatever* coherent set of ends an agent might have.

19. By "appropriate" here, I mean only that it counts benefits positively and costs negatively. I have already suggested that on plausible moral views, BCA will not employ the appropriate *weights* in making its final recommendation.

20. This argument depends on the assumption that the information contained in a benefit/cost analysis does not "count as noise rather than information" and does not "hinder rather than help rational social decision making." David Copp speculates that this assumption may be false (1987, p. 81).

21. This insight offers the core of a plausible response to the issue of the possibility of a Paretian liberal—that is, a person who believes both that all Pareto-efficient changes should be made and that there are some issues over which the individual should exercise veto power. See Sen (1970).

22. J. J. C. Smart (1978), for example, is completely unmoved by such criticisms.

23. If there were *any* case in which BCA considered all morally relevant factors and weighed them properly, then it is trivial that there is a class of cases for which there are no outcome-oriented objections to having BCA be determinative. (Indeed, if BCA ever got the right answer in any way—even by "dumb luck"—this would be true.) But the interesting issue is whether that class can be identified in advance in such a way as to be helpful.

24. This point receives sustained emphasis by Mark Sagoff (1988).

25. It is sometimes charged that decision-makers are subject to "bewitchment by numbers," so that even if the results of benefit/cost analyses are only to be used as information for the decision-maker (rather than a rule to follow), they still skew the decision in an inappropriate way. The idea is that decision-makers have a tendency to accord the BCA recommendation undue weight because of its rigor (or apparent rigor). This is, in effect, a charge that there are (moral) costs involved in using BCA information apart from the cost of securing it. It is not clear if there is any truth to the charge, and, if so, what the appropriate solution is. It may be better to educate decision-makers about what is incorporated in a benefit/cost analysis and what is not, rather than to avoid the reliance on BCA information. If so, the above is not an argument against using BCA but against using it poorly.

26. Allocation of scarce resources can have moral implications that are of a sort not well handled by BCA, of course. This is why, even here, there are legitimate concerns about employing BCA as a determinative procedure.

27. Even prior to its repair, the Hubble telescope was apparently returning valuable information despite the distortions produced by the improper design of the telescope.

28. This intriguing analogy was presented to me by David Copp (correspondence).

29. One standard view of utility identifies utility with certain behavioral dispositions. On this view, it is difficult, to say the least, to see what it might mean to sum utilities over persons, since individual utility is measured only on an entirely idiosyncratic scale. If this is the point of the objection, then the problem is not that BCA gives everyone "a different colored crayon," but precisely that it gives everyone the same color crayon to represent information that is not commensurable.

30. Contrary to what is suggested by MacIntyre (1979).

31. The fact that the assumptions mentioned in the previous paragraph are defeasible is probably reason enough, though, for a utilitarian to refrain from conferring this status on BCA.

32. This sort of view is suggested by *some* of what Leonard and Zeckhauser (1986) say. Unfortunately, their discussion is not clear enough to be sure what theory the authors have in mind.

33. Many, but not all. While Rawls (1971) holds such a view, Harsanyi (1977) believes that contractors would not be risk averse and would, consequently, agree to utilitarian principles unaided by any distributive principle.

34. I suspect that the distinction is not ultimately sustainable, unless Sagoff takes the notion of "costs" to be defined by some political (or other) process that doesn't take individual preferences to be relevant. Furthermore, and importantly, even if the "official" role of BCA is confined to "cost-effectiveness analysis," this doesn't undermine the claim that BCA provides morally relevant informational input into a broader decision-making procedure. BCA may still provide decision-makers—whoever they might be in this political decision-making procedure—with information that *they* deem morally relevant to their decision. So, while the government may operate entirely by direct majoritarian decision-making, the citizens may, in casting their votes, be moved by moral considerations that lead them to be interested in the information conveyed by a good benefit/cost analysis.

35. Indeed, I take the sensitivity of the theory to the degree of intrinsic preference satisfaction to be a plausibility condition itself. That is to say, a theory is *eo ipso* less plausible if it does not take intrinsic preference satisfaction to be morally relevant. The argument in the text does not require this assumption.

References

Bentham, Jeremy. 1948. *Principles of Morals and Legislation*. Darien, CT: Hafner Publishing Co.

Byrne, John. 1983. "What's Wrong with Being Reasonable? The Politics of Cost-Benefit Analysis." In *Ethical Theory and Business,* edited by Tom L. Beauchamp and Norman Bowie, pp. 568–76. Englewood Cliffs, NJ: Prentice Hall.

Copp, David. 1987. "The Justice and Rationale of Cost-Benefit Analysis." *Theory and Decision* 23:65–87.

Elster, Jon. 1983. *Sour Grapes*. Cambridge: Cambridge University Press.

Gauthier, David. 1986. *Morals by Agreement.* Oxford: Clarendon Press.

Gibbard, Allan. 1986. "Risk and Value." In *Values at Risk,* edited by Douglas MacLean, pp. 94–112. Totowa, NJ: Rowman & Allanheld.

Hare, R. M. 1969. *The Language of Morals*. Oxford: Clarendon Press.

Harsanyi, John C. 1977. "Morality and the Theory of Rational Behavior." *Social Research* 44:625–56.

Hobbes, Thomas. [1651] 1969. *Leviathan: Or the Matter, Forme, and Power of a Commonwealth Ecclesiasticall and Civil.* London: Collier-Macmillan Ltd.

Hubin, Donald C. 1986. "Of Bindings and By-Products: Elster on Rationality." *Philosophy and Public Affairs* 15:82–95.

Hubin, Donald C., and Michael Perkins. 1986. "Self-Subverting Principles of Choice." *The Canadian Journal of Philosophy* 16:1–10.

Leonard, Herman, and Richard Zeckhauser. 1986. "Cost-Benefit Analysis Applied to Risks: Its Philosophy and Legitimacy." In *Values at Risk,* edited by Douglas MacLean, pp. 31–48. Totowa, NJ: Rowman & Allanheld.

Locke, John. 1960. *Two Treatises of Government.* New York: Mentor Books.

MacIntyre, Alasdair. 1979. "Utilitarianism and Benefit/Cost Analysis: An Essay on the Relevance of Moral Theory to Bureaucratic Theory." In *Ethical Theory and Business,* edited by Tom L. Beauchamp and Norman E. Bowie, pp. 266–76. Englewood Cliffs, NJ: Prentice-Hall, Inc.

Mill, John Stuart. 1968. *Selected Writings of John Stuart Mill,* edited by Maurice Cowling. New York: Mentor Books.

Nozick, Robert. 1974. *Anarchy, State, and Utopia.* New York: Basic Books, Inc.

Parfit, Derek. 1984. *Reasons and Persons*. Oxford: Clarendon Press.

Rawls, John. 1955. "Two Concepts of Rules." *Philosophical Review* 64:3–32.

———. 1971. *A Theory of Justice*. Cambridge, MA: Harvard Press.

Sagoff, Mark. 1988. *The Economy of the Earth.* New York: Cambridge University Press.

Schwartzman, Daniel. 1982. "Cost-Benefit Analysis in Environmental Regulation: Sources of the Controversy." In *Cost-Benefit Analysis and Environmental Regulations: Politics, Ethics and Methods,* edited by Daniel Schwartzman, Richard Liroff, and Kevin Croke, pp. 53–86. Washington, DC: The Conservation Foundation.

Sen, A. K. 1970. "The Impossibility of a Paretian Liberal." *Journal of Political Economy* 78:152–57.

Smart, J. J. C. 1978. "Distributive Justice and Utility." In *Justice and Economic Distribution,* edited by John Arthur and William Shaw, pp. 103–31. Englewood Cliffs, NJ: Prentice-Hall.

Weinrib, Ernest J. 1980. "Utilitarianism, Economics and Legal Theory." *University of Toronto Law Journal* 30:307–36.

INDEX

ABOUT THE CONTRIBUTORS

Elizabeth Anderson is associate professor and Arthur F. Thurnau Professor of Philosophy and Women's Studies at the University of Michigan, Ann Arbor. She is the author of *Value in Ethics and Economics* (1993) and numerous articles in ethics and political philosophy.

Tyler Cowen is currently professor of economics at George Mason. He has written *Explorations in the New Monetary Economics* (1994) with Randall Kroszner. He has just finished a book, *Enterprise and the Arts,* on the economics of music and the arts, and is currently working on the economics of multiculturalism.

David A. Crocker is Senior Research Scholar at the Institute of Philosophy and Public Affairs in the School of Public Affairs at the University of Maryland, College Park. He is a founder and current president of the International Development Ethics Association. He has published extensively on development ethics in professional journals. His most recent book, coedited with Toby Linden, is *Ethics of Consumption: The Good Life, Justice and Global Stewardship* (1997).

Robyn M. Dawes is The Charles J. Queenan, Jr. University Professor, Department of Social and Decision Sciences, Carnegie-Mellon University, Pittsburgh. His current research spans five areas: intuitive expertise, human cooperation, retrospective memory, methodology, and U.S. AIDS policy. He has published *Rational Choice in an Uncertain World* (1988) and *House of Cards: Psychology and Psychotherapy Built on Myth* (1994) in addition to numerous articles in professional journals.

Jon Elster is R. K. Merton Professor of Social Sciences, Columbia University. His many books include *Ulysses and the Sirens: Studies in Rationality and Irrationality* (1979), *Sour Grapes: Studies in the Subversion of Rationality*

(1983), *Solomonic Judgements: Studies in the Limitations of Rationality* (1989), and *Local Justice: How Institutions Allocate Scarce Goods and Necessary Burdens* (1992).

Amitai Etzioni is America's communitarian-in-chief, the most prominent figure in the movement to balance rights with responsibilities, shore up the family, and knit together neighborhoods. A liberal intellectual worried about the decline in civic virtue in America, Etzioni teaches sociology at George Washington University in Washington, D.C., is a prolific author noted for *The Moral Dimension: Toward a New Economics* (1988), and the founder of the new discipline of socio-economics.

Jerry Evensky is associate professor of economics, Maxwell School of Public Affairs, Syracuse University. He works on Adam Smith's moral philosophy, ethics and economics, and education and economics. He has published widely in professional journals.

Robert H. Frank is Goldwin Smith Professor of Economics, Ethics and Public Policy at Cornell University, Ithaca. His recent book, *The Winner Take All Society* (1996), studies the expansion of special markets where the top performer, whether a rock star or a piece of software, garners nearly all of the rewards. His earlier book, *Passions within Reason* (1988), explores rivalry and cooperation in economic and social behavior.

Thomas Gilovich is professor of psychology at Cornell University, Ithaca. He is most widely known for his research that debunks the "hot hand" in basketball and for his book on the causes of erroneous beliefs, *How We Know What Isn't So: The Fallibility of Human Reason in Everyday Life* (1991).

Virginia Held is professor of philosophy at the City University of New York. She is the author of numerous books including *Rights and Goods: Justifying Social Action* (1984), and *Feminist Morality* (1993).

Roland Hoksbergen is professor of economics at Calvin College, Grand Rapids. He is the author of a number of professional articles and the editor of *Through the Eye of a Needle: Readings on Stewardship and Justice* (1988).

Donald C. Hubin is associate professor of philosophy at Ohio State University, Columbus. He has published widely in professional journals on the nature of reasons for acting and the connection between rationality and morality.

Glenn C. Loury is professor of economics at Boston University. In addition to numerous journal articles, he has published *One by One, from the Inside Out: Essays and Reviews on Race and Responsibility in America* (1995).

Richard P. Nielsen is a professor in the Organizational Studies Department at Boston College. He has published in the areas of the politics and aesthetics of ethics as well as action, learning, leadership, negotiating, and change methods. His most recent work is *The Politics of Ethics: Methods for Acting, Learning, and Sometimes Fighting with Others in Addressing Ethics Problems in Organizational Life* (1996).

Dennis T. Regan is associate professor of psychology at Cornell University, Ithaca, working in experimental social psychology, especially attribution and interpersonal influence.

Steven Shulman is professor of economics at Colorado State University, Fort Collins. His most recent published work is *Unlevel Playing Fields: Understanding Wage Inequality and Discrimination* (1996).

W. David Solomon is associate professor of philosophy at the University of Notre Dame. He has published *The Synoptic Vision: The Philosophy of Wilfrid Sellars* (1977) in addition to studies on medical ethics and virtue theory.

James P. Sterba is professor of philosophy at the University of Notre Dame. He has published numerous books including *The Demands of Justice* (1980), *How to Make People Just* (1988), *Contemporary Ethics* (1989), *Earth Ethics* (1994), *Morality in Practice,* Fifth Edition (1996), and *Feminist Philosophies,* Second Edition (1996).

Paul Streeten has taught at Oxford and Boston Universities and has been a consulting economist to the World Bank and a variety of other international organizations. One of the founding fathers of development economics, he has published widely in professional journals and World Bank reports. His books include *The Frontiers of Development Studies* (1972), *Development Perspectives* (1981), *What Price Food?* (1987), and *Strategies for Human Development* (1994).

Richard H. Thaler is Robert P. Gwinn Professor of Behavioral Science and Economics at the University of Chicago. He has published widely in experimental economics, game theory and applied microeconomics. His most widely known work is *The Winner's Curse: Paradoxes and Anomalies of Economic Life* (1992).

Samuel C. Weston is assistant professor of economics at the University of Dallas and works in history of economic thought in addition to methodological issues.

Charles K. Wilber is professor of economics at the University of Notre Dame. He has published numerous articles and a number of books, mainly on issues of economic development, economic methodology, and economic ethics. His books include *The Soviet Model and Underdeveloped Countries* (1969), *An Inquiry into the Poverty of Economics* (1983), and *Beyond Reaganomics: A Further Inquiry into the Poverty of Economics* (1990).